RELIGION
AND SOCIETY
IN RUSSIA

RELIGION AND SOCIETY IN RUSSIA

The Sixteenth and Seventeenth Centuries

Paul Bushkovitch

New York   Oxford

OXFORD UNIVERSITY PRESS

1992

Oxford University Press

Oxford   New York   Toronto
Delhi   Bombay   Calcutta   Madras   Karachi
Petaling Jaya   Singapore   Hong Kong   Tokyo
Nairobi   Dar es Salaam   Cape Town
Melbourne   Auckland

and associated companies in
Berlin   Ibadan

Library of Congress Cataloging-in-Publication Data
Bushkovitch, Paul.
Religion and society in Russia : the sixteenth and seventeenth
centuries / Paul Bushkovitch.
p.   cm.
Includes bibliographical references and index.
ISBN 0-19-506946-3
1. Russkaia pravoslavnaia tserkov'—History—16th century.
2. Russkaia pravoslavnaia tserkov'—History—17th century.
3. Soviet Union—Church history.   4. Soviet Union—Church
history—17th century.   I. Title.
BX489.B87   1992
281.9'47'09031—dc20   91-11540   CIP

2 4 6 8 9 7 5 3 1

Printed in the United States of America
on acid-free paper

Acknowledgments

This book has been a long while in the making, and over the years I have acquired many debts both to institutions and to persons. The International Research and Exchange Board of Princeton, New Jersey, was the primary support of the project from its inception. Yale University's A. Whitney Griswold Fund and its Center for International and Area Studies provided support for travel to West European libraries to supplement Soviet holdings. In the Soviet Union the staff of the State Historical Museum (Moscow), the Moscow University Library, the Central Scientific Library of the Academy of Sciences of the Ukrainian SSR (Kiev), the Lenin Library (Moscow), and the Central State Archive of Ancient Documents (Moscow) were particularly helpful. Moscow University was my host for most of my time in Moscow, and I am grateful both for the ties forged there and for V. V. Shul'gin's kind and helpful advice. The *kafedra* of feudalism of Moscow University's history faculty and the sector of Old Russian literature at the Gor'kii Institute of World Literature provided a forum for an early discussion of some of my principal conclusions. A. N. Robinson let a novice in the world of seventeenth-century Russian culture know at an early stage that his work had some value where it mattered most.

My debts to others are also very great. Michael McGerr took precious time from his dissertation to teach me how to use a computer. Over the years I have benefitted greatly from the knowledge and opinions of many colleagues, primarily John Boswell, Robert Crummey, D. M. Bulanin, B. L. Fonkich, Robert Harding, Nancy Kollman, Fairy von Lilienfeld, Keith Luria, George Majeska, Edgar H. Melton, Hugh Olmstead, Marc Raeff, and many others. Samuel Ramer suffered through the frustrations and rewards of research for more of this book than he perhaps realizes. My greatest debt, however, is to Leonid Betin, whose immense knowledge and understanding provided unfailing inspiration, support, and warmth over many years.

New Haven   P. B.
January 1992

Contents

RELIGION
AND SOCIETY
IN RUSSIA

Introduction: Russian History and Russian Orthodoxy

In August 1689 the young Tsar Peter, fearing that his sister, the regent Sophia, would deprive him of his throne and perhaps his life, decided to assume power in his own name. Warned by loyal soldiers stationed on Lubianka Square in Moscow, Peter galloped from his residence in Pre-obrazhenskoe near the city through the early hours of 8 August 1689 to the Trinity–St. Sergii Monastery to take refuge in the arms of the church. Calling on loyal boyars, Peter managed to oust Sophia and took the throne to begin a reign that brought about a fundamental change in the history of his country. The church made a bad choice in supporting Peter, who abolished the patriarchate, reduced the church to a hand-maiden of the tsar, and fundamentally reoriented Russian culture away from religion. In the course of thirty-six years Russia moved from an entirely religious culture to a secular one, as Peter carried out the work of centuries of European history in little more than a generation. How did he accomplish this? The traditional view of Russian culture before Peter is that it was relatively unchanging, ossified, and religious, only slightly affected by "Westernization" after about 1650. The argument of this book is that the two centuries before Peter was a period of considerable and rapid change within that religious culture. Fundamentally these changes reflected a shift in religious experience from one basically public and collective, which stressed liturgy and miracle cults, to a more private and personal faith with a strong stress on morality. In saying all this I am naturally restricting the focus to the upper classes broadly conceived: the court (both ruler and boyars), the landholding class in its various ranks, and the educated ranks of the clergy—monks and bishops—who pro-duced and read most of our sources. The existing known sources do not permit an analogous account of popular religion, though they do give us some hints and some idea of how the upper classes perceived popular religion and integrated it into their own experiences.

3

Religious belief was the center of Russian thought and culture in the sixteenth and seventeenth centuries. To make this assertion does not mean that Russian culture was "essentially" religious or that Orthodoxy was the real meaning, the culmination, of Russian culture as the Slavophiles and many religious writers have since asserted. Rather this assertion means that in a very elementary sense religious belief occupied virtually the totality of human consciousness as we know it from written sources. Religion absorbed all thought in a way that had never been true in Byzantium (which had a rich secular culture) and had not been true in the West since at least the twelfth century. In Russia there were no *chansons de geste* or law schools as in the West, and no schools of grammar and rhetoric that preserved, studied, and commented upon the ancient Greek classics as in Constantinople. The situation is readily grasped by a glance at the written works copied and composed in Russia in these times. The overwhelming mass of Russian manuscripts are liturgical or works of piety: homilies and lives of the saints and a very few theological tracts, mostly containing various monastic controversies or refutations of heresy. The closest approach to secular content is found in the chronicles and related historical works. They were written primarily to record the Russian past and demonstrate to the reader the place of Russia in world history, and though they certainly contained moral exhortations and frequent assertions of the truth of Orthodoxy, they are not basically works of piety and so may be called secular. Besides the chronicles, Russian libraries contain only a few writings that might be called secular, such as herbals, guides to the interpretation of dreams, or similar marginalia together with a few secular tales. Only in the seventeenth century does the number of secular works increase, with the appearance of grammars, rhetorical treatises, geographical and historical writings, and other compositions without religious aims, many of them translated from Western languages. Scholars have been diligent in tracing these writings, but the total number is quite small, and 90 percent of the contents of Russian libraries, as before, consisted of liturgical texts, works of the Greek and Byzantine fathers, and the lives of the saints.

Like many topics in Russian history, the story of the religion of these centuries has not been the object of extensive research, with the result that the accepted ideas rest on methodologies and ideas now fifty to a hundred years old. Before 1917 Russian historians who treated these matters were primarily concerned with three areas: the institutional development of the church (mainly church-state relations), the church as a bearer of Russian nationality, and the special problem of the schism of Old Belief. These were not trivial problems, but they were not the only ones worth studying, and we need now to go beyond that subject matter.

Although ideas on the religion of the seventeenth century appear in the work of the main Russian historians, church historians and literary historians have produced most of the literature. Church history was not a strong area in the academic culture of prerevolutionary Russia.[1] Most historians of the Russian church understood their subject to be primarily the history of the institutional structure of the church and its role in Russian history as an expression of Russian national consciousness. Archbishop Makarii (Bulgakov) is perhaps the first relatively modern historian of the church, and his superb knowledge of sources has rendered his work valuable even today; however, his choice of themes severely limits its usefulness to the modern historian. In the last three volumes, dealing with the years 1589–1667, almost half of the space was devoted to the history of Orthodoxy in the Ukraine and Belorussia, or "West Russia" as Russian nationalist scholars then called those countries. His theme was the "reunification" of the nation under the church. His younger colleague E. E. Golubinskii was perhaps more thoughtful and critical, but shared the same emphasis on the institutional history of the church. Neither of them spent much time on the religious life of the laity, or even on the traditions of theology and spirituality within the church. Both were understandably concerned with the points at issue with the Old Belief, but the result was that much time was spent on issues (such as the history of the sign of the cross) that have not the same importance to the historian.[2] Russian church history has not flourished either in the Soviet Union or in the West, and there has been little systematic attempt to go beyond the nineteenth-century pioneers.

The other major group of scholars to attack the history of religion were the philologists studying Old Russian literature. The philologists came much closer to studying the religious life of Old Russia, as their attention was drawn to the texts that could be seen as "literary," the chronicles, saints' lives, and religious tracts that formed the background to these works. It was the philologists who gave us the extensive text publications and studies of the great monastic literature of the period 1350–1530, which forms the immediate background to the period studied here. The philological tradition was not interrupted in 1917, unlike church history, and has succeeded in introducing some new ideas that are quite useful to the historian. D. S. Likhachev, in particular, has provided a scheme of evolution of Old Russian literature that is really the first to break with the Slavophile notion of Old Russia as an essentially unchanging timeless essence of true Orthodox Russia. In Likhachev's scheme the fourteenth and fifteenth centuries are marked by the influence of the Southern Slavs, and form a sort of "prerenaissance" whose hallmark is a certain inwardness and an emotional style. The sixteenth century is the era of the "second monumentalism," an official culture that stressed celebration of achievements, and the seventeenth by Baroque style and a stress on didacticism.[3]

Like any schema this succession of stages has its problems. The very complex sixteenth century seems to receive particularly short shrift. The basic problem for the historian of religion, however, has nothing to do with the adequacy of the schema as a way of understanding the history of Old Russian literature but with the inevitable need of the philologists to concentrate on major written expressions of the period. Phenomena of central importance such as the miracle cults of the sixteenth century of necessity have no room in the schema because they have no literary form of expression. In the seventeenth century the match is better simply because the sermons and tales of the time are both "literary" and central expressions of religious experience and feeling. Likhachev's schema has not found universal support among Western Slavists, many of whom prefer to stress the common typological features of Old Russian and Old Slavic literatures, but for the historian of religion his observation of continuous change is an invaluable opening to new avenues of research.

Other Soviet philologists, particularly A. N. Robinson, have reopened many of the old debates on the seventeenth century, pointing out the very close ties of the innovators of the period (like Simeon Polotskii) to the Russian court and even to particular boyar patrons. Thus many of the religious writers need to be seen in a context that is not only one of the church but of society at large and the court in particular.[4]

Western Slavists have concentrated their attention on earlier periods of the history of the church and religious literature, and have also usually followed the lead of prerevolutionary Russian historians. So did those Russians who emigrated, with some notable exceptions. Virtually the only historian to concern himself with the history of religion, not of the church or literature, was G. P. Fedotov, writing in Paris in the interwar era. For Fedotov, the high point of religious feeling in Russia was the monastic movement of the later fourteenth and fifteenth centuries, marked by a moderate asceticism and the absence of mysticism. A decline in the sanctity of the Russian church began in the time of Joseph Volotskii and then continued from about 1550 until Peter's time. The period witnessed a reduction in the number of new saints and a loss of monastic discipline and fervor. Without this decline in spirituality, the break (*sryv,* that is, the Petrine reforms) at the end of the seventeenth century could not have taken place.[5] It is not difficult to find fault with this schema: the terminology is vague and frequently unhistorical, and Fedotov's modern concerns are as obvious as Golubinskii's. His account of the period suffered from his inability to consult manuscript sources, as well as from relative neglect of the social and political foundations of the religious changes he describes. On the whole, however, he was able to break out of some of the less helpful traditional interpretations of the period. His basic contention, that the sixteenth century saw not merely a process of ossification of a tradition but an actual decline of the fifteenth-century religious ideal, is an extremely suggestive idea. In my view, the phenomenon that he observed was real, although I prefer to think of it as the decline of the importance and spiritual authority of monasticism. Unfortunately, Fedotov provides only a few suggestions and not a complete account of the history of Russian Orthodoxy. Many of the basic questions remain to be asked.

The present work does not and cannot attempt to fill the gap and to provide a definitive account and interpretation of all religious experience in the Russia of that era. It attempts only to trace the character of the changes in religious life of the landholding elite of Russian society. It does not try to present in any systematic fashion the experience of other sectors of society, and it ignores some important areas, principally the inner life of the monasteries after about 1530. Although the monasteries were much less important to society as a whole after that date, their records are still so voluminous and neglected that they require investigation by themselves. That would be another book, or perhaps even several, and is beyond my scope.

To reach even this more modest goal, one basic issue needs to be cleared away, the notion of the "Westernization" of Russia in the seventeenth century. It is one of the contentions of this book that the notion of Westernization is unhelpful and too general, and conceals a quite complicated process of selection and adaptation.

The traditional view of Old Russian culture (and thus religion) from Kievan times to the seventeenth century is that it was traditional, unchanging, ritualistic, Byzantine, isolated from the West, xenophobic, and suspicious of change. Normally it is held that only in the reign of Peter's father Aleksei (1645–1676) can the beginnings of "Western influence" be detected, but they are superficial and insubstantial until 1689. Recent research has shown, however, that throughout most of the seventeenth century Russia was the recipient of powerful cultural impulses from Kiev and the other Orthodox centers of the Polish state. These impulses do not appear only on the eve of Peter's reign but as early as the 1620s, only gathering greater force after 1650. Much of this is already known, but the present work attempts to show that this movement was much deeper and more significant than previously thought, and that the impulses were as much religious as "cultural." I have also tried to point out that the interaction of Russia and the Ukraine was not merely the passive acceptance of "influence" but a series of conscious choices. As far as culture is concerned, what Russia chose to receive from the Ukraine was essentially a reflection of European Baroque culture, or rather a mixture of Renaissance and Baroque elements, all reformulated to fit a basically religious, not secular, worldview. The Russian case is only an extreme example of the reworking of Renaissance culture outside its main heartland.[6] This cultural impact was secondary to the impact of religious ideas, particularly the importance of sermons in the Ukrainian church.

Before 1689 the dividing line was between a largely secular post-Renaissance Europe and a largely religious Russia. It was not a line of nationality, with Russia opposed to the West and Russia equated with Orthodoxy. Seventeenth-century Russians worried about learning and faith, not about Russia and the West. Previous historians, in stressing the national element, have come across all sorts of inconsistencies that are rarely explained, merely stated. Why did so many Russian "traditionalists," from Avvakum to Ivan Nasedka and Patriarch Ioakim, systematically use and quote so many Ukrainian religious books, allegedly tainted with Catholicism? Why is it so hard to place the writers of the period in neat Grecophile and Latin camps? Historians usually assert that the Russian churchmen of the time looked with horror on the heretical books coming from Kiev or Wilno, yet these books circulated in large numbers in Russia. It is my contention that these difficulties arise only from the persistence of the essentially Slavophile notions of Old Russia, and that the Russians of the seventeenth century looked at a book based on its content, not its place of publication. They read and used books that they liked; if they found errors of faith, they sometimes rejected the whole book but sometimes only part (such as the works of the Uniate Stavrovetskii).

The Russians often reacted vigorously to the books they read from the Ukraine or farther West because their world was not absolutely remote from that of their neighbors. This is not the way most Russian historians have seen the country's history, for particularly in the West they have tried to argue that Russian history is unique, radically different from that of Europe. Here contemporary Western and Slavophile historiography agree, and Orthodoxy would seem to be their best example. The fall of Constantinople in 1453 indeed left Russia the only major Orthodox state to possess an elite culture and at the same time to control its own destiny. A fundamental discontinuity in the history of the Orthodox church resulted, for neither Byzantine Orthodoxy nor the largely folk religion of the Balkan peoples under Ottoman rule operated under political and cultural conditions similar to those of sixteenth- and seventeenth-century Russia. In the religious sphere, Russia would seem to be unique, and indeed in some aspects it was. The notion of "deification" (*theosis/obozhestvlenie*), for example, was much more important in Russian religious thought of this period than elsewhere even in the Orthodox world. On the social level, however, the Russian religious experience was hardly unique. Miracle cults, for instance were much the same as elsewhere. Rooted in the experience of late antiquity, the cults revolved in Russia as elsewhere in Christian Europe around demonstrations of the power of the saint and of healing. Comparison with other European experience reveals differences as well, for Russian miracle cults were distinguished by the virtually total absence of the elite of society, in sharp contrast to those of Poland or Central Europe. Only by recognizing what Russian miracle cults had in common with those of the rest of Europe can one see what was unique to Russia. To this end I have made use of the work of numerous historians of medieval and early modern Europe. Many historians of Russia will find this approach to be fundamentally incorrect, but I cannot agree. For it is precisely in the study of the social context of religious experience that the study of European and other societies is essential for the historian of Russia's religions.

The sixteenth and seventeenth centuries witnessed rapid religious change, at least among the elite of Russian society. In 1530 elite religious experience revolved around the religious rituals of the court. These rituals were extensive and all-embracing, public and collective. The sixteenth century saw the rise of the miracle cults, church- and state-sponsored phenomena of public piety. These healing cults, replacing the earlier miracles of power by living holy monks, were public cults that celebrated the action of divine grace in individual lives, thus making a small move from the public to the private. These healing cults were described in stories written mostly by monks. The stories had wide circulation among the reading public of Russia—that is, the elite, broadly defined, although the very elite, the boyars, seem not to have been direct participants. They remained in the political world of the court and its religious rituals and patronized the monasteries that maintained the shrines, but themselves were not cured.

For the elite the greatest changes began with the increasing influence of Ukrainian religious writings in the 1620s, a process that would reorient the elite's religious world away from ritual and miracle cults toward sermons and other moralizing writings, both at court and elsewhere. This change was a response to the elite's changing political and social circumstances, the growth in power of tsar and court, and the gradual formation of serfdom. The new nobleman needed to restrain his pride and greed to be both successful at court and just toward his serfs. The sermons represent the final move toward individual religious life, for in a very direct way they tell the individual to be personally a good Christian, not merely a participant in liturgy and ritual or an outside admirer of the monks. At the same time, probably under pressure from Old Belief, the state and the church moved to deemphasize the miracle cults as early as the 1660s, long before Peter's ascendancy. It is this movement from public to private, from ritual and miracle to morality, that prepared the way for Peter.

1

Orthodoxy in the Sixteenth Century

The Orthodox church of medieval Russia was a monastic church. This does not mean that the monasteries exercised a prescribed power over the church, or that monasticism absorbed all spiritual impulses. It means simply that the monk was the most authoritative spiritual figure in the church and that he exerted a purely charismatic authority over clergy and laity alike. Around the year 1500 the role of the monk in Russian Orthodoxy began to change. On the one hand the monasteries seem to have reached a peak of influence as well as material prosperity, and ordered their internal life with considerable success. On the other hand, their very success led to a withdrawal from their previous role in the church and the concomitant rise of the bishops.

The decline in spiritual significance of monasticism in the Orthodox church of Russia in the course of the sixteenth century was a change with profound religious and social implications. The resulting vacuum at the heart of Orthodoxy required the church to strengthen episcopal and priestly authority in order to bring its message to the laity in ways that had never before been necessary. The decline in authority of the monk had social implications as well, for it went along with a certain plebeianization of the monasteries (and inevitably also of the episcopacy), and the withdrawal of the aristocracy of the Russian state from direct participation in most religious activities (other than public ritual and attendance at the most important liturgical observances). The decline in influence of monasticism also led to the decline of the significance of the monastic saint, hitherto the primary type of medieval Russian saint. The phenomenon that filled this vacuum seems to have been the rise of the popular miracle cults, which celebrated a kind of direct contact of the believer with divine power that was rare before the mid-sixteenth century. In these popular cults the role of the elite of Russian society was almost completely passive, but in the seventeenth century and mainly at the Russian court a new type of elite religious experience began to emerge.

The Decline of Monastic Authority

From the beginning of Christianity in Kievan Rus' the monasteries were the most prominent feature of religious life. As Gerhard Podskalsky recently observed, "The inner history of Kiev Rus' is in its essential parts the history of monasticism." The Primary Chronicle does not even name the first metropolitan of Rus', and barely mentions many of his successors, but the story of the foundation of the Kiev Monastery of the Caves takes up many pages. Other sources tell us the metropolitans' names, but we usually find out little more than their dates of office and a few facts about their involvement in political affairs. The monasteries overshadow the bishops through the whole pre-Mongol era: alongside the magnificent Paterikon of the Kiev Caves Monastery and Efrem's life of the monk Avraamii of Smolensk stands only the brief account of the finding of the relics of Bishop Leontii of Rostov in the 1160s. The same was true of the early Novgorod church, for the hegumen (abbot) Varlaam was the subject of a thirteenth- or early fourteenth-century life, but the archbishops were venerated only from the sixteenth century. Parish priests are essentially nameless.[1]

The bishops do not emerge out of this almost total obscurity until the fourteenth century, with the cults and written lives of the Moscow metropolitans Peter and Aleksei. Perhaps as a reply to Moscow's efforts, Pakhomii Logofet and others produced lives of the greater Novgorod archbishops in the fifteenth century, although many of the earlier archbishops had to wait until the sixteenth century, when largely mythical lives of the eleventh- and twelfth-century Novgorod archbishops were composed. All of these episcopal lives stressed the subjects' political and ecclesiastical activities as much or more than their holiness of life. (The other main type of Kievan and early Russian saint, the saintly princes such as Boris and Gleb or Aleksandr Nevskii, was also mainly political in content.) The great saints' lives of the fourteenth and fifteenth centuries, however, were neither those of holy bishops nor of saintly princes. These were the lives of holy monks, containing some political elements to be sure, but basically images of Christian life. The written life of St. Sergii of Radonezh, for example, played down his political activity in favor of a more thorough portrait of a proper monastic life. The absence of lives of most bishops and metropolitans was not compensated by great attention to their activities in the chronicles. Here too they were mere names, if they were mentioned at all. The bishops seem also to have expended little time in recording their ideas or actions. Almost no sermons, letters, or other documents not purely administrative or legal survive, and only

with difficulty can a picture be formed of the basic powers and activity of
the bishops.[2]

The monastic saints of the fourteenth and fifteenth centuries were
part of a long tradition reaching back to the Kievan monks of the eleventh century, specifically to Antonii, the founder of the Kiev Monastery
of the Caves, and Feodosii, its principal saint. The Caves Monastery,
cenobitic and largely free of lay control, was the major center of Kievan
monasticism. Feodosii and the other brothers of the monastery led a life
of exemplary holiness, and at the same time were important purveyors of
divine power. They cured the sick, foretold the future, defeated the
magic of heretic Armenians and Jews, and exerted power and influence
over the Kievan princes. It was these monks, not the faceless metropolitans and bishops, who dominated the landscape of Kievan religious
life.[3]

The domination of the monks in the church grew stronger in the
fourteenth century under the influence of hesychasm, the movement of
mystical revival among Byzantine monks led by St. Gregory Palamas. It
was, in Smolitsch's words, an "ascetic age." The metropolitans Peter and
Aleksei, though they were strong figures in their own right, did not
challenge the monks, and Aleksei even aided them. Monastic dominance
was not an institutional dominance: the monks had no power over the
rest of the church in canon law, and indeed were supposed to obey the
metropolitan and bishops. The monks exercised a power that was purely
charismatic, but no less strong for its informal character. St. Sergii of
Radonezh repeatedly intervened in Russian politics, using only his personal authority, not any specific powers as monk or hegumen. He was
the first of the powerful monastic saints of the fourteenth century, and in
his life Epifanii Premudryi depicted him mainly as the founder of new
monasteries throughout the Northeast. (It is the secular princely chronicles that describe his actions on the behalf of the Moscow dynasty.) Epifanii devoted comparatively little space to Sergii's style of monasticism,
and almost no space to the saint's inner life. He was careful to depict the
respect shown him by both princes and peasants, as well as his supernatural power and his ability to heal the sick, revive the dead, and punish
the wicked. These stories, however, were overshadowed by the accounts
of the founding of new monasteries, which were Epifanii's main theme.[4]

The career of St. Sergii marked the beginning of a revival of monasticism, partly under the influence of Byzantine hesychasm, that had
far-reaching implications in Russian religious life. The foundation of this
revival was the growth of the great independent monasteries, which
replaced the predominant type of Kievan times, the private monastery.
The independent monasteries were also cenobitic, and thus doubly continued the traditions of the Kiev Monastery of the Caves. They provided
an institutional base for the movement, which in turn allowed the spread
of monastic influence beyond monastery walls. It is at this time that the
typikon (the order of services) of Jerusalem began to replace the typikon

of Constantinople as the basis of Russian liturgy. This meant not only a change in geography, for the earlier typikon followed the practice of the Great Church of St. Sophia in Constantinople, while the liturgy of Jerusalem was that of the Monastery of St. Sabbas near Jerusalem and, as a liturgy designed for monks, was thus much more elaborate and complex. It now came to be used in all Russian churches, monastic or not. Monastic influence extended to the physical appearance of nonmonastic churches as well. The development of the five-tiered icon screen (iconostasis) concealing the altar in a wall of icons from floor to ceiling, which reached final form in the late fifteenth century, was first developed in monastery churches, spreading from there to cathedrals and parish churches. In all this the spirituality of the monks was spreading to the white clergy and the laity.[5]

The inner life of the monk and a detailed account of monastic life were the themes of two later lives of monastic saints, Kirill Belozerskii (1337–1427), whose life was written by Pakhomii Logofet (the Serb) about 1462–1463, and Pafnutii of Borovsk (died 1477), written by Vassian Sanin about 1500–1515. Of all the late medieval monastic lives it was Pakhomii's life of Kirill that devoted most space to the subject's inner life, which was close in spirit and letter to Greek monastic spirituality. It was not specifically hesychast spirituality, but Greek spirituality nevertheless, for Pakhomii stressed again and again Kirill's mourning for sin (*penthos/umilenie*) and his gradual ascent along St. John Climacus's ladder of perfection. At the same time Pakhomii did not omit Kirill's spiritual power, for Kirill defended the monastery against predatory neighbors, noble and peasant, by supernatural means, and in the same way healed the possessed and the sick. Pakhomii also noted his adherence to the monastic typikon, and his observance of fasts and ceremonies.[6] Kirill was in all the perfect monastic saint, combining inner life, traditional observance, spiritual power, and organizational skill and finding the respect and love of the Moscow dynasty.

Pafnutii of Borovsk represented the next generation of monastic saints. In his life of Pafnutii Vassian Sanin put much less emphasis on inner life and more on the observance of monastic rules and on political relations with the Moscow and Volok dynasties. At the same time he showed Pafnutii as a healer and a man who wielded his power to punish the wicked and reward the good, especially those in his own monastery and his allies in the church and in lay society. This was still the charismatic model. Though Pafnutii, like his pupil Joseph Volotskii, grew closer to the princes, his power derived not so much from his alliance with lay rulers but from his personal authority.[7]

These three lives represent the Russian monastic saint at the height of his significance in church and lay society, a period that runs from the middle of the fourteenth to the end of the fifteenth century. Around 1500 a process of rapid change set in, part of which was the gradual cessation of the recognition of holy monks as saints. The last important monastic saint was Antonii Siiskii, who died in 1556 and was recognized as a saint of national importance by 1610 at the latest. None of the many monks who lived after him were ever recognized for more than local festivals, and most not even that. This represents a major change in the role of monastic saints and needs to be explained. Most historians have not looked at the sixteenth century in the context of the decline of monasticism, and have instead tried to account for what they perceived as a general decline in the vitality of religious life and literature. G. P. Fedotov saw the change as one of the gradual decline of holiness in general, a conception that (aside from its vagueness) does not account for the decline of the monastic saint, the primary type of saint in the period before 1550. Other historians, most recently D. S. Likhachev and Ia. S. Lur'e, have seen the decline of monastic life as well as Russian culture in general in this period as the result of the victory of Josephism, an ideology that was narrow-minded, intolerant, and allied with the "autocratic" tsar.[8] This conception probably exaggerates the power of pure Josephism after 1530. It also rests on a very traditional view of the power of the grand prince/tsar, a view that has come under increasing criticism in recent years, and in any case does not explain exactly how the decline was supposed to have occurred without recourse to a model of the state closer to the reality of the twentieth century than the sixteenth. The conception that stresses the Josephite alliance with the grand prince/tsar also reduces a religious problem to a political one. Finally, the decline of the monastic saint as an ideal was part of the general decline of the authority of the monasteries, a phenomenon that has been scarcely touched by scholars. Our task is first to describe this process of decline in authority and then to try to explain it.

The lack of any new monastic saints after about 1550 seems all the more surprising since the fifteenth and early sixteenth centuries were times of great expansion in the number of monasteries, particularly in the Russian North. This is a phenomenon that is very well known, and already noted by V. O. Kliuchevskii over a century ago. The expansion of the monasteries not only produced numerous minor foundations but also many great monasteries, those of Sergii and Kirill as well as the Solovetskii Monastery and the more modest Vologda monasteries. By the middle of the sixteenth century the monasteries were very rich, owning altogether perhaps a third of the populated land in the state.[9] The monasteries were also assiduous in the task of self-glorification, writing up the lives and deeds of their founders and famous brothers. Nevertheless, the monasteries lost the central position they once held. The controversy between Joseph and the so-called nonpossessors does not easily account for this loss. The victory of the Josephites in the early sixteenth century was designed to strengthen the monasteries, and their victory would seem to provide a basis for the great age of monasticism, not the reverse.

The Josephites were the followers of the teaching of Joseph Volotskii, the hegumen of the Monastery of the Mother of God in Volokolamsk, known after his death in 1515 usually as the Iosifo-Volokolamsk Monastery. Joseph's writings had been originally inspired by the challenge of the heresy of the Judaizers, a small group who were alleged to reject the Trinity, and his principal work, the *Prosvetitel'*, is largely devoted to refuting their teachings. Joseph not only tried to demonstrate the falsity of the Judaizer doctrine, but specifically called for the extermination of the heretics, meeting here the opposition not only of sympathizers at court but also of the hermit Nil Sorskii.[10] Nil asserted (quite incorrectly) that there was no traditional sanction in the church for the execution of heretics, only a requirement for their admonition. Joseph thus not only restated the traditional Christian doctrine of the Trinity, he also restated the traditional intolerance of the church toward heresy and the policy of physical extermination of heretics. Josephism gave birth to a narrow Orthodoxy, closely allied with the princes against any suggestion of wrong teaching.

A subtler challenge to Josephite Orthodoxy came also from Nil Sorskii in the other great dispute of the century, over monastic life and the landholding issue. Here the issue was not one of heresy. In the argument over monastic landholding, the best-known feature of this controversy, Nil denied that such landholding was proper or necessary. (For this reason the party of Nil was known as the "nonpossessors," or *nestiazhateli*, while the Josephites were also known as the "possessors," or *stiazhateli*.) Nil's hermitage, or *skit* as it was called, was not a cenobitic monastery but a collection of hermitages where he and his fellow monks lived in cells at some distance apart and supported themselves mainly by their own labor together with modest gifts from visitors. They assembled only for divine service but ate, worked, and prayed separately. Such hermitages had existed before in Russia, and the novelty of Nil's position was contained in his assertions that such a system was desirable for all monks and that the vast landholdings of the Russian monasteries were wrong and contrary to the tradition of the church (here he was obviously mistaken). Joseph, on the other hand, defended the landholdings as permitted by tradition and also as necessary to support the charitable work of the monasteries, to take care of the poor. Nil's retort, that better care for the poor did not depend on monasteries' owning their land, did not impress Joseph, who differed from the hermit in his basic conception of monastic spirituality as well. The difference between the two monks was not an absolute contradiction but rather a matter of emphasis. Joseph did not reject the notion of hermitage but rather subsumed it within the general life of the monastery. Nil did not absolutely reject the common life, but considered the individual hermitage more conducive to salvation as it did not offer the distractions that came from the wealth of the monasteries, from the land they owned, and from the fact of common life itself. These differences of emphasis however, led ultimately to different views of the nature of monastic life, and on matters of both organization and spirituality: Nil's rule, his *ustav*, was almost entirely concerned with the

monk's inner life, while Joseph's concentrated on matters of discipline
and organization. Joseph's was the more popular position in the church
hierarchy, for the chief hegumens had a direct interest in supporting
him, as did the bishops, and perhaps as early as the 1503–1504 church
councils Nil's position was rejected. For the rest of the century Joseph's
teaching on these and other subjects was the dominant one in the
church, while Nil's writings, though never wholly forgotten, sank into
obscurity.[11]

Nil's followers did not give up the fight after the councils or after Nil's
death in 1508, and found in Vassian Patrikeev a leader more combative
than the retiring Nil. A Gediminovich prince in origin, Vassian had been
forcibly tonsured in 1499 when he had come out on the losing side of the
court intrigues over the succession to Ivan III. Monastic life seems to
have suited him, however, and after Nil's death he became the leader of
the group, both at court (where he eventually regained access after 1509,
rising to prominence by 1511) and in the hermitage as a leading monastic publicist. The views he expressed were directly derived from those
of Nil Sorskii, but Vassian was less interested than his master in the inner
life of the monk. For Vassian, monastic landholding was the crux of the
issue and it was for that perceived wrongdoing that he attacked Joseph
and the great monasteries. This enterprise was not as dangerous as it
might seem, however, as he enjoyed for many years the protection and
tolerance of Grand Prince Vasilii III, and Metropolitan Varlaam (1511–
1521) seems to have been tolerant as well, though whether he supported
Vassian's views is not clear. The new metropolitan Daniil (1521–1533),
however, was a firm Josephite and in 1531 the tolerance of Vassian came
to an abrupt end with his condemnation by a church council. Unfortunately the text of the council decision is incomplete, but it is clear that
Vassian lost; he died a few years later, imprisoned in the Iosifo-
Volokolamsk Monastery.[12] In his later years, however, Vassian did not
oppose monastic landholding alone.

His support had come from no less than Maksim the Greek, one of the
most important religious writers of sixteenth-century Russia. Born
Michael Trivolis about 1470 in Arta, a town in Ottoman Epirus, he
studied in Corfu and then Venice, where he met Aldo Manuzio and Pico
della Mirandola in the process. A Dominican monk and admirer of Sa-
vonarola for several years, he returned to Orthodoxy and to Greece in
1504, entering the Vatopedi Monastery on Mount Athos. Grand Prince
Vasilii III wanted a learned monk to correct the translations of the liturgical books in Russia, and in 1518 Maksim arrived in Moscow. Maksim
flourished under Metropolitan Varlaam, but under Varlaam's successor
Daniil he was tried twice for heresy, in 1525 and 1531. The latter trial led
to a long but not very onerous confinement in the Tver' Otroch' Monastery, where the favor of the local bishop Akakii made his life bearable and
productive. Ivan IV had him released to the Trinity Monastery about
1547, where he died in 1556.[13]

Maksim seems to have had three main interests, though his writings covered a great variety of themes. One was the theology of the incarnation, which he addressed both in general writings and in polemics with Judaism, Islam, and Catholicism. Historians have not made much of this aspect of his work, presumably considering it to be technical theology, but in the *Ispovedanie very* of about 1534, which he put at the head of his collected works, he stressed this point and also claimed that his views on the matter were the reason for his condemnation. The Russian church, in his view, did not stress adequately the divine side of Christ's nature. His polemics with Islam, Judaism, and even Catholicism revolve around Christology rather than any other sides of his opponents' views. Maksim also devoted a number of his writings to attacking the belief in astrology (the 1551 church council followed him in this) and secularized notions of fate. Finally, the third theme was the nature of monasticism. Maksim wrote long paeans to monasticism, but they were coupled with extremely critical remarks about the greed for wealth and land of the Russian monasteries. Maksim is considered a "moderate" on the land issue because he does not appear to have called for large scale surrender of monastic lands, but his language is extremely harsh, in the same vein as Vassian Patrikeev's. Furthermore Maksim thought that greed was not only a monastic issue but a defect of society as a whole, affecting church, boyars, and even rulers. His solution was naturally a call to repentance by the monks, but also to call on the bishops and the tsar to lead the people in casting off sin, greed, pride, and drunkenness.

The appeal to the bishops was most clearly stated in a "dialogue" between Bishop Akakii of Tver' and God on the occasion of the fire in Tver' of July 1537. Here God explicitly calls on Akakii as bishop to fulfill his duties as pastor and prevent the spread of greed and moneylending among the people. In epistles to the young tsar Ivan IV, Maksim called on him as well to help in this task by practicing justice, meekness, restraint, and generosity, and in this obeying his fathers the bishops of the Russian church.[14] Maksim called on the bishops, aided by the tsar, to reform the monks, evidently feeling he could not rely on the monks alone. Maksim's views on the respective role of the bishops and the monks in the church were not those of an isolated foreigner. As we shall see, Josephism was not nearly so dominant by the 1550s as is normally claimed, and Maksim's views were entirely in accord with the decisions of the 1551 *Stoglav* church council. Maksim recognized the decline of the authority of the Russian monasteries, though he found its cause in monastic wealth and greed, and saw the cure in the bishops.

The historians of the nineteenth century thought the "external" quality of Josephite monasticism was enough to explain the spiritual decline of the church that they noted in the sixteenth century, but that is a transparently nineteenth-century explanation that depends on post-Romantic notions of literary creativity and religious experience, both irrelevant to the sixteenth century. The best way to understand the problem is to

examine closely three important monastic lives of the first half of the
sixteenth century: the life of Zosima and Savvatii of the Solovetskii Monastery, Savva Chernyi's life of Joseph Volotskii, and the anonymous life of
Daniil of Pereiaslavl'. Zosima and Savvatii were recognized as saints officially in 1547, and therefore their lives are more than provincial literary
compositions. The two latter texts in particular should express the views
of the dominant Josephite party among Russian monks and the metropolitan of Moscow's chancellery.

All three of these accounts of monastic life represent a change from
the fifteenth-century lives in that much less attention was devoted to
supernatural events and much more to the spiritual perfection of the
monks. The lives of Zosima and Savvatii already show a complete lack of
the traditional healing miracles or other acts of divine intervention carried out by the living saint. The miraculous events in the lives became
curiously "institutional" and include angels driving out the fishermen
from the Solovki Islands or helping Savvatii to reach Novgorod to be
made hegumen of the monastery. Such incidents take up less space than
in the lives of Kirill or Sergii, and more space is devoted to the organization of the monastery, its construction, and even the early lives of the
saints as hermits. The result is that the saints are much less "public"
figures than their predecessors and much more confined to exclusively
monastic concerns. Their relations with Novgorod, the metropolis of the
monastery in their time, are often negative rather than positive, stressing
the hesitation of the Novgorod boyars in helping the monastery and the
resistance of their servants in the North to the monastery's land claims.
Nowhere is there the suggestion of patronage or even close relations with
either princes, boyars, or local peasants, other than the occasional conflict.[15]

The 1546 life of Joseph Volotskii by Savva Chernyi (bishop of Krutitsy
1544–1554) describes Joseph's relations with the princes but in a more
"realistic" manner. This is in keeping with the entire life, which is re-
markably free of supernatural events. In it Joseph's learning is noted
again and again, as is his obedience to Pafnutii of Borovsk and his loyalty
to his parents, but not his supernatural powers. He neither cures nor
smites his opponents with God's power. Instead, he proceeds by normal
earthly means, learning the rules of the common life for monks at the
Monastery of St. Kirill in Belozero and enforcing them in Volokolamsk
by his wisdom. God points to the correct place for the monastery of the
Dormition that will be ultimately the Iosifo-Volokolamsk Monastery, but
it is built by Joseph's efforts and Prince Boris of Volok's favor and contributions, including the physical labor of the prince and his boyars. Indeed
the patronage of Prince Boris and (after his son Fedor's falling out with
Joseph) of Grand Prince Ivan III is stressed throughout the life, as the
natural result of his holy life and successful direction of his monastery,
not of his supernatural powers of favor. Joseph is also not afraid to
reprove the prince and intervene in the internal squabbles of the Moscow

dynasty. Savva's life totally ignores the dispute with the nonpossessors, which shows that by the time of writing the church was moving away from pure Josephism. Nil Sorskii is not even mentioned. The Judaizers, on the other hand, come in for the severest and most violent condemnation, and Joseph's position is presented as fully justified. In the conflict with Archbishop Serapion of Novgorod, Savva entirely takes Joseph's side, presenting his hero's motives as practical in the situation and Serapion's motives as ignoble (based on wounded pride) and his actions as uncanonical.[16] In this incident Savva is fully traditional, supporting the monk against the bishop. As we shall see, this attitude would give way to support for the bishop.

Finally, the life of Daniil of Pereiaslavl', written about 1553, illustrates these trends as well. Like the Solovetskii saints and Joseph, Daniil spent most of his time simply establishing his monastery. Divine intervention occurred not to demonstrate his charismatic authority over the surrounding community but to help build the monastery and to show the surrounding community that the building of the monastery was a good idea. In this task Daniil had the cooperation of the two Cheliadnin brothers, Ivan Andreevich (died after 1523) and Vasilii Andreevich (died 1516), both important boyars of the early sixteenth century.[17] The boyar Semen Ivanovich Vorontsov (died 1521/1522) had great faith in Daniil as well. Daniil's efforts to build the monasteries around Pereiaslavl' do not seem to have been enough to attract the kind of support he felt he needed. Toward the end of his life he discovered the relics of Prince Andrei of Smolensk in his monastery cemetery and tried to get the possibly mythical prince recognized as a miracle worker. The holy man was never recognized as a saint by the church. This in spite (so claims the life) of a commission led by Archimandrite (abbot) Iona of the Chudov Monastery around 1540.[18] Hegumen Daniil was in many ways a transitional figure to the next stage in the decline of the monastic saint. Though his life was included in the Book of Degrees, he never himself came close to being the object of a cult or festival. Like most of his contemporary monks, he tried to promote a miracle cult obviously designed to increase the prestige of his monastery, but unlike better-established monks he failed. Daniil did understand the problem. He could no longer claim himself or a predecessor as a living miracle worker, so he had to find relics. At the same time his efforts at building the monastery had not the same success as those of his predecessors, even though his life tried to glorify those efforts, and reminded the reader of the support of both princes and boyars. In Daniil the power of the monk as well as the charismatic was beginning to weaken by the time of his death in 1540.

The decline of the charismatic authority of the monk left the church without a powerful ideal for laymen and without living holy men to direct laymen onto the right path. Into this vacuum moved the metropolitan and the bishops, the obvious remaining source of authority. The church hierarchy now had to instruct the laity in the proper Christian life and also to establish its authority over both monk and layman alike. The first to try to do this was Metropolitan Daniil, the former hegumen of the Iosifo-Voloklamsk Monastery. Historians generally paint Danill as a Josephite fanatic, the persecutor of Maksim Grek and Vassian Patrikeev. This he was, but he was also perceptive enough to see that the church needed to turn its attention to the daily life of the laity. He did this in a series of epistles and sermons—the last major sermons before the 1650s—which covered three topics: the dogma of the incarnation (presumably against the Judaizers), monasticism, and the problems of lay morality. The type of lay morality that he advocated and his audience on that subject will be examined in the next chapter. It is his views on monks and bishops that concern us here, for they reveal a conviction that monastic life was in decline. The purely monastic works concern the virtues of the common life, but also the lapses of the monks, even in Volokolamsk, who seem frequently to have fallen prey to greed in violation of their vows. Their other besetting sin was, not surprisingly, lust, and Metropolitan Daniil authored what is probably the largest corpus of writings on the evils of lust in Old Russian religious literature, most of them apparently directed at monastic audiences. If the monks were as bad as he maintained, then someone had to take charge, and Daniil naturally called on the bishops of the Russian church to exhort and supervise the laity. He did this himself in his extensive series of sermons, almost entirely directed at an elite audience. His sermons were the inevitable consequence of the problems with monasticism that he himself underscored.[19]

The gradual decline in authority of the monks and their increasing concentration on internal problems of the monasteries paralleled the attempts of the grand princes and tsars of Russia to restrict the purely material wealth of the monasteries. This process has been the object of considerable research and has been noted frequently in connection with the impact of Josephism on the church as a whole. The successive waves of attempts by the crown to restrict the monasteries' judicial and financial privileges have been seen as the result of the impact of tendencies critical of Josephism in the church as well as in the state. There is considerable evidence for this point of view, and indeed the rhythms of crown policy from restriction to relaxation of privilege and back again seem to parallel the decline in monastic authority.

The first serious attempts to restrict monastic privilege came in the latter part of the reign of Ivan IV, from the 1480s. These quite timid attempts lasted until the end of 1513, and coincided with the ending of the practice of issuing judicial and tax immunity charters to great boyars. In 1514 Vasilii III resumed the practice, and it continued after his death in the period of boyar regency, though the regents did not resume the practice of granting such immunities to boyars. The coronation of Ivan IV as tsar in 1547 marked the end of that wave of new immunity charters.[20] Indirectly these changes in policy reflect the fortunes of the monasteries and their reputation in lay society. Dominant before the end of the fifteenth century, they are increasingly discredited after about 1490, the period of the greatest activity of the "nonpossessors." In 1514 the policy was reversed, though not to the generosity of the pre-1490 period, for many taxes routinely exempted before 1490 are not exempted after 1514.

The beginning of the reign of Ivan IV saw a coherent attempt by the young tsar and his advisers to reform the monasteries and restrict their material prosperity. Although this second feature of the reign has been the subject of considerable scholarly discussion, the attempt to reform the monasteries has not. The problem is that historians have seen the conflict as largely a church-state matter, the financial interests of the crown coming into collision with a largely Josephite church.

The variations of policy under Ivan IV are quickly disposed of. The early years of his majority saw a number of actions regarding the church, starting with the church council of 1547 that recognized many new saints. In early 1550 Ivan's new *Sudebnik* (law book) asserted the decision to recall all the old immunity charters and not issue new ones, a decision not immediately carried out. On 15 September 1550, the church agreed not to erect new privileged settlements. Ivan's government seems to have felt it needed still more of a consensus of the church, for the *Stoglav* council in early 1551 proposed a whole series of measures to strengthen episcopal authority to be discussed shortly and at the same time to reform the monasteries. Ivan proposed to the council restrictions on monastery immunities, but the council does not seem to have gone along; Ivan began on his own to restrict the immunities in the spring of 1551.[21] This policy did not prove possible to retain in succeeding decades. The whole period of Ivan IV's *Oprichnina* (1564–1572) and the years after it was one of gradual increase in the granting of immunities, in spite of the acute needs of the Livonian War. Kashtanov believes that it was the internal conflicts of Ivan with the boyars that led to the crown's retreat, though again it was not a complete retreat. At the end of the reign, in 1580 and again in early 1584 (after Ivan's death), the crown was able to convince a church council to restrict the immunities of the monasteries.

Whether the crown's financial needs were the main motivation for restricting monastic immunities or not, the policy had implications beyond financial or political issues, for it was precisely the material wealth of the monasteries that had been criticized by the nonpossessors. The compromises over the attempts to restrict monastic immunities paralleled exactly the ideological evolution of the church establishment of the second half of the century, for the dominant attitude on the issue of monastic wealth was one of compromise. There was no victory of pure Josephism, as stated in most accounts of the period. This compromise ideology was part of the decline in authority of the monasteries, as it ultimately benefited the episcopacy, in some ways quite specifically.

The Church Council of 1551: Clergy and Laity

The church council that took place in the early part of the year 1551, known as the Council of a Hundred Chapters, or *Stoglav* Council from the name of the book of its proceedings and decisions, was a serious attempt to reform the church and to introduce simultaneously Christian practices into the daily life of the population. The reform of the church was primarily an attempt to increase the power and influence of the bishops, especially over the parish clergy, and to arrest the decline of monastic life.

One of the basic problems for the bishops was the simple lack of staff to supervise the parish clergy. In 1551 Russia had only ten eparchies (dioceses) including that of the metropolitan, with the result that each one was enormous in size. These eparchies were divided into "tenths" (*desiatiny*), each of which was under the eye of a lay "tither" or *desiatil'nik*. In turn the bishop seems to have frequently resorted to appointing a locum tenens or *namestnik* to oversee the tithers. The surviving sources that refer to the tithers all deal with various dues owed the bishop, not with spiritual or disciplinary questions, until the early sixteenth century. In 1545 Archbishop Feodosii of Novgorod wrote to the clergy of the small market town of Ustiuzhna Zhelezopol'skaia to complain of their misdeeds and shortcomings. They had made unauthorized changes in the liturgy, married people within prohibited degrees of consanguinity, remarried divorced people, moved to other eparchies, and continued to celebrate mass when widowed. All this was done without the authorization of the archbishop's tithers, who had complained to him of the clergy's behavior. These are clearly disciplinary issues, which were assumed to fall under the jurisdiction of the tithers.[22]

The system was too small and imperfect to be of much use, and so the *Stoglav* council proceeded to change it. The problem was addressed in the seventh question to the council from the tsar, which stated that the tithers' courts were both ineffective and corrupt, ruining the people and clergy with fines and taxes while paying heed to slanderers (*iabedniki*) and permitting priests to have mistresses (*zhonki i devki*). The council justified its actions with long quotations from the fathers and the decisions of the early ecumenical councils to the effect that clergy should be judged only by clergy and thus the system of delegating episcopal administration to lay tithers was wrong in principle. In the new system members of the clergy of each town or district were to elect from their midst priests' elders (*popovskie starosty*) who were to take care of disciplinary, liturgical, and financial matters. The office of tither was not to be abolished but henceforth only priests were to be chosen for it. In spite of the declarations from the fathers and canon law, members of the clergy were not to be entirely autonomous from the crown, for some matters (murder and certain forms of theft) still came under lay courts, where the priests' elders would sit together with the land elders or the tsar's officials. The new tither, now a priest, would be accompanied on his duties also by the land elder and his assistants. Nevertheless, disciplinary matters short of serious crimes by the clergy were to be handled by the priests' elders, not by episcopal officials.[23] This whole system gave the bishop a more effective instrument of supervision of the clergy, while at the same time placing much of the day-to-day control into the hands of the clergy itself. It thus both helped the bishops and raised the prestige of the clergy, something much needed in the presence of the perceived decline of the monasteries and the need to combat pre-Christian beliefs and practices among the population.

The decline in the authority of monasticism had already led Metropolitan Daniil to see the monasteries as morally lax and in need of reform. His exhortations presumably had little effect, for the monasteries came under considerable criticism at the council in the tsar's questions. Of the first group of thirty-seven questions from the throne, no less than eleven concerned monasteries wholly or in part. One of these was about monastic privileges in landholding, and the rest concerned basic aspects of monastic life, such as obedience to the hegumen, permanent residence in the monastery, and observance of the typikon. The moral shortcomings of the monks, drunkenness, the presence of young boys in the monastery, and contact with women outside the monastery all came in for the tsar's disapproval. The reaction of the council to these strictures was complicated. To the whole group of eleven questions the council compiled two chapters of decisions in which they agreed with the criticism but established no new institutions or procedures to deal with the problems. The churchmen only exhorted the monks to improve their behavior and cautioned the hegumens and archimandrites to be more careful in accepting novices and monks tonsured in other monasteries. The church recognized the problem but did little about it.[24]

The council was similarly cautious in the matter of the immunities and privileges on the monasteries' lands. The 1550 Book of Laws, the *Sudebnik*, had already forbidden certain types of privileges (tax immunities called *tarkhan* charters), and the decree of the tsar and the church of 15 September 1550 forbade the establishment of new privileged settlements (*slobody*). The text of the 1551 council proceedings indicates that the issue came up again (question 16 of the first group), where the young tsar stated that these privileges led to the excessive involvement of the monks in worldly affairs and thus to the corruption of the monks. Normally historians see this attempt as part of the crown's efforts to increase its revenue in the face of Josephite-inspired opposition in the church, led by Metropolitan Makarii—this despite Makarii's acquiescence in the decree of 15 September 1550, which was included in the *Stoglav* as chapter 98. Furthermore, in the early months of 1551 the crown reissued the monastery land charters whose time had elapsed but with far fewer immunities than before.[25] Ivan IV evidently thought that the monasteries not only needed reformation but also did not need the extensive privileges that they had previously enjoyed. These restrictions affected to some extent episcopal property, but the main losers were the monasteries, not the metropolitan or bishops. In one respect the latter even gained revenue and authority. Ivan also greatly restricted the judicial immunities of the monasteries, but not in his own interest, as in the case of financial immunities. Early judicial immunities had exempted the monasteries from the courts of the grand prince's provincial governors, allowing them to come to the grand prince himself in Moscow for nonspiritual matters, both criminal and civil. The *Stoglav* (article 67) transferred this jurisdiction over the monasteries to the bishops and metropolitan of the relevant eparchy, in principle bypassing the tsar's court altogether.[26] Thus the crown increased its revenue from taxes that were no longer exempt, but the metropolitan and bishops increased their authority over the monasteries and to some extent their revenues from the courts. The transfer of the monasteries to the courts of the bishops and metropolitan was a diminution in power of the crown as well as a loss of privilege by the monastery: it also increased the autonomy of the church as a whole.

In this issue, episcopal jurisdiction over the monasteries, may lie one of the main reasons that Makarii was so ready to compromise with the crown in church matters. Further, if we accept the statement of the text of the *Stoglav* that the "tsar's questions" were prepared by Makarii before the council, we may indeed question the usually accepted notion that Makarii resisted Ivan. More likely the council represents a collaborative effort to restrict the wealth and improve the life of the monasteries and simultaneously to raise the authority of the bishops. This interpretation of Makarii's efforts would also explain his patronage of ecclesiastical writers like Varlaam-Vasilii of Pskov, whose writings are hard to square with the pure Josephism usually asserted to be the basis of Makarii's worldview.

The further strengthening of the clergy, the bishops and the parish clergy, was also a component in the council's attempt to reform popular religious practices. This attempt was not new, but it was one to which the monasteries could not easily contribute. The relationship of the monasteries to the mass of the population (as revealed by the lives of the monastic saints) was charismatic—that is, it was noninstitutional. The Russian church in the fourteenth and fifteenth centuries was aware of the need to bring Christianity to the masses and drive out the old ways, but it did little more than exhort the priests to greater effort, primarily on the fringes of the Russian state. To some extent this pattern persisted, for the known exhortations to the clergy to stamp out pagan practices in 1534, 1543, and 1548 all came from Novgorod (which had more non-Russians and therefore presumably was less Christianized) and were directed at the Orthodox clergy of the Finnish Vod' and Karelians. In one important respect this passivity began in the first half of the sixteenth century to give way to greater activity. The establishment of the Epiphany ceremony as a principal ritual of the Russian court around 1520 was partly an attempt to combat pagan practices and at the same time to reinforce the authority of the metropolitan in a public ceremony in Moscow before the whole people of the city.[27] The decisions of the Council of a Hundred Chapters show the same combination of the reinforcement of episcopal authority and the attempt to combat popular ritual.

The issue of popular rituals and practices was addressed in the second group of "tsar's questions," largely about issues of liturgy and practice. Many of these dealt with technicalities of liturgy the significance of which is obscure and unresearched, but others were direct attacks on popular practices. Question 16 described the folk musicians and players that came to the church before weddings, and the council ordered the priests to forbid them to appear. Question 19 raised the general issue of *skomorokhi* (popular musicians) with the same answer from the council: forbid them to perform. Commemoration of the dead on Trinity Saturday (with dancing and singing), the Rusalia on St. John's Day (midsummer), the Christmas-Epiphany rituals called *sviatki,* and various rituals in the spring from Easter to St. Peter's Fast (questions 23–27) were likewise condemned. Most of these practices are known in detail from the nineteenth and early twentieth centuries, so clearly the condemnations were quite ineffective. This is not surprising since no mechanism is suggested other than the actions of the local priest, and no mechanism is set up to help him in his task.[28]

As far as it is known, the attempt to set up priest's elders in place of lay officials was relatively successful at least in the sense that it was done, whereas the attempt to influence the masses away from traditional rites in favor of Christian ritual was not. The instructions to Gurii, the new archbishop of Kazan', mainly concern his relations with the governor of the new province, but his letter to the monks of the Sviiazhsk Monastery of the Mother of God reasserts his right to name priests among the monks and his jurisdiction over them. In 1561 Archbishop Nikandr of Rostov, Iaroslavl', and Ustiug gave his opinion on a case of spiritual consanguinity, and the opinion was addressed to the priests' elder and the *desiatil'nik,* the tither of Velikii Ustiug. Three years later Nikandr wrote to the cathedral archpriest (*sobornyi protopop*) of Velikii Ustiug ordering him to instruct the cathedral priests of the city to go to Sol' Vychegodsk (then the capital of the Stroganov domains!) to ensure that the liturgy was properly celebrated and to educate lax priests. These references show the new system in operation. Nevertheless, everything could not have been so well organized, for in 1594 another church council had to repeat the same injunctions to elect priests' elders to take care of both discipline and liturgy, primarily in Moscow itself.[29] As for the attempts to replace popular rituals, this was simply a failure, for already in 1581 Possevino reported that the common people rarely went to church and thought that church attendance was for the higher orders of society. Little seems to have changed since the fourteenth century in this regard. In 1627 and 1648 Tsar Aleksei repeated the same injunctions against the same popular festivals and rituals, again to no effect, as they persisted another three hundred years.[30]

Religious Thought after 1551

The traditional view of the Russian church from midcentury onward is one of the dominance of Josephism, incarnated in the figure of Metropolitan Makarii. In opposition to Makarii and the rest of the church were only a few remaining nonpossessors, including the priest Sil'vestr of the Annunciation Cathedral, and the heretics, who continued the traditions of the Judaizers in a modified form. The heretics were very few in number and easily suppressed, so that the church presented a picture of almost complete uniformity of thought. Churchmen like Sil'vestr could only be successful because they had the support of Ivan IV until the *Oprichnina*, after which the Josephites had virtually complete control.[31] The traditional view considerably exaggerates the uniformity of thought and action in the church after 1551, as well as the dominance of Orthodox Josephism. The "Josephite" ideology of the period roughly 1550–1570 was in fact a compromise ideology that acknowledged the correctness of some positions of Joseph's opponents. The writings of the half century after the Council of a Hundred Chapters also show a persistent desire to raise the authority of the episcopate, not only over the monasteries but even in relation to the tsar himself.

The heretics, in contrast, were certainly critical of monasticism, but in general they also rejected the existing hierarchy and many basic aspects of Christian dogma. There were only three known heretics: Matvei Bashkin; Artemii, the archimandrite of the Trinity–St. Sergii Monastery; and Feodosii Kosoi, a slave. All were arrested and tried in 1553–1554. Bashkin was the most obscure: he was accused of disbelief in the Trinity by the foreign office secretary Ivan Mikhailovich Viskovatyi. He was imprisoned and possibly executed. Artemii was a much more important figure, and was accused of disbelief in the Trinity, opposition to persecution of the Judaizers, and praise of the Latin faith. These charges obviously have something wrong with them, for Artemii could not simultaneously support anti-Trinitarianism and Catholicism. Furthermore, after his escape to Lithuania he defended the Trinity against real anti-Trinitarians in Poland and asserted that this charge against him had been manufactured by his opponents in Moscow. Artemii did, however, express skepticism about miracles and asserted that true faith was to be found in the scriptures, a position that Makarii and the church were bound to condemn. The third of the heretics, Feodosii Kosoi, had been the slave of one of the tsar's "servants" (a boyar?), who had run away to Belozero and become a monk. According to Zinovii Otenskii, Feodosii's theological opponent, the ex-slave also denied the reality of the Trinity, the need of monks or a church hierarchy (and the landed wealth that supported them), and the devotion to icons and the cross, and he thought miracles a deception by the clergy, greedy for the pilgrims' money. In Lithuania Kosoi joined real anti-Trinitarians, the Polish Arians.[32] None of these heretics (if that indeed is what they all were) had any significant following, and Artemii and Feodosii are more part of the history of Orthodoxy in Lithuania than in Russia. The radicalism of their views has attracted much attention from historians, but it does little more than highlight the possible discontents in the Russian church. More significant was the criticism of miracles in the writings of Artemii, who does seem to have been Orthodox in belief, for it shows that the consequences of the decline of monasticism did not meet universal acceptance. His crime was most likely his refusal to curse the Judaizers (in this case meaning any anti-Trinitarian), which took him back to Nil Sorskii's original ideas and separated him from the moderate Josephism of the 1550s.

The clearest example of the attitude of church writers to Josephism after midcentury is in the second life of Joseph Volotskii himself, usually attributed to the Serbian monk Lev-Anikita Filolog. The text begins with the quite explicit statement that there are many paths to the cure of the spiritual disease of sin, and the ensuing account makes clear that he means that Joseph's path was one, while Nil Sorskii's path of hermitage was another that was just as good. The text goes on to describe Joseph's life in a manner concordant with the beginning. After describing Joseph's apprenticeship in the Monastery of Pafnutii of Borovsk, it goes on to describe his stay at the Monastery of St. Kirill of Belozero, to which he retreated to escape the disharmony in Borovsk. Joseph learned virtue, labor, fasting, and obedience from Pafnutii, but not the common life. The author attributes Joseph's love of the common life to his stay at Belozero, and explicitly connects the typikon of Joseph's monastery at Volokolamsk with Belozero and St. Kirill. The text handled the issue of the nonpossessors with great delicacy. He mentioned Nil Sorskii by name only once, to note that Prince Dionisii Zvenigorodskii, after his tonsure, "loved isolation [*uedinenie*] and asked the father [Joseph] to be allowed to go to father Nil, who shone then like a light in wilderness at Belozero." The issue of landholding was more complex, but Lev-Anikita described Joseph's views at some length, attributing to him a moderation he probably did not possess in reality. In this account, Joseph even begged the prince not to give him land and wealth in view of the poverty of the people! The conflict with Archbishop Serapion was likewise presented in a compromise form, stressing the virtue of Serapion and attributing the dispute to the bad advice of the grand prince's men.[33]

This story of Joseph's life was not included in the *Chet'i minei* of Metropolitan Makarii, for he preferred the more conventional work of Savva Chernyi. Other writings, however, showed a similar conciliatory spirit, such as the life of the hegumen Daniil of Pereiaslavl' mentioned previously. In this otherwise rather conventional Josephite text the author asserts that at the beginning of Daniil's monastic career some "trans-

Volga elders" from the hermitages of that area came to him and expressed their approval of his efforts. Again, both the hermitage and the common life are shown as possible routes to salvation. Other texts from the middle of the sixteenth century reveal very clearly the shift away from monasticism, and even a rather critical view of the Russian bishops. These are the works of Varlaam-Vasilii of Pskov, normally considered to be an ally and supporter of Metropolitan Makarii.

Varlaam-Vasilii stated in the life of Nifont and other works that he had written it at the request of Makarii, and on this basis he is assumed to be a supporter of the official church position (in turn assumed to be pure Josephism). If Varlaam-Vasilii really shared all of Makarii's views, then Makarii was not entirely the dogmatic follower of Josephite Orthodoxy depicted in the literature. This conclusion is inescapable after a careful examination of Varlaam-Vasilii's life of the Novgorod bishop Nifont, written about 1558. Nifont was bishop during 1131–1156, a former monk of the Kiev Monastery of the Caves. These few facts are virtually all that we or Varlaam-Vasilii know about him, but the Pskov monk managed to produce an entire life around them, and with a definite purpose. In Varlaam's account his hero's life as monk and then bishop is briefly summarized, and the core of the work is Nifont's conflict with Klim Smoliatich, the metropolitan of Kiev. In Varlaam's version, the conflict arose because Klim's elevation was not confirmed in Constantinople: he became metropolitan "not by the patriarchal blessing of the Ecumenical Patriarch of Tsar'grad [Constantinople] but by his own wish." Klim tried to force Nifont to celebrate the liturgy with him, but Nifont refused. This account was precisely the opposite to that given in the quasi-official Book of Degrees, where Klim was presented as wholly legitimate, and the relic of the head of St. Clement of Rome served in place of the blessing from Constantinople.[34] This was a controversial issue in the middle of the sixteenth century, for Maksim Grek had been accused (among other things) of not accepting the legitimacy of the Russian hierarchy without confirmation from Constantinople. No Russian metropolitan after Fotii a century before had been so confirmed, and in 1588–1589 the Russians would extract recognition of their autonomy from the Greeks with some difficulty.[35]

Varlaam's other writings primarily glorified other Novgorod and Pskov saints, both monks and bishops. This hagiography, especially of the bishops, became a small industry in the second half of the sixteenth century, culminating in the composition of the life of Archbishop Antonii the Roman after his relics were discovered in 1581 and a local festival established in his honor in 1597. The story of Antonii is basically a fabulous adventure, the core of it being his miraculous journey on a rock over the sea to Novgorod from Italy. The point of the story was to demonstrate the holiness of the Novgorod archbishop, God's direct protection of him, and his association with Nifont.[36] None of this was in itself at all "subversive" (except for the life of Nifont), though it does not fit

with the image of centralization of the church after 1547–1551 common
in the scholarly literature. It was an attempt to build up the importance
of Novgorod, and one that was successful, for Antonii appeared in the
printed *Ustav* of 1610.

The most dramatic attempt at the glorification of a holy bishop, and
one that is radically at odds with the traditional picture of the submissive
Josephite church, was the life of Metropolitan Filipp. Never published
until this day, the text (written in the 1590s in the Solovetskii Monastery)
presents the most negative picture of Ivan the Terrible (Ivan IV) to be
produced in Old Russia, and the clearest argument for the central role of
the episcopacy and its leader, the metropolitan. The text is not close
enough to the events to tell us much that is reliable about the events of
Filipp's metropolitanate (1566–1568), but that is not its value nor its
intent. The text opens with a brief account of Filipp's early life, followed
by a somewhat longer account of his days as monk and then hegumen of
the Solovetskii Monastery. It moves quickly to his appointment as metropolitan of Moscow, and then spends three-quarters of its space on Filipp's
reproof of Tsar Ivan for his cruelty and injustice. The text uses the sixth-
century work on kingship by Deacon Agapetus, curiously reversing its
intent by citing it against Ivan rather than for him. A text in praise of
imperial autocracy is used to denounce the tyranny of the tsar. Essentially the life of Filipp is a pamphlet against Ivan with an introduction
about Filipp's life followed by a brief account of his murder. It not only
presents arguments against Ivan's rule and a verbal portrait of the bad
tsar, but also a portrait of the virtuous metropolitan, a man of such
spiritual strength and authority that he dares to reprove the tsar to his
face. It is the metropolitan, not the monk, that is here the defender of the
Russian land.[37]

Filipp had to wait until 1646 for recognition as a saint, but Archbishop
Serapion of Novgorod, a figure clearly at variance with the Josephite
tradition, did not. In the older Josephite literature (by Savva Chernyi),
Serapion was a negative character, the opponent of the holy and correct
Joseph. In the 1550s a life of Serapion was composed that presented
him in a wholly different light, as a pious and righteous man maligned
by his enemies. In this account Joseph was at fault, for the devil had
caused a quarrel between him and Prince Fedor Volotskii, and Joseph
had answered the prince's anger not with humility but with self-will
(*samovol'stvo*). Serapion's just anger at Joseph's self-will was answered by
Joseph's deceitful persuasion of the "meek and quiet" metropolitan Simon to remove Serapion. Joseph thus appeared in a most unpleasant
light. At the same time the text did not endorse the position of the
nonpossessors, and defended monastic landholding while not attributing
base motives to the nonpossessors. Indeed the text is quite respectful,
ascribing their ideas to their great piety and desire for complete removal
from the world. In this version the council merely decided that landholding was useful to maintain the monasteries, for there were needs that

piety alone could not satisfy.[38] Again, this was an attempt at compromise, and one that was officially recognized in the typikon of 1610, which included Serapion among the Russian saints.

Serapion was included in this number, but Joseph Volotskii himself was not. This fact is rarely noted, though some scholars are accurate enough to record correctly that the "canonization" of 1579 mentioned by Golubinskii was merely the establishment of a local festival at the monastery of Joseph of Volokolamsk. Joseph first appeared in service books issued under the official eye of the Moscow patriarch with Metropolitan Filipp in 1646, evidently the result of the influence of the Zealots of Piety (see pages 54–59). At no time in the sixteenth century did the Russian Orthodox church recognize Joseph as worthy of a national feast day, though by 1610 it did so recognize his opponent Serapion. In the texts about monasticism, especially those about Joseph and his life, every effort seems to have been made to present a compromise ideology on the main points that had been in dispute: monastic landholding and the common life were accepted as legitimate, but the hermitage was accepted also and the motives and virtues of the nonpossessors recognized. The life of Serapion went so far as to condemn Joseph and simultaneously to propound a moderate form of Josephism. While the influence of Josephism was thus being moderated, and the questioning of monastic landholding legitimated if not imitated, a concerted attempt was made, especially in Novgorod, to glorify the archbishops over the monks. Virtually unknown, semimythical figures of the past were resurrected to exemplify the virtues of the good archbishop, which in Nifont's case even included a glorification of the supreme authority of the Greeks in the Russian church. The life of Filipp glorified not only the good and wise metropolitan but even resistance to and reproof of the tsar himself. Not surprisingly, Nifont was never accepted as a saint, and Filipp had to wait until the 1640s. Nevertheless, both lives show the desire to see the bishop as the central figure in the church, replacing the monk. In the life of Serapion, Joseph's ultimate sin was that he did not obey his bishop.[39]

The sixteenth-century Orthodox church in Russia had most of all to deal with the decline in importance and spiritual authority of monasticism. This decline took two forms, one being the withdrawal of the monks into almost exclusive concern with inner-monastic affairs, and the other being a perceived decline in the morals and spiritual level of the monasteries. As Metropolitan Daniil perceived, this meant that he and the bishops would have to step into the gap and try to improve the moral and spiritual life of the laity. The *Stoglav* council and its decisions were the result of that attempt, as were Daniil's sermons and the lives of holy bishops that appeared in such numbers after 1550. The attempt was not a success, even though a number of bishops were recognized as saints. The problem was that at this moment the elite of Russian society, the boyars and the court, entered a period of great political turmoil that absorbed their attention until after the Time of Troubles. Interest in the holy bishops was concentrated in provincial Novgorod and the North, and Daniil had no imitators. The attempt of the *Stoglav* council to re-order popular religious life away from the traditional rituals was an utter failure, and so the miracle cults became the main avenue of integration of the masses into the religious life of the church.

2

*The Landholding Class
and Its Religious World*

The religious changes of the early sixteenth century, the decline of the authority of the monasteries, and the concomitant attempts to raise the power of the bishops affected the laity as well as the clergy, especially the elite of Russian society: the boyars (and court society in general) and the lesser landholding class. This elite was more greatly affected because it had been more deeply involved in religious life than the townspeople or peasants: as we shall see, the monks came largely from the landholding class, mainly the lesser landholders but also some boyars. As the monasteries declined in spiritual importance, other forms of religious life became more important for the boyars, such as participation in court ceremonies and involvement in the religious disputes and writings of the time; they even became the object of Metropolitan Daniil's sermons. However, the second half of the century was more a period of withdrawal from active involvement in religion than of change of form: the boyars in particular seem to have concentrated their attention on the turbulent politics of the era. Of the lesser landholding class we know less, and only the *Domostroi* sheds some light on what their attitudes and actions were supposed to be.

The composition of the elite of sixteenth-century Russian society is the object of some scholarly debate, and it is not my intention to resolve or even to describe all of these disputes. Nineteenth-century tradition focused on the service of the lesser landholders in the army and the allegedly conditional character of their landholdings. Similarly the boyars were also seen mainly in relation to the grand prince/tsar, in the traditional view an absolute ("autocratic") ruler little different in power from Nicholas I. More modern historians have noted that the sovereign of the sixteenth-century Russian state was more a referee among powerful boyar clans, and others have suggested that the traditional idea of conditional service is, to say the least, exaggerated. The landholding aristocracy of Russia may have lacked the legal apparatus of the Central European *Ständestaat* but it possessed remarkable stability of family and property at the level of the clan. Its greatest families, the boyars, in fact ruled the state up to 1547 and after 1584, and the interval between of Ivan IV's challenge to them was ultimately a bloody failure.[1] To understand the forms of religious life of the various layers of the landholding class it is necessary first to briefly review the institutional structure of their political and social life.

The Russian boyars of the sixteenth century formed the aristocracy of one of Europe's more archaic states. In 1500 the administration of the "state" was virtually equivalent to the administration of the grand prince's household. Only the treasury and the palace itself under the majordomo (*dvoretskii*) had become distinct offices: the foreign office, the *posol'skii prikaz*, did not come until the 1550s, and other offices were added only in the course of the second half of the century. These tiny offices were responsible for the whole of the Russian state apart from the few remaining appanage principalities, hardly a major exception by mid-century. The army was equally primitive in structure, however successful in the field. It consisted almost entirely of the landholding class mobilized for war, from great boyars to provincial landholders, each expected to provide his own food, equipment, and armed retainers, a considerable number in the case of great boyars. Once again, it was not until the 1550s that Ivan IV introduced permanent (infantry) formations into the army. At the pinnacle of the aristocracy and the state stood the boyar duma. The name is a scholarly invention of the nineteenth century (contemporaries referred merely to "the boyars"), but the importance of boyar aristocracy was no less real. The boyars dealt with all important affairs, foreign policy, war, and internal problems. The treasurer and majordomo handled routine matters, but their offices alone did not convey political power. Traditional views of the significance of the boyars are rather contradictory, as historians have devoted much time to analyzing the boyar duma but have also insisted on presenting the grand prince tsar as a powerful absolutist monarch decades before this type of monarchy became a reality. A more realistic view of relations between the crown and aristocracy in this very archaic state shows that the grand prince was essentially a referee among traditionally powerful boyar clans. This was a consensus system that presented to the outside a mythic unity under the hand of the sovereign.[2]

The summit of Russian society was formed by a very small group indeed. The core of this aristocracy was the boyar duma, which included both those few men who held the rank of boyar as well as some lesser ranks.[3] Those with boyar rank rarely exceeded forty in number in the sixteenth century, and in the reign of Ivan III the number was closer to eight or ten. Below the boyars were those holding the rank of *okol'nichii*, similar in number. The boyars formed the core of the elite military unit known as the *Gosudarev dvor*, literally the "Sovereign's court," which con-

sisted of all the landholders who served the sovereign directly either in
the army or the administration, as well as their armed servants. Although
the overwhelming majority comprised landholders and soldiers, the Sovereign's court also included the secretaries (*d'iaki*) of the greater administrative offices in Moscow. At midcentury the total number in the Sovereign's court reached about twenty-six hundred men. Very roughly
speaking, this was the elite of the Russian state, together with their own
elite servants. Beyond this privileged group was the bulk of the landholders, mostly *deti boiarskie* in rank, who served in the army "from the
towns," that is, from districts other than Moscow. These numbered about
thirty-five to forty thousand in the early years in the reign of Ivan IV.[4]
These latter constituted the bulk of the landholding class and were much
less important politically than the Sovereign's court. The distinction was
not entirely one of wealth, however, for humbler members of the Sovereign's court might be poorer than the wealthier *deti boiarskie* who
served from one of the provincial towns. The very wealthy landholders,
however, were exclusively to be found in the highest ranks of the Sovereign's court. These distinctions, though military in origin, formed the
basis of the ranking system of the landholding class.[5]

The elite of elites, the boyars and officials who made up the inner circle
of the Sovereign's court and who had actual power, was quite small. It
consisted of the boyars and *okol'nichie*, a few army commanders of lesser
rank, and the holders of the important court offices, like that of *dvoretskii*.
Almost all of these men came from the families traditionally powerful in
the Moscow and other principalities, and like the Russian state itself,
came together to form a single national aristocracy comparatively recently. Some were the scions of the boyars of the Old Moscow principality
of the fourteenth century, others were princely families that had come to
serve the grand prince of Moscow at various times after about 1400.
Some were descendants of the princes of Rostov and Suzdal', ancient
families of northeastern Russia. Others sprang from branches of the
Lithuanian ruling house, the Gediminovichi. Most were merely great
magnates serving the Russian tsar, but others, like the princes
Riapolovskii or Obolenskii, still possessed semisovereign rights over their
small original territories in the first half of the century. An exotic touch
was provided by the Tatar tsarevichi, many still Muslims and all descendants of Ghengiz Khan, who in dignity, if not in wealth or political power,
stood ahead of all the Russian noble families. These aristocratic families
stood in relationship to one another in a system of rank that only partly
coincided with the ladder of political, military, and palace offices that
made up the Sovereign's court. Certain princely families were equal or
superior in dignity to the old Moscow boyar families but not necessarily
as powerful in politics. At the same time there were hundreds of families
with ancient princely titles that languished in provincial obscurity. The
institution that kept this loose and messy system together was the body of
precedent known as *mestnichestvo* (precedence), a set of rules that roughly

determined what members of what families could hold what office. Rigid enough to ensure important office in the army and administration for the great families, it was flexible enough to allow the tsar to deal with incompetents and slowly promote the deserving, even if not very far. Thus the combination of tradition, wealth, and *mestnichestvo* kept the elite of Russian society small and stable.[6] Most of our knowledge of the religious world of the laity concerns this aristocracy, while that of the lesser landholders is much more obscure.

As far as we can tell, the religious world of the boyars had several components. One important area was the religious life of the court, its ceremonies during the main church festivals, the pilgrimages to the Trinity and other monasteries, and even the messages contained in the physical appearance of the main churches and palace buildings in the Kremlin. Here the ruler played a central role, and the elite were presumably more participants than actors. Members of the elite were also involved in the religious controversies of the time as supporters, enemies, or mere correspondents of the main religious leaders. A great deal is known about this aspect of religious life, but it has been approached not from the side of laymen but rather from that of the church leaders. Finally, the monasteries played a role in the religious life of the boyars. This is one of the few areas in which it is possible to get some sense of the elite's personal religious life and to go beyond the possibly untypical friends of Joseph Volotskii or Maksim Grek. In the absence of extensive knowledge of private devotions or reading among the boyars, their relations with the monasteries offer a rare window into their world.

In Kiev Rus' princes and boyars played a central role—maybe the central role—in the foundation and maintenance of monasteries. Of the approximately seventeen monasteries in the city of Kiev, most were princely foundations, essentially house monasteries of one or another branch of the ruling dynasty. These seem to correspond to the private monasteries of the Byzantine Empire. The Kiev Monastery of the Caves, by contrast, was an independent foundation, following the example of Mount Athos among the Byzantines, the predominant type of monastery in later Byzantium. Its independent status did not diminish its attractiveness to great boyars, however, who both gave land to the monks and joined their ranks. This role was to be expected from the Byzantine example, since many Byzantine aristocrats also became monks and patronized monasteries, including the great independent monasteries that grew up following the example of Mount Athos. In the late Byzantine period such an aristocratic monk was none other than St. Gregory Palamas, the leader of the hesychasts.[7]

At the beginning of the sixteenth century the aristocracy of the Russian state was still involved actively in monastic life, but by its end the role of the aristocracy was largely passive. The period of greatest involvement by princes and boyars in the monasteries was the fifteenth century: St. Sergii seems to have had fewer such relations, though he did cure a

boyar possessed by demons. St. Kirill, by contrast was closely tied to the
appanage prince Mikhail Andreevich of Mozhaisk, Vereia, and Belozero
(c. 1445–1486) and his family, who visited the saint in his lifetime and
were cured afterward at his shrine. A local boyar named Fedor initially
tried to attack the monastery, but afterward Kirill's ability to call on
divine aid caused Fedor to "have great faith" in Kirill and give him
fishing rights. The saint also cured a princess of Kargopol' and received
donations (with miraculous aid) from the boyars Roman Aleksandrovich
and Roman Ivanovich.[8] The saints' relations with the outside world were
to a large extent with the aristocracy.

The boyars' relations with the monasteries changed in the course of
the sixteenth century, following the decline in authority of the monks. In
Josephite literature the ties to the aristocracy seem to gradually weaken.
Pafnutii Borovskii's relations with the appanage princes are cool or hostile, and his visions are of members of the ruling Moscow dynasty. He also
cured the wife of a Moscow boyar who held the office of *stol'nik* (table
assistant), Aleksei Burun. Savva Chernyi's life of Joseph Volotskii shows a
similar picture. Joseph founded his monastery with the encouragement
of Prince Boris Vasil'evich of Volok, who attended the dedication with his
boyars and continued to visit and patronize the monastery. His son
Fedor, however, was hostile, leading to Joseph's transfer to grand
princely authority. The two boyars mentioned in the life (Prince Andrei
Golenin and Andrei Kvashnin-Nevezha) both served appanage princes
in Volok and Ruza rather than the grand prince.[9]

Zimin's data on the Iosifo-Volokolamsk Monastery confirm the picture
in Savva Chernyi's life. Zimin analyzed both the social origins of the
monks and the records of donations to the monastery (land, money, and
objects) and came to the conclusion that both monks and donors were
the same group of people: the lesser landholders of the Volokolamsk
area. These *melkie votchinniki* made up the majority of the monks through
the whole period from the founding of the monastery in 1479 until the
end of the sixteenth century, both in the early years when the appanage
prince Boris Vasil'evich of Volok was both immediate lord and patron of
the monastery, and after 1507, when Grand Prince Vasilii III of Moscow
took it under his protection. Thus, throughout the sixteenth century,
even as the monastery worked with the grand prince and the church to
try to uphold Josephite principles, the monastery itself remained essentially a local center, with both monks and donors coming from the lesser
landholders of the immediate area. The most aristocratic of the monks
were the boyars who served Prince Boris: Andrei Kvashnin, Prince Andrei Golenin, and Prince Danilo Zvenigorodskii. (Some princes of this
line served the grand princes.) As Zimin observed, even these local nota-
bles were the monastery's troublemakers: Kvashnin tried to wear better
clothes than the rule allowed, and Danilo (Dionisii) opposed Joseph over
the issue of the nonpossessors. Most of the monks were from families
unknown outside of the district, names that appear in the service records

of the grand princes and tsars rarely if at all. Such are the Polevs and Rugotins, who gave monks to the monastery but do not figure in the Moscow service records (the Rugotins were servants of the princes Penkov who themselves rarely appear) or only appear after the lifetime of the monks (Polev). The exceptions confirm the rule: the Obolenskii family produced at least one monk of boyar rank, Prince Dmitrii Ivanovich Nemoi Telepnev-Obolenskii, but his tonsure was ordered by Ivan IV. Prince Obolenskii's family had once served the Volok princes, so the choice was natural. The typical monk, however, who entered the monastery fairly early in life without a secular career, remained the son of local landholders throughout the century. Indeed there seem to have been more monks of humble origin, even peasants, than there were representatives of the great families. The donors, curiously enough, followed the same pattern. Of course the grand princes and tsars gave many gifts, and three of the great families did too: the princes Obolenskii again, whose connection with the monastery went back to the Volok appanage, and the princes Bel'skii and the Godunovs, both of whom seem to have simply wanted to give to this particular monastery. Nevertheless, the bulk of the gifts came from local landholders of the Volok area. The other great families of Russia gave nothing. To the end of the century the Iosifo-Volokolamsk Monastery, though the seat of currents of thought of national importance, remained the monastery of the small and middle-level Volok landholders.[10]

The Monastery of St. Kirill at Belozero had a more complex relationship to lay society in the sixteenth century, for the boyars seem to have been more involved in its monastic life. Situated on the White Lake in the North, it was very near the northern limit of productive agriculture. The old Belozero (White Lake) principality was essentially a projection of an agricultural settlement jutting into the northern forests, and until about 1530 most of the land granted to the monastery was in this area, in spite of its fifteenth-century ties to the Mozhaisk princes. The donors then were local landholders as in the case of the Iosifo-Volokolamsk Monastery. About that time, however, the monastery began to receive grants of property and make purchases farther south, reaching into the valley of the Upper Volga, in the heartland of the Russian state and of boyar landholding. This expansion continued until about 1570, after which most new monastery property was to be found in the North and was generally not agricultural land but holdings in the northern trade and industries, such as fishing and salt boiling.[11] Clearly important boyar families in Moscow were giving land only after about 1530. Monetary gifts seem to have started about the same time, for Nikol'skii was able to find them only from the 1540s (Prince Ivan Ivanovich Kubenskii, a local family that had become important in Moscow, for example). About 1550 several important boyar clans—the princes Vorotynskii and the Sheremetevs—began to give to the monastery, and their gifts increased in the 1560s and 1570s, when many were exiled or executed by the tsar. However, their gifts did not cease after Ivan's death, and they continued to give money to the monks into the seventeenth century, joined by a few more clans, notably the princes Golitsyn; exile was not the main factor. Similarly, the same clans gave money to the monks to say a mass for them after their death; in this category were the Vorotynskiis, Sheremetevs, Bel'skiis, Shuiskiis, the princes Kemskii (a local family), and lesser families like the princes Paletskii. Burial records from the early part of the seventeenth century show that many of the donors were buried in the monastery churches, as is natural since the money was often given so that the name of the donor be mentioned in masses for the dead.

Nikol'skii did not set out to collect information about the social origin of the monks, but the same burial records give some clues. Not all monks were identified beyond their monastic names, but those that were either have names suggesting birth in the northern towns ("Kargopolets") or have surnames that do not appear in the service records, suggesting that if they did come from the landholding class, they were from fairly lowly sectors of it. Nikol'skii was able to identify some townsmen from towns not in the North, such as Pskov or Viaz'ma. Many of the nicknames recorded also point to monks probably not from the boyar elite: Krivoi Klobuk or Baboedov.[12] One case of a monk from a greater family than this was the hegumen Afanasii (1539–1551), who came from a minor branch of the princes Paletskii, not (it seems) from the branch that made its way into the lower ranks of the boyar duma in the 1540s and 1550s.[13] Though a prince, Afanasii did not come from the boyar elite. In his epistle to the monks of the Monastery of St. Kirill the tsar Ivan IV himself heavily criticized two monks of boyar rank, I. V. Sheremetev (Bol'shoi) and I. I. Khabarov. Although Khabarov apparently had a reputation for piety as a layman, both he and Sheremetev chose monasticism as a refuge from political disgrace or execution. There were also two Kolychevs among the monks. Sergei and Ivan Ivanovich Umnoi-Kolychev, from the elder Kolychev line of boyars and *okol'nichie*. These results are far from complete, but they suggest that some monks of the Kirillo-Belozerskii Monastery were less humble in origin than those of their rival in Volok, and perhaps not quite as local in origin. Both monasteries attracted few monks from the boyar elite, though in this the Kirillo-Belozerskii Monastery was the more successful. The burial records distinguish quite clearly between "career monks," called *startsy* (singular, *starets*), and the noblemen who took the tonsure at the end of their lives, called *inok* so-and-so, followed by their name in the world with title. The deathbed tonsure seems to have been the most common form of monasticism for the elite, and although it shows a certain respect for the monastic vocation, it was a rather distant admiration indeed. Some boyars did become monks in the Monastery of St. Kirill, but the boyar elite's respect was better reflected in its donations to the brothers. Here Belozero was clearly different from

Volokolamsk, where most donors as well as monks tended to come from the petty nobles described by Zimin.

The relationship of the boyar clans to the monasteries could be problematic as well, as shown by the case of Prince Vladimir Ivanovich Vorotynskii. An important military commander and boyar, Vorotynskii had been active in the Kazan' campaign and had been loyal to Ivan in the dynastic crisis of 1553. Shortly thereafter, however, Vorotynskii died, and was buried in the Kirillo-Belozerskii Monastery. There is no hint here of disfavor in the eyes of the tsar, but rather the opposite. His wife gave money to build a church over his grave and then in 1554 a small church, really a *pridel* (side altar) in the Dormition Cathedral. Decades later in his epistle to the monks, Tsar Ivan reproached them for this, asserting that there was no such church over the grave of the miracle worker Kirill. The church was too grand for a monastery, and its construction set Vorotynskii above even St. Kirill.[14]

Finally, the Trinity–St. Sergii Monastery, close to Moscow and the object of annual pilgrimages by the court, would seem the natural place for the Moscow boyars to express their religious interests. Unfortunately this major institution of the Russian church has not received the detailed attention of its brother monasteries in Volok and Belozero, but burial records allow some comparisons, and can be checked with reference to the published land charters of the monastery. A small number of clans of boyar rank were represented (princes Vorotynskii, Gorbatyi, Glinskii), and in the later sixteenth century other clans replaced them (princes Bakhteiarov and Priimkov-Rostovskii, the *okol'nichie* Buturlin, princes Khvorostinin, Tatev, Velikogo-Gagin), with the princes Golitsyn, Trubetskoi, and Odoevskii coming in the early seventeenth century. As might be expected from location alone, the number of clans of boyar rank buried in the Trinity Monastery is greater than the other two, and hence the number of donations was large from these sources as well. Most of these clans were prominent in the boyar duma, and at the same time they are all princely clans, representing the Gediminovich, Suzdal', and Rostov princes. The old Moscow boyar clans, by contrast, are not represented in the Trinity Monastery's burial lists. The burial records show many names of landholders who never rose above the level of minor generals and provincial governors (Zacheslomskii, Osor'in, Volynskii), as well as names that do not appear in service records at all (Butenev, Durov, Stogov). As a rule, it is from these latter families that the monks listed in the records come, not from the elite or even the lesser landholders mentioned in the service records. Like the Volokolamsk Monastery, the monks were of humble origin, but the donors reflect a pattern similar to the Kirillo-Belozerskii Monastery.[15] The monks mentioned in the burial records are from families like Stogov or the Kurtsevs, both small landholder families of Pereiaslavl', the Kurtsevs even producing a Novgorod archbishop (Serapion, 1551–1552). The Kurtsevs were related to the Funikov-Kurtsev clan, which produced a keeper of the seal (*pechatnik*) and treasurer of the Russian state in the years 1549–1570, but these were not high positions in dignity, and Funikov-Kurtsev was essentially a secretary (*d'iak*). The records of land donations show both the great princely clans and the humbler local landholders, but only the local landholders became monks.[16]

Boyars did not usually become monks. A few exceptional cases, mostly of forced tonsure, seem to be recorded, and of course the practice of deathbed tonsure was widespread. As a result, monastic saints and holy men mostly came from lesser landholder families, if not more humble origins. This had been the origin of Sergii of Radonezh and Kirill Belozerskii, and the pattern continued: Daniil of Pereiaslavl', Aleksandr Svirskii, and Arsenii Komel'skii were petty landholders. Kornilii Komel'skii was a *d'iak* of the grand prince of Moscow, Nil Stolbenskii was a peasant, and other founders of monasteries were former merchants or even slaves.[17]

Another result of the relative absence of the boyars among the monks was that boyars also never became bishops in the sixteenth century. Earlier on there were exceptions. In the fourteenth and fifteenth centuries there were some aristocratic bishops, mostly notably Metropolitan Aleksei, the son of Fedor Biakont who had come to serve the Moscow princes from Chernigov. The metropolitan's younger brother Aleksandr Pleshchei founded the boyar clan of the Pleshcheevs, prominent in Russian history from then on. In 1477 Vassian of the Tver' Otroch' Monastery became bishop of Tver', a see he held until 1508. Vassian had been born Prince Vasilii Ivanovich Strigin-Obolenskii. His cousin Ioasaf became hegumen of the Ferapontov Monastery near Belozero and later archbishop of Rostov (1481–1484). Bishop Vassian of Tver' had a nephew, also Vasilii-Vassian, the son of Prince Ivan Repnia Mikhailovich Obolenskii, who entered the Kirillov Monastery as monk around 1500. These are the only hierarchs of aristocratic family that can be found in the Russian church for the whole of the period 1300–1600, and they are very few indeed. As Kollmann puts it, "As a rule, men from boyar clans from the fourteenth to the sixteenth centuries seldom pursued a religious vocation." They cluster around the end of the fifteenth century, and all were Obolenskii princes. Why this should be the case is not clear, but there is a sarcastic reference in the chronicles to Bishop Vassian's father Prince Ivan Striga Vasil'evich Obolenskii as a "new miracle worker" who came to rule Iaroslavl' for Ivan III and proceeded to confiscate the land of local boyars. The reference was to the land acquisition of the monasteries, who acquired land in theory for the saints to whom the monasteries were dedicated. The remark would not have been made if Prince Ivan Striga Obolenskii had not acquired a reputation for piety that the chronicler wished to deflate, and perhaps the Obolenskiis were simply a particularly pious family. However untypical they may have been, there were no similar families later on, for there are no known bishops or hegumens of similarly aristocratic origins (excluding forced tonsures).[18]

The sixteenth-century metropolitans whose lives are known to us came from similar humble origins, the lesser landholding group. Metropolitan Daniil apparently was a townsman of Riazan' who had been a monk in both the Pafnut'ev-Borovskii Monastery and the Iosifo-Volokolamsk Monastery. Metropolitan Filipp (Fedor Stepanovich Kolychev) is often described as a boyar. In fact he came from a lesser branch of the old Moscow boyar clan Kolychev, in his case a branch that had received *pomest'ia* (land grants) in the Novgorod district by 1495. According to the life of St. Filipp that was composed in the 1590s, Filipp's grandfather Ivan Loban Kolychev was an important general, and this information is confirmed from other sources. His father, however, does not appear in the service records, nor does the young Filipp's service at court, where his biographer asserts he won the friendship of the boy Ivan IV. The Novgorodian estates of the family suggest that it could not have been too high up, for Novgorod was not the territory of the highest elite. His uncle Ivan Ivanovich Umnoi-Kolychev, on the other hand, started as major-domo of the Staritsa appanage and became an *okol'nichii* at the court of Ivan IV in 1549 (and died 1553–1554). Filipp's upbringing was that suitable for a lesser landholder serving his sovereign, for in addition to learning to read and being introduced to religious literature he learned to ride and to fight. Evidently he was on the lower fringes of the elite, attached to it perhaps more by family than by personal achievement, when he left for the North to become a monk around 1537. Only as metropolitan does Filipp enter the elite of Russian society and hobnob with the boyars: before his elevation he was only a humble monk of undistinguished origin.[19] Filipp was probably the most exalted in social origin of the important churchmen of the sixteenth century, and even he was barely among the lower fringes of the real elite, which remained in many ways aloof from the monastic world. Happy to donate money and be buried in the monastery church, they were somewhat less willing to donate land. They rarely became monks themselves.

As far as can be traced, the elite formed a more important part of the religious life of the court. The court's religious activities fell into several types. The most fundamental was the cycle of the liturgical year, in which the court participated as did every other Orthodox believer in Russia. Our knowledge of the yearly liturgical cycle at court tends to come from the late sixteenth century if not later, but the general outlines are valid for most of the sixteenth century.[20] Essentially the court followed the cycle that all other nonmonastic Orthodox Christians did, with the main festivals falling on Easter, Christmas, and other principal days. On these days the court went to church in the Dormition Cathedral in the Kremlin, where the service was normally conducted by the metropolitan or patriarch. This was a more elaborate version of the same service everyone attended, and surrounding it were feasts and rituals of greeting of churchmen and aristocrats that can hardly have been different in substance from those of ordinary people, even if vastly superior in magnificence and dignity. At Easter the tsar gave alms to the poor and an amnesty to imprisoned criminals, but the actual day was spent in the Kremlin churches accompanied by the boyars. The tsar greeted the patriarch and clergy of the Dormition Cathedral and exchanged Easter eggs with them. He prayed at the tombs of his ancestors in the Archangel Cathedral, moving on to the Annunciation Cathedral, the house church of the palace, where he gave eggs to his confessor and the rest of the clergy. The day ended with a formal reception in the Gold Room of the palace, where he received the patriarch while surrounded by his boyars.[21] These Easter ceremonies were basically the same, though of greater splendor, as those of the ordinary faithful, but their celebration at court attached a public, even political character lacking elsewhere. The tsar was almost as much the main "character" in the drama as Christ, and the boyars almost as much as the apostles.

Two of the festivals were new and were unique to the court as they were unique to the ruler of the Russian state: the ceremony of the blessing of the waters at Epiphany (6 January, with a lesser but similar ceremony on 1 August), and the Palm Sunday procession of tsar and patriarch. The Epiphany procession and ceremony was the most magnificent that the court put on in the course of a normal year, rivaled only by coronations and weddings. It also clearly existed from at least 1525. The action was fairly simple: after a morning service in the Dormition Cathedral, tsar and patriarch, went in procession, accompanied by the highest-ranking aristocrats and churchmen, to the frozen Moscow River, where a hole was cut in the ice over which was built a small square wooden structure called a *iordan'* (commemorating the Jordan River where Christ was baptized), with the four evangelists depicted on the corner posts and hung inside with icons, including one showing the baptism of Christ. Here the patriarch plunged a cross into the water, some of which was brought back to the palace to be sprinkled through rooms and on icons. He also sprinkled the banners of the army regiments, the tsar (who stood bareheaded before him), and the boyars, while the people watched until the ritual ended and they, too, could partake of the holy water of the river. The ceremony demonstrated the respect of tsar, boyars, and people for the church.[22] The Palm Sunday procession demonstrated a similar notion. Here the tsar led the patriarch, seated on a donkey in remembrance of Christ's entrance into Jerusalem, around the Kremlin squares and streets from church to church. The tsar thus expressed his respect for the church and patriarch in particular as the successor of Christ.[23] The boyars supported their sovereign in his role, accompanying him to the river on 6 January and providing an audience and a following on Palm Sunday, thus expressing their own respect for the church as the elite of the Russian court. The great court ceremonies, Epiphany, Palm Sunday, and the annual September pilgrimage to the Trinity Monastery, were also political in that they were expressions of the unity of the Russian state, of the often fictitious consensus of ruler, church, and aristocracy that was supposed to characterize political life. They were equivalent in function to the earlier patronage of the Russian state by monastic saints such as Sergii or Kirill, a collective expression of unity and protection by God. In the increasingly charged political atmosphere after the middle of the century, these public ceremonies and private attendance at church became the main form of religious experience of the boyar elite.

Not all boyars and landholders limited their religious life to contributions to monasteries and participation in court ceremonies. Some of them were involved in varying degrees in most of the religious controversies of the period. Boyars were rarely themselves polemicists and left almost no writings of their own, but epistles to them and records of their activities do exist in sufficient quantity to establish some patterns. In general, most of the lay actors in the religious controversies were not boyars and came from the same group of lesser landholders that formed the backbone of monastic life. One group that was especially involved was the *d'iaki* (secretaries), whose status was relatively humble until late in the sixteenth century, but who were well educated and at the center of Russian administration. Although they worked among the elite, they were not yet part of it. The most usual role of the boyars in religious controversies was that of partisan patrons using their influence at court to support the interests of one side or the other. In this case the boyar's religious opinions were open to various interpretations, as we shall see. The few aristocratic connections of Joseph Volotskii fit this pattern. The one case in which the elite was involved beyond the role of patronage was that of Maksim Grek, in whose writings boyars took an active interest, which may tell us something about their own religious concerns.

Only one trend seems to have totally excluded the boyars, the heresy of the so-called Judaizers, the anti-Trinitarian group that appeared in the 1480s in Novgorod and Moscow. In Novgorod the group almost entirely consisted of clergy, and in Moscow as well, with the addition of the Kuritsyn brothers, both *d'iaki* in the princely administration. There is some evidence that Grand Prince Ivan III himself tolerated the heretics for some years after their appearance in Moscow, but there is no evidence that such tolerance reflected sympathy for their general views. Most scholars see this toleration as the result of the desire to retain the freedom to maneuver against the church rather that actual sympathy with the heretics' ideas.[24]

In the Orthodox camp, Filofei of Pskov wrote his famous epistles either to the grand prince or to M. G. Misiur'-Munekhin, a *d'iak,* not to boyars. Nil Sorskii's personal origins are disputed, some claiming him to be a peasant and some a minor landholder, while Ia. S. Lur'e argues for a family of *d'iaki*. His correspondents were mainly monks of the monastery of St. Kirill, as well as Kassian of Mangup, a Crimean Greek descendant of the erstwhile princes of tiny Mangup, who came to Russia in the entourage of Sophia Paleologue and entered Russian service. The only member of the movement of the *nestiazhateli* of any real elite origin was of course Vassian Patrikeev, the monastic name of Prince Vasilii Patrikeev, a Gediminovich and the son of one of Ivan III's principal generals. Vassian was undoubtedly the most aristocratic religious writer in Russia in the century, but his own origins are so atypical that they do not warrant much attention. His milieu as a monk was much humbler, and he seems to have functioned for most of his life after Nil Sorskii's death as would a layman of boyar rank, for he lived at court and functioned as patron to the movement.[25]

Joseph Volotskii and his followers had only slightly more aristocratic connections than their rivals. Joseph had four lay correspondents that are known. Two of them, Princess Golenina and B. V. Kutuzov, came from the milieu of lesser landholders that were closely connected with Joseph's monastery. The letter to Golenina addressed actual religious issues, whereas in the letter to Kutuzov Joseph defended his move from the jurisdiction of the Volok appanage princes to that of the grand prince. Higher up in the ladder was Ivan Ivanovich Tret'iakov, later the grand princely treasurer, but not of boyar rank, however personally influential. Joseph wrote to him in reply to a letter urging the monk to make up his quarrel with Archbishop Serapion of Novgorod (Joseph rejected the advice). Joseph also wrote to one real member of the elite, V. A. Cheliadnin, a boyar and majordomo (1507/1509–1516). This letter was a request to the boyar to defend Joseph against the slanders of Vassian Patrikeev before the grand prince, and thus shows Cheliadnin to be the hegumen's patron at court. The relationship was as much political as religious, and we do not know what Cheliadnin thought about the punishment of heretics, the nature of the Trinity, or the internal life of the monastery, all topics to which Joseph devoted much of his effort.[26]

Correspondence of boyars and other members of the elite with churchmen on themes touching both politics and religion was not uncommon. Metropolitan Daniil (1522–1539) corresponded with F. I. Karpov (died 1540, in the rank of *okol'nichii*) on the nature of princely power, and in the 1550s Sil'vestr wrote to the boyar Prince A. B. Gorbatyi on the theme of the just administrator, as the prince departed to govern the newly conquered territories of Kazan'. In a more strictly religious context, Prince Andrei Kurbskii seems to have approved of the hegumen Arsenii in the 1550s, but the other heretics of the era, Matvei Bashkin and Feodosii Kosoi, operated in a strictly nonelite context: Bashkin was at least a *syn boiarskii*, but this was unusual.[27]

Of all the religious figures of the century it was Maksim Grek that seems to have had the greatest contact with the actual elite. Until his first trial in 1525, he was friendly with V. M. Tuchkov-Morozov, himself later a religious writer, the son of a boyar but himself only Riazan' majordomo. It was his brother Mikhail Mikhailovich who continued the line in the duma.[28] Maksim's connections with the Shuiskiis, however, brought him in contact with actual boyars. In 1542 he composed an epistle to Prince Petr Ivanovich Shuiskii, whose father was at that moment one of the powerful regents for the boy Ivan IV. This letter survives in both an Old Russia and a Greek version, a nearly unique case of Maksim's Greek writings from the Russian period. The letter itself is mainly an appeal to the prince to lighten the burden of his imprisonment so that he could take communion. Shuiskii himself was quite junior (he was mentioned as being in military service in 1539 for the first time) but Maksim presumably wanted the young man to speak to his father. Again this is a case of patronage of religious writers by the elite (Prince P. I. Shuiskii attained boyar rank by 1549/1550, and was killed in battle at the Ula River 26 January 1564). In the 1550s, after Tsar Ivan IV had freed Maksim from his sentence, Maksim wrote also to the *okol'nichii* Aleksei Adashev on religious questions. Most significant, however, was his correspondence with Fedor Ivanovich Karpov, the *okol'nichii* and diplomat. Maksim devoted a dozen epistles to Karpov, and they are all on major themes, such as the falsity of Catholicism and astrology. They include a large proportion of his major writings, and Karpov responded to him as well. Maksim here dealt with a man whose education brought him close to his own world, for Karpov had read Aristotle and even cited him in his epistle to Metropolitan Daniil. These men of the elite were not Maksim's only correspondents. He wrote to a variety of monks and priests, and to the German physician Nicholas Bulow, most of the time on religious issues of some substance.[29] Maksim seems to have evoked a response from at least some members of the Russian elite that was greater than that of any of his colleagues.

After the middle of the century the ties of the main religious writers to the boyars and perhaps even the lesser landholders weakened. This is not surprising, as the writers of saints' lives were largely the provincial bishops (Iov of Kazan', later patriarch) or monks (Varlaam-Vasilii), whose origins lay among the lesser landholders. The saints and holy men they glorified were also mostly of local significance, especially in Novgorod and Pskov. Nevertheless, it does seem as if the boyars and lesser landholders were simply less involved in the production of religious writings after midcentury.

Finally, the sixteenth century saw the first systematic attempts to construct and propagate a moral code and pattern of religious life for the landholding class. This attempt was made in the sermons of Metropolitan Daniil and in the *Domostroi*, a handbook of behavior and housekeeping possibly compiled under the direction of the archpriest Sil'vestr of the Annunciation Cathedral in the Kremlin.

Metropolitan Daniil was the author of the last major series of sermons in Russia before the 1650s. His sermons and epistles concerned the dogmatic and monastic issues mentioned in the previous chapter but also addressed lay morality in considerable detail. His sixth epistle already prepared the ground for dealing with lay concerns by stressing that monasticism and married life in the world were both paths to salvation, though monasticism was the more perfect and the more difficult. Daniil seems to have been writing to an unnamed boyar who was trying to decide whether he should enter a monastery. The metropolitan apparently tried to discourage him, stressing the difficulty of the monastic life and exhorting him to pursue a chaste married life in the world instead. Daniil then set out to provide more detailed advice to the layman in his twelfth and thirteenth sermons. Essentially his aim was moderation. As in the case of marriage, Daniil recommended restraint rather than total abstinence. Drink was permissible, but drunkenness was not; the same moderation was needed in eating, dress, and other aspects of daily life. Much space was devoted to sexual purity, stressing the avoidance of both female prostitutes and young men who pay more attention to their dress and appearance than do women.

He also commended charity to the poor and love of one's fellow man. The latter in particular may seem like a banality, but there was more to it. Love of one's fellow man was the virtue opposed to hostility and discord, the only sins other than sexual misconduct to which he devoted entire sermons. He had two groups in the audience in mind here: clergy (second sermon) and laymen (ninth and tenth sermons). But what laymen? Other than clergy, the references in his sermons make it clear that he addressed mainly the boyars or more generally the elite of Russian society. By hostility he meant intriguing, spreading of false rumors, slander, and all the arts of palace intrigue. The boyar clans must have been the primary audience, because hostility grew naturally out of the situation of the court described by Kollmann, where the grand prince exercised only a general control over powerful boyar clans who competed with one another. The types of excess he condemns also reinforce the impression of an aristocratic audience. Drunkenness was presumably a democratic sin, but gluttony implied a certain prosperity. Ostentatious display of wealth in dress and building was clearly the sin of the boyar, not the peasant, as were pride, greed, and injustice. The general prosperity of the first half of the century noted by agrarian historians provided the basis for the now problematic wealth of the elite.[30] Even the sexual sins were those of the elite, for the evil ways of prostitutes and effeminate young men were revealed most clearly in their refinements of dress and manner. Daniil was basically concerned with the effects of wealth and of competition for power and office at court.

He rarely touched on life of the people and their sins. His few remarks on the lower classes were exhortations to work honestly with God in mind and, more often, recommendations to the upper classes to treat their inferiors with kindness. The one area of popular life that he seemed to address was the popular festivals—all of which he opposed. His main statement on the issue, however, came in a sermon to the clergy of the Dormition Cathedral in the Kremlin, where he condemned musicians and dancers as well as the playing of chess. It was the participation of boyars and nobles in certain aspects of the traditional popular culture (such as the music of the minstrels, the *skomorokhi*) to which he objected; popular culture itself was beneath his notice.[31]

The *Domostroi* was written for a much humbler layer of Russian society and reflected its needs. The tract has received much less attention than its putative author or compiler Sil'vestr, who is a major figure in the historiographic controversies surrounding the politics of the 1550s. Sympathetically described by Kurbskii, the priest is normally associated in the literature with the "reformers" of the early reign of Ivan IV, who fell from power in 1560–1562. In all this discussion the *Domostroi* has figured hardly at all, and then only as a possible example of Sil'vestr's social and political views.[32] It is primarily a book on how to behave, divided into three areas: religious observances, moral behavior, and housekeeping, with a concluding epistle from Sil'vestr to his son Anfim. Not all manuscripts include the names in the final epistle, a fact that has given rise to doubts about authorship. The date of the text, however, is more secure: the earliest manuscript was written in the 1560s, and the details of the text point to the middle of the sixteenth century (mention of the tsar, the details of Russian administration). The most likely hypothesis is that Sil'vestr (or an unknown writer of the 1550s) compiled the text from earlier sources, adding his own epistle at the end. The authorship of the text makes little difference to its value as a source for the religious ideas of the sixteenth century.

The addresses of the text have provided some disagreement. Zimin, following Nekrasov, saw the text as directed at urban social groups, mainly merchants, largely on the grounds that there are numerous references to markets and buying of household supplies. The final epistle of Sil'vestr in particular seems to reflect an urban environment, since it frequently refers to commerce. The rest of the text, however, is quite clear in its addresses, as chapters 24 and 25, on the just and unjust life, demonstrate. The unjust man oppresses others by delays in government offices, lays heavy exactions on his peasants (*v sele na svoikh khristiian*) or extorts heavy taxes for the crown, takes the land, arable, meadow, forest, or fisheries, from his neighbor, enslaves others by guile, judges unjustly, and practices usury. All of these sins imply a landholder, not a merchant, except for usury, and a landholder who serves the tsar in some office to boot. The just man is the reverse: he is kind to peasants, refrains form coveting his neighbors' land, and is just in his functions in office. This is clearly a picture of a lesser nobleman, one who has some local or central office, serving perhaps as a secretary in the crown offices or a local judge or administrator, such as a *gubnoi starosta*. It should not be surprising that the same man goes to an urban market to buy food and supplies for his household, for most Russian landholders of the period maintained a town residence, and indeed that was still probably their main residence. The final epistle does seem to be applicable to a more commercial milieu,

but it was obviously tacked on, as its literary form is quite different from
the rest of the text. Even if Sil'vestr compiled the whole text, it must be
admitted that his epistle does not fully accord with the previous sixty-
three chapters, which were addressed to the lesser landholder.

The *Domostroi* recommended to its readers an entire code of behavior.
It opened with a series of prescriptions for relations with the clergy and
church attendance, starting with the proper treatment of the eucharist. It
went on to commend love of God and one's neighbor, and respect for (in
this order) the bishop, the priest, and the monk. Monasteries were to be
visited, but mainly to give alms to the prisoners in them. The good
Christian was to serve the tsar faithfully and live in harmony with all
men. He should put icons in his house and make gifts to churches and
monasteries. He should invite priests to his house to bless the house and
to pray for the tsar, all Christians, and the householders. The priest and
others were to be fed properly, without excess or improper singing and
dancing, or games such as chess. On the moral side, the text put much
emphasis on moderation, especially in food and drink, on sexual purity,
and on good relations within the family. This is the aspect of the text that
most embarrassed nineteenth-century writers, for it laid great stress on
the need for obedience, chiefly by the sons. It recommended that fathers
beat their sons rather than allow them to sin and endanger their souls.
The daughters, by contrast, received much less attention, their chastity
being the main concern. The wife was naturally to obey her husband and
listen to his moral exhortations, but most of the space on the role of the
wife was devoted to her economic functions as the primary housekeeper.
Her duties were mostly to oversee the servants, although she was also to
be skilled in women's work and pass on her knowledge to her daughters.
Harmony and good morals were the responsibility of the husband, who
was to lead the family in prayer and periodically instruct them in Christian behavior.[33]

The *Domostroi* did contain a brief section on proper behavior in
church, but its emphasis was on prayer and observance within the household. In this it indirectly confirmed the observation of Possevino and
other foreigners that sixteenth-century Russians did not seem to go to
church very often, and suggests that private family prayers and the visits
of the priests to the house were the center of religious life in the lower
levels of the landholding class. The moral code that it recommended was
different from that which Metropolitan Daniil designed for the boyars.
General hostility was much less prominent and more specific, tied to the
social behavior of the Christian landholder in relation to his peasants and
his fellow landholders. Daniil spent little if any space on the behavior of
boyars as officials, as was proper: boyars commanded armies and debated
foreign policy, but less often met the population in routine administration. Their sins arose more from competition with one another than
from their treatment of their inferiors. By contrast, the lesser noble
needed to be exhorted to treat his peasants and neighbors properly, and

to discipline his sons so that they too would learn to act in a Christian manner. Neither Daniil nor the *Domostroi* showed the particular concern with the sins of pride and greed that were to occupy so greatly the moralists of the seventeenth century. The *Domostroi* also relied on family discipline and obedience to the father to enforce morality, not the preaching that was to come in the seventeenth century.

The relationship of Russian boyars and lesser landholders to religion and the church changed a great deal over the course of time, especially after about 1540. From the middle of the fourteenth century to the early sixteenth century, boyars took a modest but persistent part in the life of the Orthodox church. While they rarely entered monasteries themselves, they were the patrons of monasteries, often more than one. The monks, especially the great monastic saints, were the spiritual patrons of many important boyars as they were to Russia as a whole. Boyars and their families went to the monasteries for simple pilgrimages to pray, to be cured of disease and other ills, or simply to show their "great faith" in the holy monks. The monasteries performed a spiritual function that the parish churches and the episcopal cathedrals did not, and did so more for the boyars than for other classes of society, which are more infrequently mentioned in the lives of the great monastic saints. Peasants rather than pilgrims are more likely to be the monasteries' opponents over land rights. In return the boyars gave land to the monasteries and paid the monks handsomely for masses for departed relatives, and themselves were often buried in the monastery cemetery. A very few even became monks.

At the beginning of the sixteenth century the decline in authority of the monasteries necessitated a change. The boyars continued to be buried in monasteries, to ask the monks to say masses for the family, and to give gifts, but they no longer were cured by living saints or their relics. The spiritual patronage had gone. Boyars were the patrons of the contending monastic parties in the period 1490–1530, and correspondents and associates of the better-educated monks. While the church tried to deal with the problem created by the decline of the monasteries by increasing the authority of the bishops and (to a lesser extent) the parish clergy, the boyars seem to have withdrawn from serious interest in religion for some two generations. If we knew more about the libraries of the boyars in this period, we might be able to see the change more clearly, but almost nothing is known. The few libraries mentioned were donated to monasteries, sometimes unwillingly.[34] The known religious writings of the second half of the sixteenth century seem to have been mainly a product of the provinces, the Novgorod-Pskov area, Kazan', and the northern monasteries like the Solovetskii Monastery. The only religious activities of the second half of the century in which boyars participated for certain were the court ceremonies, which seem to have changed relatively little between the introduction of the Palm Sunday procession around 1550 and the end of the Time of Troubles. As we shall see, the boyars and the elite in general reentered religious life after 1620, but in very different ways from earlier times.

This withdrawal of the boyars is not difficult to understand. The idea that the decline of religious literature after 1550 is due to "censorship" or the victory of Josephism has been seen to be inadequate, in large part because the type of Josephism dominant after 1550 was not the militant variety, and seems to have meant mainly hostility to anti-Trinitarianism.[35] A better explanation lies in the general political history of the period. The years from the accession of Ivan IV to the throne in 1547 until the end of the Time of Troubles (the truce of Deulino in 1618) were years of almost continuous political turmoil. Not only were there periods of considerable internal violence, but the years of peace were a time of unceasing intrigue and maneuver at court among the shifting alliances of boyar clans. This is as true of the 1550s as of the years 1572–1604, which have been most recently chronicled by Zimin and Skrynnikov. The issues contested in these years were not minor. Between 1547 and 1618 the basic institutions of the later Russian state—autocracy and serfdom—were laid down, as well as a host of lesser social and institutional forms. Russia fought several major wars with its neighbors Poland and Sweden, and maintained diplomatic ties with England, Denmark, the Holy Roman Empire, Turkey, Iran, and lesser states. The interests of the boyars in this period were primarily political, and indeed practical more than theoretical. Exiles like Kurbskii could afford to spend time writing political tracts and religious works, but the boyar at home was more concerned with survival and daily politics. Only after the Time of Troubles was there again the time to try to reformulate religious belief and practice. This reformulation was stimulated more than anything else by the political events of the whole period beginning in 1547 and is another example of the dominance of politics in those years.

Less information is available about the lesser landholders. We do know that they provided the largest single groups of monks, and in that sense the decline of monastic authority inevitably affected them. At the same time there were certain compensations. The Novgorod-Pskov writers that defended the honor of the local archbishops were also promoting Novgorod's honor and its miracle cults as well. Novgorod was an area where landholders came almost exclusively from among lesser nobles, with little if any boyar property. As we shall see, localism was an element in the miracle cults, and lesser landholders, as opposed to boyars, did participate in those cults. Finally, the evidence of the *Domostroi* suggests that the religious life of the lesser noble was essentially private, centered on the household and its observances, and local as well. The great boyar, by contrast, was a public man and his observances, especially after mid-century, were public, part of the official religious life of the state.

3

The Church in
the Seventeenth Century

The most important changes in the religious experience of the upper strata of Russian society in the seventeenth century were the result of internal intellectual trends and the reorientation of court life by Tsar Aleksei Mikhailovich, both in response to a changing society and politics. The church's relationship to these changes was complex, for at different times it both encouraged and discouraged the changes themselves or as aspects of them. At the same time the church was equally or more concerned with other issues, principally its attempts to remold popular religious practices and to check the spread of the schism of Old Belief, as well as with defending its own rights and dignity against the tsar. The church's agenda was thus different from the court's, but the two regularly impinged on one another and in some cases actually overlapped. The changes in the religious experience of the laity are not comprehensible without an understanding of the church.

The history of the church in seventeenth-century Russia falls into two periods of unequal length and importance. The years between the election of Michael Romanov as tsar in 1613 and the accession of Tsar Aleksei in 1645 were relatively quiet, a calm broken only by a few minor disputes. From 1645 to 1690, however, the church was riven by two of the greatest quarrels of its history: the schism of the Old Belief and the patriarchate and deposition of Nikon.[1] Before that period we know relatively little about the church because the peace within it was so great. Of the patriarchs of the earlier century only Filaret Romanov (1619–1634), the young tsar's father, is a fully developed political figure to the historian. Ioasaf I (1634–1640) is no more than a name and Iosif (1642–1652) only a bit more. The issues that emerged in the middle of the sixteenth century seem to have abated or stalled. The attempts to raise the importance of the episcopacy and the clergy in general were forgotten until a few parish priests began to revive the issue in the late 1630s.

Patriarch and bishops do not seem to have reacted to this ferment until at least midcentury. The miracle cults seem to have reached a peak and then ceased to expand, for the *Ustavy* (the typika) of 1610 and 1633 were nearly identical in spite of Patriarch Filaret's condemnation of the 1610 version. There was no revival of the monasteries. It is as if the shock of the Time of Troubles meant that the church virtually ceased to develop in this period, and this may be another reason for the rise of lay religious writers, to be described in chapter 6. Only after 1645 did the old issues of bishops and parish clergy, popular piety and elite piety reemerge, with quite unexpected results.

A dispute over the liturgy of the Epiphany provided the first disagreement after the Time of Troubles. After the death of Patriarch Germogen in January 1612, there was no head of the Russian church for seven years. The young tsar ruled at first without a patriarch, but that did not mean that the affairs of the church came to a halt. The Printing Office resumed its operations, and that meant it needed a staff knowing enough Greek to be able to check the texts of the liturgical books that it printed against the Greek originals. In the circumstances of 1613 the appropriate knowledge was found only in Russia's greatest monastery, the Trinity–St. Sergii Monastery, which had recently played a distinguished role in the Troubles. Unfortunately the Trinity monks, mainly the archimandrite Dionisii, fell afoul of Iona, the Sarskii and Podonski (Krutitskii) metropolitan, who was acting as head of the church in the absence of a patriarch. Iona accused Dionisii and his associates, Arsenii Glukhoi and Ivan Nasedka, of corrupting the texts, especially of the liturgy of the consecration of the waters at Epiphany. In 1618 at Iona's insistence, Dionisii was imprisoned as a heretic. Here matters stood when Filaret, then metropolitan of Rostov and the obvious candidate for the patriarchate, arrived in Moscow from Polish imprisonment in the summer of 1619. Filaret was chosen patriarch of Moscow by the Russian church and Theophanes, the Greek patriarch of Jerusalem (1606–1644), bestowed the dignity upon him. This was a new role for the Greeks, a stronger one than had existed at any time since 1437. Filaret reviewed the case of Dionisii, relying in part on the evidence of Theophanes, and found the accusations groundless.[2] The meaning of the affair seems to concern the relationship of Russian texts to Greek rather than in the substance of the ritual.

   In the following year of 1620, another council made a decision that was to cause minor problems throughout the next decades—namely that the ritual of baptism required triple immersion and that pouring water was not enough. This meant that all Catholic converts would have to be rebaptized, something that had not been required in recent years. Normally this incident is seen as a "nationalist" response to the Time of Troubles, but it may equally be seen as Filaret's response to Catholicism, in his eyes not a schism but a heresy. Furthermore, Ukrainian Orthodox polemicists took the same position as Filaret, who also required rebaptism of Orthodox Ukrainians and Belorussians, as they mostly followed the Catholic practice in this matter. Perhaps it is more helpful to see this incident as part of the general hardening of confessional lines in Europe at this time, among Catholics and Protestants as well as Orthodox.[3]

Patriarch Filaret appears in a similar light some years later when the Ukrainian monk and scholar Lavrentii Zizanii appeared in Moscow with his catechism, at the height of attempts by the Ukrainian church to gain support from Moscow. After the union of Brest (1596), the Orthodox hierarchy went over to the papacy. The mass of believers remained faithful to Orthodoxy, however, and under the wings of Orthodox nobles and urban brotherhoods. To escape this situation, Zizanii wanted the book printed in Moscow, but Filaret found a number of passages to criticize in the text and condemned the book in February 1627. In December of the same year Filaret and the Russian church also condemned the *Evangelie uchitel'noe* of the Ukrainian monk Kirill Trankvillion Stavrovetskii. Stavrovetskii had sent the book to Moscow in 1622, but it had been condemned by the Ukrainian church. Perhaps Filaret's action was sparked by news of the author's conversion to the Union and acceptance of the position of archimandrite of the then Uniate Elets'kyi Monastery in Chernigov. On Filaret's request Tsar Michael ordered the book burned and forbade the importation of books from Poland, including Orthodox books.[4] Much has been made of the this decree by some historians, but in fact it was unenforceable and unenforced. There are hundreds of copies of books from the Ukrainian-Belorussian presses known to have been in Russia, and dozens of manuscripts; as we shall see in later chapters, this was a period of intense interest in Ukrainian Orthodoxy, during which its culture was extremely influential. Even the works of a known Uniate like Stavrovetskii circulated in Russia, including the *Perlo mnogotsennoe* of his Uniate period (1646). The Russians were interested in the whole range of Ukrainian-Belorussian Orthodoxy, beginning with the period that ran from the Orthodox Ukrainian revival in the 1580s to the election of Peter Mohyla as metropolitan of Kiev in 1632. This was the period of polemic and persecution. The Orthodox of both Belorussia and the Ukraine produced a large polemical literature defending their religious and legal positions. At the same time the Orthodox schools went on producing graduates who were Orthodox but were imbued with "Latin" learning and post-Renaissance conceptions of language, style, and culture.[5] The "Mohylan" period of Ukrainian Orthodox culture (1632–1648) had an impact as well, though mainly after 1648, for it provided texts for the Moscow presses as well as the intellectual formation of the leading teachers and scholars in Moscow, Epifanii Slavinetskii and Simeon Polotskii.[6] The Russians continued to read Ukrainian books in spite of Metropolitan Peter Mohyla's politically pro-Polish stance.

In the 1640s the period of calm in the Russian church came to an end. A generation of almost complete absence of internal dissension gave way both to popular ferment (the followers of the ascetic Kapiton) and to a reform movement of increasing strength, the work of the so-called Zealots of Piety. The latter were a small group of secular priests and a few monks who sought to bring religion closer to the laity and to make it a more significant part of their lives. Out of this group came the principal leaders of the two sides in the great schism, Patriarch Nikon and the archpriest Avvakum. Kapiton, by contrast, was an obscure provincial monk whose extreme asceticism and opposition to church authority acquired a substantial popular following among the peasants of the Kostroma and Vladimir districts. His influence in the region lasted from his first conflict with the church in 1639 to his death in 1662/1663. The schism that emerged in the 1650s was apparently the result of Avvakum's and Neronov's opposition to Nikon and the Kapiton movement, the two flowing together by the 1660s to form Old Belief. Ultimately the schism led to the formation of a whole series of related religious communities in sharp opposition to the Orthodox hierarchy, communities with a variety of beliefs and practices but having in common the conviction that the Russian Orthodox church under Nikon had strayed from the fold and become a heretical tool of the Antichrist. These communities are known as *staroobriadtsy,* "old ritualists," but usually translated in English as Old Believers.[7] The story of the schism has been often told and will not be repeated here in detail. The schism presented Orthodoxy with a serious challenge, the first for the Eastern churches since the time of the Bogumils. The persistence of the schism gave to Russian Orthodoxy a hard and determined opposition that no other Orthodox church faced in modern times. Furthermore, it was not a small opposition. From relatively modest beginnings, it spread from the 1680s with great speed, and by the nineteenth century the various Old Belief groups embraced perhaps 40 percent of the Great Russian peasantry, giving to Russian peasant culture a coloring absent in that of its Orthodox brethren, not only among the Balkan peoples but even among the Ukrainians.[8] At the same time, Patriarch Nikon not only precipitated a schism in the church, but also came into sharp conflict with the tsar that ended with Nikon's formal deposition in 1666. This was the first episode in a struggle culminating in Peter the Great's abolition of the patriarchate.

The schism was the ultimate outcome of the activity of the Zealots of Piety, but in the 1640s it must have seemed only that the Zealots had revived all the old issues of the middle sixteenth century: the need to strengthen the role of the clergy, mainly the parish clergy, and the need to establish more control over the religious life of the laity, particularly popular piety. They objected to many of the popular religious festivals, were appalled at the drunkenness and generally unchristian morals of the people, and felt they needed to improve the liturgy and introduce sermons to Christianize the Russian people properly. They seem to have directed their attention to all social classes, but mostly to the lower classes. The Zealots of Piety only came into their own with the accession to the throne of Tsar Aleksei Mikhailovich in 1645, for their acknowledged leader was the priest Stefan Vonifat'ev, the priest of the Annunciation Cathedral in the Kremlin, traditionally the palace church. However, they began to agitate for reform almost a decade earlier, for we first hear of their platform in a petition sent to Patriarch Ioasaf in 1636 by a group of parish priests of Nizhnii Novgorod. The group included Ioann Neronov, later a prominent leader of the group, but in the petition his name was listed last, and there is no hard evidence that the petition was his idea. It was significant not only as part of Neronov's biography but as evidence of the time of the formation of the Zealots' platform and its appeal beyond the elite of the clergy grouped around Vonifat'ev. The petitioners produced a long list of what they saw as shortcomings in the religious life of the town. First on the list stood *edinoglasie*, the practice among priests in parish churches (but not in monastery churches) of shortening the service by chanting several parts of it at once, making the words incomprehensible to the congregation. Also, the priests made a number of arbitrary changes in the services that had no justification in the service books. Finally, the typical priest did nothing to ensure the proper atmosphere in church, even during the liturgy. The congregation was not even quiet, much less reverent, and worst of all, hordes of beggars regularly invaded the church.

> The deceivers and beggars [*prokuraty i shpyni*] do not allow [the congregation] to listen to divine things in church with awe and silence. They walk through the church without obstacle and with fearlessness and uncleanness, like ferocious bandits, ruining the church with banging and shouts and squealing, making great riot in the churches; they go in gangs of ten and more, some leaving and others coming in, and there is unceasing trouble and riot in the churches from them, sometimes they fight and curse in the churches; and some deceivers go about with the Savior's image hung about their neck, and others with towels and candles on a plate collecting (they say) for the building of churches, but later they are seen with drunks. Some say that they have sold themselves and beg for money to pay the debt, and give various names and towns [of origin]; some pretend to be mad, but later are seen fully sane; and some go about in the dress of hermits, in black clothes and in chains and wild strands of hair, and some smear their legs with excrement, blood, and brains and crawl about the church squealing and offering great temptation to the simple folk.[9]

The other main objection of the petitioners was to the manner in which many church festivals were celebrated. The customs of the people between Christmas and Epiphany caused particular ire.

> From Christmas to Epiphany they have games in their houses and men and women assemble for the evil games [?]; and they perform these games of the devil's imagining with evil images, blaspheming God's mercy and his Mother's holidays. They make wooden figures like horses and bulls and decorate

them with linen cloth and strips of silk and hang bells on the horse; and on themselves they put hairy animal masks and clothes to fit and in back they put tails, looking like devils, and on their faces they carry the shameful members and bleat devilish things like goats and reveal their shameful members; and some beat tambourines and dance and do other inappropriate things. They do this not only at home but on the streets of the city and go about the villages. . . . [G]reat crowds follow them. And on Christmas eve and Epiphany eve they go in the streets in crowds and sing devilish songs and shout *koledy* and do devilish things.[10]

Further, the petitioners complained that the celebrations of the "altar festivals" of the local churches were scarcely religious at all. The Nizhnii Novgorod Pechera Monastery's church was dedicated to the Assumption of Christ, and on that day the people of the town assembled at the monastery, but rather than reverently going to church they went to the taverns and were amused by trained bears and the *skomorokhi,* the popular musicians and comedians of old Russia. Their acts as well included masks and erotic symbols. Even worse, the same trained bears and musicians appeared at Easter.

It was not the case that the patriarchs Ioasaf and Iosif did nothing. The 1636 petition produced an immediate response in the form of a patriarchal circular letter ordering an end to many of the practices mentioned in the petition. Indeed the patriarch's letter repeats much of the text of the petition word for word, though the letter is directed at the clergy of Moscow, not Nizhnii Novgorod, and does not mention the petitioners. Patriarch Iosif also admonished the clergy to read to the congregation suitable passages from the holy books so as to improve its faith and morals. Iosif followed his own advice, for he published a short book of homilies soon after his election to the patriarchate. For Lent of 1646 he also admonished all the clergy of Russia to refrain from drunkenness and concentrate on repentence, so as to bring the Russian people to repentence as well. He also reminded them to keep beggars out of the church during services, and in general to ensure the proper atmosphere.[11] A similar response came from the Printing Office, which printed more books in the 1640s than any other decade in the century, many of them of Ukrainian origin, such as Mohyla's catechism[12] or the 1648 *Kniga o vere* of the Kiev hegumen Nafanail.[13] The Printing Office followed orders from above, but at least two of the "correctors," Savvatii and Mikhail Rogov, were poets whose religious verse shows the clear influence of the Zealots (see chapter 6).

In the summer of 1648, two events, both sociopolitical upheavals seemingly far from religious concerns, dramatically accelerated the process of change in the church. One was the Moscow riot of June 1648, the other the revolt of the Ukrainian cossacks under the hetman Bohdan Khmel'nyts'kyi. The Moscow riot was a response to growing taxation, and it set off a chain of revolts throughout the towns of the Russian state and affected the church because of the long-standing objection by townsmen to the tax exemptions held by church property in the towns (a very few great boyars had similar exemptions). The tsar responded to the riots by calling a commission of boyars and *d'iaki* to frame a code of laws, and the commission and the tsar issued yet another decree trying to revoke the church's urban tax exemptions. In the fall of the year the tsar called an Assembly of the Land to discuss the projected code, and faced petitions from the landholders of the provinces asking the tsar to establish control over the church as well as voicing the usual urban complaints against untaxed church property. Clearly the church was not popular, and the criticism of its landholding was coming from large groups in Russian society, not from a few idealistic monks like Nil Sorskii. The tsar clearly did not want to go too far, and so the law code, the famous *Sobornoe Ulozhenie,* only included a prohibition on further acquisition of land by the church and established the *monastyrskii prikaz* (Monastery Office).[14] This was not the end of the story, for although the assembly concluded its work in January 1649, a church council met to consider other issues on 11 February 1649.

The subject of the council's discussions was the issue of *edinoglasie,* and its decision was negative: the services in parish churches were to remain as they were, different from those in the monastery churches. Patriarch Iosif even petitioned the tsar against Stefan Vonifat'ev, accusing him of heresy and disobedience, but unsuccessfully. Instead, evidently at Vonifat'ev's initiative, a mission was sent to Constantinople asking the ecumenical patriarch for the correct solution to the problem.[15] The deputation to Constantinople bought time. The tsar did not have to act for or against Vonifat'ev, and at the same time other projects could go forward, such as the organization of the Monastery Office, which had the duty of collecting taxes and revenues and judging major civil cases involving the church and its estates (except for the estates of the patriarchate itself). Lesser cases were handed over to the local governors, thus overturning the many immunity charters that had granted the monasteries exemption from local courts.[16] The control over the economic structure of the church was not new, for it continued the practices of the *Prikaz bol'shogo dvortsa* (Great Palace Chancellery), but a separate office had more time to devote to the church. The Monastery Office remained a bone of contention to the end of the century.

One area where immediate action was possible was that of popular religion and festivals. Here the policy of the Zealots was clear. On the one hand, a series of decrees of the tsar in 1647–1649 outlawed (in theory) a variety of rituals, from the masquerade and erotic games of the Christmas-Epiphany season to the fistfights at Shrovetide. He also outlawed trade and other normal activities on Sunday and religious holidays. On the other hand, the Printing Office, presumably under Zealot influence, further increased the number of Russian saints' festivals to an all-time high of ninety-three. This was an increase of sixteen since 1633, and reflected both extra festivals for existing saints and the addition of new ones of minor monastic saints and, for the first time, Metropolitan Filipp.[17] The addition of Filipp was a clear programmatic statement of the Zealots' belief in the dignity and exalted role of the church.

Simultaneously, Tsar Aleksei and the Zealots used the time to strengthen their ties to the Greek East and to the Ukraine. The Zealots were always interested in Kievan writings, and even the later leaders of the Old Belief show acquaintance with Kievan writings. Early in 1649 Tsar Aleksei wrote to the metropolitan of Kiev asking for learned monks to help translate works of the Greek fathers, and the Kiev monasteries sent Arsenii the Greek, Arsenii Satanovskii, and—ultimately the most important—Epifanii Slavinetskii. These requests were obviously linked to the new situation in the Ukraine as well as to the quickening of the religious controversy in Moscow. Khmel'nyts'kyi had made a triumphal entry into Kiev in December 1648 and by early 1649 was moving toward a much more definite conception of his and the cossacks' role within the Polish state as an autonomous cossack Ukrainian state. Simultaneously the abolition of the Union and the full rights of Orthodoxy began to play a much greater role in his demands on King Jan Kazimierz of Poland. The revolt had created a new political situation in the Ukraine, but also a new religious one, for the fury of the cossacks was directed at the Union and at Catholicism as much as at the Polish state and nobility. The pro-Polish, noble-oriented party of Mohyla, with its continual flirtation with Rome, had been defeated, and militant Orthodoxy came into its own, restored to the center of Ukrainian society by cossack sabers. Culturally, however, Ukrainian Orthodox scholars and religious writers did not abandon either the Polish language or the post-Renaissance conceptions of education and culture they had learned, and the cultural influence of the Ukraine on Russia entered a new phase. The process was strengthened by political events, for the Pereiaslav Treaty (1654) began the chain of events leading to the incorporation of the Ukraine into Russia and consequently, the entrance of the Kiev Academy, the cultural center of the new Ukrainian hetmanate, into the Russian state.[18] At the same time, Aleksei's and the Zealots' natural desire for as much confirmation from the Greeks as possible led to the mission of the monk Arsenii Sukhanov to Moldavia and Wallachia beginning in the summer of 1649. This paralleled the mission of that year on Vonifat'ev's initiative to Constantinople, for in the Rumanian principalities he sought out the Greek higher clergy, guided by Patriarch Paisios of Jerusalem (1645–1660), himself in Moscow in early 1649.[19] The tsar was mobilizing all the support he could find in the Orthodox world against Patriarch Iosif and the conservatives in the church.

In December 1650 Patriarch Parthenios II of Constantinople answered that there was nothing heretical in Vonifat'ev's and the tsar's desire for *edinoglasie,* and armed with this reply they proceeded to call a church council in February 1651. The principal business of the council was to ratify the desire of Vonifat'ev and the tsar for *edinoglasie,* and a number of other liturgical changes. In addition the tsar's agenda for the council included a demand for preaching by the parish clergy, the ordination of only learned priests, and the demand that the priests refrain from drunkenness and in general lead an exemplary life. Iosif's statement of the council's decisions affirmed the acceptance of *edinoglasie*, but the tsar's other concerns were not mentioned. The patriarch cited chapter 16 of the *Stoglav* as his precedent, for it asserted the role of correct liturgy in awakening repentance and fear of God in the congregation. He emphasized his own humility in acceding to the tsar's request. The document suggests that the council ended in a compromise. A rescript from the tsar to the northern Antoniev-Siiskii Monastery also restricted itself to liturgical questions, going into more detail than Iosif but not mentioning the broader reform of the parish clergy (perhaps it was not relevant to the monks).[20] If Iosif still opposed the Zealots, he was unable to do much about it, for he died on 25 April 1652. At this point the Zealots had accomplished many of their goals. They had introduced *edinoglasie* into the liturgy and had made a beginning on raising both the status and significance of the parish clergy, particularly by requiring them to preach. Long-range success, however, was to elude them.

With Iosif's death the main issue for the Zealots was the selection of his successor, and the successful candidate was Nikon, then metropolitan of Novgorod and the former archimandrite of the Novospasskii Monastery in Moscow, traditionally the burial ground of the Romanovs and still closely tied to the dynasty. Nikon, still earlier in his life a parish priest in the Nizhnii Novgorod area, came from the same milieu as the Zealots and clearly shared their ideology. At the time of Iosif's death, Nikon was returning from the Solovetskii Monastery, where he had gone to collect the relics of Metropolitan Filipp to bring them to Moscow so they could be placed in the Dormition Cathedral with the remains of the other metropolitans and patriarchs of Moscow. On 25 July Nikon was formally enthroned. Within a year, his actions were to precipitate a split in the church, and his elevated conception of the rights and power of the church was to bring about a conflict with the tsar that led to his abandonment of the patriarchate in 1658 and his formal deposition in 1666. At the same time, the original goals of the Zealots of Piety were largely lost during Nikon's patriarchate. On both sides, the goal of bringing religion closer to the lay individual dissolved in a struggle over what that religion should be; Nikon added to it the desire to strengthen the role of the clergy in Russian society, but for him that meant the episcopate, not the parish clergy.[21] The implication of the split among the Zealots is that Nikon's opponents were not all or even mainly "traditionalists," but in fact innovators, both from among the Zealots and from their associates, the Printing Office poets such as the monk Savvatii.

The split began in reaction to a rescript of Nikon that Ivan Neronov, the priest of the church of the Mother of God of Kazan' on Red Square, received just before Lent of 1653, less than a year after Nikon assumed the patriarchal throne. According to Avvakum, writing some twenty years later: "In the rescript Nikon wrote: 'Year and date. According to the tradition of the holy apostles and holy fathers, it is not proper in the church to bow on your knees, but to bow from the waist, and you should also cross yourself with three fingers.' We thought when we met that we could see winter coming; our hearts froze and our legs shook." Here, apparently for the first time, were the classical issues of the schism of Old Belief. Neronov, Avvakum, and a number of other priests refused to obey the rescript. Nikon responded immediately: they were forbidden to hold services, Avvakum taking refuge in a barn where he was arrested by musketeers sent to capture him. Nikon's first victim was the archpriest Longin of Murom, condemned for slander and disobedience, unfrocked, and sent back to his native village near Murom. Neronov's defense of Longin led to his own condemnation, unfrocking, and exile to the Spaso-Kamennyi Monastery near Vologda. The more obstreperous Avvakum was exiled in September to Siberia. Both men tried to get Vonifat'ev to intercede on their behalf but to no avail. Vonifat'ev was either unable to oppose Nikon or unwilling to do so, and soon retired to monastic life. The exiles then turned to the tsar but again to no avail.[22] At this early date the dispute seems still to have been an arcane disagreement among priests. The laity were not yet involved in any numbers and remained so until the 1660s. Until then the dispute did not impinge much on the greater issues of the religious experience of the elite.

In early 1654 Nikon turned to the church to ratify his decisions, holding a council that affirmed the need and right of the patriarch to correct the existing liturgical books. According to the accounts of the council in the *Skrizhal'* and the 1655 *Sluzhebnik,* Nikon decided to correct the books when he came upon the documents of the establishment of the Moscow patriarchate (1589) and the council of Constantinople (1593) in the patriarchal library. Since the Greeks had here commended the Russians to keep the correct faith, free from innovation, Nikon took this as a justification of his actions, for innovations had (in his view) crept into Russian liturgical books. No mention was made in either account of Neronov and Avvakum or orders to change any practices in 1653: from these accounts the 1654 council appears as the first move in the process of correcting the books. In any case, the council confirmed the church's right, even duty, to correct the books, and considered six particular liturgical issues, most of them fairly minor. The list did not include the correct form of the sign of the cross but did include the question of bows during Lent, where no decision was reached but Nikon was given authority to investigate earlier practices. Little opposition seems to have existed, and the only bishop to oppose Nikon, Pavel of Kolomna, was deprived of his see and exiled to the Paleostrov Monastery on Lake Onega after the conclusion of the council.[23] He was soon tranferred to the Khutynskii Monastery near Novgorod, where he disappeared from view, believed murdered by Nikon's agents, according to Old Believer reports circulating in the

1670s. Neronov too was tranferred on Nikon's orders, from the relative ease of Vologda to a small monastery near Kandalaksha on the White Sea.

What was at issue in this famous dispute? This is no place to review the complex history of interpretation of the schism, but most explanations have seen it as either the result of the "literalism" of Old Russian Orthodoxy, continued by the Old Believers, or as a sort of social protest movement. That the latter was an element is beyond doubt, but the religious side of the dispute deserves more serious attention. Recently Karl Christian Felmy has argued that Nikon's liturgical reforms reflected a change in the understanding of liturgy in Russia, from the older "theophanic" perspective to one more "commemorative." Certainly it is the case that fifteenth- and sixteenth-century interpretations of the liturgy in Russia were in keeping with the notion of deification or, in Felmy's terminology, theophany. The basic idea was that the liturgy, the mass in particular, was an aspect of the presence of God in the world, similar to the icon screen and the church building. Nikon, by contrast, using the work of the sixteenth-century Greek priest Ioannes Nathaniel (who in turn compiled the ideas of Nicholas Cabasilas and Symeon of Thessalonika), moved toward a more commemorative understanding, one that stressed the mass as only a commemoration of Christ's life on earth, however real the presence of Christ in the actual eucharist. From Felmy's perspective, the Old Believers represented a continuation (or more likely a revival) of the old theophanic interpretation. Thus for the schismatics liturgy would remain central, no matter how much they may have preached, whereas Nikon (along with Epifanii Slavinetskii) was more concerned to build on the liturgy to awaken repentance and deeper faith in the congregation, something that made sermons a natural accessory to liturgy.[24]

At the same time, events that would fundamentally affect the outcome of the dispute were going forward in other realms. Khmel'nyts'kyi's revolt against Poland had initially gone well, but after the battle of Berestechko (20 June 1651) he had suffered a series of reverses. By early 1653 he was ready to ask the Russian tsar for an alliance in return for recognizing the sovereignty of the tsar over the Ukraine, and the tsar was ready to accept. In early 1653, at the very moment when Neronov was leading his followers against Nikon, a Ukrainian embassy was laying the groundwork for Russian involvement, and an Assembly of the Land—the last, it turned out—met on 1 October 1653 to ratify the decision of tsar and boyars. Nearly a year of negotiations bore fruit on 8 January 1654, when Khmel'nyts'kyi and the Ukrainian cossacks accepted the agreement with Russia at a cossack *Rada* (assembly) at Pereiaslav in the Ukraine. The news reached Aleksei roughly at the time of the church council, and after its conclusion, in May 1654, he departed for the army, for Russia was now at war with Poland, and was the new overlord of the Ukraine, including Kiev. The war went well, and Smolensk fell to Russia on 23 September.[25] The new situation undoubtedly eased Nikon's task of

correcting the liturgical books, and it also took the tsar away from
Moscow, leaving Nikon as the most prestigious and perhaps the most
powerful figure in Moscow.

The Pereiaslav Treaty and the Russian victories suddenly brought into
the Russian state millions of Orthodox believers, up until that time under
the metropolitan of Kiev and ultimately the patriarch of Constantinople.
In 1654 the attitude of the metropoliton of Kiev, Syl'vestr Kosiv (1647–
1657), and his clergy to the treaty seems to have been largely negative,
and they remained loyal to the Polish king. This attitude began to change
only in late 1657, when the Polish state seemed to have completely col-
lapsed: then Kosov and the bishops became more cooperative. Unfortunately we know little of Nikon's attitude toward these events. One would
expect (from his role in government) that he supported the war, and the
Swedish resident de Rodes reported in October 1654 that he indeed
pressed the tsar to liberate the oppressed Orthodox brethren of the
commonwealth. The negotiations with Kosiv seem to have involved
solely the tsar's emissaries, and we do not hear of Nikon's involvement
until late in 1657. Whether this situation reflects Nikon's lack of involvement with the issues or his opposition to the tsar's policy of incorporating
the Ukrainian-Belorussian church—of course, it may also be that historians have not looked at the relevant sources—cannot be determined.[26]

From Moscow Nikon supported the tsar's war effort, roping in money,
men, and supplies from the monasteries. An outbreak of the plague in
the late summer of 1654 brought a crisis, as the tsar's family and then
Nikon left the city, its population and government decimated by disease.
The confusion brought out the religious opposition to Nikon in the
town, for a number of townspeople petitioned the remaining officials
against Nikon and threatened riot, disturbed not only because the patriarch had left the city but also because of the content of the newly
corrected books coming from the Printing Office and Nikon's effort to
reform Russian icon painting. Nikon was not disturbed, however, and
the threats came to nothing.[27] In March 1655 he held another church
council, apparently with the advice of Makarios, patriarch of Antioch, to
establish further changes in the liturgy. The agenda of the council is not
perfectly clear to us, but the result was the appearance of a new book of
basic liturgical texts (*Sluzhebnik*) with a corrected version of the text of the
mass.[28] Once again, Aleksei set off for the war in spring, his armies this
time conquering the whole of the grand duchy of Lithuania and captur-
ing Wilno and Grodno. Nikon remained in Moscow, running the Russian
state, preparing the new service books and keeping down his opponents.
Neronov was still a problem, for he had left the monastery at Kandalaksha for the Danilov Monastery in Pereiaslavl', closer to Moscow, and
became a monk with the name of Grigorii on Christmas Day 1655.

The church councils of 1656 set a seal on Nikon's reforms, pronounc-
ing an anathema on the supporters of the old rituals, and specifically
condemning Neronov, now the monk Grigorii. The council specifically

declared that the old manner of the sign of the cross was incorrect, for Nikon asked Makarios of Antioch for information on the subject and was told that three fingers were proper. Three years after the presumed date of the beginning of the dispute, the church in council had finally made a decision.[29] Once again the tsar set off to war shortly after the council, this time against Sweden. The Swedes had taken advantage of Poland's virtual collapse in 1655 to invade the heart of the country, and Russia now made a truce with Poland and moved against Sweden in Livonia, the prize being Riga. Once again, Nikon was left in charge of the state.[30] The success of Nikon in imposing his will on the church and the obvious support of the young and victorious tsar evidently took its toll on the opposition. Neronov had been hiding in Moscow with Vonifat'ev; perhaps the latter's death in November 1656 was the last straw, since about that time Neronov offered to submit, the ceremony taking place when the tsar returned from the wars in January 1657.

The year and a half that followed, from January 1657 to July 1658, was a period of apparent calm and harmony. Neronov's submission seemed to end the schism, for the more rebellious Avvakum was far away in eastern Siberia. On the Polish front, the situation was stable, and Russia retained its earlier gains. Sweden was more successful, but mainly because the death of Khmel'nyts'kyi in 1657 made trouble for the Russians in the Ukraine and Aleksei found it advantageous to surrender his gains to Sweden and make a truce (at Valiesari in 1658). This allowed him to deal successfully with the Ukrainian hetmanate. Thus the tsar, now twenty-eight and flush with victory, remained in Moscow throughout the rest of 1657 and all 1658, side by side with Nikon. The only event that might have given the tsar some grounds for dissatisfaction with Nikon was the church council of October 1656, devoted to the seemingly neutral issue of reorganizing Russia's vast eparchies. Their excessive size had been recognized as a problem in the sixteenth century, but they had remained with virtually the same boundaries as in 1589. At the 1656 council Nikon succeeded in establishing a new bishopric in distant Viatka, but at the expense of absorbing the rich eparchy of Kolomna into the patriarchal district, thus increasing both his income and power over the church. Plans were afoot at the same time to remove the metropolitanate of Krutitsy (Sarskii and Podonskii) from Moscow to the southwestern border, the emerging Sloboda Ukraine, but the metropolitan obstinately refused to move, and Nikon's "abdication" in July 1658 found the metropolitan still in Moscow.[31] Nikon's schemes here did not directly challenge the tsar, but they did involve a strengthening of his position within the church, and therefore an indirect threat.

The actual break seems to have occurred over matters of honor and rank, for in the crush accompanying the reception for the Georgian king Teimuraz on 6 July 1658, the *okol'nichii* Bogdan Matveevich Khitrovo struck on the head Prince Dmitrii Meshcherskii, the patriarch's *striapchii* (adjutant). Khitrovo was clearing the way for the procession, and seems to have struck Meshcherskii accidentally, but when the prince took offense, Khitrovo made it clear to him that a patriarchal official was too humble to be entitled to such a sense of his own dignity. Meshcherskii complained immediately to Nikon, who wrote to the tsar to no avail. During the next few days, the tsar failed to appear at a number of important church services in the Dormition Cathedral. Nikon took offense. On 10 July, after the liturgy in honor of the festival of the Robe of the Lord, Nikon removed his patriarchal vestments and put on the black robe of a monk, thereby symbolically abandoning the patriarchate. He then said quietly to a few surrounding clerics that he was leaving the patriarchate—or that he was unworthy of it, according to some. His exact words later became a matter of contention, for it was not clear whether he meant a formal abdication or something short of that. The crowd prevented him from leaving and sent to the tsar, who swiftly dispatched the boyar Prince Aleksei Nikitich Trubetskoi (an important general) to the scene. Prince Trubetskoi was unable to stop Nikon or to get much of an explanation. Nikon merely said that he was unworthy of the office and had never intended to be patriarch more than three years. Trubetskoi let him go, and Nikon retired to the Resurrection Monastery west of Moscow, his own foundation of a few years back. As with the split between Nikon and Ivan Neronov before Lent 1653, there is no contemporary documentation for the events, and the historian must accept the evidence of later years, when the events had become a matter of contention. The immediate reasons for his actions are somewhat unclear, though the Khitrovo incident was usually mentioned later on.[32] It was also mentioned by Nikon later without contradiction, often enough so we may presume that it really occurred more or less as he described it.

The deeper causes of the split cannot so easily be determined. In the 1660s, before his final deposition, Nikon maintained that he left the patriarchate in anger over the Khitrovo incident but also because the tsar's officials had taken control over the church courts and administration (usually interpreted as refering to the Monastery Office). Unfortunately, the published documentation on the period 1652–1658 is so thin that it is difficult to evaluate that charge. A few documents exist where the tsar commanded monasteries to provide troops and supplies for the war by issuing instructions through the Monastery Office, but this is no different from the practices of the Great Palace Chancellery in the Smolensk War (1632–1634). It is also difficult to find any hard evidence of any interference on Nikon's part in the affairs of state. A few official documents from the period have Nikon's signature, but almost all are rescripts to monasteries or relate to church affairs.[33] Tsar Aleksei formed the Privy Chancellery in the war years precisely to retain contact with the administration (especially the *Razriad*) and seems to have succeeded in his aim. Nikon may have felt some pressure, but only on the assumption that he wished to exercise power in political matters or routine administration.[34] In the absence of any hard evidence from 1653–1658 Kapterev and other scholars have concentrated on Nikon's ideology and conception of the church, but they rely mainly on statements from the 1660s. Strictly speaking, it is only conjecture that he held these views while patriarch and did not develop them after leaving the office to justify his actions. The principal evidence cited for his early adherence to an exalted view of his office in his use of the title *Velikii gosudar'* (great sovereign) beyond the bounds granted to him by the tsar, such as in his 1657 correspondence with the Rumanian hospodars (princes). It is by no means obvious that this was an issue: it was not cited in the councils of 1660 and 1666–1667 when Nikon's case was discussed. The letters to the hospodars themselves cannot be seen as overstepping Nikon's prerogatives, for the documents concerned church affairs primarily and political matters only incidentally. In any case, the title had been granted by the tsar.[35] On the other hand, the absence of any record of clashes over particular policies in 1652–1658 suggests that the main cause was in Nikon's new views of the dignity and power of the church. Aleksei improved a previously existing control over the church, while Nikon reacted on the basis of ideas on the patriarchal throne that were new. The clash was thus inevitable.

The de facto abdication of Nikon led to a standoff between him and the tsar. The difficulty was that Nikon did not simply and clearly abdicate the office. What he said on 10 July 1658 was not agreed upon even by his opponents, and by spring 1659 he was making clear to the tsar that he had not fully abandoned the dignity of patriarch. On Palm Sunday of that year Pitirim, the metropolitan Krutitsy (Sarskii and Podonskii), took the patriarch's place in the Palm Sunday procession and Nikon objected vigorously when he heard of it, asserting that only the patriarch could take part. The tsar immediately sent his officials to Nikon to inquire what he meant by all this, and received in March the reply that Nikon had not abdicated his office but did not intend to return to it, proposing that tsar and church elect a new patriarch. In May 1659 Aleksei sent Dementii Bashmakov, the chief *d'iak* of the Privy Chancellery, to Nikon for further information. Nikon explained he had indeed left the *office* of patriarch, but that with the office came an episcopal dignity conferred by God's grace that neither Nikon nor Aleksei could remove from him.[36] Here matters stood until the church council of February 1660 was called to deal with the situation and depose Nikon. The council resulted in some confusion. Depositions were taken from the lay officials and clergy present in the Dormition Cathedral on 10 July 1658, with a view to determining Nikon's precise words, but to no avail; the evidence was contradictory. The matter was referred to some Greek prelates present in Moscow, but their answer was also ambiguous, for they accepted the testimony of Nikon's enemies (in accord with the tsar's wishes, it seems). They produced two possible conclusions: one pair of documents from the Greeks judged that Nikon had fully left the office, and that tsar and church could choose a new patriarch. The other said that he had left the office but since he had made no errors of dogma or faith he should be left with the episcopal dignity as a kindness. A further complication arose when Epifanii Slavinetskii, the chief Greek and Latin translator of the church and its main preacher at court, suddenly declared that some of the precedents cited by the Greeks to support the deposition of Nikon were false, and that he could find nothing in the decisions of the church councils to support the deprivation of Nikon's episcopal dignity. In August 1660 the church met again and declared it legal to choose a new patriarch, but nothing happened. The stalemate remained.[37]

Tsar Aleksei's motives in delaying the selection of a new patriarch are unknown, but he may have hoped for a compromise to avoid turmoil in the church in the face of rising discontent over the replacement of the old rituals with new ones. A new generation of supporters of the old rituals had arisen, including the priest Lazar' in Borisoglebsk (exiled to Siberia in 1661), Nikita Dobrynin "Pustosviat" in Suzdal', Fedor the deacon in the Cathedral of the Annunciation in the Kremlin (Aleksei's own church!), and the monks Epifanii and Avraamii in the North and the Nizhnii Novgorod area. None of these men had been seriously involved with the Zealots of Piety, and most had been unknown in the clashes of 1653–1654. They had emerged from the provinces beginning in 1659, and by 1665 they were major actors in the drama and supporters of Avvakum.

Meanwhile Aleksei tried to work out some sort of compromise with Nikon. The arrival of Paisios Ligarides (c. 1609–1678), metropolitan of Gaza, in early 1662 spurred a new effort to define the situation. The tsar had his trusted boyar and general Rodion Streshnev put a series of questions to Paisios about Nikon's behavior, and received answers more or less in accord with his desires on 15 August 1662.[38] Nikon in turn produced a vast reply to Paisios, in which he defended his actions and his retention of the episcopal dignity on grounds of canon law and church tradition. Nikon now shifted his ground, and took the position that he could not be removed from his office, and that in particular the tsar and other laymen had no authority to remove him. Nikon discussed this and related issues at some length, but his greatest wrath was aroused by the existence of the Monastery Office, perhaps because he still believed the Greek patriarchs would support him and thus he did not fear actual deposition. Whatever the reason, his discussion of the Monastery Office occupied somewhat more than half the text of his refutation, and was perhaps the most vitriolic as well. He heaped scorn on Aleksei's law code, the *Ulozhenie*, maintaining that the committee appointed to search precedents was corrupt and biased:

> The sovereign Tsar ordered Prince Nikita Ivanovich Odoevskii and colleagues to report to the boyars, but he, Prince Nikita, is a most proud man, and does not have the fear of God in his heart. He does not read or understand divine scripture, and the rules of the holy apostles and holy fathers,

and does not live by them, and hates those who do as enemies, himself being an enemy of truth. And his colleagues are simple people, not knowledgeable in the divine scripture, and the secretaries, known enemies of God and daytime bandits, destroy God's people without fear in broad daylight.

Nikon denied that the precedents they found were correct, and devoted hundreds of pages to providing his own.[39] Of course, it was not common for the ruler to depose the head of the church, and even in those few instances that did occur the ruler normally had some part of the church behind him; however, examples are known from sixteenth-century Russia, during the rule of Ivan IV as well as the boyar regency.

Needless to say, Nikon's arguments did not convince the tsar and his supporters. On 26 December 1662, Tsar Aleksei invited the Greek patriarchs to come to Moscow for a council that would finally replace Nikon as patriarch of Moscow. The negotiations were extensive, for Patriarch Dionysios II of Constantinople (1662–1665) was willing to accommodate the tsar but was unenthusiastic, while Nektarios the patriarch of Jerusalem (1661–1669, died 1676), a much more substantial figure in the Greek church, even wrote to Aleksei suggesting that Nikon be returned to office, whatever his misdeeds. In Moscow 1663 and most of 1664 were passed in an exchange of increasingly hostile messages between the two antagonists. The final break seems to have come in December 1664, before the Greeks arrived. The boyar N. A. Ziuzin, the patriarch's chief (and perhaps only) friend among the boyars, wrote him that if he came to Moscow to the Dormition Cathedral a reconciliation might be effected. After some persuasion, Nikon came, apparently won over by Ziuzin's suggestion that the proposal came from the tsar's closest advisers. Nikon's appearance on 18 December 1664 achieved nothing, however, for the tsar would not see him, and Nikon returned to the Resurrection Monastery. In further negotiations Nikon restated his position that he had ceased to exercise the office of patriarch but could not be removed from his episcopal dignity, the result of consecration. The incident strengthened Aleksei's determination to call a church council to deal with the matter. Some delay was caused by further correspondence with the Greek authorities in Constantinople, but eventually a relatively favorable answer was received and patriarchs Paisios of Alexandria and Makarios of Antioch came to Moscow for the council, arriving only on 2 November 1666.[40]

The council, called to discuss both the schism and Nikon, finally opened its discussion of Nikon on 1 December 1666 and Nikon took an aggressive stand from the beginning, rejecting the authority of the council without the patriarchs of Constantinople and Jerusalem. Then he demanded that Pitirim of Novgorod and Pavel the Sarskii and Podonskii (Krutitskii) metropolitan, withdraw because they had tried to poison him. Pitirim, Pavel, and the tsar rejected the charges, and then the council went on the offensive, asking Nikon why he had abdicated (*otreksia*)

the patriarchate. Nikon then recounted the story of Khitrovo and his
servant, putting the blame for the incident on Khitrovo and indirectly on
the tsar. Then followed a long and intricate review that considered all the
various aspects of the Khitrovo incident and possible grounds for Nikon's
bad relations with the tsar. The council brought up Nikon's letter to
patriarch Dionysios of Constantinople, and his complaints in it: the unjust murder of Filipp by Ivan IV, the interference by Tsar Aleksei in the
church's business, and the tsar's anger against him. The climax of the
first day came when the council accused Nikon of impugning the faith of
Paisios Ligarides, and Nikon readily admitted it, calling him a Catholic in
disguise.

> And the Tsar and the holy council and the Tsar's boyars said to the most
> holy patriarchs that the former patriarch Nikon wrote and called them all
> heretics, and not only the metropolitan of Gaza, and that they [the pa-
> triarchs] should make a decision according to the rules of the holy apostles
> and the holy fathers.
> And Nikon the former patriarch said to the Tsar: "If only you feared
> God, you would not have done this to me."

After this exchange the council dragged on several days, but the outcome was decided, as indeed it most likely was at the outset. The last
meeting was on 5 December, and three days later the council members
consulted with the tsar. A decree was prepared, and on 12 December a
last meeting was held to communicate to Nikon his formal deposition.
The patriarchs also told him that he

> was to live in a monastery quietly and without disturbance and that he
> should pray to the all-merciful God for his sins.
> And the former patriarch Nikon said to the holy patriarchs, "I know how
> to live without your teaching and they should take the cowl and panagia
> from him and divide the pearls from the cowl and the panagia among
> themselves, and they would get pearls weighing five, six, or more *zolotniki*
> and ten gold pieces."

Nikon went away defiant.[41]
The tsar thus settled the dispute to his own satisfaction and a new
patriarch, Ioasaf II, was chosen on 10 February 1667. Things did not run
perfectly smoothly, however, for Metropolitan Pavel Krutitskii (whom
Nikon had accused of trying to poison him!) and Ilarion, the metropolitan of Riazan', refused to sign the council decisions. The leaders of
the Greek church, the Jerusalem patriarchs Nektarios and later Dositheos (1669–1707) were obviously hostile, and repeatedly condemned
Ligarides. The result was a definite cooling of relations, but there was
little the Greeks could do for Nikon.[42] The metropolitans Pavel and
Ilarion did not pursue the issue, and as a result Tsar Aleksei was able to
determine his own religious policy for over a decade, from 1658 until the

appointment of Ioakim in 1674. During this period the Ukrainians became the strongest influence in religious affairs at court and sharply reoriented religious life there, with considerable consequences for the elite of Russian society who participated in court events.

At the same time resistance to Nikon's liturgical changes, which Tsar Aleksei supported, appeared among the lesser clergy in Moscow and beyond, so that in this sphere, too, changes were taking place that would soon affect a large section of the laity. During this period Tsar Aleksei also failed to apply the full rigor of repression to the movement. Perhaps his hesitation came from a certain lack of confidence in his position. Hostilities between Russia and Poland resumed in the fall of 1658, and in the summer campaign of 1660 success was entirely on the side of the Poles. By 1661–1662 they had reconquered Lithuania and most of Belorussia, nearly erasing Aleksei's gains of 1655. Russia's conquests were reduced to eastern Belorussia, Smolensk, Kiev, and the left-bank Ukraine, no small gains but far from the situation of 1655. The long war brought inflation, and in July 1662 the people of Moscow revolted, calling Aleksei's relatives and close associates (the Miloslavskiis, Rtishchev, Khitrovo, Bashmakov) traitors. The rebels reached the tsar's suburban palace at Kolomenskoe, only to be suppressed by the new "regiments of foreign order" commanded by mercenary officers.[43]

Aleksei clearly could not afford to add to his troubles, and in June 1662 Avvakum was brought back to European Russia, to Ustiug Velikii, and then in February 1664 to Moscow. Avvakum stayed in the capital less than a year, for he did not temper his opposition. In the autumn he was again exiled to the far North, but this action did no good. The years 1664–1665 saw the appearance of the first known detailed expositions of the Old Belief platform, petitions from the pens of Nikita "Pustosviat" and the priest Lazar'. Nikita focused his attention on Nikon's *Skrizhal'*, his 1656 defense of his liturgical innovations, listing at some length the deviations from past practice. His did not merely address ritual, for a large part of his objections were to passages that touched on the incarnation. Lazar' concentrated more on the issues of ritual.[44] The authorities responded to the petitions by arresting their authors and other leaders. At the same time, musketeers were sent in 1665–1666 to search out and arrest the Old Believers and followers of Kapiton among the townsmen and peasants of the provinces, especially in the forests of Viazniki (Vladimir district), Kostroma, Nizhnii Novgorod, and Vologda. The prisoners seem to have believed in a doctrine that combined both Kapiton's belief in abstinence from sexual relations and meat (at least for some in the community) and his rejection of the priesthood with Avvakum's rejection of Nikon's liturgical changes. Central to both streams of thought was the absolute rejection of both church and state authority, expressed for the first time in suicide by fire, self-starvation, and the consistent refusal, even under torture, to provide any information. Several hundred people (it seems) were arrested and suffered various penalties, death by fire for the leaders and lesser penalties for others. This series of arrests and investigations, a joint effort of church and state, was the first such action known to historians, and coincided with the arrest of Nikita Pustosviat and Lazar' and the rearrest of Avvakum.[45] With the arrest of the leaders of the opposition as well as many followers in the winter of 1665–1666, the church and the tsar were ready for the council when it opened in February 1666.

The church council proved to be a great show, lasting until mid-1667 and taking time out only to depose Nikon. Lazar', Nikita, Avvakum, and other opponents of the hierarchy were hauled before the council, denounced, lectured, and asked to repent. Lazar' had a moment of weakness, and Grigorii (Ivan) Neronov surrendered completely. Nikita was a stranger case, for he repented at the council but reemerged as an Old Belief leader in 1682. Avvakum, of course, was steadfast. The official council report was laconic:

> The evil-tongued Avvakum the former archpriest of Iurevets Povolzhskii stood before them, he who in former years had been sent to prison in Siberia for his schisms, rebellions, and false teachings. . . . He had not left off spreading his evil thoughts and false teachings by speaking and writing nor [had he ceased] to ensnare the simple people. . . .

Avvakum's errors were listed, and "he was tested by the sacred council, but the slanderer and rebel did not submit, and adding anger to anger, reproved the whole sacred council, calling them all not Orthodox." The council declared him unfrocked and pronounced an anathema against him. Avvakum's own account is more colorful:

> They dragged me into the Chudov Monastery and placed me before the ecumenical patriarchs, and our people all sat there, too, like foxes. I spoke a lot with the patriarchs from scripture; God had opened my mouth and Christ shamed them. They said their last word to me, "Why are you stubborn? All our Palestine, and the Serbs, the Albanians, the Wallachians, the Greeks [*rimliane*, i.e., *romaioi*], and the Poles [presumably the Ukrainians], all cross themselves with three fingers, you alone stand in your stubbornness and cross yourself with five."

Avvakum then gave them a lecture on the Third Rome, and went on: "The wolf Nikon and the devil told us to cross ourselves with three fingers, but our first shepherds, who crossed themselves with five, also blessed with five in accord with the tradition of our fathers." He then cited the Byzantine and Russian precedents, ending with the *Stoglav* council, praising the piety of the Russian saints (including Metropolitan Filipp). "And the patriarchs fell to thinking, but our people, they jumped up like wolves and howled and spit on their own fathers, saying, 'Our Russian saints were stupid and did not understand, they were not learned. How can we trust them, they could not even read?'" After more such exchanges Avvakum reports that "Evfimii, the cellarer of the Chudov Monastery, said, 'You are right, we have nothing more to say to one another.' And they led me away to the chain."[46]

A number of the schismatics, including Lazar', who had recovered his courage, had their tongues cut out at the place of execution in Moscow, and Avvakum was exiled to Pustozersk north of the arctic circle, which was to become the prison of most of the leaders of the movement. Thus began the centuries of oppression of the Old Belief in Russia and, at the same time, the spread of the movement among the population, for if ever the blood of martyrs was the seed of the church, it was these martyrs and this church. The mutilation of Lazar' and the monk Epifanii in 1667 was only the beginning. The deacon Fedor suffered the same fate in 1668, but sympathizers remained in Moscow in spite of this. In 1670 the government decided to smash some of the centers of resistance. In the North two of Avvakum's fellow prisoners, Luka and Fedor the Holy Fool, were hanged, and Avvakum and his family were placed in underground cells where they remained for twelve years. Throughout the country, in the North, around Nizhnii Novgorod and Vladimir, wherever the followers of the old piety had fled, military expeditions were sent to hunt them out, try to force them to recant, and execute the recalcitrant. In Moscow the church took a leading role in the proceedings, interrogating the prisoners and helping the tsar. Two boyar women, the sisters Morozova and Urusova, joined the ranks of the martyrs when they were arrested in 1670 and confined in pits in Borovsk, where they died in 1675.[47] None of this was very effective and merely forced the movement underground. Moreover, Avvakum and his party in Pustozersk used the time in prison to write the history and doctrine of the group, Avvakum's autobiography, and a variety of theological tracts.

The resistance was not merely passive. The news of the council sent the monks of the Solovetskii Monastery into revolt, resulting in a siege lasting from 1668 to 1676.[48] Fortunately for Aleksei the treaty of Andrusovo put an end to the Polish war in 1667, leaving him in control of Kiev and as overlord of the Ukrainian hetmanate, but in 1670 Stepan Razin and his cossacks on the Volga began the first of Russia's great peasant revolts. There is little evidence that Razin was connected with the Old Belief, but from Aleksei's point of view the Russian masses were slipping from his control, following either Razin or Avvakum. Razin was defeated, as were the Solovetskii monks, but the Old Belief was stronger than ever. The new patriarch Ioakim (1674–1690) was determined to put a stop to the movement, but the increased repression in the late 1670s only further aroused a response with which neither tsar nor church could effectively deal: mass suicide. Some cases had already occurred of small groups burning themselves to death in houses or barns in 1665–1666, and another such case is known from 1672, near Nizhnii Novgorod. A similar incident took place near Olonets in 1677, but the first large mass suicide came near the Siberian town of Tiumen' in 1679, when the inhabitants of an entire hermitage set it afire and perished rather than submit to the tsar's soldiers. From then on it was a standard practice for decades, even if opposed by some Old Belief leaders and discouraged by Avvakum. Ioakim was stymied, and at the church council of February 1682, it was decided to put an end to the nest of opposition in Pustozersk: Avvakum, the deacon Fedor, the priest Lazar', and the monk Epifanii were burned at the stake in the spring of 1682.[49]

No matter how acerbic and violent the conflict with the Old Belief, the church had other matters to deal with, particularly after the long period without a patriarch. Until the appointment of Ioakim in 1674 the tsar had a fairly free hand in religious matters, influenced more by his religious entourage (Simeon Polotskii and others) than by the hierarchy. The patriarch Ioakim was not well disposed toward that entourage and was able to exert his power. In 1678 he was able to get Tsar Fyodor to reverse his initial hostility to the Greek clergy in Moscow, and in 1681 it was certainly his initiative that caused the tsar to ask the Greek church to "forgive" Nikon, a task for which it was only too ready. As Kartashev put it, "Patriarch Ioakim clearly was carrying out the program of Nikon."[50] Ioakim was much stronger than Ioasaf or Pitirim in his brief (1672–1673) patriarchate, and he also managed soon after his accession to convince Aleksei to allow him to abolish the Monastery Office. A church council in 1675 made the declaration, though the decree implementing the change came only in 1677.[51] This time the jurisdiction over the church estates did not go back to the Great Palace Chancellery; instead a new system was set up in which the clergy alone had charge of affairs, the elected "priests' elders" at the lowest level and various hegumens and archpriests substituting for the higher patriarchal officials. This system persisted until Peter's reestablishment of the Monastery Office in 1700 and represented more autonomy for the church than Nikon had ever achieved.

If this autonomy was to be effective, and if the church was to fight Old Belief and bring Orthodoxy into the inner life of the population (the original goal of the Zealots of Piety), then it had to be better organized, and that meant more bishops to cover the vast extent of Russia. The problem, as before, was that any such creation of new eparchies would have to be at the expense of existing ones, especially the vast patriarchal district. The 1667 council had called for such measures, but only the creation of a new eparchy of Belgorod for the Sloboda Ukraine was actually carried out, at the expense of the patriarchal district but in a politically vital area. The eparchy of Kolomna was also restored. Even the undistinguished patriarch Ioasaf seems to have been able to stop further reform, and Tsar Aleksei used the occasion of Ioasaf's death in 1672 to create a new eparchy of Nizhnii Novgorod in the hotbed of Old Belief. Again the new creation cut down the patriarchal district. In partial compensation Tsar Fyodor agreed in 1677, shortly after the decree implementing the abolition of the Monastery Office, to force nobles who built churches to give land to support them, a benefit both to the parish clergy and the hierarchy, which received revenue from such lands. In general Ioakim was able to maintain his position, and when Tsar Fyodor proposed in September 1681 to establish a total of seventy-two new bishoprics, this was too much for the church. After deliberation extending into the next year (and after the tsar's death) the church council agreed in principle to fifteen new bishoprics. Only four, however, came into existence: Velikii Ustiug, Kholmogory, Voronezh, and Tambov, all in 1682 and none at the expense of the patriarch. Once again, Ioakim was the victor, apparently aided by Tsar Fyodor's untimely death.[52]

Patriarch Ioakim also returned to the policy of asserting control over popular religion, in part to combat Old Belief, as the councils of 1677 and 1679 on the sainthood of Anna of Kashin reveal. In 1682, shortly before the death of the cooperative Tsar Fyodor, the church council dealt with matters of the conduct of priests, monks, and beggars, the proper conduct of church services, and the care of relics. At about the same time Ioakim re-edited the *Ustav.* He increased the number of festivals of Russian saints to sixty-three over Nikon's forty-eight, but at the same time he demoted some nineteen saints, all of whom had had national festivals in 1641 but were now honored by merely local festivals. His aim was to monitor and regulate the popular devotions while effecting a modest revival of some official, national festivals.[53] The last eight years of Ioakim's patriarchate, though they had their own share of strife and ended in a bloody victory for the old man, nevertheless were really part of a different story, in which the claims of the patriarchate were entangled with a whole series of other cultural and religious issues.[54]

4

Saints and Miracles
in Church Policy

The sixteenth century saw the decline of the basic type of medieval Russian saint, the holy monk. He was not supplanted by any new sort of saint, however, for the decades after about 1550 saw the decline of sainthood in general. This phenomenon was noticed by G. P. Fedotov half a century ago and described metaphorically as the "escape of sanctity" (*utechka sviatosti*). The Soviet historians of Old Russian literature, Ia. S. Lur'e and D. S. Likhachev, observed a related phenomenon when they noted the relative silence and official character of the writings that appear after midcentury, their seemingly mindless adherence to older norms: Fedotov's *ustavnoe blagochestie*, "piety of the typikon."[1] As I shall argue in the ensuing chapter, the century after about 1550 was marked nót only by silence or an ossified official religious culture, but by the explosion of miracle cults. These cults were not merely part of popular piety but also were part of elite religious experience as well.

These two phenomena, the decline of the monastic saint and the rise of miracle cults, presented the church with a series of tasks. The church still had to codify and regulate the cults of the saints who had lived in earlier centuries, as well as decide on the holiness of the few more recent saints. At the same time the explosion of miracle cults, while desirable in general, posed a specific problem of recognition, control, and regulation as each new cult appeared. The decisions of the church on these issues traditionally have been analyzed under the rubric of "canonization," a term foreign to the church in this period and the result of nineteenth-century scholarship. Unfortunately the literature on this subject is extremely misleading, mixing up in one term quite different types of decisions and frequently using very unreliable sources: the dubious church council of 1549 is a good example of this. In order to put some order in the existing mass of confused and unreliable information on sainthood, it will be necessary first to review the history of "canonization" in the sixteenth century. This review will demonstrate that the number of officially recognized saints has been considerably inflated in the literature, and that important decisions that did recognize saints have been buried under a mass of highly dubious claims. It will also demonstrate that Fedotov's decline of sanctity was even more extreme than he realized, misled as he was by the scholarly literature. Once a more accurate history of church policy in this area has been established, we will examine some of the holy men who were and were not recognized as saints, so as to uncover the religious ideas of the second half of the sixteenth century, a period up until the present relatively unknown. Finally, the policies of the church in the seventeenth century on sainthood and miracle cults will provide a framework for later chapters.

The Recognition of Saints to 1551

The scholarly history of sainthood in Russia goes back primarily to two historians, both considered among Russia's greatest: V. O. Kliuchevskii, whose pathbreaking study of the texts of the lives of the saints provided a basic framework in the sources, and E. E. Golubinskii, who tried to summarize the whole process of canonization. Kliuchevskii's work touched on canonization as part of the history of the texts of the lives of saints and was cautious about its conclusions. A case in point was the council of 1549, for which Kliuchevskii's evidence was the principal but highly questionable source. Kliuchevskii laid out all the basic difficulties with the council, and it was not his fault if later scholars took as simple fact something that he presented as the result of a complex chain of reasoning. Much more misleading was the work of Golubinskii, Russia's premier church historian. Golubinskii was committed to a number of assumptions, all clearly laid out in his book and all of them wrong. First was that canonization was an identifiable procedure throughout the whole of Russian history. The conclusion was that any reference to a feast day for a particular saint, even on an undated icon or a manuscript of unknown provenance, represented evidence of an official canonization of unknown date. Thus, he assumed what he needed to prove. Second, he assumed that all cults, national and local, were evidence of canonization, the recognition of a saint. Even though he noted that some cults were local and their festivals restricted to a certain locality, he listed obscure local miracle workers together with well-known saints to arrive at his totals. While this approach may have been theologically correct as far as the modern Orthodox church is concerned, it concealed the very serious issues taken into account by the sixteenth-century church when deciding who should be included among the ranks of its holy men and women and at what level. Third, Golubinskii assumed that the crucial issue was the presence of miracles at the shrine of the saint, an assumption in direct contradiction to the evidence of the *Stoglav*. The issue here is not that

Golubinskii was careless or dishonest. His citations were accurate and his breadth of coverage exemplary, but his assumptions required him to read the sources in ways that were fundamentally misleading.[2]

Golubinskii began his work with the earliest canonizations of saints in the eleventh century, thus giving the impression that this procedure was known, at least in principle. In fact, the incidents of the recognition of saints are known only from rare chronicle references and more frequently from references in the lives of saints or stories of the translations of their relics, where services in their honor are mentioned. No canonization documents are known before 1339, so in fact nothing certain is known about the recognition of saints, either the procedure or the time and place of recognition. The case of saints Boris and Gleb illustrates the problem, for the time of their canonization is the subject of scholarly debate to this day as the result of the lack of any formal documents. The two brothers were murdered in 1015, and sometime in the course of the next century they began to appear in service books. The tale of the martrydom of Boris and Gleb merely states that after some miracles at their tomb Grand Prince Iaroslav and Metropolitan Ioann "and the clergy and the people" established a festival, which in the generalized language of such stories could mean a great deal or nothing at all. Many historians prefer 1072, after Iaroslav's death as the actual time of canonization, but the time does not tell us anything about the procedure. Furthermore, the obvious political utility of the cult of Boris and Gleb as dynastic saints has attracted the attention of historians to the political aspects of the cult rather than the criteria of sainthood.[3]

The story of the gradual establishment of festivals for the two eleventh-century monks of the Kiev Pecherskii Monastery, St. Feodosii and St. Antonii, is equally typical. Antonii and Feodosii were prominent in both the early chronicles and the *Paterik* of the monastery and were thus ideal candidates for sainthood. The cult of Feodosii developed at the end of the eleventh century, and in 1108 the hegumen of the Pechera Monastery convinced Grand Prince Sviatopolk to have Feodosii's name included in the *Sinodik*, the list of saints read on the Sunday of Orthodoxy. The chronicle asserts that Sviatopolk ordered the metropolitan (Nikifor I) to add the name, and it was done. Was this a typical canonization, even in part? Chronicle references suggest that a miracle cult existed at his tomb, but the decline of Kiev and the monastery around 1200, followed by the Mongol destruction of Kiev in 1238, brought an apparent end to the cult. Nevertheless Feodosii retained his feast day, and the cult was revived with new relics under wholly different circumstances in the late sixteenth century, when the now Ukrainian monastery became a center of Orthodoxy, with dozens of uncorrupted remains of saintly monks.

Antonii, who appears in the earliest stories of the monastery as its founder, was nevertheless a rather shadowy figure and had no cult until 1394, when it appeared in the northern principality of Tver', apparently the result of the Tver' clergy's desire to revive the traditions of Kievan monasticism as part of their support of hesychasm. From about 1400 the feast appears in Moscow service books, and Antonii was clearly recognized as a saint. No relics existed, for the Kiev Pecherskii Monastery was still an obscure semi-ruin and Kiev a small provincial town in the Grand Duchy of Lithuania, and only the revival of Kiev and the monastery after about 1550 brought relics, when (as occurred with Feodosii) an uncorrupted body was found that was identified as Antonii's.[4] In none of these cases was the establishment of sainthood proclaimed by a council of the church, and the role even of the metropolitan seems to have been sometimes obscure, yet feasts and liturgies of these saints came into being and seem to have been widespread.[5]

In Russia the first documentary evidence on the character of the recognition of saints is the letter of Patriarch John XIV to Metropolitan Feognost in 1339. The letter came in response to Feognost's letter informing the patriarch that Metropolitan Peter (1308–1326) was a healer (*therapon*) and had worked miracles, and requesting instructions on what to do with the relics. Patriarch John replied that Feognost already knew what was the "order and custom" (*takseos kai synetheias*) of the church in such matters: he was to honor the healer with sacred hymns and serve him with praise, for now and the future.[6] The patriarch seems to have been puzzled by the request, and to have thought that Feognost knew perfectly well how to proceed and did not need his advice or confirmation. This reaction would seem to imply that the metropolitan Feognost's decision was the crucial element, though a council is not excluded by the language of the letter. Though John mentioned miracles (only healing miracles), he did not state or even imply that they were the main criteria for sainthood. The letter also reveals nothing about John's own procedure. Did he call a council in Constantinople? Did he consult anyone at all? We know the answers to none of these questions, but we do know that Metropolitan Kiprian (1381/90–1406) included a Slavic translation of the letter in his life of Metropolitan Peter. He also asserted that Patriarch John had called a council of the church to discuss Feognost's letter: "The Patriarch assembled a council and when the Metropolitan's letter had been read, all unanimously praised God, who glorified His saints." Kiprian then went on to assert that Feognost took the letter to the prince (Ivan Kalita) "and they established a bright holy day for the saint. And from then until now we celebrate the saint according to his worth."[7] This letter and its use by Kiprian is the only case of documentary evidence on the recognition of a saint in medieval Russia. The fact that Kiprian went into such detail suggests that Byzantine and Balkan practice was unknown in Russia up until this time. Obviously Feognost in 1339 had felt the need of Greek support, while Kiprian a generation later wanted to add the element of conciliar decision. However, Kiprian also described the final establishment of a festival as the act of Feognost and Ivan Kalita alone, leaving the role of the church council very unclear.

In the cases of the other most important Russian saints we do not even possess this scanty evidence. St. Sergii of Radonezh was listed in a chronicle reference under 1448 together with saints Peter, Aleksei, and Leontii of Rostov as one of the "saints and miracle workers of our land," but how did he acquire that status? A pastoral letter of Metropolitan Iona of 1448 substituted St. Kirill of Belozero for Metropolitan Aleksei, but neither of these references gives the slightest clue as to when and with what procedures these saints were recognized. All that can be said is that the 1448 references do seem to be fairly clear evidence that by that year metropolitans Peter and Aleksei, Bishop Leontii of Rostov, and the holy monks Sergii and Kirill were considered saints and miracle workers. Later practice would suggest that this meant an officially accepted, universal feast day, but that is only an assumption based on later practice and may be wrong entirely or in part.[8] Thus the procedures and criteria of canonization remain unknown to us as late as the middle of the fifteenth century. The criteria for sainthood can be inferred to some extent from practice, mainly from the history of the cults of Antonii and Feodosii of the Kiev Monastery of the Caves, and the evidence of the case of Metropolitan Peter. Fundamentally the basis for the recognition of saints was charismatic. It rested on the virtuous life and spiritual power of the individual in question, and only in part on miracles performed in life as well as afterward, in the presence of the person's relics. The church naturally strove to be certain of the truth of the miracles, but there is no sign of a formalized procedure. No clear evidence exists for conciliar discussion of sainthood. The few references in narrative sources suggest that the metropolitan and the grand prince simply established festivals by themselves, consulting only with each other. In one case of exceptional political sensitivity (Metropolitan Peter), the issue was referred to Byzantium, though the Greek patriarch's reply suggests that he was puzzled by the request, which seemed to him unnecessary. This situation lasted until 1547.

Golubinskii believed to the contrary. He asserted that by the middle of the fifteenth century the church had begun to require an investigation and verification of the miracles attributed to a saint.[9] As ever, the miracles were the main issue in Golubinskii's mind. Unfortunately the four cases that he adduced in support of this position cannot be sustained as evidence, since he used in all cases not documents that were or even claimed to be contemporary but incidents in lives of the saints written after the council of 1547, where the procedures and criteria seem to have been spelled out for the first time. Post-1547 narrative sources reinterpreted the past in light of the new ideas.

The first case of an investigation by the church to establish the truth of a claim of miracles at the shrine of a miracle worker allegedly came in 1467. In 1463 the uncorrupted relics of Prince Fedor Rostislavich and his two sons were found in the Spas monastery of Iaroslavl', and the monastery's hegumen Khristofor had them buried in the church. "Many miracles" took place, and the incident is reported in most chronicles. As far as the fifteenth century and early sixteenth century chronicles (Voskresenskaia and Ioasaf) are concerned, this is the end of the story. Golubinskii, however, found material in two mid-sixteenth-century chronicles (L'vov and Second Sophia, a Novgorod source), as well as the Book of Degrees (about 1560), which added other elements. These later chronicles based their story on the late fifteenth-century lives of Iona, the anonymous version and the version of the monk Antonii. In these versions the skeptical archbishop of Rostov, Trifon, investigated the relics in 1467 and was apparently convinced of their authenticity. The story of Trifon's investigation seems to confirm Golubinskii's belief in a procedure of investigation, but on closer inspection it was nothing of the kind. Trifon sent a deputy to look into the matter rather than do it personally as he did not reside in Iaroslavl': this was not a "commission." Trifon also did not represent the church as a whole but merely the bishop of the diocese. Basically this story was only the usual topos of the skeptical bishop that occurs in many miracle stories, and says nothing about official procedure. The core of the story is that Trifon's skepticism was overcome by the saint's cure of his disease, not by any formal investigation. Neither the metropolitan nor any churchmen other than Trifon were involved. Finally, the texts say nothing about feast days or canonization, only that Trifon believed in Prince Fedor's miracle-working powers.[10] The evidence is too late to be convincing.

The next case of an investigation of miracles that Golubinskii (here followed by Zimin) adduced and that seems to be reported in sources close to the events was the recognition of the cult of St. Makarii of Kaliazin in 1523. Makarii's body was discovered to be miraculously uncorrupted in 1521 when workmen were digging a ditch on the monastery's grounds. Nothing happened, it is presumed, because of the negative attitude of Metropolitan Varlaam. So far the chronicles. Again, the life of Makarii tells a further story. Here the miracles were reported to the new metropolitan Daniil, who sent Archimandrite Iona of the Chudov Monastery to investigate. He was convinced and a local feast day was established by the church. Other sources tell us that the cult aroused skepticism in Vassian Patrikeev, and Makarii was officially proclaimed worthy of a national festival only in the council of 1547.[11] This story is less impressive when the fact is taken into account that the life of Makarii was written in 1546–1547, on the eve of the council, and may reflect the idea of procedure evolved for the council. Further, if the life is believed, all it says is that Daniil personally approved a local festival; it says nothing on the procedure for establishing universal festivals for saints of national importance.[12]

Two other incidents, in 1539–1540 and 1544, revealed to Golubinskii a similar concern with the verification of claims of miracles that did not lead to canonization but in his view demonstrated the nature of the procedure. The first incident comes from the life of the hegumen Daniil of Pereiaslavl', which was written in 1553. According to the life, around

1539 Daniil tried to convince Tsar Ivan IV and Metropolitan Ioasaf to recognize the miracles of Prince Andrei of Smolensk, whose body had been found on the territory of Daniil's monastery. The metropolitan's emissary, Archimandrite Iona of the Chudov Monastery, remained unconvinced: he accepted the miracles and noted the existence of a liturgy (a *stikhir'* and a *kanon*) as well as a supposedly ancient icon, but no life of the prince. Supposedly Andrei failed the test. While the story is not inherently improbable, it comes from a document written six years after the 1547 canonization council and again may reflect the procedure adopted there and projected onto earlier events. Furthermore, the story does not make clear what Daniil wanted to do with the relics.[13]

The story of the discovery of the relics of Iakov of Borovichi in 1544 seems to offer greater authenticity and thus reflects the procedures of canonization. According to the story quoted by Golubinskii, in that year a corpse was washed up on the river bank in Borovichi, a small town near Novgorod. After the townspeople buried it, it appeared in a dream to one of them and informed the townsman that its name was Iakov, who in life had been a holy hermit. Then the tomb began to work miracles, and the town petitioned Archbishop Feodosii of Novgorod to sanction a feast day. He in turn wrote to Metropolitan Makarii in Moscow, who sent the hegumen Konstantin of the monastery of St. Anthony in Novgorod to investigate. The result of Konstantin's investigation was only partly in favor of Iakov, for Makarii allowed only a local service in the monastery in Borovichi where Iakov's body lay. Barsukov also asserted that very official-sounding "documents of the Novgorod archbishop Feodosii" about the events existed in the synodal library, the nineteenth-century successor to the older patriarchal library. On closer examination, neither Golubinskii nor Barsukov had a real case. The text to which Golubinskii referred was Trinity Monastery MS 654, a sixteenth-century miscellany donated to the monastery by one Princess Sudskaia, who died in 1572. There is no evidence that the manuscript is much older than that date, though it could be. Barsukov's "documents" are no better, for they are simply the letters found in another copy of the tale of the discovery of the miracles, as they are in Trinity 654.[14] There is no reason to conclude that the tale of the discovery of the relics of Iakov of Borovichi reflects anything more than the ideas of the 1550s. Thus no secure evidence exists on the nature of the recognition of saints in Russia before 1547. Golubinskii's idea that a clear and recognized procedure in which the confirmation of miracles played a crucial role from Kievan times cannot be sustained; instead a procedure seems to be established for the first time in 1547, and miracles are not the main criterion.

The church council of 1547 is the first occasion on which we know the church made a decision recognizing a series of holy men as miracle workers. It is also the first such recognition since 1339 for which there is certain documentary evidence. The same is not the case for the council of 1549, and the two should therefore not be grouped together. As we shall see, although a church council did take place in February 1549 and miracle workers seem to have been discussed, there is no evidence that reliably informs us of the council's decision.

The evidence for the council of 1547 is relatively straightforward. In the early nineteenth century Karamzin published in the notes to his history a list of saints from a Volokolamsk Monastery manuscript (Moscow Spiritual Academy MS 362). The Imperial Archeographical Commission published another, from a miscellany of the Krasnogorsk Pinega Monastery (an obscure northern monastery). Another is found in Trinity MS 241, which remains unpublished. In 1910 Kuntsevich published the last to be found, from a miscellany in the St. Petersburg Public Library. The last is part of what seems to be miscellany originating from the Savva-Storozhevskii Monastery library, and was considered by Kuntsevich to be the most reliable. All of these seem to be messages from the metropolitan to various eparchies informing the clergy of the 1547 council and its decisions. The lists of new miracle workers differ in the four versions, the longest being the Kuntsevich text. This document names four holy men "great miracle workers": Metropolitan Iona, Ioann the archbishop of Novgorod, Pafnutii of Borovsk, and Makarii of the Kaliazin Monastery. Fifteen holy men and women are called "new miracle workers": Nikon of Radonezh, Mikhail Klopskii, Zosima and Savvatii of the Solovetskii Monastery, Dionisii Glushitskii, Aleksandr Svirskii, Maksim the holy fool of Moscow, Prince Konstantin of Murom and his sons Mikhail and Fedor, Bishop Arsenii of Tver', Prince Petr and Fevroniia of Murom, and Prokopii and Ioann the holy fools of Ustiug. Three are called merely "miracle workers": Aleksandr Nevskii, Pavel Komel'skii (Obnorskii), and Archbishop Iona of Novgorod.[15] (The significance of these distinctions is not clear.) One further distinction is that all the saints but Prokopii and Ioann of Ustiug are granted universal feast days throughout Russia, whereas the two holy fools were apparently to be commemorated only in Velikii Ustiug.

A further indication of the authenticity of the document is the presence of these saints in the printed liturgical books from 1602–1610 to the middle of the seventeenth century, books printed under the direct supervision of the patriarchate.[16] The other texts present variations that have never been analyzed or discussed. The Krasnogorsk-Pinega Monastery version omits the name of Aleksandr Nevskii, and established only local festivals for the Murom princes, Maksim of Moscow, Arsenii of Tver', and the holy fools of Ustiug. The Karamzin (Volokolamsk) text omits the Novgorod archbishop Iona. The Trinity Monastery MS 241 unaccountably adds Bishop Nikita of Novgorod and Savva Storozhevskii, but other evidence suggests that these additions are possibly fraudulent. The 1610 service book lists only the festival of the Discovery of the Relics of Nikita, which took place in 1558. Mention of Savva Storozhevskii did occur in seventeenth-century service books, but that does not prove he was recognized in 1547: his life seems to have been composed in 1550 or 1552.[17]

The four versions of the 1547 council's decisions thus have a core of names in common, but they also present differences that are hard to explain. The least reliable appears to be the unpublished Trinity Monastery version, which seems to have included two holy men recognized only after 1547. It is difficult to draw a distinction, however, between the Kuntsevich version and the Krasnogorsk-Pinega version: both have almost identical prefaces describing the council, but a quite different order of listing the miracle workers, apart from the other differences in the list. Although Kuntsevich's asserted that his list was more authentic, he offered no actual proof of that statement. The only evidence in his favor (which he did not himself adduce) is the evidence of the early seventeenth-century service books, which do include Aleksandr Nevskii. We know so little about the administrative and record-keeping practices of the church in such matters that it is hard to evaluate these texts, and the skeptic might wonder if the 1547 council even took place. Fortunately, the 1547 council is mentioned in the *Stoglav*, in the section containing the tsar's speech to the clergy in 1551, referring to the previous two councils. Here the tsar says that the clergy and laity of Russia collected the lives and miracles of the miracle workers of the Russian land in the seventeenth year of his reign (1547). Ivan IV does not then say what happened, but the rhetorical character of the "speech" does not call for such precision.[18] It does confirm the existence and the agenda of the 1547 council, and thus indirectly substantiates the evidence of the Kuntsevich and Krasnogorsk-Pinega documents.

The situation with the council of 1549, however, is less promising. The passage of Ivan IV's speech to the *Stoglav* council is the only evidence that miracle workers were a subject of discussion and decision in 1549. That there indeed was a council in February 1549 is confirmed from a quite different source, the trials of Maksim Grek and Isak Sobaka. In this text the lengthy account of Maksim's trials precedes a short account of the trial of the Chudov archimandrite Isak Sobaka, one of Maksim's associates, and Isak's trial took place at a church council in February 1549.[19] Thus there really was a council, which seems to have discussed both Isak's alleged heresies and new miracle workers. All modern historians of the sixteenth century, however, go on to provide a list of saints allegedly recognized at the 1549 council, a list that has no reliable basis in sources. The list is found only in one late text of the sixteenth or early seventeenth century, and in a form that is highly suspect: a part of a brief summary of the story of both councils is inserted into the third redaction of the life of Metropolitan Iona of Moscow. The text was discovered and published by Kliuchevskii in 1871 from a manuscript in his personal collection. It groups the 1547 saints with an additional sixteen saints, arranging them all by their "occupation" (princes, bishops, monks, holy fools) rather than by the council at which they were recognized. The third redaction of the life of Iona containing the passage on the councils was both the latest redaction and the rarest in number of manuscripts. Since the third redaction depends on the second, and the second appeared in the Book of Degrees, the very earliest date for the third redaction is the 1560s.

There is nothing wrong with such a source a priori, for many such events are known from narrative sources rather than official documents in sixteenth-century Russia, and the late dates of the manuscripts in themselves mean nothing. Kliuchevskii cannot be faulted, especially since he clearly stated the relevant facts about the manuscript and the text. Golubinskii, however, eschewed Kliuchevskii's caution and accepted the list as simple fact. The problem is that, unlike the 1547 Kuntsevich list, only four of the sixteen new "1549" miracle workers appear in all or almost all the early seventeenth-century service books: Archbishop Evfimii Viazhitskii of Novgorod, Bishop Stefan of Perm', and the hegumens Avraamii of Smolensk and Evfimii of Suzdal'. These four appear in the books of both 1602 and 1610, as well as the succeeding books until midcentury. Eight of the saints are lacking in the 1602 service book, but appear in 1610 and stay until midcentury: Archbishop Iona Otenskii of Novgorod, Bishop Iakov of Rostov, Prince Vsevolod-Gavriil of Pskov, Prince Mikhail of Tver', and hegumens Grigorii Pel'shemskii, Savva Visherskii, Evfrosin of Pskov, and Efrem Perekomskii. One, Archbishop Nifont of Novgorod, does not ever appear in any seventeenth-century service books, and the three "Lithuanian martyrs," Antonii, Evstafii, and Ioann of Wilno, do not appear until 1633. Furthermore, at the *Stoglav* council of 1551 Tsar Ivan IV asked the assembled clergy to decide how to celebrate the feast day of Evfrosin of Pskov and Avraamii of Smolensk (both in the "1549" list), which sounds if they were being recognized for the first time. The council answered that they were to be remembered "like the other holy and worthy fathers," which again sounds like a new recognition of sainthood.[20] If these two holy monks were recognized as saints only in 1551, the "1549" list looks even more suspect.

The list of saints, however suspect, does allow some light to be thrown on the puzzle. As will be seen below, the *Stoglav* council made extremely clear that the church and the tsar considered the presence of a properly written life of a saint essential to his recognition. In the list of "1549" saints there are several anomalies in this area. Bishop Iakov of Rostov, for example, had no known life at all: he did not appear in Kliuchevskii's book on saints' lives, and Barsukov was able to find only a service for him but no life. Even more suggestive is the inclusion of several Pskov and Novgorod saints, Prince Vsevolod-Gavriil, Evfrosin of Pskov, and Archbishop Nifont of Novgorod. The lives of these saints were all the work of the Pskov monk Vasilii-Varlaam of the Krypetskii Monastery in Pskov. They are also dated. Vasilii's life of Prince Vsevolod comes from 1550–1552, that of Evfrosin in 1547, and of Nifont in 1558. Two of these were thus written after the events of 1549, and there was no known life of these saints available in 1549. A similar case in the "1549" list is Efrem of the Perekomskii Monastery (near Novgorod), a compilation from earlier works on other monastic saints with numerous errors in chronology, and which mentions Archbishop Pimen of Novgorod, who held that office in 1552–1570. None of these facts are by themselves conclusive, though they are difficult to explain away. This is especially true of the inclusion of Nifont, a twelfth-century archbishop who is mentioned in the *Paterikon* (the lives of the fathers) of the Kiev Monastery of the Caves, but was not sufficiently regarded even to appear in a single service book in the seventeenth century.[21]

The other saints listed as recognized in 1549 are a mixed bag. The four that appear in all later service books were clearly well established by that time, but the date of recognition is known only for Avraamii of Smolensk (1551). The other three in that group (Stefan of Perm', the hegumen Evfimii of Suzdal', and Archbishop Evfimii of Novgorod) could have been recognized at any time before or after 1547; we just do not know. The eight that appear in the service books of 1610–1648 seem to have been the object of a local feast day of some sort before 1610, so they must have had some standing in the church as miracle workers. This evidence, imperfect as it is, suggests that the list of 1549 saints is open to very serious question. There is no hard evidence that these saints (or any others) were recognized at the council of that year, and the text used to provide such evidence includes saints most likely recognized (if at all before 1610) in the 1550s. As the third redaction of the life of Iona cannot be earlier than 1563, the story of the councils with the list of saints thus seems to have been put together at the earliest in the middle 1560s, and inserted into the life of Metropolitan Iona possibly as late as the 1580s or 1590s. The conclusion must be that we do not know what happened at the 1549 church council beyond the condemnation of Isak Sobaka and the discussion of new miracle workers. Our first hard evidence for the recognition of saints after 1547 is found in the 1551 *Stoglav* council and the printed service books of 1602–1610.

The hard evidence on the recognition of new miracle workers, the 1547 documents, and the *Stoglav* of 1551 do provide a fairly clear account of the process and results of canonization for the years 1547–1551. Fortunately the *Stoglav* was a widely copied document even in the sixteenth century, and Jack Kollmann's exhaustive study of it found no major textual problems. Within the limits of the genre, it is hard evidence, and it suggests that several issues were in the mind of Tsar Ivan IV and the church at that time. The tsar's "speeches" to the council brought out these issues. The third chapter, with Ivan IV's injunctions to the council and its response, emphasizes that the existence of miracle workers proves the piety and Orthodoxy of the Russian land, and in the fourth chapter the tsar reminds the council that the saints intercede with God for the remission of punishment for sin and that they work miracles as well. In 1547 he therefore ordered the clergy and people, great and small, to search out "canons, lives, and miracles" of reputed miracle workers. Even though the new saints were called "miracle workers," the presence of miracles was not enough: a miracle worker was not necessarily a saint and vice versa. The bishops were to assemble these materials, each in his own eparchy. The young tsar demanded that the saints' glory must be proved both by their good deeds (presumably known from the written lives) and by their miracles. In 1549 he had all evidence concerning the canons, lives, and miracles brought to the church council in Moscow and witnessed, and ordered that these documented saints be celebrated in all churches, on the days of their death or the finding of their relics.[22] In explaining the grounds for canonization Golubinskii maintained that the only crucial element was the presence of miracles, but the text of the *Stoglav* here directly contradicts him, for it mentioned three things that were needed: "canons," that is, a liturgical text; a life, that is, a written life; and evidence of miracles. As we have seen, the story of Daniil of Pereiaslavl''s attempt to obtain recognition for Prince Andrei of Smolensk (compiled 1553) suggests that the need for a credible written life was taken quite seriously: in the story Andrei was rejected because Daniil could show only miracles and a liturgy but no life. Makarii also saw to it that saints whom he wanted to recognize had a life not only credible but sufficiently elevated in a "literary" sense. This was the case of Mikhail Klopskii, whose life had been composed half a century before the council but was redone under Makarii's supervision because the metropolitan found the earlier version too "simple."[23] The image of a holy life rather than the presence of miracles seems to have been the most important criterion, at least at the councils of 1547 and 1551.

There seem to have been two reasons for this emphasis on the holy (written) life: one being the earlier disputes with Maksim Grek and Vassian Patrikeev about sainthood, and the other being the general problems caused by the decline of the monastic saint in the course of the sixteenth century. The issue of sainthood appeared in the trails of Maksim Grek and Vassian Patrikeev in 1531. The form of the charges and their replies suggest that not miracles per se but rather other aspects of the cult of saints, primarily the moral qualities of the saints' lives, were at issue. Both Maksim and Vassian were accused of disbelieving in the Russian miracle workers, and in both cases the charge was probably untrue in the form that the prosecution, primarily Metropolitan Daniil, presented it. Vassian had used the example of the Russian miracle workers to substantiate his opposition to monastic landholding, citing a long list of monks from Antonii and Feodosii of Kiev to those of more recent times and claiming (incorrectly) that their monasteries held no land. At his trial Daniil accused him of denying Makarii of Kaliazin the title of miracle worker and saying that Makarii was merely a peasant (*sel'skoi muzhik*). Vassian replied that indeed Makarii had been only a simple man, and as far as miracles were concerned the matter was up to Daniil. Vassian similarly evaded a question on Metropolitan Iona of Moscow. Maksim Grek was accused of generally disbelieving in the Russian miracle workers, a charge he strenuously denied at his trial of the same year. The context of these questions makes clear that the issue here was not miracles or sainthood but monastic landholding. The saints in question were mostly monastic, and the differences between Daniil on one hand and Maksim and Vassian on the other were over the lives of the saints, not their posthumous miracles.[24] In his trial Maksim admitted that he had criticized Pafnutii Borovskii for owning villages, practicing usury, and beating monastery servants; for these reasons, he concluded that Pafnutii could not have been a miracle worker. Maksim claimed to have learned from Pafnutii's life, which Vassian had given him (Vassian denied the latter point). It was the written life of Pafnutii that gave offense to Maksim and, as in the case of Makarii, his real life, known to Vassian, threw doubt on his ability to be a miracle worker. Neither Maksim nor Vassian were interested in the validity of the posthumous miracles, for the lives had already cast doubt in their eyes.[25]

The other reason for the concern with the lives has to do with the implications of the decline of the monastic saint. The fact of this decline was clearly present in the minds of both the tsar and the church at the 1551 *Stoglav* council. In the first group of thirty-seven questions from the throne, no less than eleven concerned monasteries wholly or in part. Only one of those was about monastic privileges in landholding, the subject that has occupied the virtually exclusive attention of historians. The rest were matters of monastic life: the basic details of obedience to the hegumen, remaining in the monasteries, and observance of the *ustav*. The moral life of the monks—especially topics such as drunkenness, allowing young boys in the monastery, and consorting with women outside the monastery—all came in for comment by the tsar. The reaction of the council to these strictures was complex. To the eleven questions of the tsar the church gave two fairly detailed chapters in answer, agreeing with his strictures but establishing no new institutional structure or procedure to deal with the problems. The church only exhorted the monks to good behavior and cautioned the hegumens and archimandrites to be more careful in accepting novices and monks from other monasteries. This cautious reaction is in distinct contrast to the church's reaction to the tsar's remarks about the need to improve the morals and life of the laity and the parish clergy. Here a whole new institutional arrangement was made to allow closer supervision of the parish clergy, an arrangement that allowed ultimately for more effective episcopal control. In the same vein the council strengthened the autonomy of the episcopal courts.[26] In a word, the church was trying gradually to substitute episcopal control for the declining charismatic authority of the holy monk. At the same time neither Makarii nor his colleagues showed any inclination toward criticism of monasticism as such. That was the point of view of heretics. The collection, redaction, and copying of the lives of the monastic saints, as well as their recognition as new miracle workers, was all part of the policy of exhortation to virtue so clearly revealed in the *Stoglav*. The result was the intense activity in hagiography noticed already by Kliuchevskii, an activity that died down after Makarii's death in 1563, which coincided with the beginning of Ivan IV's *Oprichnina*.

The Recognition of Saints after 1551

The history of the recognition of saints after 1551 makes these trends even more obvious, for fewer and fewer saints were recognized for national feast days (the last in 1619) and a larger proportion than before were bishops. This conclusion arises naturally from considering the saints recognized in the period 1551–1610, but only after the inflated list provided by Golubinskii is pared down to those for whom some evidence suggests that a national festival was established, as shown by their presence in the *Ustavy* printed under supervision of tsar and patriarch in 1602 and 1610. Golubinskii simply listed in chronological order all occasions known to him from some source, however late or inadequate, grouping together nationally established feast days and extremely obscure local commemorations of a miracle worker. Recognition in the official printed books of 1602 and 1610 should be taken instead as the only clear evidence of recognition by the higher authorities in the church for a national festival. (Local festivals present an interest of an entirely different kind, and will be considered separately later.) Using this criterion on the sources of the second half of the sixteenth century reveals that eighteen saints were probably recognized in the interval 1551–1610, though almost all belong only in the period 1602–1610. First of all, there are the saints for whom some evidence exists of the establishment of a local festival in this time period and who appear in the 1610 book. These are (with Golubinskii's dates of the establishment of local festivals): Peter, the tsarevich of the Horde (1553), Iakov of Borovichi (1572), the hegumen Antonii Siiskii (1579), the hegumen Efrem of Novyi Torzhok (1584–1587), Vasilii the Blessed, the holy fool of Moscow (1588), Archbishop Gurii of Kazan' and Archimandrite Varsonofii (1595), and Archbishop Antonii the Roman of Novgorod (1597). For the first four the sources are particularly shaky, and Golubinskii's data are not even convincing evidence of the establishment of a local feast day. These four do not appear in the 1602 *Sluzhebnik* and appear for the first time in the *Ustav* of 1610.[27] The last three look a bit better, though the data about the festivals are all in narrative sources, not documents of the church. Vasilii the Blessed also appeared in the 1602 *Sluzhebnik*, the only saint in this first group to be so recognized before 1610.[28]

The second group includes those found in the "1549" list in the story of the two councils included in the life of Iona. While this list cannot be used for a source on the 1549 council, it does show that the compiler in the late sixteenth century wanted these saints recognized. As they were not included in the 1602 service book but were included in the 1610

Ustav, it is even possible that the story was composed in that interval, but there is too little evidence for this to remain more than a hypothesis. These saints, let us remember, were Archbishop Iona of Novgorod, Bishop Iakov of Rostov, Prince Vsevolod-Gavriil of Pskov, Prince Michael of Tver', and hegumens Grigorii Pel'shemskii, Savva Visherskii, Evfrosin of Pskov, and Efrem Perekomskii. Finally, three saints appeared in the 1610 *Ustav* but are not in the life of Iona and escaped Golubinskii's attention: Archbishop Fedor of Rostov (died 1394), Nikolai Kochanov the holy fool of Novgorod (died 1392), and Archbishop Serapion of Novgorod (died 1516).[29]

The geographic grouping of these saints is quite striking. Three (Peter of the Horde and Iakov and Fedor of Rostov) come from the eparchy of Rostov, both shrines near the town itself. Vasilii the Blessed was a local Moscow saint, Prince Michael of Tver' was naturally associated with that town where his relics rested, and Gurii and Varsonofii were Kazan' saints. Eleven were saints of Novgorod and Pskov: Efrem of Novyi Torzhok, Antonii the Roman, Archbishop Serapion, Nikolai Kochanov the holy fool, Iona Otenskii, Prince Gavriil-Vsevolod of Pskov, the four hegumens Grigorii Pel'shemskii, Savva Visherskii, Efrem Perekomskii, and Evfrosin of Pskov, and finally Iakov of Borovichi. No other subgroup emerges with such clarity as the Novgorod and Pskov saints, and this is something new, since the saints recognized in 1547 and 1551 do not show such an emphasis on Novgorod and Pskov: there the largest group was the monastic saints, mostly from central Russia and the North.

Historians of Russia and its church have not spent much time on the interpretation of the recognition of saints at the church councils. The normal explanation is that the results were determined by the need to centralize the church as the handmaiden of the autocratic tsar, as well as the desire to raise the prestige of the Russian church.[30] This thesis may account for the fact of the recognition of new miracle workers, but it accounts very poorly for the specific saints recognized. Centralization, if it is to be a meaningful concept, would necessarily imply the abolition of local cults in favor of national ones, or the widespread imposition of "central" saints over local ones. This is not what happened, either in 1547 or after. In 1547, of the whole group of new miracle workers, only four (Metropolitan Iona, Aleksandr Nevskii, Maksim the holy fool of Moscow, and perhaps Pafnutii Borovskii) could be considered central "Moscow" saints imposed upon non-Muscovites in 1547. The others were local saints, from Novgorod, Vologda, and the North, whom Muscovite and provincial alike were expected to revere. This was a process that made the church and its liturgy more uniform throughout the country, but not more centralized. A much better explanation of the 1547 and 1551 recognitions of new miracle workers is that it was an attempt to maintain the prestige of the monastic establishment by recognizing a whole series of new monastic saints. At the same time, recognizing the new miracle workers was a call to remember the glories of the monastic past, an attempt to arrest the decline of the monasteries and their authority. This attempt ran parallel to the proposals in 1551 to strengthen clerical discipline. Furthermore, the notion that the 1547 recognitions of miracle workers were part of a policy of territorial centralization depends to some extent on the acceptance of A. A. Zimin's view of Ivan the Terrible's reforms as directed against the last appanages and toward the unity of the state. R. G. Skrynnikov, however, sees Ivan's enemy not as territorial appanages but as boyar clans, and if his view is adopted then there is no need to force the 1547 decisions into the mode of territorial centralization. Indeed the 1547 council indirectly strengthens Skrynnikov's argument.

In the period 1547–1610 it is also very difficult to trace a policy of territorial centralization through the use of the recognition of saints. The recognition of Vasilii the Blessed in 1588 meant the introduction of a Moscow saint throughout the country, but the saints added in the *Ustav* of 1610 (as noted previously) included a preponderance of Novgorodians. Archbishop Serapion could even be considered to some extent an anti-Moscow saint because of his conflicts with St. Joseph of Volokolamsk. Again, local holy men were being imposed on Moscovites, not the other way around. Why such a need to placate the provinces? The political context of the 1610 *Ustav* renders the preponderance of Novgorodians perfectly comprehensible. The *Ustav* was begun on 1 January 1607, only a few months after the expulsion of the first False Dmitrii and the enthronement of Vasilii Shuiskii. It was prepared under the watchful eye of Vasilii's supporter, the new patriarch Germogen, author of the lives of St. Gurii and St. Varsonofii of Kazan' and the tale of the Kazan' icon. It was completed late in 1610, thus bridging the short reign of Vasilii Shuiskii. Above all, Shuiskii needed national unity in the face of Bolotnikov, the second False Dmitrii, and their Polish allies, and this unity was lacking in Novgorod and Pskov as well as some other areas.[31] In the political context of 1607–1610 the inclusion of so many Novgorod and Pskov saints made perfect sense, though again this was not the imposition of central practices on the localities. It was an attempt to placate the people of Novgorod and Pskov with the recognition of their local saints, filling out the list of Novgorod archbishops and local monks alongside the Moscow metropolitans and the monks of the center and north.

From the beginning of the seventeenth century, enough sources survive to follow the process of establishment of festivals closely in a few cases. Such records are not numerous, in part because of the smaller number of confirmations of sainthood in the seventeenth century. On 21 February 1600, the dignitaries of the church led by Patriarch Iov assembled to judge the qualifications for sainthood of Kornilii Komel'skii, a sixteenth-century northern monk. They had read out the written life of the saint and were offered testimony to the authenticity of the miracles, which was sufficient to convince them. They also noted that the liturgy and written life were "*pisano po obrazu i podobiiu, iako zhe i prochiim sviatym* [written according to form and propriety, as for other saints]." Kornilii Komel'skii's feast day was established for Vologda alone, and he never acquired a national festival in the seventeenth century.[32] A more important cult approved in 1618–1619 was that of Makarii Zheltovodskii (died 1444). A monk who was the founder of the Zheltovodskii Monastery a few miles down the Volga from Nizhnii Novgorod, Makarii was called a miracle worker some years before, but the cult was officially recognized only in 1618–1619, as we learn from the correspondence of Patriarch Filaret with his son the young tsar Michael. Filaret did so only after an investigation of the miracles, as well as after the intervention of Prince D. M. Pozharskii, who submitted proof that an icon of Makarii in a village church on his estate had worked miracles. In this case, a national festival followed that lasted the century.[33] The decision of the patriarch or a council had been the usual form of recognition of a saint since 1547. However, the increasing control of the church by the tsar, as well as the bureaucratization of the church itself, often lead to the recognition of sainthood by the government or church office with jurisdiction in the area of the country where the saint's relics (or the miraculous icon) were to be found. The 1627 confirmation of the miracles of the Solovetskii monk Daniil came from the *Prikaz Bol'shogo Dvortsa* over the signature of its secretary Gerasim Martem'ianov, not from Patriarch Filaret.[34] A miraculous icon of the Mother of God in a village near Tsarevo-Kokshaisk was investigated in 1647 by the *Prikaz kazanskogo dvortsa*, the Office of the Kazan' Palace, again an office of state, not of the church, but also not a local government office. By contrast, a miraculous icon of the *Zhenymironositsy* in a village near Suzdal' was dealt with in the same year by the patriarchal *sudnyi prikaz* (judicial chancellery), in response to a petition of the archbishop of Suzdal'.[35] All these were only local celebrations.

But whether the investigation took place in the offices of tsar or patriarch the results seem to fit the same pattern, one of general tolerance for miracle cults of saints and cults securely placed at the top of the hierarchy. Such was Metropolitan Filipp in 1646 and 1653 or the Robe of the Lord (*Riza Gospodnia*) sent in 1625 from Persia.[36] In the case of miracles of icons or obscure holy men in the villages, however, both church and state were more cautious. The relics of Adrian Poshekhonskii (investigated 1626) and the two miraculous icons of 1647 mentioned already were treated with mild caution, and the authorities would only grant a local liturgy for the icons and Adrian. But the church and state, while more cautious in the case of popular cults, were not careless about more dignified cults either. Nikon investigated the miracles of Daniil of Pereiaslavl' and only in 1653 approved a local cult.[37]

A restriction in the number of saints' days in the Russian Orthodox church took place after 1653 in a series of stages, first the patriarchate of Nikon, then the councils of the 1666–1667, and finally the councils of 1677–1679. Nikon's patriarchate seems to have brought a radical reduction in the number of saints recognized as worthy of a national feast day. Nikon did promote two cults in his early years, that of Metropolitan Filipp, whose relics he brought to Moscow while still metropolitan of Novgorod, and Iakov Borovitskii, whose relics were brought to the principal shrine of Nikon's new monastery on Lake Valdai. As noted in the next chapter, even these cults were centered not on cures but on the moral virtues of the saint. Nikon seems also to have early found a use for relics other than as the object of miracle cults. At the church council of 1654, among the various liturgical issues and the condemnations of Ioann Neronov, Nikon brought up the issue that the ecumenical councils had ordered relics of saints and martyrs to be placed under the altar when new churches were consecrated, and that this order had not been carried out in Russia. When the council ordered it to be done,[38] surely this action changed the meaning of relics in Russian religious life, de-emphasizing the uniqueness of the relics at miracle-working shrines and at the same time spreading the aura of holiness to the ordinary parish church. Even more basic perhaps was the patriarch's reduction in the number of saints listed in the printed service books prepared under his supervision. These books reduced by more than half the number of saints' days over the 1610 book (see Table 4-1). Thus the time of Nikon's patriarchate represented an all-time low in the number of festivals. The saints whom Nikon eliminated were a mixed bag, but the common thread seems to have been that they were mainly of local significance, such as Gurii and Varsonofii of Kazan' and Petr and Fevroniia of Murom (the latter recognized only in 1646). Nikon reversed the policy of 1610 and later years that included many local cults in the national pantheon. His reduction in the number of saints also seems to signify a certain shift away from the cult of saints in general, a trend exemplified in the sermons of Epifanii Slavinetskii.[39]

The second stage was the condemnation of Old Belief at the council of 1666–1667. It inevitably affected the status of the cults, directly and

Table 4-1. Number of Saints' Days, 1602–1682

Year	Saints' Days
1602	45
1610	76
1633	67
1641	77
1646	101
1648	101
1655	57
1656	30
1658	48
1667	48
1668	48
1682	63

Source: Golubinskii, *Istoniia Kanonigatsii*, 229–43.

indirectly. One indirect way was through the various measures agreed upon to improve administration and discipline in the church, such as increasing the number of bishops (thereby decreasing the size of the eparchies) and reestablishing the jurisdiction of bishops over the clergy (with a better apparatus for that purpose). Perhaps because the tsar felt a threat to his prerogatives, many of these measures were not carried out right away. (The abolition of the *monastyrskii prikaz*, for example, clearly a consequence of the measures, did not occur until 1677.) The council also reiterated the need for caution in the recognition of sainthood. This had been a concern all along, but the appearance of Old Belief obviously further alarmed the church with the prospect of uncontrolled popular cults that might act as a rallying point for the Old Believers. The passage on relics of saints follows immediately upon the refutation of St. Evfrosin of Pskov's contention that the hallelujah in the liturgy should be said twice (the *sugubaia alliluia*) rather than three times, as appeared in the post-Nikonian service books. The council concluded:

> And also dare not to honor newly found uncorrupted bodies without trust-worthy verification [*svidetel'stvo*] and conciliar command: for there are many whole and uncorrupted bodies that are not so from holiness, but who have died excommunicated by episcopal or priestly curse, or are whole and un-destroyed because of their violation of divine rules and laws. And if you wish to honor someone among saints, it is proper that you investigate and verify such bodies that have been found before the great and perfect council of bishops.

The council also increased the climate of skepticism in regard to the holy fools, taking an even more restrictive position than the 1547 council, which generally relegated them to local cults. At the end of a long series of decisions designed to strengthen monastic discipline, the council rail-ed against

> certain hairy hypocrites and ensnarers, who live in cities and villages in the form of hermits and recluses and in monastic garb. Some even are in chains. Also they go begging naked and barefoot in cities and villages for the sake of vanity, and get great glory from the people who honor them as saints, as a snare to the simple and ignorant.

The council found such people not in their right minds (*ne zdravym umom*) and also contrary to tradition, for in the holy books it was written that such people passed their time in the desert so as to flee the world, not in towns begging. Such were St. Andrei (of Crete?) and St. Simeon (Stylites?), who did not imitate the hairy hypocrites, "nor did they go among the yards and houses of the powerful and well known, but where no one knew or honored them." The council made no specific recom-mendation, but clearly suggested that such activity should be confined to distant monasteries, and that people who are afflicted with weakness of mind are worthy of condemnation, not praise and honor.[40] These words referred to living examples of holy fools, but such a negative view could not help but increase the distrust of the Russian holy fools of the recent past, who had lived in towns and begged for a living.

Patriarch Ioakim followed the lead of Nikon in reinforcing his own authority and that of the church against the tsar, and in trying (as the Zealots had earlier) to improve the church's influence over popular life and religious practices. Important cases involving the attempts to control popular religious practices were the church councils of 1677 and 1679, which discussed the cult of Anna of Kashin. Anna was a fourteenth-century Tver' princess, the wife of St. Michael of Tver', the latter recognized as a saint in the 1610 *Ustav*. Her miracle-working relics lay in a church in Kashin near the city of Tver'. Her cult had been investigated in 1647, but only recognized in 1650 or 1652, and then only for a local liturgy, and she never appeared in the printed service books. On the other hand, Epifanii Slavinetski himself wrote a *kanon* for her in the 1650s, and in 1674–1676 a life was compiled with accounts of the miracles.[41] All this activity seems to suggest a move toward recognition of Anna as a saint.

The proceedings of the councils on this subject are unusually detailed, and mark the only occasions on which the church devoted its full attention to an otherwise obscure local miracle cult. Ten people—townsmen, clergy, and peasants—who claimed knowledge of her miracles were interrogated, and most asserted certain knowledge of the miracles. The councils, however, paid more attention to the written life, which was examined with great care and compared with reports in the Russian chronicles, since as a Tver' princess she appeared in their pages. The council of 1677 found no less than thirteen places where the life contradicted the information in the chronicles, and the 1679 council found another three such places. In one place the chronicles contradicted the year of Anna's death given in the life, and in another the names of the Tver' princes who journeyed to the court of the Khans of the Golden Horde. The council took the chronicles to be accurate accounts of the past, and concluded that the life's deviations from the chronicles proved its falsity (in this conclusion they were correct). This was an unprecedented procedure, and a potentially dangerous one, for most of the tales of miraculous icons (Tikhvin, Fedoroskaia) and many saints' lives (for example, Antonii the Roman) contained precisely such inconsistencies or even worse. This was the basic problem, but some miracles also came in for criticism. In particular the council rejected the story of the Kashin archimandrite Sil'vestr, who claimed he had seen Anna's fingers forming the gesture of blessing, had unbent them, and seen them return again to the blessing. The council found that, in the first place, Anna's corpse was not completely uncorrupted (and therefore the position of the fingers was irrelevant) and, in the second place, the gesture of blessing was that of a priest or bishop, and as a lay person and a woman Anna could not possibly have been either. The 1677 council also referred explicitly to the 1666–1667 council's decision on the need to investigate relics carefully: the issue of Old Belief and the authority of the church was central to the proceedings.[42]

Another issue at the council was that of the cults of saintly princes. Anna was after all a princess, and the church included an elaborate defense of its position on the subject, listing thirty-five Russian and Byzantine saintly tsars and princes who had no liturgy, cult, or written life to honor them. The fathers reminded the faithful that the virtues of good men and women were remembered in heaven, and that not all good people, however virtuous, could have cults devoted to them. The council ruled that "if someone wants to pray for his own health and salvation, let him pray to the Lord God or the most holy Mother of God, but for the Grand Princess the nun Sofia [Anna] let him have a funeral service said and let him perform acts of charity." Thus Anna would be remembered like other saintly princes, not like a saint. This emphasis was entirely in keeping with the time, the general emphasis on moral teaching over miracle cults that was characteristic of the religiosity of the court, aristocracy, and church elite.[43] The rejection of Anna of Kashin was a blow at the Old Belief, but Ioakim did not go as far as Nikon in removing other Russian saints. In fact, Ioakim restored some whom Nikon had rejected.

In early 1682 another church council met to discuss a number of issues.[44] The church responded favorably to the tsar's request that some attention be given to making the cult of saints more dignified by prohibiting construction in cemeteries, prohibiting the bringing of food and drink to church on major festivals, and taking better care of relics. The tsar's proposals (worked out the previous fall with Patriarch Ioakim) touched only on the Kremlin cathedrals, on the large number of small relics in the Annunciation Cathedral and on the relics of the Robe of the Lord and part of the True Cross in the Dormition Cathedral. The many relics in the Annunciation Cathedral were brought every year for blessing to the Dormition Cathedral on Good Friday and then returned "for the enlightenment and healing of those who accept them with faith," while the Robe and Cross had been divided and placed in various places in the Dormition Cathedral where they had worked many miracles. In this situation the relics lacked sufficient respect, so the tsar proposed to take the many small relics from the Annunciation Cathedral and distribute them among the parish churches and monasteries so that they might have greater honor. The Robe and Cross, on the other hand, he proposed to bring together with all their fragments in one reliquary, to be raised (*vozdviziat*) on Good Friday but during the rest of the year kept on the western wall of the cathedral so that people might be cured of their diseases. The church, not surprisingly, accepted this proposal, for it was in accord with the policies of the previous decades. The effect of the decisions was to substitute one central miracle cult of the Robe and True

Cross for a number of smaller ones of the same relics and to integrate that cult into the liturgical cycle of the main cathedral church of Russia and its court. Dispersal of the smaller relics concentrated the liturgical cycle of the Annunciation Cathedral on the Mother of God, reducing the importance of relics in the tsar's own church. The dispersion of smaller relics gave smaller churches objects of devotion that were approved by the church authorities and would be the object of a dignified cult, since the relics were to go only to stone churches (that is the wealthier and more important churches). The church, as before, was not prohibiting the miracle cults, merely restricting and controlling them.

The council also approved a new *Ustav* for church services that included some sixty-three Russian saints, an increase over the numbers found in the service books of the 1650s and 1660s. The *Ustav* restored only some fifteen saints omitted in 1658–1668. Under Adrian a further revision in 1695 added eight and dropped two, and the sixty-nine saints listed in the 1695 *Ustav* were the only ones ever to be the object of recognized national cults into the nineteenth century. The two revisions added no really new saints and thus Ioakim and Adrian, in institutional matters so close to Nikon's policies, combined the new restrictions on popular cults with a return to some of the saints of the pre-Nikonian era.[45]

The decision to regulate the local miracle cults was made by the tsar and the ecclesiastical authorities, but in Russia enforcement of such decisions was often a problem. How were these policies carried out? The attempt of the church to de-emphasize and even restrict local popular miracle cults in the later years of the seventeenth century met with a certain amount of opposition, not all of it from the Old Belief. The attempts on the part of local groups to maintain their cults are very helpful in revealing the attitude of the church authorities. Through the middle seventeenth century, when the church was beginning to restrict the recognition of local saints, the popular cults, especially of icons, continued to grow in number in spite of official policy. The two cases from 1647 were early examples. Another was the case of the miraculous icon of the Smolensk Mother of God in the small town of Shuia near Suzdal', a newly painted icon (*novopisannaia*) that began to work miracles during Passion Week of 1666 (6–10 April). The miracles started among the townspeople who came to the icon in the church of the Resurrection (Voskresenie), a Shuia parish church, the first to be cured being a boy (*otrok*) possessed by the devil. Then many people began to come: "[M]any sick, deaf and blind and paralyzed in the arms, and lame, and paralyzed, and bothered by unclean spirits and possessed by various passions were cured and became healthy." The townspeople as a community (*vsem mirom*) informed the *voevoda* (governor) of the district, Semen Stepanovich Ushakov, listing 103 miracles from April to October. The townspeople were by then not alone, for the peasants of the surrounding villages had begun to come and be cured, and the icon began to work miracles not only in the church but in outlying parts of the district (*v dal'nykh okrestnykh mestakh*). The townspeople made sure their case would be heard, for in addition they presented it to the clerks of the archbishopric of Suzdal' and in Moscow personally to Metropolitan Pavel Sarskii and Podonskii (Krutitskii), who was in charge of the church in the absence of a patriarch. Pavel turned the matter over to the patriarchal *razriadnyi prikaz* (service records office), so in both Moscow and Suzdal' ecclesiastical officials handled the case.[46] The petitions, strengthened by accounts of the miracles, did not work at first and were repeated in the summer of 1667. Ioasaf, the new patriarch, then instructed his clerks to write Archbishop Stefan of Suzdal' instructing him to take five archimandrites and an archpriest and investigate the miracles in Shuia, requiring an oath from those who were cured or witnessed cures. Stefan did his duty, compiling books recording his investigation and sending them to the patriarchal *razriadnyi prikaz*, the boyar Nikifor Mikhailovich Beklemishev, and the clerk Ivan Kalitin. A few weeks later Stefan (that is, his chancellery) wrote to the town government, the *zemskii starosta* (land elder) Ivan Gerasimov asking for another copy of the complete list of miracles and for further information on one disputed case. The decision is not recorded. The townspeople were not wholly satisfied with the result of their labors, however, for in November 1669 the town government, the *zemskii starosta* Luka Andreev and others, sent a petition to the *voevoda* of Shuia Ivan Ivanovich Borkov, informing him that in the past months great crowds of men, women, and girls had come possessed by evil spirits and were cured at the icon. Many of them had begun to call out (*klikati*) against various people; in particular, Irina, the daughter of Fedor and the wife of the Shuia townsman Ivan Maurin, had called out against one Fedor Iakimov. What she had said is not explained, but it was enough to cause him to be taken to Suzdal', where he had died (under torture, apparently). The townspeople begged for mercy, saying that they had not done anything wrong and supporting the petition of Ivan Andreev Telegin made to the town authorities on 23 November 1669. Irina Maurina had evidently called out against him as well. The *voevoda* of Suzdal', Aleksander Petrovich Mitropolitov, evidently believed Irina had been possessed by an evil spirit or was enchanted (*porchena*), for he ordered the clerk in the Shuia branch of the Suzdal' local administration, the clerk Roman Ivanov in the Shuia *s"ezzhaia izba*, to communicate his desire that the Iakimov case not be repeated with Telegin, but that he investigate who was enchanting Irina Maurina. This question the townspeople could not answer, and here our sources end.[47] The whole episode illustrate the rise of the cults, the attitude of state and church, and the dangers involved. The cult of the Smolensk icon arose spontaneously but was furthered by the town government and the parish priest. The townspeople appealed to both secular and ecclesiastical authorities, but it was the church, or more particularly the patriarchal chancellery, that handled the case. The chancellery of the Suzdal' archbishop was involved as well, but the actual investigation of the miracles was made by a rather high level group of churchmen, including Archbishop Stefan of Suzdal' himself, Pavel, the archimandrite of the Evfimiev monastery, Suzdal's most important monastery, and Varlaam, the archimandrite of the Danilov Monastery in Moscow. The town government of Suzdal' was called in as well. The cult seems to have been approved only as a local cult. The episode of Irina Maurina in 1669–1670 at first frightened the (presumably secular) authorities, who investigated the unfortunate Iakimov with such enthusiasm that he died of it. It was the secular authorities, in the person of Mitropolitov the Suzdal' *voevoda* who finally put a stop to the arrest of persons accused by Maurina or other women. The caution and ultimate skepticism of the authorities, secular and ecclesiastical, are clear: they were only a short step away from the later campaigns against popular superstition.

The Shuia records are especially useful because they illustrate the reaction of the church and local administration, but there are numerous cases in which merely the history of the cult survives, often recorded only by later local historians who used local archives. Suzdal' itself was not only an archbishopric, but also the scene of numerous local cults in the seventeenth and eighteenth centuries. The primary local cult seems to have been that of the relics of Ioann and Fedor of Suzdal', two bishops of Suzdal' of the fourteenth and tenth centuries, respectively. Liturgical and other documents of the Suzdal' archbishops reveal the existence of a well-organized local cult from at least 1598, when bishop Galaktion had the coffins of the two saints covered in silver. However, almost nothing was known of them. Fedor was certainly mythical, for there were no Christians in Suzdal' that early, and the only references to Bishop Ioann seem to have been in the written life of Evfimii of Suzdal' as well as in an early sixteenth-century written life of Ioann himself. Miracles do not seem to have been recorded before 1738, in spite of the flourishing liturgical cult, and even though the cult was confirmed by the Holy Synod in 1755, Fedor later was dropped from the list of permitted cults because it could not be proved that he existed.

A cult that did have recorded miracles from the beginning was that of Sofia, the wife whom Vasilii III divorced and who became a nun in the Pokrov Convent in Suzdal', where she died in 1542. The list of her miracles, twenty-one in number, begins in 1602 and ends in 1656. They are a typical collection of miracle stories; all but one (in which she saved the town from the Poles in the Time of Troubles) are miraculous cures and with the usual social-geographic pattern. All the cured come from Suzdal' or nearby villages, six are clergy or their families, two are townspeople, and twelve are peasants. In spite of these very typical miracles, the church never recognized the cult and Sofia never became a saint, though the Suzdal' archbishops do not seem ever to have interfered with it. Perhaps the divorced wife of the sovereign did not seem an appropriate candidate for sainthood, and furthermore no written life existed.

Somewhat more successful was Efrosinia of Suzdal', supposedly the daughter of Prince Michael of Chernigov, whose uncorrupted relics were revealed under the auspices of Patriarch Adrian in 1699. Evfrosinia thus acquired recognition for the establishment of a local cult, but not enough to secure her a permanent place in the *Ustav* of Russian saints after the 1699 ceremony. Finally, in the village of Aleksino near Suzdal' at about the same time, a local cult existed of a prince Fedor of Starodub, who supposedly had been buried there. An investigation was started in 1722 at the instigation of the Suzdal' archbishop, and in 1745 it ended unfavorably for the cult: the miracles reported at the coffin were declared false, and in 1746 repeated pilgrimages to the site led the Holy Synod to order the relics and icons of Fedor destroyed.[48]

Somewhat similar events took place west of Moscow in the small town of Viaz'ma in 1677–1680. Here conflict arose over Arkadii of Novyi Torzhok, a quite obscure local holy man alleged to have lived in the eleventh century.[49] He had already appeared in a dream to the local governor's cook in 1525 and asked that a church be erected in his honor, and in response the Church of the Savior was built with a side altar to honor Arkadii. It seems to have flourished until the *Smuta* but was then abandoned until 1661, when the townspeople decided to rebuild it to honor Arkadii. However, Arkadii himself appeared in a dream to Sergei, a "pious shepherd" of Viaz'ma, and instructed him to build a church to the Savior instead. Sergei went even farther, becoming a monk and constructing a small monastery in the town to the All-Merciful Savior, later the locus of the cult. In 1677 Arkadii's relics were uncovered, and an icon was painted by a monk from a monastery in nearby Iukhnov. The icon now became the primary object of the cult. Processions were held to honor the icon, apparently in conjunction with the celebration of the defeat of the Old Belief in the area (not an impressive victory, for it had been very weak). In 1679 Archimandrite Pitirim of the Monastery of John the Baptist (*Predtechev monastyr'*) in Viaz'ma was ordered by Varsonofii, the metropolitan of Krutitsy, to investigate the miracles claimed for the icon. Pitirim was clearly not convinced that the icon worked any true miracles, for he decided to keep the icon in his monastery for safekeeping and further investigation. This decision did not sit well with the townspeople, and after the Ascension Day procession in 1680 a retired cavalryman named Stepan Kovalev and a great crowd came to Pitirim to ask for the return of the icon to the Church of the Savior where it had rested before. Pitirim reported back to Moscow that Kovalev had said that because the icon had been taken away to the monastery "great difficulty had come on the town, and great sadness on the community, for there was no rain." Thus Kovalev "aroused the people and raised up murmuring against [him]." On 28 July another procession passed by Pitirim's monastery and one Sen'ka Mukha, the priest's son, cried out that Pitirim did not believe in the icon and threatened him with death. Another townsman, Vasilii Bubnov, even claimed that in the past Arkadii had kept snakes away from the town. Two days later an open revolt threatened, when Kovalev, some musketeers, and the town poor abused Pitirim in public and threatened his life for the second time, frightening the archimandrite so much that he was afraid to go to the cathedral. When Metropolitan Varsonofii heard of all this he ordered the icon brought to his residence in Moscow to decide the case. The townspeople of Viaz'ma petitioned in favor of the icon, asserting that the real reason that Pitirim did not believe in it was that his own monastery, the chief one of the region, feared the Savior Monastery as a rival. This argument did not convince Varsonofii, and the case was decided in favor of Pitirim and denial of official recognition of the icon.[50]

In these cases of such local cults as Shuia, Suzdal', and Viaz'ma, the church and the state seem to have followed the direction marked out by the church councils of 1666–1667 and 1679. They drew a clear line between the officially recognized cults and those merely tolerated. Although they did not yet expressly forbid them (this came in the eighteenth century), they made it clear that the cults had no official recognition, and that the miracles claimed for them were not confirmed as true miracles. Thus the church, some decades before Peter, put a damper on local miracle cults. This was the policy of both Ioakim and Adrian, though it was not as strong as Nikon's. The reasons are not hard to find. The miracle cults had expanded in the sixteenth century, in the wake of the decline of monastic authority, and had been kept under the control of the church authorities. When the Old Belief challenged that authority, the church responded with a tightening of control. The fate of the local cults was different from that of the great national festivals after 1682. While both Ioakim and Adrian restored the saints excluded from service books in Nikon's time, they continued to be suspicious of local cults and allowed them only as local cults and under close supervision.

5

The Era of Miracles

The most visible example of change in the character of religious experience in the wake of the decline of monastic authority was the swift and tremendous increase in the popularity of miracles in the sixteenth century. These miracles were of two types: the more public miracles that involved the whole community (aid in battle, defense against fire and plague); and miracle cults, both of the relics of saints and of miracle-working icons. The latter worked cures of particular individuals, normally in association with a particular shrine. The two types of miracles are reflected in two different types of sources. The public miracles were recorded in chronicles or in tales of the miraculous occurrences, which were essentially brief historical narratives. The miracle cults were recorded in appendices to the lives of saints or to tales of the appearance of miraculous icons, long appendices that gave considerable detail about the persons and places involved. These appendices appear at the end of the fifteenth century; earlier Russian saints' lives do mention the existence of shrines and cures, but only very rarely give specific examples. Later on, starting in the sixteenth century, miracles at shrines begin to include miracles of power, where the saint protects the monastery's property. These types of miracles replaced the predominant types of the earlier era, public miracles alongside those worked by living holy men who were almost all monks. It is the miracle cults that are our primary concern.

The increase in the frequency of both types of recorded miracles at shrines cannot be attributed merely to more numerous sources, for older saints' lives did occasionally include stories of posthumous miracles. In the sixteenth century the number of saints and miracle-working icons increased, and the size of the appendices to the saints' lives and icon tales grew as well. In chronicles the number of public miracles also grew, which suggests that we are dealing with a real increase in the interest in miraculous events, not merely in the appearance of a new type of source in the miracle appendices to saints' lives.

The public miracles in the chronicles do not seem to have changed much in character in the sixteenth century: they merely became more frequent. The miracle cults not only increased in number, they also changed in character, from miracles worked by living holy men to miracles at shrines, and from a seemingly random mix of miracles of power and healing to predominantly healing miracles. Here Russia passed through changes in the character of miracle cults similar to those that had occurred in Western Europe during the twelfth to thirteenth centuries.[1] Miracles of power, the predominant type in early medieval Western Europe, were those in which the saint at a particular shrine showed his power in the world, often by vengeance on the skeptical or by protecting the material possessions (land or treasure) of the monastery or church where the saint's body rested. They expressed, as Thomas Head has put it, the patronage of the saint over a particular community, monastic or lay. In the twelfth century such miracles gave way to miraculous cures, in which the believer was cured of some physical or mental disease either at the shrine or through prayer elsewhere. Further, there seem to have been social distinctions in the types of miracles, for only about one third of those affecting nobles were cures, as opposed to about four fifths of those involving the popular classes. Nobles experienced primarily miracles of power. Russian experience before about 1470 was quite different, in large part because of the absence of large numbers of miracles at shrines. In Kiev Rus' and later Russia, the living saint exercised power and patronage as well as cures. In addition, Kiev Rus' and Russia witnessed numerous public miracles, when the Mother of God or the saints interceded for a whole land or state, also as in Western Europe. The miracles worked by the early Russian saints as living holy men seem to have been predominantly miracles of power rather than cures, and thus were directed at the community more than the individual. The essence of the shift, in Western Europe of the twelfth to thirteenth centuries and in sixteenth-century Russia, was from miracles on behalf of a group (monastery, town, village, country) to miracles that helped an individual. There is neither reason to believe nor any evidence to suggest that sixteenth-century Russia was influenced by Western Europe in this regard: the similarity in types of miracles should be put down to common Christian roots. There was also one important social difference. Russian aristocrats were not the objects of miracles at the shrines, and only a few lesser landholders were cured among a crowd of peasants, soldiers, townsmen, and lesser clergy.[2] The causes of the increase in attention to miracles in sixteenth-century Russia and the changes in type of miracle were internal, and had nothing to do with fashions from outside, even from Byzantium and the Greek church.

The history of the miracle cults and their shrines is more complex than that of the public miracles. Miraculous relics and icons certainly existed from the earliest times of Christianity in Russia, but the sixteenth century saw a tremendous change in scale. The stories of miraculous icons and saints from before the fifteenth century regularly include some brief comment to the effect that many people visited the icon or the shrine of the saint and were cured, but they give little or no detail. The saints, predominantly monastic, also worked miracles during their lifetimes, and these miracles are recorded as episodes in the written life of the saint, not as posthumous miracles at the shrine containing the saint's relics. The icons worked great political miracles recorded in chronicles or special tales, not at their shrines. The Kievan monastic saints Antonii and Feodosii had been this type, as were the two most important monastic saints of Moscow, Sergii of Radonezh and Kirill of Belozero. The changes in the sixteenth century were spontaneous, arising from the increase in sheer number of cults, but also from an increase in interest and record- ing of the cures by the clergy and eventual conscious sponsorship by the hierarchy. The church both ratified and further encouraged the cults at the church councils of 1547 and 1551, when it recognized many Russian holy men and women as miracle workers. In the seventeenth century the miracle cults continued to flourish until about the 1660s, when there was a gradual change to miracles of power, a symptom (in this case) of de- cline. These were crass attempts to sanctify the monastery's property against rival landholders or neighboring peasants. Such miracles seem to be concentrated in the years about 1640–1670, after which the church inaugurated a policy of suspicion and restraint on both sainthood and miracle cults. Popular miracle cults continued to exist as healing cults, as we have seen, but were not emphasized in elite religious culture and were ultimately discouraged in the eighteenth century.

The social context of sixteenth- and seventeenth-century Russian mir- acle cults presents a complex problem. The evidence of the miracle sto- ries provides a very clear social context, which varies surprisingly little from shrine to shrine: the cured were mainly merchants and artisans in the towns and peasants (at least the more prosperous peasants), provin- cial landholders, and a variety of soldiers, clergy, and petty officials. Strik- ingly absent are the upper aristocracy of the court, the boyars and other ranks, who were prominent in the patronage of the monasteries and were the principal participants in the court religious ceremonies. At the same time, the very poorest peasants and townspeople do not seem to be prominent, but that may be only because they were too humble to be recorded. Such an explanation cannot account for the absence of the boyars: on the rare occasion when members of the elite did appear at shrines, much was made of it in the lists of miracles.

The miracle cults seem at first glance to record a popular layer of religious experience. The problem is that the miracle stories were written by educated people (mainly monks, like Simon Azarin or Patriarch Iov) and for people not only basically literate but even educated (at least in religious matters). No large proportion of the humble folk cured at the shrines can have read these stories, however optimistically we assess the level of literacy in sixteenth- and seventeenth-century Russia. Most of the known authors of the saints' lives were monks, whose origins normally lay among the lesser landholders and whose institutions were also wealthy. At the same time their audience was not extremely narrow, as the number of copies of the texts of saints' lives and icon tales was considerably greater than that of chronicles or secular tales. Saints' lives were usually in the dozens of copies, chronicles in only a handful of copies, and secular tales even fewer. Admittedly this is a crude index, but the numbers suggest a much wider audience for saints' lives with their records of miracles than for chronicles or other written works.[3] Nevertheless, the saints' lives and tales of miraculous icons required literacy, for they were too long to be read in church on the relevant festival. The paradoxical result is that a "popular" cult was described and possibly known more to the landholding class than to the people who actually participated in it.

The miracle cults after about 1470 were healing cults, with only one case involving primarily miracles of power (Sts. Zosima and Savvatii) in the sixteenth century. The earlier predominance of public miracle stories in the chronicles and other tales, such as the legend of the intercession of the Vladimir Mother of God in 1395, served to underline the piety of the Russian land as a whole. They were also in a sense "aristocratic," for inevitably the prince and the boyars were the main actors in political events. The chronicle tales, in contrast to the miracle cult records, were public political events that reflected the political piety of the aristocracy and the court and were written for an audience similar to the actors in the events.

The miracle cults were rather more complex. On one hand, the sixteenth-century healing miracles from the saints' lives were about the faith and healing of series of single individuals, and they glorified the roles of those saints in the individual piety of the believer. The healing miracles were a step on the road from a more public to a more private and inward Orthodoxy. The long lists of individuals with the details of their lives and diseases gave the reader a vivid impression of the workings of God on the individual level. On the other hand, a miracle cult was a public, community institution, approved by church and tsar. That approval, and the composition of a written record of the cult in many copies, incorporated the ordinary people into the religious experience of the elite, as the objects of a divine power that did not fall on that elite itself. In this respect, like the great religious rituals of Epiphany or Palm Sunday, the miracles were expressions of a religious notion of social and political solidarity as well as of the power of God in individual life. Private in essence, they had an important public side to them.

Miracles in the Sixteenth Century

Before the fifteenth century the lives of the saints do not include long appendices of the cured, and the saint, usually a monk, worked his miracles while alive. Even miraculous cures are often really miracles of power, as in the Kiev *Paterik,* where the holy monks cure the sick in rivalry with Armenian physicians. The public, political function of the miracle-working icons was even clearer. The two most important were the Mother of God of the Sign (*Znamenie*) in Novgorod, and the Mother of God of Vladimir in Vladimir and later Moscow. Both were essentially political symbols of local patriotism and dynastic loyalties. The *Znamenie* icon was the instrument through which the intercession of the Mother of God was successfully sought by the Novgorodians when Mstislav, the son of the Vladimir Grand Prince Andrei Bogoliubskii, besieged their city in 1170. In later times the Vladimir icon's most famous act was the protection of Moscow and its territories in the Northeast of Russia from the army of Tamerlane in 1395. There are occasional notices that these icons worked other miracles, but detailed written accounts were provided by medieval churchmen only for these two central incidents. Many of the sixteenth-century legends about other miraculous icons (the Mother of God of Tikhvin, for example) assert that the icon was miraculously found earlier on, normally in the late fourteenth century, but there is no evidence from earlier (fourteenth- or fifteenth-century) sources to confirm these assertions, and it seems clear that these dates are mere legends.[4] In reality the number of icon cults did not expand noticeably until about 1500. Furthermore, the earlier confirmed icon cults that have left any significant record are not healing but political cults, whose miracles are those of power, and represent a public piety centered on the land and the community. The sixteenth-century cults of miraculous icons are almost exclusively healing cults.

The same pattern exists in the case of the relics of saints: before the end of the fifteenth century they are few in number and the recorded miracles they effected at each shrine are few. The cults of the most important saints (Sergii, Kirill, metropolitans Peter and Aleksei) simultaneously reflect monastic and political interests. Whereas their written lives represent the holy monk and the holy prelate, their posthumous cults are largely manifestations of their political importance, and include no long lists of healing miracles as they later did. This pattern is illustrated in the life of St. Sergii of Radonezh. Epifanii Premudryi's early fifteenth-century life of St. Sergii records a small number of miracles that the saint worked in his lifetime, mostly miracles of power, but includes no stories of posthumous miracles worked at his tomb. The impression is given, however, that a cult did exist, for the oldest lives state that "Many cures happen from his coffin up to our day, for those who come with faith but burdened with various diseases are cured."[5] The first accounts of specific cures are found in Pakhomii Logofet's second version of the life from the third quarter of the fifteenth century. Here the text describes seven cures, two of great noblemen (*vel'mozhi*), one of a merchant, one of a lesser nobleman (*voin*) or soldier, and three of people listed without social or geographic origin. A significant healing cult did not develop until later, however, for the 1646 life of Sergii records only the very early healing miracles and follows with a long list of public, political miracles of power, which change to healing miracles only in the 1600s.[6]

The life of Kirill of Belozero is similar, which suggests that during the late fifteenth century the cults of the monastic saints began the shift to miracles of healing. Pakhomii Logofet's life of Kirill lists sixteen posthumous miracles, all but the first healing miracles. Seven of them happened to persons of low status, servants, priests' sons, or merchants, while eight were boyars or princes. This list includes three boyars or their wives mentioned only by Christian names, Prince David Semenovich; Princess Elena (cured three times), the wife of Prince Mikhail Andreevich of Mozahisk, Vereia, and Belozero; and Prince Mikhail himself. The cult of Kirill also shows an involvement of boyars not to be found in later posthumous cults.[7]

In the sixteenth century the elite of Russian society was mainly involved in public, political miracles, continuing the pattern of earlier centuries. These miracles were recorded in the principal official records of events, the Voskresenskii and Ioasaf chronicles. These were primarily miracles that occurred to aid the Russian army fighting the Muslim Tatars: victories over Christian opponents, whether the Novgorodians in 1471–1478 or the Lithuanians at Smolensk in 1514, took place without supernatural assistance. The "Standing on the Ugra" of 1480 and various lesser conflicts with the Tatars involved divine aid. In 1480 the Mother of God defeated Khan Ahmed on the Ugra, though the rather similar encounter with the Crimean Khan Mehmed Girei in 1522 was explained naturalistically: "The Khan, hearing that the Grand Prince was at Kolomna [with the army] did not attack Rus'."[8] These military encounters necessarily required the presence of the larger part of the elite, boyars and lesser nobles as well, as well as the grand prince himself. The chronicle accounts, quasi-official as they were, recorded the elite's perception of the events, both church and lay elite. The Voskresenskii chronicle was sympathetic to the princes Shuiskii and their faction, and the Ioasaf chronicle seems to have been compiled in the entourage of Metropolitan Daniil. As we shall see, the historical narratives compiled in the period 1547–1564 under the direct eye of Metropolitan Makarii and Ivan IV will radically increase the role of miracles in describing the events of the past.

The shift toward the spread of popular healing cults began at the end of the fifteenth century. The type of miracle stories appended to the lives was not much different from those in the older lives, giving the Christian name, the disease (or type of possession by devils), and usually the social status and geographic home of the cured. The change comes in the sheer number of saints' lives with such appendices, and the size of the appendices, from a dozen or so in the fifteenth century to many dozens in the sixteenth and after.[9]

An important example of the early sixteenth century miracle cults is contained in the first version of the lives of Sts. Zosima and Savvatii. This shrine, in the Solovetskii Monastery that they founded in the fifteenth century, was the most important in the Russian North. The earliest life was compiled about 1503, and describes twelve posthumous miracles at the shrine of the two saints. Of the twelve persons healed, two were monks of the Solovetskii Monastery (one originally a Novgorod boyar), five were peasants from the estates of the monastery in the North, and one a merchant from those same estates. Three more were merchants of the city of Novgorod, and one a tax collector for the grand prince of Moscow among the Lapps of the Kola peninsula (but who had his home on the Umba River where the monastery owned land). The three merchants in Novgorod did not travel to the shrine and were cured when some monks from the monastery prayed to the saints on the merchants' behalf. The cult of Sts. Zosima and Savvatii seems to have been primarily a local northern cult, involving northern peasants and merchants and Novgorod merchants, traditionally the most active in northern trade. The regionalism of the cult contrasts with the "national" quality of the earlier cult of Sergii.[10]

The spread of the miracle cults to become one of the basic forms of Russian religious life had been greatly accelerated by decisions of the church councils of 1547 and 1551. Metropolitan Makarii and the young tsar Ivan IV not only sponsored the recognition of new saints but they also sponsored an unprecedented introduction of the miraculous into the historical narratives of the period. A comparison of the Nikon chronicle and the *Stepennaia kniga*, the Book of Degrees, with earlier chronicles makes this abundantly clear. For example, both substituted a long story of visions of Russian saints for the earlier simple account of the 1522 campaign of Khan Mehmed against the Russians. In the later version a nun of the Voznesenie convent in Moscow saw a vision of metropolitans Petr, Aleskei, and Iona, Sergii of Radonezh, Varlaam of Khutyn' and others praying to the Vladimir icon to save Russia from the Tatars. Other miracles were inserted elsewhere in the place of earlier naturalistic accounts of events, such as the intercession of St. Sergii that led to the birth of Grand Prince Vasilii in 1479, absent in earlier chronicles. According to the Book of Degrees, the great Moscow fire of 1547 was stopped by the intercession of the Mother of God, signaled by the refusal of the Vladimir icon to be removed from the Dormition Cathedral in the Kremlin. All this was nothing in comparison with the accounts in both narratives of the conquest of Kazan', where the miraculous aid of the Mother of God and the Russian miracle workers was a regular and frequent occurrence. In the winter campaign of 1547–1548 no miracles occurred, but then the campaign was a failure. The same was the case in 1548–1549 and 1549–1550, but in 1550–1551 there were already portents of the Tatars' defeat. The final victorious campaign of 1552 was accompanied by a series of visions. During the siege in August of that year a servant of the treasurer of the Russian state, the *okol'nichii* Ivan Petrov Golovin, saw the apostles Peter and Paul and St. Nicholas. A soldier of Nizhnii Novgorod saw St. Nicholas as well, and a priest the hegumen Daniil of Pereiaslavl'. The Nikon chronicle and Book of Degrees also brought the miraculous into the Livonian War at the capture of Narva in 1558, though not at the capture of Polotsk in 1563. Later in the century the *Kazanskaia istoriia* amplified the description of the saints helping the Russian army against Kazan'. This was not a product of the palace or the metropolitanate and gives a slightly different picture of the role of the saints. In one version of the text the same miracles that appear in the Nikon chronicle and Book of Degrees (Sts. Peter and Paul, Nicholas, and the hegumen Daniil) were recounted, while the other introduced St. Sergii of Radonezh as well.[11]

The hundred years between the middle of the sixteenth and the middle of the seventeenth century was also the period of greatest importance for the cults of relics and icons in Russia. Many had arisen in the years 1470–1550 to find recognition in the church councils, and many more seem to have appeared on the local level in the years after 1550, some to find recognition only as local cults, others to find their way into the printed liturgical books, in almost all cases as national cults. In the first half of the seventeenth century the evidence suggests that fewer major cults arose, but the church continued in the liturgical books of 1610, 1633, and 1646 to recognize the older ones. The 1646 *Sviattsy* represented a high point in the liturgical celebration of saints and icons. Although not all (such as Joseph of Volokolamsk) had a cult at the shrine, most did, and that year was the high-water mark of official recognition of the miracle cults. Nikon's radical pruning of the liturgical books was followed by the church's decision to regulate popular miracle cults more carefully, a major change in church policy. The result was that our source of information runs out about that time. The cults survived, but no longer did clerics carefully keep lists of the cures to append to the texts of the saints' lives or the icon tales, so that even eighteenth-century copies of the miracle lists end in the seventeenth century.

The first important group of cults came into prominence by the middle of the sixteenth century. Besides the cults recognized at the councils, a number of others sprang up or increased in the 1550s. The Pskov saint Savva Krypetskii began to work various miracles after his relics were uncovered in 1554, the records running from 1551 to 1597 (fifty-six miracles in all). Most were healing miracles involving monks, townspeople, and even some princes and boyars, but there were also some miracles of power where the saint protected the monastery of St. Savva from misfortune. This was a typical local monastic cult, for Savva never appeared in the printed liturgical books. A bit later a similar mixture of miracles can be found in the cult of St. Antonii the Roman, supposedly a bishop of twelfth-century Novgorod who had been miraculously carried to the city from Rome on a large rock that sailed across the sea. The cult actually began between the time the relics were uncovered in 1581 and their translation in 1597, and Antonii appeared in the 1610 *Ustav* with other Novgorod saints added that year. A more archaic cult, smaller in extent but still a healing cult was that of Prince Aleksander Nevskii, recognized as a saint in the 1547 council. At his shrine there were eighteen miracles, the third from May 1491 and the sixteenth in 1572. Most of the cured were anonymous, but at least one was a peasant and two were *deti boiarkskie*.[12]

The saints of Kazan'—bishops Gurii and Varsonofii, and the miraculous icon of the Mother of God of that city—were the most striking examples of the new wave of cults at the end of the century. Both cults were (in theory) good candidates for a largely public, political cult, as they arose in a city recently conquered from the Muslim Tatars in 1552 during the reign of Ivan the Terrible. His victory over the Tatars in that year was recounted in numerous sources, all mentioning the intervention of various Russian saints on his behalf. After the victory Ivan largely rebuilt the city and repopulated it with Russians, relegating the native Tatars to a *sloboda,* or suburb, on the edge of the Russian town. This victory and rebuilding represented a great victory for Orthodoxy, but not a complete triumph, since the Tatars—both peasants and part of the native elite—remained in the countryside, and most nobles and all peasants held fast to Islam. The other peoples of the old Tatar Khanate—the Chuvash, Mari, Udmurt, and Bashkirs—held to their traditional beliefs as well, so that Orthodoxy in Kazan' was surrounded by a hostile population. However, in the first decades after the conquest the Russian state asked mainly political obedience: attempts at conversion came later, and the lives of St. Gurii and St. Varsonofii, as well as the tale of the Kazan' icon, contain almost no anti-Muslim passages, only the most cursory remark that the power of the Christian God awed the Tatars (but not enough to convert them).[13]

The life of the two bishops Gurii and Varsonofii was the work of the later patriarch Germogen, who devoted most of his work to the monastic lives of its heroes and their general piety, but little to their activity in Kazan'. Their shrine in Kazan', however, was quite active, and by the early seventeenth century sixty-six miraculous cures (no miracles of power) were recorded. The social background of the cured was notably nonaristocratic, since twenty-seven were townspeople, seventeen were clergy (monks, priests, deacons) or their servants, four were *strel'tsy* or soldiers, and one a *podd'iachii* or minor government secretary. (The identities of five were not specified.) Only four were *deti boiarskie* ("boyars sons," that is, lesser nobles) or members of their families and none came from the boyar aristocracy or even close to it. The geographic radius was quite small, with the peasants all living in the Kazan' *uezd* (district) and apparently some on the estates of the archbishop of Kazan'. The *deti boiarskie* were also local, only one coming from as far away as the nearby Arzamas *uezd*. Some of the clergy were resident in Moscow, but most were cured on trips to Kazan', and the rest were residents of Kazan'. Only the townspeople came from farther afield, though, again, from towns that traded with Kazan': the Volga towns of Kostroma and Tetiushi, and towns roughly in Kazan's trading area, Viatka, Rostov, and Vologda. One icon painter of Vologda was cured in Moscow where he lived by obtaining some holy oil from the saints' relics from Archimandrite Arsenii. The impression is inescapable that the cult of Sts. Gurii and Varsonofii, even though it was approved by the authorities in Moscow, was local in importance and confined to townspeople, clergy, peasants, and the lower provincial gentry.[14]

The cult of the Kazan' icon was of the same type. It worked sixteen miracle cures in the town from its discovery in 1579 until 1594, when an altar was built in the convent church of the Dormition to house the icon. This was the beginning of the official local cult. The cured included only one noble, the wife of the *syn boiarskii* Ivashko Kuz'minskii, together with five townspeople, five clergy, two peasants (one likely a peasant merchant), and three unspecified persons who happened to be in the convent church. The geographic range is ever narrower than that of the cult of the two bishops: one townsman and one priest's wife came from Sviiazhsk across the Volga from Kazan', another priest's wife lived in the village of Tagashevo some twenty miles southeast of the city, and Koz'ma Okulov came to the shrine from Laishev, a small town on the Kama River about forty miles south and east of Kazan'. The person from the greatest distance was one Trofim the son of Larion, who lived on Listerostrov (Kholmogory *uezd*) near the White Sea, but who fell ill in the Volga town of Samara and was cured when he stopped in Kazan'. Evidently Trofim was also a peasant merchant, for the northern peasants were quite enterprising in those years, often going thousands of miles into Siberia to hunt and trade in furs.[15]

This restricted social and geographic range of the miracle cults was not an exclusive characteristic of these cults, for the cult of Vasilii Blazhennyi in the capital of Moscow itself shows exactly the same pattern. Vasilii the *iurodivyi,* or holy fool, died in 1557 and was buried in the Cathedral of the Intercession of the Mother of God (*Pokrov Bogoroditsy*) on Red Square, the church known from the seventeenth century as the Cathedral of St. Basil the Blessed (Vasilii Blazhennyi). His relics were discovered to be uncorrupted in 1588, and shortly afterward a life was composed with thirty miracle cures at the end. Twenty of these took place in Moscow at the shrine of Vasilii, eight involving townspeople, four peasants, one *syn boiarskii,* one minor official at court, two clergymen, and four of unknown social origin. Ten more miracles occurred in the town of Likhvin south of Kaluga on the steppe frontier in 1590–1591. Here Gavrilo Lodyzhenskii *ot roda boiarska* (from a boyar family) built in the Church of the Resurrection a side altar (*predel*) in honor of Vasilii after the saint had cured him of possession by a devil. All the miracles at this shrine cured women who were apparently of humble status, though the account is extremely brief. Vasilii is found in the 1610 typikon, and his story also reflects some elite interest in the cult beyond liturgical celebration. The author was Archimandrite Pafnutii of the Chudov Monastery in the Kremlin, the monastery most closely connected with the court and the boyar elite. It first appeared in the *Chet'i-minei* of 1600, a luxurious manuscript intended for the court and church elite. Since Pafnutii knew relatively little about the life of Vasilii, he borrowed large sections from the Slavic translation of the early Byzantine life of St. Theodore of Edessa, and produced a document of some literary sophistication, if little historic reliability, a document that furthermore emphasizes wherever possible the great respect that tsars Ivan IV and Fyodor had for the saint and his shrine.[16] Thus an apparently popular cult was recorded mainly by an elite that did not participate in that same cult, as the records of healings demonstrate.

A pattern quite different in one crucial respect is to be found in the miracles of Sts. Zosima and Savvatii at the great center of Russian monasticism in the North, the Solovetskii Monastery. The middle and late sixteenth-century miracles are miracles of power, and they also take in a somewhat larger area. The earlier group of miracles associated with Sts. Zosima and Savvatii had been healing miracles and primarily of northern origin. Later manuscripts of the lives of the two saints include twenty-six additional miracles that extend in time from 1534 to 1632. Six of these involve monks and the rest involve various northern laymen, peasants or merchants, and a few people from central Russia. Two characteristics of the miracle stories stand out in the collection, one the unusually "realistic" detail and the other the relative paucity of straightforward healing miracles. One such clear healing miracle was the cure of Prince Ivan Aleksandrovich Obolenskii's wife, whom the prince struck in a fit of rage during his tenure as governor of the Velikii Ustiug district. Another case of a simple cure was that of Fekla Kostakova, a noblewoman from the Suzdal' district, who was cured of injuries on a pilgrimage to the Solovetskii Monastery that had taken her first to the Pechery Monastery near Pskov. (These two are also the only nobles among the cured.) The more typical cases are those like that (in the 1550s) of Melentii the son of Kozma, a peasant on the Onega River who promised land to the monks but went back on his promise until illness and a vision of the saints caused him to change his mind. A number of cases involve the children of merchants of the villages of the White Sea coast who vowed to enter the monastery but for one reason or another failed to carry out the vow and continued to trade until the saints rescued them at sea. In other cases the vow involved a promise to work for the monastery at manual labor, and the cure was not effected until the promise was fulfilled. Other miracles protected the monastery from fire. Curiously, the last few miracles from the early seventeenth century were again cures. The continuous intervention on the part of Sts. Zosima and Savvatii to increase the monastery's land and the number of brothers (who, it should be remembered, brought in money or land when they took the monastic vow) is without precedent in the sixteenth-century miracle stories. The reason for the greater acquisitiveness in the miracle stories of the Solovetskii

Monastery does not arise from the sources: perhaps it comes from the greater development of commercial relations in the sixteenth-century North that N. E. Nosov has described. This was the period of the greatest expansion of the monastery's property, and in conditions certainly more "commercial" than those of central Russia. Whatever the reason, the character of the miracle cult of Sts. Zosima and Savvatii anticipate the changes in the character of the cults that took place in central Russia only in the middle years of the seventeenth century.[17] The local focus of the cult, however, and the social status of the healed puts the Solovetskii cults among the general type of sixteenth-century cult.

These miracle cults were among the most important in the Russian state, and they show that a basic type of cult had come into existence by the last decades of the sixteenth century. This type was a healing cult that appealed primarily to the peasants, townspeople, clergy, and lesser land-holders, and seems to have excluded the boyars. Its appeal, furthermore, was local, with long pilgrimages the exception rather than the rule. The cults were not only local but often "localist," demonstrating the piety and glory of some particular area. At the same time the stories of the icons or saints and their miracles could carry a very different message as well, one celebrating more "national" causes. The story of the Kazan' icon tells us that the icon was indeed found by a girl of humble origin, the daughter of a soldier, but the cult was soon approved by the tsar and patriarch, and a convent was built with the tsar's money around the church that housed the icon. In the Time of Troubles none other than Prince Dmitrii Pozharskii himself carried the icon into battle, and it was said to work miracles, especially at the decisive battle against the Poles in October 1612. In spite of this success, recorded in the chronicles, it did not become the object of a national festival right away, but seems to have remained a local affair in Moscow until 1646.[18] However, the use of certain cults, or at least of certain icons, as political symbols by the tsar and court was not accompanied by devotion to the healing cults, even those that seemed to have official patronage. The tsar and the church were apparently happy to give their sanction to these cults and even to participate in the ceremonies celebrating them, but they were not themselves interested in benefiting from their healing powers. This attitude remained unchanged throughout the seventeenth century, whether the shrine was in the Kremlin, a great monastery, or a rural church.

Miracles in the Seventeenth Century

After the Time of Troubles the miracle cults reappeared as society calmed down following more than a decade of turmoil. Political miracles had already reappeared in the historical narratives of the Troubles. The *Skazanie* of Avraamii Palitsyn and most of the anonymous tales continue to present miraculous intercessions of the Mother of God, St. Sergii, or others, while Timofeev, Khvorostinin, and Shakhovskoi do not present any such miracles. The greatest number of miracles was in Palitsyn's story, not surprisingly since much of it was given over to a detailed account of the siege of the Trinity–St. Sergii Monastery by Sapieha's troops in 1608–1610. St. Sergii appeared to the Russian troops at virtually every major battle, as well as at other occasions in the story. The so-called *Inoe skazanie*, "Other Tale," was more restrained than Palitsyn, but it also included a vision of the Mother of God on 12 October 1606, a voice singing psalms in the Cathedral of Michael the Archangel on 20 October 1609, and a candle that flamed spontaneously in front of an icon of the Mother of God on 18 February 1610. No miracle accompanied Pozharskii's decisive victory over the Poles in October 1612. There are at least three stories of particular visions, one of the archpriest of the Annunciation Cathedral (the palace church), Terentii. Terentii describes the vision just mentioned of the Mother of God from 1606, saying it occurred to a "holy man, whose name is known to God." A group of townsmen heard voices and weeping in the Archangel cathedral on 27 February 1607, and told the *okol'nichii* Vasilii Petrovich Golovin about their experience. Another story tells of one Grigorii in Nizhnii Novgorod, who heard God in a church promise to save the Russians if they would repent (May 1611). In the same story Melaniia, the wife of Boris the butcher in Vladimir, saw a woman in church who told her roughly the same thing a few months later. She told the town authorities about it. Finally, in July 1611 the monk Varlaam of Novgorod saw the Mother of God and the Novgorod saints in church, again with the same sort of message. Strictly speaking these were warning signs and promises of miraculous help rather than actual miracles as in Palitsyn's story. Real miracles reappear in the "Novyi Letopisets," which was an official chronicle, unlike the previous tales. Here St. Sergii helped the army of Minin and Pozharskii to overcome fear as they marched toward Moscow, though no miracles featured in the battle itself; however, a note later on in the text mentioned that the icon of the Mother of God of Kazan' had helped. In a similar fashion the Mother of God, Sts. Zosima and Savvatii, and others appeared in visions and helped out the Russians against the Swedes in the siege of the Tikhvin Monastery in 1613. The anonymous sources, both official or from the palace staff, like Archpriest Terentii's or the more humble provincial tales, still contained a strong miraculous element. Palitsyn, the "Novyi Letopisets," and Terentii were all directed at the landholding class, Terentii very explicitly so. The members of that class themselves, however, were beginning to produce tales of a different type, which stressed the moral character of the actors rather than divine intervention.[19]

The healing cults resumed after the Troubles (many were uninterrupted) and in the form inherited from the sixteenth century, as mainly healing cults, where the healed came from the middle and lower layers of Russian society and were drawn from a small geographic area. The cults had these same characteristics in a variety of areas and social contexts. The most important (and possibly the only) new cult to appear at court was that of the Lord's Robe, the *Riza gospodnia*, a gift of the Persian Shah in 1625. The story was inserted in the *Dvortsovye razriady*, the official record of court occasions, a fact that demonstrates its importance in court life. The location of the shrine in the Dormition Cathedral in the Kremlin also put it at the center of court religious life, as is also shown by the existing icons of the deposition of the Robe. These portray very clearly a specifically court religious ceremony, with the tsar and his family, the boyars, lesser nobles, servants, and clergy all assembled in the church for the installation of the shrine. The text of the miracle stories, however, was precisely the opposite, for the healed at the shrine of the Robe are beggar women, townspeople, secretaries from the Moscow *prikazy*, or clergymen, but not noblemen. Of the fifty miracles, only one involved a minor nobleman, Ia. A. Dem'ianov, who had once been the *voevoda* of Berezov in Siberia, and one other the son of Fedor Pushkin, who really was a prominent boyar in those years.[20] Even a cult centered in the main Kremlin cathedral attracted boyars only as spectators, not as participants.

These cults, wherever they existed in the Russian state, reveal the same localism and the same appeal to the middle and (to some extent) lower layers of Russian society. There is at least one case, however, of a more aristocratic miracle cult that did exist at the end of the sixteenth century and continued into the seventeenth. This is the cult of St. Savva Storozhevskii (died 1406), the founder of the Savva-Storozhevskii Monastery near Zvenigorod, a small town a few miles to the southwest of Moscow. A cult of St. Savva already existed when he was recognized as a saint in 1602. His life with miracles had been included in Metropolitan Makarii's *Chet'i minei*. Precisely the same text was printed in Moscow in 1646 as *Zhitie i sluzhba sv. Savvy Storozhevskogo*, thus elevating St. Savva to the select company of saints whose life and miracles were printed in the seventeenth century as a separate book. That event was certainly connected with the renewal of the monastery in the 1640s, and its close association in those years with the family of the tsar, so that here if anywhere there should have been an aristocratic cult. In a way, that is the case. Of the twenty-five miracles, nine involved monks of the monastery, eight involved unidentified people, and all the rest, eight in number, involved *deti boiarskie*, some of whose descendants attained much higher rank. Some of them can be identified as landholders of the Zvenigorod *uezd* in the second half of the sixteenth century. Dalmat Fedorov Karpov was the former lord of a number of villages that by the registers of 1573–1574 and 1584–1586 had passed to other hands, but the family of Dalmatov-Karpov was still prominent in the seventeenth century, with one *okol'nichii* (Lev Ivanovich) and one boyar (Fedor Borisovich, made boyar 1649, died 1659/60). Two miracles involved the family of Ivan Rtishchev, his son Georgii, his servants, and eventually Ivan himself. The

Rtishchev family in the 1640s was a lesser landholding clan that made its way into the highest court circles, for F. M. Rtishchev was an important official, tutor to the tsar's son and one of the patrons of the Ukrainian scholars brought to Moscow. His life (see chapter 6) is one of the central texts of the newer trends in religious life of that time, but in rank he never rose beyond *okol'nichii*. The printing of the life of St. Savva thus added not only to the glory of the saint but also to that of the Rtishchev family. It did not, however, directly add to the popularity of the miracle cult of the saint in the mid-seventeenth century, for it contained no new miracles, only those in sixteenth-century versions. The cult as recorded in the latter sixteenth century was one that involved only a few provincial noblemen, and the later prominence of their descendants does not change the fact that it was a cult that did not involve the elite of the nobility, but only a few provincials who later entered court circles. The elite of Russian society thus patronized the cults from a distance but did not participate.[21]

The city of Iaroslavl' in the seventeenth century was one of the richest in the Russian state, and was also a primarily commercial city. In the past it had been a minor principality, and in the fifteenth and sixteenth centuries the "Iaroslavl' princes" were a major aristocratic grouping at the Moscow court who still held land in the area but whose political and religious life was at court. The Monastery of the Savior in the center of the town was still the monument of the older aristocratic Iaroslavl', but after 1615 all of the churches of the town were merchant foundations. This was no mean achievement, for even today Iaroslavl' is a living museum of church architecture and painting of the seventeenth century, a monument to the taste and wealth of the merchants and simple townspeople who fostered it. The town's prosperity was founded on its location at the intersection of two crucial trade routes, the land and river route from Moscow north to Archangel, the entrepôt of the Western European traders (mainly the Dutch) in Russia, and the Volga route from Iaroslavl' and other Russian towns to Astrakhan at the river's mouth, where Russian merchants traded with the steppe peoples and merchants of Central Asia and especially Persia. Needless to say, these routes were crucial to Russia's internal trade, especially that with the Russian North, the Urals, and Siberia, all rich stores of furs, salt, and other essentials. No wonder then, that the merchants and artisans of Iaroslavl' could endow such magnificent churches, and their actions were imitated on a lesser scale by their counterparts farther down the river in Kostroma and Nizhnii Novgorod.[22]

Along with this church building and decorating went the development of the local miracle cults. In Iaroslavl' the chief miracle cult was in the Tolgskii monastery on the edge of town, where the church kept the icon known as the Tolgskaia Bogoroditsa, the Tolgskii Mother of God. The story of the miraculous appearance of this icon is a typical sixteenth-century story that asserts the apparition to have taken place in 1378 but whose internal structure betrays much later composition. The first group of miracles (only four) includes one dating from 1547, and the story was probably written about that time. In the 1640s another four miracles were added to the text; this was the time of the rise in popularity of the cult, the time when most of the monastery's buildings were constructed. The miracle stories are not very informative, one priest and one merchant being healed, but there is one interesting aspect to the fourth miracle of the 1640s group: a man was healed when he fell ill on the way back from a pilgrimage to the Solovetskii Monastery and sought out the Tolgskii Mother of God. This is a sign of the increasing rivalry among the monastic miracle cults in the seventeenth century.[23]

Kostroma down the river from Iaroslavl' was another ancient princely center, with the Ipat'ev Monastery to remind visitor and resident of that ancient glory, but in the seventeenth century the town was mainly a center of commerce. The town's cathedral contained the icon of the Fedorovskii Mother of God, like the Tolzhskii icon in that a clearly sixteenth-century text asserted that the icon was found by an (otherwise unattested) prince Vasilii Georgievich as he fled from the Tatar armies of Batu in 1238. The author here was clumsier even than his Iaroslavl' counterpart, for the text is full of sixteenth-century terminology such as *voevoda* and other anachronisms, and no chronicles refer to the icon earlier on. Most of the thirty-five miracles are dated and occur between 1636 and 1646. The cured include fifteen peasants, eleven townspeople, two clergymen, one church servant, and the wife of one *syn boiarskii*. Nearly all these people come from in or near Kostroma: all the peasants came to the shrine from villages in Kostroma *uezd* except for one from the Iaroslavl' *uezd*. The townspeople are all residents of Kostroma itself save one man from the nearby small town of Liubim to the northeast. Only the wife of the *syn boiarskii* had come to Kostroma from her estate in the Bezhetskaia *piatina* (fifth) of Novgorod, a considerable distance but one easily navigated by river.[24]

In the Russian North the landholding class was absent, and the northern miracle cults were thus closer to a relatively pure popular religion. If the landholders were absent, however, the clergy was not and the miracle stories were presumably composed by clerics (mainly monks). Furthermore the North was not as isolated as might seem, as some of the stories reveal. Not surprisingly the northern miracle cults were similar in type to those farther south from great towns or monasteries, although they do show occasional interesting variations. The cult of St. Makarii Zheltovodskii at the Khergozero hermitage near Kargopol' was a good example of this sort of cult. The monastery was extremely obscure, and there is no question of any significant elite audience for the cult, but the icon of St. Makarii formed a healing shrine that worked some forty cures from about 1640 on to the end of the century. The cured were peasants from the area and some clergy.[25]

The shrine of the miracle-working icon of the Savior at Krasnyi Bor, a trading village on the Northern Dvina, in the *uezd* of Velikii Ustiug, was much more unusual. In 1641 a series a miracles took place in the church, which gave birth to an essentially rural cult whose records were kept (it seems) by the parish priest. The miracles were associated with a miraculous icon of the *Nerukotvornyi Spas*, the Savior Not-created-by-human-hands, but curiously enough it was not Christ the Savior who appeared in the village but the Mother of God. The sixteen miracles almost all occurred in the summer of 1641, and many involved the same people, most of them women from the village or villages nearby. The most important of the miracles happened on 9 July 1641, when Mary appeared to three women, one of whom reported their experiences: "The woman Akilina began to speak standing in the altar area (*trapeza*) and crossing herself before the priests and the whole people [she said] that a woman brilliant with light gave me, Akilina, orders and told me to say in the whole community [*mir*] that the priests and clergy should come with the icons and with all Orthodox Christians to Krasnyi Bor to the all-merciful Savior to pray and beg mercy of him; and that drunken people should not come to church and they should not drink tobacco nor swear obscenely [*materno by otniud' ne branilis'*] and they should live by the rule of the holy fathers and have no anger against one another," and that if the people did not repent their sins she would send down storms to destroy churches and crops.[26] Thus Mary's commands to the peasants were essentially moral. About a month later, on 16 August of the same year, Mary appeared to a different woman who had been cured of paralysis at the shrine a few days before and repeated the same injunctions. In September a man who violated them and "drank tobacco" was struck dead before the church, and the last miracle in the collection, in 1651, concerned a deacon who smoked and was stricken with fits that only the icon could cure. The direct punishment of sin is unusual, though not unknown in Russian miracle stories, and naturally reinforces Mary's commands and the role of her peasant prophets.

The theology of the story is a bit confused, for it was Mary who appears even though the icon was of Christ, and in fact the text tells us that it was the Tikhvin Mother of God who appeared. Mary's commands to the people were, as noted, moral, and emphatic prohibition on smoking and the concern with drunkenness and swearing resembled the ideals of the Zealots of Piety as well as the later asceticism of the Old Believers. The later patriarch Ioakim shared virtually the same moral code, as did Simeon Polotskii, so the Mother of God's instructions as to the peasants of Krasnyi Bor should not be seen as exhortation to heresy or disobedience. The woman's description of Mary's appearance and commands was made before the village priests, who may well have been the authors of the anonymous text. The tale gives more than usual detail about village life, and tempts the historian to see it as the voice of the silent, but there is no evidence that the peasants wrote the story. It appears in various collections emanating from the upper orders of society, chronicles, and miscellanies. The story of the Krasnyi Bor miracles is not a direct reflection of the ideals of the northern peasant. More likely it is one of the few cases of the reflection of the ideals of the reformist parish clergy in the literature of miracle stories.[27]

The subsequent history of the church shows that the church hierarchy accepted and even exploited the miracles. When the *voevoda* of Ustiug's court was called upon to judge a dispute in the 1640s, in which the Krasnyi Bor parish administrator was accused of stealing church funds, the court simply assumed the validity of the miracles. It looks as if the lay parish administrators (*tserkovnye starosty*)—in the North usually rich peasants, frequently peasant merchants—were using the miracle cult to produce revenue for the parish and then stealing it for themselves. Throughout the period from 1641 to at least 1686, the church was more or less the property of the local Ozhegov family, clearly among the richest of the village. The revenue that the miracles produced for the church is beyond question, and by 1678 it was so great that some of that revenue was granted to the Antoniev-Siiskii Monastery to increase its income. The Antoniev-Siiskii monks did not hold onto the income, and it seems that the church had passed to the Solovetskii Monastery by 1724, when the Holy Synod investigated a new series of miracles reported at the shrine. This was Peter's time, however, a new age, and the Synod passed the case to the officials of the eparchy of Kholmogory, who found the miracles to be fraudulent and forbade their recognition or publication. Although the records do not say so, the Synod may have suspected the Solovetskii monks of fabricating miracles to increase the number of pilgrims to Krasnyi Bor.[28]

Miracles of Power and Opposition to Miracles

The first signs of a de-emphasis on miracles appear in the historical narratives of the Time of Troubles composed by the secretary Ivan Timofeev and princes Ivan Khvorostinin and Semen Shakhovskoi. They are notable in that their accounts of the events, in contrast to that of Palitsyn or the "Novyi Letopisets," completely lack any miracles, visions, or other supernatural explanations of events. Their explanations revolve around the moral character of Boris Godunov and the Russian people in general, but miracles are just not part of the narrative. This was not just an accident, for we shall see later that Khvorostinin and Shakhovskoi were both innovators in their conceptions of religion, both with a strong moral emphasis. More generally, their narratives are the beginning of a trend in this respect at least, for the historical writings of the second half of the seventeenth century are also lacking in miracles. This is the case with Fedor Griboedov's very official history of Russia of 1669, as with the anonymous chronicles composed in that period. The Russo-Polish War of 1654–1667, for all its victories, was the first major conflict in centuries completely lacking in miracle stories.[29]

In the middle of the seventeenth century, miracles of power similar to those of early medieval Europe appeared in some Russian miracle cults, though with quite different backgrounds and results. As far as we know the change affected only monastic shrines, and the miracles of power reinforced the monasteries' land claims as well as their internal discipline. This change was not universal, as the cult of the Virgin of the Tolgskii Monastery shows, but it did take place both at the Trinity–St. Sergii Monastery and at least one obscure provincial monastery as well, the Oranskii Monastery near Nizhnii Novgorod.

The Oranskii Monastery was indeed an obscure provincial foundation in the Nizhnii Novgorod area, but its fame was enhanced by the possession of a miraculous copy of the Vladimir Mother of God. Petr Gladkov, a nobleman of the district, founded the monastery in 1634–1635 and supported it by his own donations of land and serfs and those of his family, but it never grew enough to accommodate more than a dozen or so monks, including, eventually, Gladkov himself. The miracles of the icon, however, brought the monastery some fame, and the existence of a healing cult is noted in the story of the monastery that Gladkov composed about 1662–1663, but what he recounted in some detail was not the cures but the icon's defense of the monastery's more mundane interests. The icon gave the monks help against the Mordovian peasants of the area who objected to the monastery's seizure of their land, and later helped secure for the monks legal title to the land in face of bureaucratic hostility in Moscow. The Mother of God also inclined the *voevoda* of Nizhnii Novgorod, V. P. Sheremetev, toward friendship with the monastery, and already in the 1630s it prospered: Patriarch Ioasaf ordered some local churchmen to investigate the icon's reputed miracles. Their verdict was favorable. Petr Gladkov (under the monastic name Pavel) crowned this campaign in the 1660s with the composition of the story, and possibly to good effect, for about this time the tsar confirmed the little monastery's landholdings. This effort at influencing the Moscow bureaucrats cost Brother Pavel his life, however, for the Mordovian peasants whose land he had seized and whom he had presumably enserfed in the process murdered him in 1664 or 1665.[30] In the history of the Oranskii Monastery the miracle cult has been reduced to the defense of the monastery's economic interests, and there is a certain openness in Gladkov's account that earlier stories of conflict between monastery and peasantry lack.[31]

In the seventeenth century Russia's principal monastic saint, St. Sergii of Radonezh, finally acquired a healing cult at his shrine. As noted before, Sergii had performed miracles in his life time, but his posthumous cult was largely public and political. Since the early sixteenth century the monastery was the object of an elaborate pilgrimage of the court and the tsar's family twice yearly, and the churches and graveyards provided a burial ground for many of the country's oldest and most powerful boyar clans: the Golitsyns, Odoevskiis, Glinskiis, and many of lesser stature. St. Sergii had taken a central role in the religious interpretation of the main events in Russian history, aiding the Russian armies at Kulikovo (1380), Kazan' (1550–1552), and the Time of Troubles. In 1646 the *kelar'* (cellarer) of the Trinity Monastery, Simon Azarin, had published a printed book with his new redaction of the traditional life of St. Sergii and added a long list of miracles. The political miracles ended in 1619, and were simply compiled from various chronicles and tales, but he added to them eighteen miracles that were mostly cures of disease. Azarin asserted that the work was done at the behest of the new tsar Aleksei Mikhailovich, but there is no way of knowing if this is truth or merely flattery of the tsar's piety combined with Azarin's self-interest. Azarin claimed that he brought the secretaries of the Printing Office the pages that were eventually published and many more miracles, which they refused to print. He wrote them up in manuscript and supplied them with a preface recounting the incidents, and they circulated in this form.[32]

The eighteen new miracles of the 1646 printed text are typical in most respects of the miracle records of other saints that were compiled in decades before: they are cures of disease or miraculous rescues from drowning or other disaster. Most of the cured or saved—the three artisans, three clergymen, one peasant, and (naturally) the five monastery servants[33]—did not come to the shrine from far away. Not surprisingly, the soldier and cossack saved by the saint had traveled farther, but the two noblemen who were cured lived in the vicinity. Two miracles, however, were not cures or miraculous rescues but clear interventions by the saint in the monastery's attempts to maintain its authority and discipline. In one case, a nun of the Khot'kov Convent subordinate to the Trinity Monastery wanted to leave the convent in despair over the envy and spite of her fellow nuns, who resented her great piety. St. Sergii appeared to her in a dream and told her to remain. She obeyed and was rewarded with a calmer life from then on. The other case involved the monk Feodosii, who had the task of *khlebodar'* or distributer of grain in the Trinity Monastery. Feodosii decided to leave the monastery together with a fellow monk from Kiev and not to ask permission from the hegumen. Clearly the two planned to join the numerous ranks of wandering monks that seventeenth-century sources so often complain about. When Feodosii and his comrade had just made good their escape across the monastery fields, the saint struck Feodosii blind. He wept over his sins and called on God, Mary, and St. Sergii to restore his sight and vowed to visit the holy places of Russia if his sight was restored. It was, but the two did not return to the monastery right away: they continued on to Kostroma, where the Kievan decided to return to the Trinity Monastery but Feodosii did not. Again his disobedience to his monastic vows was punished, and he began to bleed continuously at the nose, so he went north to the Solovetskii Monastery to ask Sts. Zosima and Savvatii to stop the nosebleed. They did not. Only as he was leaving the Solovetskii Monastery and had just decided in his mind to return to the Trinity Monastery did the bleeding stop. Feodosii returned and told the story that Azarin recorded. In both cases St. Sergii intervened to restore monastic discipline. The two cases stand out against the stories of miraculous cures and are more like the stories about which the secretaries of the Printing Office displayed doubts.[34]

Azarin himself described these doubts in the preface to the manuscript of supplementary miracles at the shrine of St. Sergii that the Printing Office would not publish. He tells us that the secretaries rejected the miracles even at the peril of their eternal life, "for they said that truth was a lie, and that it was an accident, not a miracle (*v sluchai, ne v chudo*) that occurred at the appearance of a spring by the porch wall of the church of the Mother of God, and they only printed it under compulsion."[35] Indeed some copies of the book have an extra page with the miracle of the spring glued into it, the Printing Office evidently not taking the trouble to reprint the book, and never printing the other miracles that Azarin recorded. He cited other instances of disrespect for the monastery, such as the refusal of the Greek patriarchs to visit it in 1619 and offer gifts. He saw the monastery's status as intimately bound up with its shrines. The shrine that he wished to advance the most was the miraculous spring that appeared in 1644. In that year the monks decided that they needed a new water supply and sent north to the towns of Tot'ma and Ustiug Velikii to find workmen to locate a spring and build a well. Before they arrived, other workmen repairing a wall in the church of the Mother of God came upon a spring gushing forth, a not especially remarkable event and one easy to explain without supernatural causes. One monk was cured of an eye disease right away, and a monastery servant who mocked the miraculous powers of the spring was struck down. Azarin heard of these incidents and was moved to tell of them to the tsar and to Patriarch Iosif, who responded with the order to print the life and miracles of St. Sergii. Evidently Azarin worked fast, for the miracles occurred between September 1643 and September 1644, Tsar Aleksei came to the throne on the death of his father in July 1645, and the book was printed in November 1646. Azarin's swift work may have been partly an attempt to influence the tsar in the face of the many legal disputes and the attempts to restrict monastic landholding by the state in the mid-seventeenth century.[36] In spite of the Printing Office's hesitation, Azarin got his way, for the spring became a pilgrimage site after 1645 and even had a special chapel built for it in the 1680s or 1690s, which survives to this day on the monastery grounds. The pilgrimage certainly brought more "business" to the monks, adding a new object of devotion precisely at the time (as we shall see) that miracle cults were being called into question, and on the eve of another major attempt by the state to restrict monastic landholding.

The spring itself was not unprecedented but somewhat unusual, and the Printing Office may have been put off by the spring as the center of attention instead of simply St. Sergii's tomb. In addition to the role of the spring, twenty-five of the seventy-seven miracles recorded by Azarin have nothing to do with healing and represent the crassest use of spiritual authority to support material interests. St. Sergii no longer aids the Russian army against its foes, but rather aids the monks in securing land and serfs against rivals in Russian society. The saint himself came to the aid of the monks in the law courts, both in land cases and cases of *poklep* (false accusation). The five land cases all involve important aristocrats: in Tsar Michael's time with a Sheremetev's peasants, in 1633 with V. I. Nagoi and the boyar Semen Golovin over the will of B. M. Nagoi, in 1644 with the *okol'nichii* F. V. Volynskii, in the 1640s with the boyar B. M. Lykov's peasants, and in 1653 with N. I. Sheremetev's peasants.[37] The suit over B. M. Nagoi's will dragged on for several years, with his cousin, his widow, and his relative Golovin keeping the land (and therefore the serfs) and other property promised to the monastery for as long as they could. Vasilii Nagoi (the cousin) surrendered only after an injury suffered during one of the Moscow fires brought him to a deathbed repentence, undoubtedly encouraged by a dream of St. Sergii that came to the monastery's *kelar'* Aleksander, and which Aleksander related to Vasilii Nagoi. In 1644 F. V. Volynskii repossessed a village given to the monastery in his sister's will, but after repeated attacks of blindness he surrendered it to the monks at his own death in 1646. The incident in the 1640s with the Lykov peasants was more complicated. On the boyar's estate in the Zakudemskaia *volost'* near Nizhnii Novgorod the bailiff Zhukov lead the peasants in the seizure of forests and fields claimed by the monastery. At first Lykov supported them, but after some time the monks persuaded him to order the lands returned to them. The peasants, however, managed to keep part of what they had taken, but God punished Zhukov: the peasants murdered him for his cruelty to them. Lykov gave all the disputed land to the monastery in his will in 1646. In the 1653 case, the saint aided the monks in court by helping them to produce better written evidence against the boyar Sheremetev's peasants again in the Nizhnii Novgorod district. St. Sergii also obliged the monks some years later by striking dead the parish priest Iakov, who had taken the peasants' side.

The monastery's other disputes were with people of similar rank. One was a simple case of disrespect from an unnamed noble holding the rank of *rynda* (bodyguard) at the court of Tsar Michael. Another took place in the late 1640s, when the peasants of boyar Nikita Ivanovich Romanov complained (with the support again of the parish priest) of the actions of the monastery's servants. The saint won the case for the monks by striking down the peasants' representative with a fit. In 1632 during the Smolensk War, the gentry of the Alatyr' district brought suit against the Trinity monks before the judge Grigorii Zlovidov, himself a *moskovskii dvorianin* (gentleman of Moscow) in rank. They complained that the monastery was harboring their runaway serfs and settling them on monastery lands, and Zlovidov decided in the gentry's favor: the monks were ordered to return the serfs in question. According to Azarin, Zlovidov was later captured by the Crimean Tatars and languished in prison praying to St. Sergii for aid, until, as it happened, he was ransomed with money contributed by the monastery. He repented of his earlier injustice to the Trinity monks and died among them in 1640. This particularly crass case of monastic self-interest is presented in the company of endless interventions by the saint to prevent damage from falling buildings, fires, and other disasters in the monastery, as well as the saint's involvement in disciplinary cases. For example, a monastery servant who had left its service to join that of a boyar who had seized some of the monks' land was punished by having various ills inflicted on him by the saint. In another case, one of the monastery's enemies was punished by God and St. Sergii in the form of a popular rebellion: an unnamed boyar (probably P. T. Trakhaniotov) had seized numerous monastery lands and met his supposedly deserved fate when the mob murdered him in the 1648 revolt in Moscow. Fortunately for the fate of his soul, he had had the time to repent his crimes and beg forgiveness of St. Sergii.[38]

Azarin's zeal in defense of his monastery is extremely valuable to the historian, for he unwittingly clarifies the context, both sociopolitical and religious, of the cult of St. Sergii. The Trinity–St. Sergii Monastery, the largest and richest in the country, was faced with an internal breakdown in discipline and external challenges by the 1640s. Monks were trying to leave the monastery and even took their devotions elsewhere. Monastery servants were not loyal, and also caused numerous problems by antagonizing the peasants, both those of the Trinity Monastery and those of neighboring landholders. The attempt of the state to satisfy townsmen's demands for an end to the monasteries' private jurisdictions in towns brought losses in revenue and prestige. The boyars and gentry of Russia saw the monasteries as antagonists too, holders of land and serfs the nobles considered legally their own. Ironically it was in Azarin's miracle stories that boyars appeared for the first time, in most cases not as those cured but as the monastery's enemies. The atmosphere of universal hostility to the monastery that shows through the pages of Azarin's miracle stories helps explain the establishment in 1649 of the *monastyrskii prikaz,* whose duties were precisely to oversee the landholding and revenues of the Russian monasteries. This new edict was incorporated in the Law Code, the *Sobornoe ulozhenie,* that came into being in the wake of the Moscow revolt of 1648. Although that revolt brought disaster to the monks' enemy Trakhaniotov, it was a small satisfaction to contemplate for the monks hedged in by the restrictions of the new Monastery Office.

The mere fact that the Trinity monks aroused such antagonism over the mundane issues of land and revenue suggests that Russians—boyars, gentry, townsmen, and peasants—had moved still further from deference to the monastic ideal and its institutions that existed in the fifteenth century. To be sure, there were disputes over such matters earlier, and into the 1640s the Trinity and other monks received land in testaments and outright gifts, but the whole tone of Azarin's work is defensive, and the record of the laws of the time suggests that his defensiveness was justified. His work, and the reaction to it of the secretaries of the Printing Office, also reveal the growing religious doubts about the miracle cults. The Printing Office thought that his miracle stories merely described accidental events, events that need not be explained by divine intervention. As we shall see later, the Printing Office secretaries were not free-thinkers; rather they were slowly developing a conception of religious life that demanded above all a moral commitment and a solid foundation of learning. The miracles of St. Sergii had no moral content, nor did they serve to strengthen faith in the power of God, for God acted in the stories mainly as the protector of the monks' land and serfs from rival land-holders. At this stage, in the early years of the reign of Tsar Aleksei, no one believed that miracle cults were in themselves undesirable; quite the reverse, judging from the 1646 *Sviattsy* (a book of saints' days). The mistake that Azarin had made was to use the miracle cult too crassly to support utterly unspiritual aims. The confrontation that developed, however, was in embryo one of the chief religious issues of the later seventeenth century, that is, the increasing feeling that the cultivation of Christian morality by laymen was not just one side of a Christian life whose central features were monasticism and miracle cults, but an alter-native, and a better alternative at that.

Patriarch Nikon: The Spiritualization of the Cults

In the 1640s, however, this growing conflict remained only a difference of opinion and emphasis. During the patriarchate of Nikon (1652–1658) no new policy on miracle cults was enunciated by the church, but the practice revealed distinct changes. The radical drop in the number of nationally celebrated saints' days, from ninety-three in 1648 to thirty in 1656, demonstrates Nikon's policy. Nikon did found at least one monas-tery around a miracle cult, but its history reveals a shift in emphasis that parallels the decline in saints' days and foreshadows the loss of interest in the cults after the 1660s. Nikon sponsored shrines where the emphasis was on the significance of the saint to the church or to the spiritual life of the individual Christian. In this he was continuing the work of Stefan Vonifat'ev and the Zealots of Piety, as was only to be expected in a former member of the group. The ideas of Vonifat'ev on miracles are not known, but the spiritualization of the miracle cults evident in Nikon's practice continued the general approach of the Zealots. Thus Nikon continued the work of the Zealots not only by encouraging Epifanii Slavinetskii and other Ukrainian scholars to preach; he also helped redirect the veneration of saints away from the emphasis on healing miracles as well as miracles of power.

Nikon's first foray into this area looks quite traditional. In the spring of 1652, only a few weeks before his election to the office of patriarch, he was sent to bring the relics of Metropolitan Filipp of Moscow from their resting place in the Solovetskii Monastery to Moscow. This project, which took place with the full agreement and encouragement of Tsar Aleksei, was intended to raise the prestige of the patriarchate, one of Nikon's basic aims. The tsar even asked forgiveness of the saint for his predecessor's crime.[39] It was the overall political significance of the cult of St. Filipp that was the message of the translation, not the healing cult.

Nikon's first major monastic foundation was dedicated in part to St. Filipp, and here again miraculous cures played little if any role. The project arose in Nikon's mind almost immediately after he assumed office, for he had often seen Lake Valdai, or Sviatoe Ozero, in his travels as the metropolitan of Novgorod, and its beauty moved him to establish a monastery on one of its islands. He began work in 1653, building a wooden church to honor the miracle-working icon called the Portaitissa (the gatekeeper) in the Iviron Monastery on Mount Athos, a copy of which was placed in the church along with some relics of metropolitans Peter, Iona, and Filipp.[40] From this wooden church of the Mother of God of Iviron, the monastery was known as the Monastery of the Mother of God of Iviron and of the Holy Martyr Filipp the Metropolitan of Moscow and Miracle Worker of all Russia, a clear statement of Nikon's intentions.

Right from the start the history of the monastery was filled with miraculous events: the saintly metropolitans Peter, Iona, and Filipp appeared to Nikon in a dream to tell him to take their relics there, and numerous peasants, clergy, and even noblemen of the area saw pillars of fire in the sky, one for each of the saints whose relics were placed in the monastery church.[41] Apparently without supernatural reminders, the patriarch also remembered the neglected shrine of St. Iakov Borovitskii, whose relics still rested in the small monastery in the town of Borovichi near Novgorod, where they were originally found in 1544. Nikon certainly knew of them from the time he had spent as Novgorod's metropolitan, and Iakov had appeared in the printed liturgical books from 1610. It was these relics, translated on the patriarch's orders to the new Iverskii Monastery, that provided the main shrine of the new establishment.[42] The cult of St. Iakov as revived by Nikon was not like the older miracle cults, for the text composed by the patriarch himself records only two healing miracles, one in Borovichi after the relics had been moved and one at the shrine in the new monastery. Nikon's tale of the miracles and the founding of the monastery is told in the first person, with many protestations of the truth of the miracles, so that the dominant tone is defensive. He records a dream he had in which he saw a wounded man lying on the ground; when he drew near to help him he saw that he was dead and that his hands were arranged in a gesture of blessing. The next day, when he opened the coffin of Iakov in the presence of a group of bishops and archimandrites, he recognized the man in his dream as Iakov and saw that his hands were making the same gesture of blessing. The emphasis throughout the story is on proving the authenticity of Iakov's miracles. Nikon's defensive attitude shows him to be halfway between the old world of unquestioned faith in miracle cults and the new world of doubt and skepticism that these events were the work of God and not the work of men or merely accidents.[43] It is therefore no surprise that Nikon's next monastic foundation, the much more elaborate Monastery of the New Jerusalem and the Resurrection near Istra (begun 1656), contained no significant relics and no miraculous shrines, but instead had as its spiritual center an enormous cathedral built in imitation of the Church of the Holy Sepulcher in Jerusalem and a smaller chapel built in imitation of the chapel on the Mount of Olives.[44] The monastery's architecture served to remind the monk or visitor of the life of Christ, in keeping with Nikon's conception of the liturgy as a continuous memory of Christ's life on earth.

If Nikon's monastic foundations show a certain shift away from the central importance of the miracle cults in religious life, the *Slovo* (homily) composed by Epifanii Slavinetskii in honor of St. Iakov Borovitskii and delivered 10 August 1658 shows the shift with equal if not greater clarity. From the title of this work, *O iavlenii chestnykh i mnogotselebnykh moshchei sviatogo i prepodobnogo Iakova* (On the Appearance of the Honorable and Much-healing Relics of the Saint and Most Excellent Iakov), the reader would expect a story of the miraculous appearance of the relics and the cures that had been effected in the shrine. Instead, Epifanii spends two thirds of his space on the power of God and on the holy life of Iakov, the latter being an example of how rhetoric can transform the merest skeleton of a story into a full-bodied and stirring (to contemporaries) life of a saint. Since Epifanii had so little information, he could only attribute to Iakov the common virtues of a hermit, describing his fasts and self-denial in general terms. He mentions only two miracles, though Nikon in the same book had mentioned others. Epifanii recounted only how several women had been cured of blindness, one separately and the others in a group, and the miracles cover only three pages out of thirty. he concluded with a call to the reader to pray to the heavenly doctor for both physical and spiritual medicine.[45]

With the phrase "spiritual medicine" Epifanii summed up the long transition from the explosion of miracle cults in the middle of the sixteenth century to the first flowering of preaching in the second half of the seventeenth century. After about 1650, ceremonial and miracle cults no longer satisfied the religious needs of the Russian elite, which, at least at court, turned increasingly to sermons, both heard and read, to satisfy those needs. That there was dissatisfaction with the miracle cults is shown in different ways by the reaction of the secretaries of the Printing Office to Simon Azarin's attempt to feather the nest of the Trinity Monastery, and by the reaction of the Oranskii Monastery's peasant neighbors to its attempts to take their land: in spite of the monks' miraculous relics, the peasants murdered the hegumen. In other ways Nikon's shrine of St. Iakov Borovitskii shows the same thing. Nikon himself was clearly defensive about it, for he was extremely careful to offer confirmation of the few miracles he attributed to St. Iakov, and his spokesman Epifanii buried the miracle stories in edifying reflections about God's power and the proper moral path of men. Although he pays formal deference to both physical and spiritual medicine, in practice Epifanii overshadowed the physical medicine (the miraculous cures) with the spiritual (the religious and moral teachings in the story of Iakov).[46] Patriarch Nikon's own religious foundations and the writings he commissioned to go along with them show in his case too a gradual shift away from the miracle cults.[47] The saint's moral and spiritual virtues had come to the fore, not his healing powers. All this was in accord with the program of the Zealots of Piety, Nikon's former colleagues.

This did not mean the immediate end of interest in the miraculous. The church did not and could not deny the existence of miraculous events, and at least some educated Russians began to read Catholic-inspired collections of Marian miracles, both in printed and manuscript form. The main printed work was the Ukrainian monk Ioannikii Galiatovskii's *Nebo novoe* (first edition, 1669), which in turn was used to make up the manuscript *Zvezda presvetlaia*. Galiatovskii's collection combined Russian and Ukrainian stories of the miracles of Mary with some purely Catholic tales such as that of he Virgin of Loretto. These collections are typical Baroque piety and have no liturgical function, nor do they exist to glorify any particular shrine. The stories shift the emphasis from the miraculous relics or icons to the actual power of Mary as a spiritual being, capable of working effects on earth through her mercy, virtue, and spiritual perfections, just as in Simeon Polotskii's sermons on Marian feasts.[48] Unfortunately, we know little of the readership of such collections.

The change in the role of miracle cults did not mean their death, and they survived as an integral part of Russian Christianity into this century. What changed was the church's attitude and their social context. At the end of the seventeenth century the cults lost the interest and patronage of the church. The eighteenth-century church was frankly hostile to them.[49] The result was that they became truly "popular," much more than they had ever been before, though their geographic appeal may have broadened with better transportation.

The sixteenth and seventeenth centuries saw the rise and decline of church sponsorship of the miraculous, parallel to the rise and decline of the recognition of saints. The rise of the miracle cults and the miraculous in general was one of the results of the decline in the charismatic authority of the monks that was the leading characteristics of the medieval church. The church, as the sixteenth-century councils show, tried to step into the vacuum left by the monks, regulating the miracle cults and trying to reform and strengthen religious life at the parish level. Judging by the writings of the reformers of the seventeenth century, the reform of the parishes was not successful, but the sponsorship of the miracle cults was. They expanded greatly in number throughout the sixteenth century, and came to attract the people of Russia's towns and villages, but few from the landholding class and virtually no boyars. The boyars were mainly absorbed by the political life of the country after the mid-sixteenth century, abandoning their earlier tenuous tie to the monasteries and other forms of religious life. Their involvement in miracles was much more distant, as actors in the political events that were interpreted in miraculous terms. The miracle cults were an expression of local and largely popular religious experience, but they were not hermetically sealed off from the landholding class. The descriptions of the cults were written down by monks from that class for literate audiences, and demonstrated to the rulers of Russia the unity of the people and the upper classes around the shrine of the miracle-working holy man. Besides manifesting the power of God in the lives of humble individuals, they provided a myth of social integration.

6

The Beginnings of Change

After the Time of Troubles new currents of thought began to appear in Russian religious literature. The new voices did not come from the boyar aristocracy or the church, yet they spoke to the elite and ultimately prepared the ground for the reorientation of elite culture after 1645. Themselves on the fringes of the elite (at best), and not themselves clergy, the innovative religious writers of the early seventeenth century faced a court and church that were fairly traditional, though not nearly as much as usually depicted. Both innovators and conservatives were open to the religious literature of the Ukraine, though in different degrees. The innovators, however, were stimulated by that literature to rethink the purposes of Orthodoxy in accord with changing Russian conditions, while the conservatives were content with a more passive role, merely republishing or circulating some Ukrainian writings.

The goals of the innovators among the laity were to reinforce and deepen the role of religion in the daily life of the laity, to move away from a religious life that stressed liturgy and miracle cults as the central religious experiences, in favor of one that stressed morality. Laymen who wrote on religious topics emerged as "reformists" before the appearance of the Zealots of Piety around 1640. They did not oppose the Zealots' program, but they lacked interest in the reform of the clergy and stressed the layman's need for virtue. They believed that men could become better by greater learning and by paying strict attention to their moral state, and in particular by avoiding the two sins of pride and greed. These had always been among the chief sins of the Christian, but in practice Russian religious writers of the previous century had said little about them. The avoidance of pride and greed and the cultivation of the opposite virtues, humility and charity, gradually became the principal moral platform of the reformers, and thus anticipated the concerns of the court preachers of the second half of the century.

This current of thought did not come out of a vacuum. Both long-range changes and specific events influenced the course of the movement for religious change. The central social change of the era was of course the establishment of serfdom, beginning precisely during the reigns of Fyodor and Boris. The effect of this change was twofold. On the one hand, it undoubtedly improved the standard of life and wealth of the middle and lesser gentry, who now had at their disposal the free labor of the villagers, and whose continuous complaints through the first half of the century reveal quite clearly their concern with preserving and expanding this new source of wealth. Those complaints also show a certain justified increase in self-confidence on their part, for in the *Sobornoe ulozhenie* of 1649 they achieved their basic goal, the (eventually) unlimited right to recover runaway serfs. At the same time the new system produced massive social tensions, revealed in the long series of popular disturbances of the century the high points of which were during the Time of Troubles and the Razin revolt. The gentry had new problems of social control to deal with and at the same time had to try to understand a different relationship to the peasantry and more generally to the masses, a relationship of much greater power and much greater danger.[1] Another significant change was the gradual increase in the power of the tsar, which meant an increase in number and broadening competence of government offices. The diminishing role of the aristocracy and gentry in politics—in a word, the beginnings of absolute monarchy—presented both groups with a different political context. For the aristocracy, the change was profound. In the sixteenth-century state the tsar, the *Oprichnina* period aside, had ruled in consultation with the whole of the boyar aristocracy, whereas the seventeenth-century tsars ruled more in consultation with selected boyar favorites and even with humble secretaries, like Dementii Bashmakov who ran Aleksei's Privy Chancellery for most of the reign. The boyar duma was expanded beyond recognition, no longer being the center of routine administration and the seat of major decisions as in the previous century.[2] The result was that the tsar had much more effective power in the seventeenth century, and his minions were correspondingly more important as well. Thus the court took on an even greater role as the road to power and wealth.

The changes in the Russian Army that took place in this century also increased the importance of the court. The sixteenth-century landholder had served his sovereign in the army, an army that was essentially a mass light cavalry composed of the landholding class. In the seventeenth century infantrymen equipped with muskets gradually took the place of the old cavalry regiments, and the landholders' service became more and more problematic. For the ambitious, the army became a much less important arena of activity, especially as many of the new infantry regiments were even commanded by foreign officers. At the same time there was an inflation of honors (mainly after 1650) that brought many more "new men" into duma and court ranks, to some extent compensating for the military changes. Many of these new men (B. M. Khitrovo, F. M. Rtishchev) were to play an important role in the religious life of Tsar Aleksei's court. All this implied a shift in the center of gravity of the life of the landholding class toward the court, but paradoxically it was accompanied by a certain privatization. No longer needed as much for the army, the landholders could devote more time to their estates (many of which were worked with labor services and required supervision) and to private life, and at the same time the ambitious were directed toward the center of all things, the tsar's court. The boyars' relation to religious life remained that of the previous century: participation in court religious ceremonies, deathbed tonsure, and gifts to the monasteries. As before, monks and prelates never came from the aristocracy and only a few from among lesser landholders (Patriarch Ioakim). The only new element seems to have been the practice of building private chapels in boyar mansions.[3] The central paradox of the religious life of the upper classes reflects this duality: on the one hand, the attempts to provide an essentially personal morality and religiosity described in this chapter, and, on the other hand, the more public court religious culture described in the next.

Two events crystallized the effects of these changes in the minds of some men in the clergy and gentry, the *Oprichnina* of Ivan IV and the Time of Troubles. The first had a complex resonance in Russian history, and in the decades after Ivan's death there were as many voices in his favor as against. The official portrait was always positive, even through the seventeenth century, for no member of the dynasty could for long be held to have done evil. Some unofficial accounts, like the *Kazanskaia istoriia*, the tale of Ivan's greatest victory, the conquest of the Tatar khanate of Kazan' in 1552, were positive as well. Works from the courts of Fyodor and Boris, the one Ivan's son and the other a beneficiary of the *Oprichnina*, naturally were favorable, and an essentially harmonic view of the state, a harmony of virtue among tsar, boyars, and people, is still to be found in Patriarch Iov's Life of Tsar Fyodor, written in the genre of the life of a saint.[4]

A slightly earlier example of these ideas was the *Zhitie*, the life of Metropolitan Filipp. Probably written in the 1590s, it put the case for the dignity and power of the metropolitanate and was part of the sixteenth-century attempts to raise the status of the episcopacy. Its portrait of the wicked tsar, however, links it more to the post-Smuta portraits of the wicked tsar Boris Godunov. The text represents a break in the traditional portrayal of the relations of the metropolitans and the rulers, one that challenged the ideology of symphony of tsar and church inherited from Byzantium. The bulk of the text is a long series of speeches by Filipp presenting the view that the tsar must be merciful and good, and not act like the evil Ivan. He must consult the church in political matters, and has no power to remove or judge the metropolitan. Ivan's execution of

Filipp is presented as simply wicked without excuse.[5] The Solovetskii monk thus presented not only a negative view of the tsar, out of harmony with his people. He also presented an exhalted view of the role of the church, or at least the higher clergy, as the moral guardians of the state, something not found in earlier Russian history and anticipating Patriarch Nikon's high conception of his duties and privileges.

The Time of Troubles was just that, an immense and confusing struggle that combined social strife with murderous warfare within the boyar and gentry class. The lesser nobles of the upper border were particularly volatile, now allying with social rebels (Bolotnikov) and now with the forces of order. The involvement of Poland and Sweden led to the final catastrophe. The ultimate recovery, with Michael Romanov's election as tsar in 1613, and peace came only at the end of the decade. The Romanov dynasty seemed to bring restoration of the status quo and, if anything, a more aristocratic air at court than had been the case of Boris's court. The court culture went on as before, the official historians celebrating the harmony of tsar, church, and people, and explaining the catastrophes of the Troubles by the actions of a few vicious men (Boris, the pretenders) and the foreign heretics. This was the Romanovs' explanation—a convenient one, for it covered up their own association with the "Thief of Tushino" in the years 1606–1610.

The Troubles produced a battery of historical tales, the first such event in Russian history to produce a large body of historical commentary outside the nearly defunct chronicle tradition. Pro-Romanov writers outside the court, like Avraamii Palitsyn, follow the court view to some extent, but paint a much blacker picture of the moral state of the Russian land in Boris's time. He suggests that there was harmony, but a harmony of evil, not of good, in which all Russians were seized with a passion for wealth and power as well as the usual lusts of the flesh.[6] The problem is in the religious realm, the moral corruption of court and people, not in the political one, for political thought as such did not exist in Russia. Herein lies the importance of the Troubles to the history of religion in Russia. The Troubles caused at least some Russian noblemen to rethink the foundations of their understanding of life, and that meant rethinking the foundations of religion. This result was only to be expected, for we have noted that after the mid-sixteenth century politics seems to have been the aristocracy's main preoccupation. Political upheaval was needed to produce religious changes.[7]

The strongest connection comes in the work of Prince Ivan Andreevich Khvorostinin, the author of both a history of the Troubles and of innovative religious works. Khvorostinin's father, Andrei Ivanovich, though a prince, was low in both rank and wealth by birth and made his mark in the world in the *Oprichnina* of Ivan IV. He first appeared as a military commander in the *Oprichnina* in 1565, and went on to command troops on the Terek River at the foot of the Caucasus, attaining the rank of *okol'nichii* in 1593. Not surprisingly, in the factional conflicts of the time he supported Boris Godunov, a fellow former *oprichnik,* and seems to have died around 1595/1596. His son the author served both Boris Godunov and False Dmitrii I, but Vasilii Shuiskii exiled him to the Iosifo-Volokolamskii Monastery. He supported the militia of 1612, and continued into 1613–1614 to fight the Poles. In 1618–1619 he was *voevoda* in Pereiaslavl'-Riazanskii. For reasons that are not perfectly clear, he was not in favor under Tsar Michael, however, and never advanced beyond the rank of *stol'nik.* In 7131 (1622–1623) he was exiled to the Kirillo-Belozerskii Monastery on charges of heresy, and remained there about a year, being permitted to return home in January 1624. He was pardoned and died the following year.[8] His difficulties over religion have earned him the reputation in modern scholarship of a "Westernizer," or at least freethinker of sorts, but (as we shall see) the accusations against him lacked foundation and modern interpretation is thus on the wrong track. Khvorostinin was no "Westernizer" or crypto-Catholic, but within the Orthodox context he was certainly an innovator. His history, called *Slovesa dnei i tsarei i sviatitelei moskovskikh, ezhe est' v Rosii* (Words of the Days and Tsars and Bishops of Moscow, Who are in Russia), is one of the rarer stories, less common than Avraamii Palitsyn's tale, but still known in three copies (two late and all three incomplete). It presents a story of the Troubles that shares with Palitsyn a sense of the general sinfulness of contemporary Russians, but unlike Palitsyn does not dwell on the fact. Instead, Khvorostinin dwells on the vices of Boris and the False Dmitrii, the description of which falls entirely in the religious realm, with no hint of a more secularized view. Writing of Russia in the time of the 1602–1603 famine he says, "[W]ealth had rotted away, beauty and glory had grown poor, and the dynasty of rulers had left our land; they had been cast away from love of love of humanity, the towns had grown poor, the people had grown poor, [but] loathsomeness had not grown poor, and the fruit of sin had ripened, the business of lawlessness had arisen, and men hated one another." His portrait of Boris is complex, one of that series of portraits in the literature of the time that broke up the medieval conception of the character entirely good or evil. On the one hand he tried to take care of the starving in the famine, "sowing the field of his heart with the grain of mercy," and surpassing his predecessors in mercy: "No one of the previous tsars did such things, as our ruler [Boris] showed love for the poor." Khvorostinin goes on to comment: "If he was sly and power-loving, he was also God-loving: he built many churches and filled the towns with beauty, he humbled the usurers, destroyed the self-loving, and showed himself terrible to foreign countries." At the same time, Boris did many evil things: "He angered his people, and raised son against father and father against son, and made strife in their houses, and made hate and flattery among servants, and raised slave against free, and humiliated the powerful." To top it off, he consulted magicians (*volkhvy*) to determine his fate.[9] The False Dmitrii is similarly complex: "The lawbreaker, the blasphemer of monks called himself the son of the all-glorious Tsar Ivan, and, having the abomination of desolation in his heart, and having long ago tempted himself with sharpness of thought and bookish learning, he defiled the throne of the tsars." He spent too much of his time in rebuilding his palace, and Khvorostinin personally reproved him for it, only to encounter the suspicion that he entertained evil thoughts against him.[10]

If the rulers of Russia are unable to prevent themselves from doing wicked things, and do not listen to those who try to stop them, then what is the right way, the Orthodox way to act? Ultimately his religious writings come closest to providing an answer, but the history gives some hint in its account of Patriarch Germogen, the most positive character in the story. Germogen was appalled at the violence of the Troubles, but even more so at the prospect of a non-Orthodox tsar. He called on the Russians to resist, according to Khvorostinin, by arms and also by faith, turning to Khvorostinin in his despair: "As it happened I was there, he spoke to me most of all and embraced me with tears in front of everyone, 'You have labored in study most of all, you know all. . . .'" Germogen complained that enemies had accused him, a priest, of calling men to war and bloodshed, which he denied. "I said only one thing to you, to wrap yourselves in God's weapons, fasting and prayer; he who has learned letters, let him arm himself with psalms; he who has no book learning, let him wrap himself in the weapon of salvation, the Jesus prayer; he who is a bandit, let him put away banditry; he who is a robber, let him put away that; he who is a usurer, let him put that away, and he who is a fornicator, let him put away that defilement."[11] Khvorostinin continued to be troubled by the moral issue of Germogen's call to arms: was it proper for a man of God? He went to ask advice of Feodorit, the bishop of Riazan', but the tale breaks off in the first words of his answer. The whole dilemma and Germogen's own defense suggest something of the problem. Germogen's call for fasting and prayer, as well as for the rejection of a sinful life, did not solve the problem, and it was his call to arms that helped to restore order and independence to Russia. At the same time, the moral deficiencies of Russia's rulers in this period showed that a moral problem existed, which Germogen's traditionalism did nothing to solve. The only way out of the dilemma was either to abandon a religious perspective for a secular one (and Khvorostinin was not prepared to go that far) or to reinforce religion by turning it in a new direction. That was Khvorostinin's solution, to be considered in detail later.

Khvorostinin's historical works reveal the transition, but he was a religious writer as well. As such he was one of a small number of innovative thinkers of the second quarter of the seventeenth century, most of them laymen, whose works are the main subject of this chapter. Besides Khvorostinin these are the monk Ivan Nasedka, the poets of the Printing Office, and Druzhina Osor'in, the author of the life of Iuliana Muromskaia, a pious noblewoman of the early seventeenth century. These three were innovators to varying degrees in both content and

style. Osor'in's innovations seem to have been homegrown, but both
Nasedka and Khvorostinin were affected by the Ukrainian writers, and
absorbed to some extent the new rhetoric that came from the West via
the Ukraine. The first of the new rhetorical handbooks was composed in
1619 by Bishop Makarii of Vologda, part of the same trend visible in
Nasedka and Khvorostinin.[12]

Ivan Nasedka

The most "conservative" of these was Ivan Nasedka (1570–1660), but his
conservatism was relative and has been exaggerated by historians.
Nasedka also used extensively Ukrainian writings in his work (and even
wrote or adapted verse) and in this sense was not at all "conservative," but
he showed no particular interest in preaching or morality. He was born
in the Trinity Monastery's nearby village of Klement'evo in 1570, and
was ordained priest in 1608. From about 1612 on he stayed in the Trinity
Monastery, supporting Archimandrite Dionisii in the liturgical controversy and attacking Dionisii's opponent Antonii Podol'skii.[13] Shortly
after he became the priest of the Annunciation Cathedral in the tsar's
palace in the Kremlin and was chosen to accompany the Russian mission
to Denmark in 1621. The mission was empowered to negotiate a marriage between Tsar Michael and the king of Denmark's niece—a marriage that never occurred but which gave Nasedka the occasion to compose a long polemic against Lutheranism based on some of the same
Ukrainian writings that Khvorostinin used as well as others which he had
not. This work, called the *Izlozhenie na liutory* was composed in 1622–
1623.[14] It must have made a good impression, for in 1626 he was made
kliuchar' (the keeper of the treasury) of the Kremlin Dormition Cathedral, and in 1638 he went to work in the Printing Office. There he
worked on such books as the *Kirillova kniga,* which was designed to provide material for another Danish controversy, the proposed marriage of
Tsar Michael's daughter Irina to the Danish prince Waldemar. This proposal was the object of negotiation in 1643–1645, and ultimately failed
for diplomatic reasons, but not before Nasedka had engaged in a series
of debates with Waldemar's Lutheran chaplain and produced a number
of works attacking Lutheran teaching and practice. These polemics concentrate an inordinate amount of attention on the subject of baptism,
presumably because Waldemar's baptism was one of the points at issue,
but they do treat a few other subjects.[15] To a large extent in response to
Lutheran charges, Nasedka defended the Orthodox view of church tradition—of the Bible, the priesthood and the eucharist, and, of course, of
fasting, the devotion to icons, and the antiquity and dignity of Russia's
faith. Perhaps as a reward for his services in these debates, Nasedka was
appointed to the Printing Office in 1638, becoming its chief in 1649 with
the dismissal of Mikhail Rogov, his former collaborator on the *Kirillova*

kniga. He remained at that post until 1652, overseeing the publication of the *Kniga o vere* and other works associated with the Vonifat'ev circle. He was thus put in the closest contact with both the Printing Office poets and the Zealots, but never seems to have shared their views. He left the office apparently out of favor with the new patriarch Nikon, retiring to a monastery. Nasedka's precise views of Nikon's reforms are not known: his apparent friendship with Neronov is ambiguous, for Neronov was an early opponent of Nikon but later the most prominent leader of the opposition to return to the fold of Orthodoxy.[16]

From 1620 until 1652, Nasedka was part of the ecclesiastical establishment, indeed one of its chief spokesman. His religious concerns were those of Patriarch Filaret, as far as we can tell: liturgical questions and the ritual of baptism. On the other hand, he was open to Ukrainian writings, in spite of his attack on Kirill Trankvillion Starovetskii, whose *Uchitel'noe evangelie* had found disfavor among Russian (and also Ukrainian) churchmen in 1627. Many of the writings that he adapted and published in the *Kirillova Kniga* were of Ukrainian or Belorussian origin and were new to Russians, such as Stefan Zizanii's commentary on St. Cyril of Jerusalem.[17]

Nasedka's compromise position meant that some writers were more innovative than he: the best example is certainly Prince Semen Shakhovskoi in the matter of the Danish marriage of 1644. Shakhovskoi got into serious trouble with the church over his views in this matter, for he made the mistake of asserting that Prince Waldemar did not really need to be rebaptized into the Orthodox faith if he were to marry Tsarevna Irina, and furthermore explained his views at some length in a memorandum to the tsar himself. Shakhovskoi's argument was primarily one of matters of state; if Russia's political interests dictated the marriage, then religion should take second place. Besides, Ivan IV had married a cousin to a Danish Lutheran prince, as diplomacy dictated, and had not required rebaptism of his new relative; Boris Godunov had tried to do the same with his own daughter, and unfortunately Prince Johan of Denmark died too soon for the match. His argument led him to disparage the difference between the two confessions, and to speak slightingly of the sacrament of baptism as well. The result was not unexpected: Shakhovskoi was tried for heresy and actually condemned to death, but the sentence was commuted to exile in Siberia, from which he returned relatively quickly. Perhaps there was some disagreement among the rulers of state and church about the seriousness of the offense, for his return was very swift for a man whose crime had once called for a death sentence.[18] Compared with the obvious freshness of Shakhovskoi, Ivan Nasedka certainly does seem to be a traditionalist, a man whose reaction to the Danish marriage is simply to bring out all the old arguments for Orthodoxy. However, this is to overstate the case. As we have seen, he was a traditionalist open to the new currents of theology and culture coming from the Ukraine. What he lacked was the specific moral emphasis of the Zealots or the Printing Office poets, and he therefore was more interested in the dogmatic polemics from the Ukraine. His writings and publications demonstrate the extent to which the Russian ecclesiastical establishment had absorbed that Ukrainian culture. The Printing Office, under close supervision of church and state, printed the Ukrainian grammars of Slavonic, collections like the *Kirillova kniga* and *Kniga o vere*, which were composed of Ukrainian writings, and other Ukrainian books.

Prince Ivan Andreevich Khvorostinin

Khvorostinin has attracted the attention of scholars primarily for the historical tale analyzed previously and the details of this life, but in fact the great bulk of his writings were religious in character. Understanding of his work, especially the religious works, has been rendered more difficult by the label of "Westernizer" usually applied to him, converting him into a seventeenth-century Chaadaev. The known reliable facts about his religious beliefs, however, do not square with the traditional portrait. Khvorostinin's presence at the court of the False Dmitrii has led to the conclusion that he was a crypto-Catholic, although at the False Dmitrii's court he could just as well have adopted Calvinist or Arian beliefs. After his exile on grounds of heresy he protested his innocence. His statement claiming his Orthodox beliefs apparently satisfied the tsar, for he was restored to his former dignity and expressly permitted to have audience with the tsar (*videti svoi gosudarskie ochi*). His religious polemics were apparently written between his 1624 return and his death in the following year.

None of this constitutes any real evidence of secret Catholic or pro-Polish sympathies. Position at the court of False Dmitrii suggests only opportunism, common enough during the Smuta when even Romanovs were to be found not in the camp of the "legitimate" tsar Vasilii Shuiskii but in that of the Thief of Tushino. The charge of heresy in 1622–1623 looks more convincing, since the document that enumerated the charges to the accused asserts that he associated with Polish priests and had Polish books and images, and forbids him to keep such items in the future. Both Platonov and V. I. Savva essentially assumed that the charges were true without really examining whether they made any sense, apparently because in their minds support of the False Dmitrii went hand-in-hand with an interest in Catholic books, and the latter in turn they assumed to imply Catholic opinion. However, Khvorostinin also was charged with rejecting the belief in the resurrection of the dead at Judgment Day, a belief certainly inconsistent with Catholicism as well as the views of most Protestant churches. Khvorostinin was also said to have forbidden his servants to go to church and to have eaten meat and drunk liquor during the fasts, again behavior not obviously connected with Catholic sympathies. Indeed, if the charges were true, then Khvorostinin's sympathies would seem more on the side of Protestant teaching than of Catholic. Either the charges against him were false, in which case there is no evidence of "Latin" sympathies, or they are correct, but in that case they do not point to any known Western church or sect. The most likely interpretation, and one that is consistent with his religious writings, is that certain aspects of Protestant teaching may have attracted him at one time, but that he remained firmly Orthodox in his own basic confessional loyalty. The importance of Khvorostinin is exactly that he did not wish to convert to another faith or found an orthodox heresy, but that he wanted to widen the intellectual and religious horizons of Russia, even if that led to the weakening of certain traditional practices.[19]

The religious works of Khvorostinin consist of two polemics, one against Catholicism and one against Protestantism. For those historians who believe him to be a crypto-Catholic, the work against Rome is taken to be insincere, written to get out of prison in the Kirillov Monastery, or the result of a last minute return to the fold in 1624. This interpretation is an unnecessary complication of a rather simple problem, since there is nothing in the text to contradict the view of Khvorostinin I have advanced, only to contradict the theory of crypto-Catholicism. The other text, a tract against Protestantism called "Against the Iconoclasts," *Na ikonobortsy*, was assigned by Platonov to Prince Ivan Katyrev-Rostovskii on extremely flimsy and circumstantial grounds, in spite of the presence in the title of Khvorostinin's usual "signature," "Duks Ivan."[20] In the preface to the anti-Catholic texts Khvorostinin refers to the two books that he has written, one against Rome and one against the Protestants, and Platonov was not able to suggest any other work to which he might be referring.[21]

All of Khvorostinin's religious works are essentially adaptations of tracts, in verse and prose, originating among the Orthodox population of Poland-Lithuania. The title of the first tract, that against the Catholics, is *Povest' ili vozglashenie k Gospodu na Rimlian* (Tale or Crying-out to the Lord against the Romans). He begins the actual work of adaptation after lengthy prefatory remarks. This "tale" is in turn followed by the version of the story of the Council of Florence that was printed at Ostrog in 1598.[22] Khvorostinin's authorship of the anti-Catholic complex of texts, original and adapted, is determined by an acrostic in one of the verse prefaces and is not in dispute. The anti-Catholic tracts demonstrate with great clarity that although Khvorostinin indeed had "Latin" books (in the sense that they were written in a "Latin" country, the Polish-Lithuanian commonwealth), they were written by Orthodox clerics defending their faith against Catholic and Calvinist alike. The Ukrainian poems are in three sections, a "Complaint of the Beggars to God," *Skarga nishchikh do Boga*, the "Kievo-Mikhailovskii" section, and the "Zagorovskii" section, named after the monastery libraries in which they were found.[23] Though the three parts are found in separate manuscripts, there is considerable overlapping of the poems, and they are believed with good reason to form parts of a single complex of polemical poetry composed probably in one place if not by the same man over two decades.

The Ukrainian originals of Khvorostinin's poetic effort present a coherent view of the evils of Catholicism, one that embraces both dogma and ritual. They cover the essential dogmatic points in the "Complaint": the *filioque* (the clause in the Nicene Creed stating the doctrine, held by Catholics and Protestants alike, that the procession of the Holy Spirit is from both the Father and the Son, as opposed to the Orthodox belief in procession only from the Father) the use of unleavened communion bread, and the doctrine of purgatory. Differences in ritual are covered as well, including the different rite of baptism and the Catholic use of organs and other musical instruments in church services. The central section, from the Kievo-Mikhailovskii Monastery, also contains a long section praising virginity and monasticism, and an equally long treatise on Christ's incarnation that seems to be directed against the Polish Arians, whose followers were numerous among the Ukrainian-Belorussian nobles of Lithuania. The primary attack on the Catholic church, however, concerns not questions of dogma or ritual but the supremacy of the pope, seen as a moral evil. All three sections, but especially the *Skarga* and the third ("Zagorovskii") section emphasize this point. In line after line the authors castigate the overwhelming pride of the pope who has assumed such a position in the church, comparing him to Satan as a rebel against God who has cast away the proper Christian humility. In all this the author or authors anticipated the adherence to the pope by much of the Orthodox clergy in the Ukraine and Belorussia after the Union of Brest in 1596.[24]

The primary moral theme of the three parts is essentially the same, the pride and greed of the Roman and Uniate clergy. This unremitting picture of wickedness is shown in contrast to the humility and poverty of the Orthodox monks and of the Orthodox people as a whole. The notion of a humble Orthodox people was in a sense accurate, for many great magnates were already Poles and thus Catholics or Calvinists, and almost all the Orthodox magnates went over to Roman Catholicism, not even to the Union preferred by the Orthodox clergy. The Orthodox church was very quickly restricted to peasants, townspeople, and the lesser nobility. Taken together, the poems represent another version of the defense of Orthodoxy in the Ukraine and Belorussia more familiar to scholars from the writings of Ivan Vyshens'kyi, the Ukrainian monk who wrote from his retreat on Mount Athos scathing accounts of the wickedness of the Latins and his fellow Ukrainians who had joined the Union.[25] His basic attitude was one of defense of the humble and the monastic virtues, even explicitly of the greater humility and poverty of Orthodox monks against the wealthy and aristocratic Catholics and their Uniate hangers-on.[26] The attack on Arianism was more complex, for the dogmatic issue was in the forefront, but the Arian rejection of monasticism combined with the aristocratic milieu of the Arians (whatever their views on apostolic pover-

ty) made it possible for the Orthodox Ukrainians to attack them on some
of the same grounds as the Catholics.

Khvorostinin's adaptation of Ukrainian poetic polemics thus injected
into Russian religious life a central concern with pride and greed, though
primarily in the form of the contrast of Orthodox clergy to Catholic clergy.
He did not merely take the Ukrainian poems and russify the language a
bit, for his work is selective, leaving out whole sections. Most of
Khvorostinin's "Tale" (*Povest' ili vozglashenie . . .*) is a summary and adaptation of the *Skarga,* perhaps better described as a poem inspired by it. The
next section of Khvorostinin's "Tale," however, is fairly closely adapted
from the third section ("Zagorovskii") of the Ukrainian poems that attack
the pride and greed of the Roman and Uniate clergy.[27] Khvorostinin also
added passages, for he inserted a section exhorting bishops to take care of
their flock, especially the priests who needed their guidance.[28] As we have
seen, this was a concern of many in the Russian church before him and
later among the Zealots.

He made clear the greater significance of the polemic against Catholicism by the prose preface with its remarks on the upbringing of children.
Here Khvorostinin tells us who all his enemies are, for he says he has
written books against the "eighth Roman council" (the Council of Florence) and against the "headless beast" Luther and other Protestants:
Calvin, Servetus, Czechowicz, and Szymon Budny. But the purpose of all
this is not only to reaffirm and defend the correctness of Orthodox belief,
but also to provide a moral foundation for the upbringing of youth. His
contemporaries, says Khvorostinin, concern themselves with giving their
children wealth to support them in this world, but they do not give them
the virtue (*dobrodetel'*) to prepare them for this world and the next.
Furthermore the proper moral upbringing of children is politically necessary, for tsars and princes cannot hope to rule justly and wisely if their
subjects, especially those who serve as administrators or generals, are not
virtuous. The preface underlines the moral significance of correct faith,
and shows that the polemic against Rome has implications greater than
merely affirmation of the truth of Orthodoxy.[29]

As Khvorostinin indicated, he was equally opposed to the Protestants,
and his attack on them, entitled *Na ikonobortsy i na vse zlye eresi* (Against the
Iconoclasts and All Evil Heresies), shows what he saw in their teachings to
oppose. This too was a work of adaptation, and the texts that Khvorostinin
took as the basis of his work ultimately go back to the Ukrainian monk
Zakharii Kopystens'kyi's *Kniga o vere,* published in Kiev in 1619. This book
combined in one volume two shorter works published in Wilno in 1602, a
tract on the Holy Trinity and a book entitled *Ob obrazekh* (On Images),
which was the basis of Khvorostinin's adaptation.[30] The selection of Protestant beliefs to attack is even more striking than that made in the case of
Catholicism. Essentially he addresses only one issue, the rejection by all
Protestants of the devotion to icons, which was such a central part of
Orthodox religious life. There is nothing in Khvorostinin's entire polemic

about *sola fide* or the doctrine of predestination, and only a short chapter on Protestant views of the eucharist. Clearly the devotion to icons was the central point of contention to him, and the dogmatic disagreements about baptism that preoccupied Nasedka had no place.[31] Finally, Khvorostinin was not merely defending icons, but also the miracle cults that surrounded them. He listed a series of such miracles, in his mind proof of the sanctity of the pictures. In this respect at least, he was a child of his time.

Khvorostinin's adaptations of Ukrainian religious literature show a definite selectivity that reveals his personal point of view. His polemic against Protestantism is largely confined to the icon questions, and for all its verbal violence, it is thus restricted in scope. There is no thorough moral condemnation of the Protestants. This is in keeping with Russian attitudes, which permitted Protestant worship in the foreign community in Moscow from the sixteenth century but forbade Catholic worship until 1684. The polemic on icons also reveals another traditional attitude, the defense of the miracle cults. Khvorostinin adapted the Ukrainian verse polemic against Catholicism much more thoroughly. He retained the moral critique of the pope and the Catholic hierarchy, but omitted the defense of monasticism and added a passage encouraging bishops to take care of their flock. This was a Russian concern from the 1550s, but also looked forward to the Zealots. Khvorostinin was no "Westerner," no secret Catholic or Protestant, but an Orthodox innovator, traditional in many ways but already moving toward an essentially moral conception of religion.

The Printing Office Poets

The poets of the Printing Office are a recent discovery, largely due to A. M. Panchenko. The existence of syllabic poetry in seventeenth-century Russia has been known for a long time, but until recently scholars have concentrated mainly on the poetry of the second half of the century.[32] Panchenko demonstrated that the more prolific of the early poets, known to one another and in close contact, formed a group that might be properly called a school. He also pointed out that all of them were secretaries in the chancelleries (*prikazy*) of the Russian state, mostly in the Printing Office. As might be expected from such a milieu, the Printing Office poets were neither religious or cultural radicals nor great reformers. Nevertheless, they were innovators: first, in literary form, for it was they who created the first large body of verse in Russia; and second, in their understanding of religious life. They expressed the essentially moral view of Orthodox Christianity that we have seen in the writings of Khvorostinin.

The poets of the Printing Office numbered probably less than a dozen men, the most prominent being the monk Savvatii, who served there as a *spravshchik* (literally a corrector, but the functions of such officials were closer to today's editors) from 1634 to 1652, when he retired to a northern monastery because of his conflict with Nikon. Another Printing Office corrector was the archpriest Mikhail Rogov, who worked with Ivan Nasedka on the *Kirillova kniga*. Poets not employed at the Printing Office but in personal and literary contact included the priest Stefan Gorchak, Petr Samsonov, a chancellery secretary apparently of the Patriarchal Palace Office in 1631, and Aleksei Romanchukov, a secretary (of the Foreign Office?), who went on the Russian embassy to Persia in 1638 and was friendly with Adam Olearius and members of the Holstein mission of that year to Russia and Persia. These do not exhaust the list, for there are anonymous poems and poems whose authors are not yet identified. Besides the clergy and government secretaries, there were nobles such as the governor and ambassador Aleksei Ivanovich Ziuzin (an *okol'nichii*, died 1618–1619), the boyar prince Mikhail Iur'evich Tatishchev (1620–1701), and probably Prince Semen Shakhovskoi himself.[33] They all wrote in syllabic, rather than accentual, verse, and the genres of poetry were limited: besides verse dedications, introductions, and conclusions to prose works they seem to have produced almost exclusively *poslaniia* (epistles) and *prosheniia*, epistles containing requests for favor from some influential nobleman.

To some extent these two basic genres offer a content appropriate to each. The epistles are epistles to friends, or more specifically to addressees bound to the author by the bond of Christian love, a notion that is both a stylistic device and a sincerely held belief. Consequently they have a more varied content, containing general reflections on man's fate, ethical advice, or consolation in grief. The *prosheniia* are more specific, with a description of the author's unhappy situation, either the result of disfavor or just of youth and lack of reputation. The boundary between the two, however, was quite fluid, as many of the requests for noble favor include the type of general moral reflections characteristic of the simple epistles (Savvatii's request to Tsarevich Aleksei's tutor, the secretary V. S. Prokofiev, for example). These poetic requests present very clearly the social situation of the poets: they are educated men to be sure, but not high enough on the ladders of wealth and career not to be dependent on someone's favor. The addressees are often men of great power, such as the boyar Ivan Nikitich Romanov-Kasha, (died 1640), Tsar Michael's uncle, or even the tsar himself. Some, however, are merely close to the seats of power, like Prokofiev, or are apparently nobles of middle rank. The view of the world—the world of court and government offices—that they offer to the reader is not attractive, for it is a world of flattery, slander, cleverness used for wicked aims, and hypocrisy. It is an unstable world, in which a man's enemies may at any point plunge him into an undeserved disfavor explainable only as evil fate. The only virtuous person in this world is, not surprisingly, the tsar, though his virtue may at any time be rendered ineffective by spiteful slanderers.[34] When Savvatii addresses the tsar himself, however, the mood is different. In place of the complaints of the wickedness of man, he praises the tsar for his power, glory, and wisdom.[35]

By contrast, the epistles among the poets—among the friends bound by

Christian love—mention the wickedness of man (especially at court) but stress the importance of learning and the proper Christian morals. Learning, and the closely connected theme of education, is an entire subject in itself in these poems. The doctrine expressed is essentially that of Khvorostinin's prose preface to his tract against the "iconoclasts," that is, the importance of learning for the understanding of Christian morality. As usual it is Savvatii who expressed the ideas most clearly, in his epistle to his pupil, the young prince Mikhail Nikitich Odoevskii. "The honor and dishonor of a man is in his mouth" (that is, in what his learning allows him to say), he insists, and also that "learning greatly beautifies the ranks of state" (*chiny gosudarskiia*), for learning and intelligence bring praise from others. Learning leads to wisdom, which is a necessary foundation for religion, but again the main lesson is that *Tsarskie dvory izriadno ustroiaiutsia ot razumnykh, khoshchu i tebe videti vo mnogoumnykh* (the courts of tsars are well build of the intelligent / I want to see you among those with much wit). The priest Stefan agreed with this view, in his epistles to the monks Arsenii Glukhoi and Fedor Kuz'mich asking them to help him learn in order to improve his *razumenie,* but meaning largely religious wisdom—his understanding of the writings of St. John Damascene, for example. But for Stefan, too, learning is the path to advancement in this world; neither God nor the tsar forgets *dobrorazumnye muzhi* (men of good reason).[36] For political life (for the young noble) and for the advancement of a bureaucratic career (for the secretaries), learning is essential. It is useful because the tsar needs educated men and it is good because it brings praise to the learned man.

But learning, as already Khvorostinin insisted, is also the path to morality, for without learning and the reading of sacred writings a man cannot really be virtuous. The morality that the poets preach is not simply general Christian morality, as understood by Russians of the time. In the first place, this morality is not monastic asceticism, even though Savvatii and possibly others were monks. Stefan specifically asks for the monk Arsenii's help in part because the monk's freedom from the passions helped him to learn wisdom, but as Stefan says,

> Free every monk of the three passions
>   and let him be saved from many snares,
> Oh, in truth this can be,
>   But not everyone can live like that.

In the second place, the poets have already made a selection from the many possible sins and Christian virtues, and do not merely offer a catalog. A few are concerned with drunkenness, but gluttony is rarely mentioned and the other sins of the flesh not at all. What does concern the poets is pride and greed, founded on wealth and power. What they want to inculcate, in themselves as well as in their friends and pupils, is humility and charity, in the sense of (primarily material) generosity.

The concern with wealth and power is expressed most clearly in an anonymous poem against pride found in a Chudov Monastery manuscript together with poems of Savvatii and one Ermolai Azancheev, otherwise unknown. Arrogance and pride darken the mind of man and take from him happiness and *razumenie*; they make him forget the life to come and turn his mind to feasting and the comforts of the flesh. Pride makes it impossible for a man to endure the reverses of fortune, for it takes away humility and meekness, such as that of Elijah in the face of the messengers of King Ahab. The context of pride is here evident in this example: the poet is speaking to the courtier, not to the ordinary man or to Man in general. In Savvatii's poem "On the World," this theme is developed.

> Tsars and other rulers add kingdom to kingdom
> and acquire praise and glory for themselves.
> Their dignitaries, seeing glory and honor for themselves
> do not think how to achieve the faces of the saints [= heaven].
> But already rich they add riches to riches
> and every day and night add profit to profit.

When he touches on the sins of the flesh he essentially castigates the sins of the rich, for the sins of the flesh in his mind are excessive eating and drinking (sexual misconduct, *blud,* is barely mentioned), by which is meant feasting, not general overindulgence. The priest Stefan Gorchak tells his friend, the monk Fedor Kuz'mich, that they will not be proud in wealth and glory, but devote themselves to learning, the ways of God, and the bond of Christian love. Petr Samsonov praises Mikhail Ignat'evich above all for his generosity, literally for giving his wealth to the needy, both in general and to Samsonov in particular. Mikhail replies sententiously that "We have a command from God our savior / who says: give what is in abundance to the poor." Only the tsar is exempt from the need to be humble, for by definition the tsar and his realm are glorious, but the tsar is supposed to be merciful and generous in this literal sense of the giving of wealth to petitioners as well as to the poor.[37]

Thus the poets continue the theme of pride and greed introduced as especially dangerous vices by Khvorostinin in his attack on the Catholic clergy. The reason that the poets should be particularly concerned with these themes is obvious, as most of them were middle-level or even lower-level officials, poorly paid and dependent for promotion on the favor of the great. Apparently many were so poorly paid that they resorted to petitioning the tsar or the great nobles for extra rewards for their services, including a poem as evidence of their talents. The condemnation of the greed of the rich was thus to some extent self-serving, but there was more to it than that. They expected moderation of themselves, especially the priest Stefan and the monk Savvatii, for whom monasticism seems to have been primarily a basis for moderate living rather than real asceticism. Pride as a more troublesome sin, for both learning and a worldly career might bring a need for reputation or a satisfaction in accomplishment that was very close to pride. Savvatii warns his charge, the young prince Odoevskii, that ignorance not only will hamper virtue, but will also give others the occasion to laugh at him and mock his ignorance and will not help his career at court or in the army. Learning too should bring praise: the priest Stefan reminded his friend Fedor that the wise are not forgotten, and his whole epistle to Fedor is a complaint that Stefan's wisdom has not yet brought the appropriate recognition. The problem all the poets faced in their lives, the need to reconcile advancement and recognition with humility, is illuminated by the rather vulgar advice given by Petr Samsonov to one Grigorii Evdokimovich, clearly a young man entering the tsar's service, presumably in the *prikazy*. He tells him to take his honors from God rather than man, and enrich himself by good deeds (rather than money), but continues:

> "You will have great honor among all men
> if you are continent in your youth.
> Keep the Tsar's secrets diligently,
> and always carry out the duties given you by superiors,
> obey in all things the dignitaries of the Tsar's realm. . . .
> Turn your ears from receiving vain rumors,
> from hearing vain whisperings and slanders.
> If you want to attain the rank of greatness,
> you should cast flattering words out of your heart.
> If you want to live peacefully in this world,
> keep peace and love with all and speak words of comfort
> If you want to achieve glory from all men,
> force yourself, as I am describing to you, to learn from all.
> Do not involve yourself from your youth in much drunkenness,
> for in old age that brings much inconvenience.
> Liquor drinking brings little pleasure to those who are used to it,
> and takes honor and eternal praise from all.

Other virtues, concludes this Russian Polonius, are to be added to these.[38]

The world view of the Printing Office poets displays a certain polarity. At the one pole are the very worldly concerns of career and the patronage of the great. The good official or courtier must acquire learning and faithfully serve the tsar, carrying out the duties of office with the skill and intelligence that comes with learning, and cultivate the favor of the great with flattery and displays of talent. At the same time learning should also be the road to faith, and more especially to good morals founded on faith; for it is the morality, not the faith itself, that is the central concern. In Western Europe at this time this problem of reconciling Christianity and service to the sovereign was an old one. In Russia, however, the problem—or rather the conception of it—was new. Certainly Russian noblemen had been faced with the practical implications for centuries, but the traditional conceptions of political life, based as they were on the notion of harmony, made them difficult to articulate. Needless to say their solution is neither clear nor profound: what they did was merely to present both sides of the problem in the same body of poetry without spelling out the potential contradiction or trying to resolve it in a theological or philosophical fashion. However, the situation did affect their thinking. They did not merely mechanically add some new notions to the old Orthodox ascetic morality. In any case, the reorganization of the traditional Orthodox Christian moral code is the most notable feature of the religious pole of their thought. Essentially they reduced the accepted list of Christian sins to two: pride and avarice, with gluttony (including drunkenness) as a poor third, scarcely worth mentioning in the same breath. All the rest—anger, gluttony, acedia, and the whole remaining Orthodox catalog of sins that fill the medieval collections of homilies of St. John Chrysostom and others—simply are not mentioned.[39] The Printing Office poets responded to a need that more and more Russians of the landholding class felt as the court and administration expanded in the course of the seventeenth century. Until the reign of Aleksei, however, these concerns do not seem to have been present in the culture of the court as a whole.

Iuliana of Murom

These religious ideas did not arise merely from the milieu of the Printing Office in this period. In the provinces, among noblemen quite removed from the hectic life of the court and government offices in the Kremlin, roughly the same religious notions were gaining currency. Government service for provincial nobles meant the lower ranks of the army and obscure provincial offices like that of *gubnoi starosta,* a local judge elected by the nobles of the district to perform a series of local police and judicial tasks. In this milieu, learning in the sense understood by the poets, which meant learning the rules of writing and prosody found in the Ukrainian grammars, did not exist. Here Old Russian religious culture survived, at least the forms of literary expression of that culture if not the entire content. Poetry was unknown, and the lives of the saints still provided the basic framework for the conception of the holy life. This did not mean that the provincial noble simply went on mechanically copying and reading the old saints' lives with nothing new to add, for within this older framework new ideas and conceptions of the holy life were spreading that bore a striking resemblance to the basic moral notions of the Printing Office poets. The newer ideas were expressed by one of the most striking documents of the early seventeenth century, and one not produced by the noble and official elite of Moscow: the life of Iuliana of Murom, the *Zhitie Iuliany Muromskoi.*

The life of Iuliana of Murom is unusual in a number of ways. It is one of the very few lives of pious laypersons other than a prince in the whole period of Russian history before Peter. The life of Iuliana, in its religious

function, is much closer to the lives of the boyar Rtishchev, of Patriarch
Nikon, and even of Avvakum later in the century, for not only does it
present the life of someone pious but not a saint, it also displays the same
compositional unity, the same departure from the topoi of saints' lives, and
the same "realism" of the detail as those later works.[40] But the feature that
most sets it apart from the few provincial lives of saints of the period is the
thematic emphasis in the text, an exclusive emphasis on humility and
charity (in the sense of almsgiving), an emphasis more exclusive than that
in any other religious writings of the seventeenth century, whether sermons, other lives, or religious poetry. Finally, the life is anchored explicitly
in the social reality of the time to a tremendous extent, and this gives it a
unique value in understanding what was at the heart of the religious
changes of those years.

In Iuliana's life almost all other Christian virtues have been abandoned
for the sake of humility and charity. Before her marriage at age sixteen to
Georgii Osor'in, a local nobleman, she fasts and has no interest in childish
games (both topoi) but primarily she is humble and obedient to her
mother and others, and cares particularly for the widows and orphans, the
beggars and the sick, who visit her parents' village. The text says nothing
whatever of virginity. After her marriage, the same is true: she is humble
and obedient to Osor'in's parents (so much so that they entrust her with
management of the estate) and takes care of the poor. In spite of her
husband's long absences serving the tsar (presumably in the army) in
Astrakhan', she is not tempted by any sexual sins: when demons visit her
in her sleep, they threaten to kill her because she cares for the poor and
devotes her time to prayer and spinning. They do not tempt her with any
of the sins of the flesh, not even the obvious sin of adultery.[41] Throughout
her adult life, Iuliana practices charity persistently. When famine comes,
she eats as little as possible in order to take care of the hungry and poor;
especially in the famine in the time of Tsar Boris Godunov (1602–1603)
does she show charity:

> In that time there was a great famine in the whole Russian land, for many
> were driven by need to eat bad meats and human flesh, and a countless
> number died of hunger. In her household there was a great dearth of food
> and all necessities, for the sown grain did not grow from the earth at all; the
> horses and cattle died. But she asked her children and servants that they not
> steal the goods of other men, and instead she sold the remaining cattle and
> clothes and vessels for grain, and from that she fed her servants, and gave
> sufficient alms, and in her own poverty she did not cease her usual almsgiv-
> ing, and let no one who asked of her leave in vain. She came to complete
> poverty, so that not one grain remained in her household, but she was not
> downcast, and put all her hope in God.

When there was no hope at all left of feeding her servants, she freed those
who were enserfed so that they could leave the area stricken by famine and

have some hope of survival, the ultimate act of charity for a serf-owning noblewoman.

Iuliana matched her perfect charity with perfect humility. Not only was she humble and obedient to her own parents and her husband's, but she showed her humility as an example to the servants, and she even washed the feet of the poor herself.[42] She was humble in the face of the servants' *bran'*, a term that meant primarily strife or quarreling but also meant conflict between states, social groups, or rival political factions. The reference is here clearly to social struggle, for Osor'in asserts that the devil envied his mother's peaceful life and "often raised quarrels among her children and servants. She, however, thinking sensibly and reasonably, calmed them. But the Enemy taught their [Iuliana and her husband's] servant, and he killed their eldest son."[43] The image of Iuliana as the calmer of social strife is strengthened by the chronology of her life, falling in the hears of the establishment of serfdom (1580–1604), and by the description of her charitable actions in the great famine of the last years of the reign of Boris Godunov. Her death in 1608 completes the image, for the Smuta began at the death of Tsar Boris in 1604, and was well under way four years later, and this was precisely the "strife" that she had met with humility and reasonable words. The Troubles are not explicitly mentioned, but every reader of the text in the 1620s or 1630s would know that the famine had been followed by the appearance of the False Dmitrii and the death of Boris, and would therefore think of all these events as "strife," and as a moral rather than political phenomenon. Iuliana's life—the cultivation of humility and charity in the face of strife—her son is telling us, is the proper Christian response to the social strife created by serfdom and other changes in the fabric of Russian rural life. He does not suggest that her attitude will solve the problem and bring universal social peace, but he does make clear that hers is the example to follow to manage serfs, run an estate, and at the same time save one's own soul.

It is clear that Druzhina Osor'in paid little deference to the clichés normal in the life of a saint. Iuliana seems to have had some difficulty getting herself to church, for example, and had to be reminded to go by the local priest, an unusual fault in a tradition where the holy person is portrayed as spending great amounts of time in church and often scarcely leaving it. Monasticism is hardly mentioned: after her husband came back from service and the children were grown, Iuliana expressed a desire to enter a convent, but her husband opposed the idea and it was dropped immediately. As a compromise they decided to abstain from "fleshly conjunction" until their deaths, a vow they carried out with little apparent difficulty. When her husband died, however, Iuliana could have entered a convent, but apparently chose not to, for she stayed in her house attending to the poor until her death.[44]

In the first half of the seventeenth century, the religious changes that came to prominence after midcentury were beginning to take shape.

True, the background of religious life looks rather grey at first glance: most of the printed books are liturgical, and there seems to be little theological excitement in the manuscript literature. There is nothing to rival the heresies and disputes of the earlier sixteenth century, the time of Iosif Volotskii and Maksim Grek, or the even more dramatic clashes of Nikon, Avvakum, and Tsar Aleksei after 1652. Nevertheless the elite of both aristocracy and church was not intellectually stagnant: new currents of ideas and new forms of learning and expression were coming to Russia from the Ukraine, and some Russian writers, perhaps not many in number but all placed at the centers of power, were responding. They responded not merely by imitation, for much of the religious culture of the Orthodox peoples of the Polish state was irrelevant to Russian conditions. Russians picked and chose among a fairly wide circle of ideas, finding most congenial the moral defense of Orthodoxy against the Catholic church. Picking up the Ukrainians' suggestion that pride and avarice were the chief dangers to man and the moral causes of the Orthodox hierarchy's desertion to the Uniate camp after Brest, Russian religious writers saw pride and avarice as the primary sins of their own fellow countrymen and of themselves. The result was a change in the form and content of religious writing. The long tradition of confessional and dogmatic polemics remained, but was enhanced by the more learned treatises of Ukrainian theologians and by the poetic form adapted by Khvorostinin. The lives of the saints, one of the most important forms of religious literature, also began to change. Druzhina Osor'in's life of his mother used an old genre to preach a new lesson. Essentially he replaced the traditional images of saintly princes and holy monks with that of the pious noble, a lay person noted more for charity and humility than for asceticism. The changes in literary form, and the appearance of new forms such as the religious verse of the Printing Office poets, thus were merely one side of a change in the religious ideas of the lower levels of Russia's elite that lay just below the court aristocracy and even extended to the provinces to some degree.

For the innovaters, morality had become central to Orthodoxy, and more specifically, charity and humility had come to be prized above all other Christian virtues. They also suggest that religious experience for that elite had become a matter of learning, in the sense that it was felt that some elementary education in grammar and rhetoric was necessary to the expression of religious ideas and feelings, and that learning was helpful on the road to salvation. Religion had become more private, not by the rejection of liturgy or of the public ceremonies of the faithful (there is no hint of that anywhere), but merely by adding a new dimension, and one that was highly valued.

This change was in large part a response to the new circumstances in which the landholding class, including the chancellery secretaries (who usually held land as well as earned a salary), found themselves. Serfdom had radically changed the character of Russian rural life, and the story of

Iuliana of Murom gives a glimpse of how deeply that fact affected the religious consciousness of the nobility. For the clerks and monks of the Printing Office, and their noble colleagues, it was the rise of autocracy and the gradual formation of bureaucratic offices of government on which the tsar could rest his rule that formed their experience. Dependent on the favor of a few courtiers or the tsar, they too began to see pride and avarice as the chief sins of humanity, in their boyar patrons as well as in their own souls; in both cases these vices were to be restrained as much as the sinful soul of man would permit.[45] The stream of texts and ideas from Kiev and Wilno arrived in a country in the midst of great social and political changes, and gave ready-made forms to express the religious ideas that arose from the new environment. The very novelty of the forms, however, confined the new ideas to a small elite within an elite, the few educated men concentrated in the Printing Office who searched out and used the books and manuscripts from the Ukraine. Druzhina Osor'in demonstrates that the new ideas existed in the provinces even without the Ukrainian forms. With the arrival of the monk Epifanii Slavinetskii from Kiev in 1649, and Nikon's ascent to the patriarchal throne in 1652, the new ideas began to spread beyond the narrow confines of the Printing Office upward into the court at large.

7

The Rise of the Sermon

At the very middle of the seventeenth century the oral delivery of sermons in churches became a basic part of the religious life of the Russian
people, at least the elite among them. This was an innovation supported
by disparate elements in the church, both the Zealots of Piety (including
the later Old Believers) and the Ukrainian-trained scholars at the Russian court. In the absence of contemporary texts or detailed descriptions
of Zealot sermons, the sermons of Epifanii Slavinetskii and Simeon Polotskii provide the main body of known sermon material, and at the same
time comprise the most important of the sermons delivered at court and
in the chief Moscow churches for the whole period from about 1650 to
1680. Since the court was the innovator of changes in elite culture in this
period and later, the ultimate significance of the court sermons goes
beyond the world of court culture. What was heard at court in 1670 was
read in the provinces by 1690, and in that sense the court sermons of the
seventeenth century are an integral part of the process of the religious
and cultural change both for the elite and for the larger circles of the
Russian landholding class.

The sermons signified a reorientation of the religious life of the upper
classes in several ways. They implied a move away from liturgy alone as
the central religious experience, for now the liturgy was accompanied by
a nontraditional homily that called the congregation to a better life. The
sermons also signified a shift in emphasis toward the moral improvement of the Orthodox Christian. The specific moral program of these
sermons put a considerable emphasis on humility and charity, and
stressed the dangers of pride and avarice. Both Epifanii and Simeon
shared this program, although their sermons were no more identical in
content than in form. As we shall see, Epifanii stuck close to this specific
emphasis, speaking generally about both pride and avarice, and calling
on priest and layman alike to avoid these sins. Otherwise only heresy

attracted his fire. Simeon's program was somewhat more complicated. A careful reading of his sermons reveals the same conviction that pride and avarice were the main threats to the Russians of his time but also provides a more elaborate sense of the moral problems of various social groups, of the clergy as well as various strata within lay society. Furthermore, Simeon's Kiev education left more of an impact on him, and occasionally he shows a certain degree of Catholic influence (greater concern with sexual sins than Epifanii, for example). On the whole, however, Epifanii and Simeon are more alike than they are different, and it was not until after their deaths, in the 1680s, that their followers quarreled and tried to exaggerate the differences between the two.

Although the interest in the sermon started with the Zealots, we know almost nothing of their sermons. Both Avvakum and Ivan Neronov had preached extensively in the 1630s and 1640s in their provincial parish churches. Our only source for this is the autobiography of Avvakum and the life of Neronov, but there is no reason to doubt these sources. They are consistent with the program contained in Iosif's circular letters, for Avvakum and Neronov not only preached but tried to establish decorum in church and fought the traditional popular entertainments. Unfortunately these sources tell us nothing whatever of the content of the sermons.[1] Some idea, however, of the probable content of Zealot sermons is provided by the publications of the Printing Office in these years, as the years from 1645 to 1652 were those of the ascendance of the Zealots of Piety over the Office. In June 1647 the Office completed work on a fat book called simply *Sbornik iz 71 slov* (*Collection of 71 Sermons*) which was obviously intended to provide guidance for priests needing inspiration or even a text to summarize. The book was a collection of mostly patristic homilies and tracts, each one entitled *slovo*, literally "word" but in Old Russian literature meaning a text of virtually any genre including the homiletic or what passed for that. The book was arranged in order of the Lenten and Easter cycle, with one or two homilies for each Sunday of Lent and all the days of Holy Week. Not surprisingly, the dominant theme of the excerpts for Lent was repentance and fasting, but there were other themes as well: love of the poor, the advent of Antichrist and the end of the world, the adoration of the cross, and the veneration of saints and icons (a particularly frequent theme).[2] After the Lenten series the book turns to the resurrection of Lazarus on Palm Sunday and finally to the description and explication of the events of the Passion, all with patristic and Byzantine homilies. Preaching in the time of Lent (or the Great Fast, *velikii post,* as it was known in Russia) seems to have been a particular concern of the Zealots, and the *Sbornik iz 71 slov* was obviously intended to provide models for sermons in this period of the liturgical year.

It also reinforced the intention of the Zealots to spread among the Russian believers their particular brand of morality. To accomplish this aim the editors broke with the medieval Slavic tradition of excerpting Chrysostom's texts so heavily as to create almost new works. In the classic medieval Russian collections of excerpts from Chrysostom, the *Izmaragd*, or the *Zlatoust*, St. John was turned into an essentially monastic writer, for the choice of excepts stressed an ascetic strictness and an emphasis on virginity that is not present in the full original text of his homilies and tracts. Chrysostom was, after all, a bishop who mainly preached to lay audiences, not monks, but, chosen in this manner, the collections not surprisingly had a primarily monkish audience.[3] In the 1647 *Sbornik* by contrast, the sermons are given not in excerpts but in the full text, as in the case of the series from Chrysostom's homilies *De poenitentia* (nos. 2, 3, and 7) or in Gregory of Nazianzus's sermon on the love of the poor.[4] In this full text the sermons stress (besides faith, of course) fasting and correct moral behavior, including almsgiving, the whole giving the impression of a morality fairly strict for laymen but far from monastic asceticism. This message was the message of the Zealots of Piety, with their concern for church attendance, avoidance of drunkenness, and the suppression of popular amusements. The Zealots tried to convince their congregations, and Russians as a whole, to adopt a morality of moderation, one that stressed pious observances, such as fasts and church attendance, and the avoidance of sin, but was not ascetic in the monastic sense. This conception of Christian morality was not only different from that of previous generations of clergy, it was also different from that of Khvorostinin and the Printing Office poets. For the Zealots, morality was central but lacked the specific emphasis on humility and almsgiving. The Zealots did have some ideas in common with Khvorostinin—an interest in the cults of saints and the desire for an improved priesthood—but the difference in moral emphasis remained. In large part this difference must have derived from the difference in audience, for the Zealots directed their message at all laymen, particularly the humble, while the poets, like the later court preachers, addressed an elite audience.

Epifanii Slavinetskii

When Epifanii Slavinetskii came to Moscow, his primary task was to assist in the correction of liturgical books, and it was his skill as a translator from Greek that was most needed. Until his death in Moscow in 1675, most of his time was spent producing fat volumes of translations from the Greek fathers and assisting Russian churchman to conform the liturgical books to the Greek standard, which was also the one common among Orthodox Ukrainians. We know relatively little about his activity in correcting the books, save that it fell in the years in which Nikon was issuing the volumes that brought about the great schism in the Russian church, and issuing them to a great extent through Epifanii's expertise. In these years he also came in contact with the monk Evfimii of the Chudov

Monastery, who worked as a corrector in the Printing Office from 1652 to 1660. Evfimii Chudovskii, as he is known, was to become Epifanii's chief Russian follower. Two important works of translation were printed a bit later, the Bible of 1663, the first complete printed edition in Russia, and a collection of patristic translations in 1665, the latter using the Western (Paris) printed texts rather than Byzantine manuscripts as a standard text from which to translate. In addition to religious works he translated parts of Book 1 of Thucydides, Pliny the Younger's panegyric on Trajan (the manuscripts of these have not survived), Andreas Vesalius's *De humana corporis fabrica* in 1657–1658, apparently for Patriarch Nikon, Willem Blaeuw's *Atlas novus*, Constantine Armenopulos's fourteenth-century Byzantine *Epitome ton deon kai hiereon kanonon* in Leuvenclavius's 1596 edition, and finally Erasmus's *De civilitate morum puerilium*. This list includes major Western European Renaissance and post-Renaissance works, and suggests interests on the part of Epifanii and his patrons that far exceeded religion and embraced specifically "Latin" culture. Epifanii seems also to have had a school of sorts in the Chudov Monastery in the Kremlin— the court monastery in effect—where he came to live most of the years he spent in the Russian capital; perhaps it is for that school that he prepared two Latin-Slavonic dictionaries based on the Calepinus dictionary.[5] The school must have been very informal, for it left few traces, but it does seem that he taught the rudiments of Latin and Greek to Russian clergymen.

Epifanii lived in the Chudov Monastery until his death, which put him in the center of the Kremlin. The monastery had two churches, one dedicated to the Miracle of St. Michael the Archangel at Chonae and the other to the monastery's founder, Metropolitan Aleksii. The tsar attended ceremonies, especially vespers, at the monastery, both on 6 September (St. Michael's day) and 20 May (St. Aleksii's) as well as other occasions. Attendance on days related to St. Aleksii were more common, and here the tsar expressed his respect for one of Moscow's greatest saints and for the church that he had led in the fourteenth century. Tsar Aleksei's early favorite, the boyar B. I. Morozov, was buried there in 1661. The archimandrites of the monastery included many important figures in the church, such as Pavel (archimandrite 1659–1664), later metropolitan Sarskii and Podonskii (Krutitskii); Ioakim (archimandrite 1666–1672), later patriarch and the self-proclaimed intellectual heir of Epifanii; and, somewhat later, Adrian (archimandrite 1678–1686), later the last patriarch. Epifanii was well connected indeed.[6] He participated in other public activities, for he was commissioned almost upon arrival in 1649 to prepare a eulogy of the newly recognized Anna of Kashin, and soon after composed another eulogy to Iakov Borovitskii, the patron saint of Nikon's new monastery at Valdai. This second eulogy was printed in the *Rai myslennyi* of 1659. Epifanii was clearly a major cultural force in the Russian church from his arrival until his death. As a religious force, he was easily left in the background in the dramatic years of the schism and dispute between Nikon and Aleksei, and his role was modest, as in the council of 1660. He was clearly primarily a scholar, a man who did not involve himself much in public controversy and probably rarely even appeared in public. What he did accomplish was to spread and deepen the acceptance by the elite of the Russian church and state of the Ukrainian religious culture of the time. Epifanii brought not only the ideas but also the tools of that culture in the form of Latin and Greek. Earlier, Russians had used Ukrainian works written in Slavonic. Epifanii used that same Slavonic for translations and sermons, but he also communicated the classical languages, as the analysis of his sermons will show. This was a radical innovation, no less so because it affected an extremely small number of people, probably little more than his personal circle in and around the Chudov Monastery.[7]

The religious culture that Epifanii conveyed in Moscow was not "Byzantine" or Greek culture, however attached he may have been to the "Byzantine" faith. What he brought was the religious culture of Kiev, Orthodox to be sure but based on the Latin curriculum of the Jesuit schools—that is, the Renaissance curriculum adapted for religious purposes, albeit in Baroque guise. This is not the usual interpretation of his role, for Epifanii is usually held to be the leader of a "Grecophile" school opposed to that of Simeon Polotskii. The Grecophile school is supposed to have emphasized Greco-Byzantine learning, Orthodoxy, and the Greek language in opposition to the "Latin" influence coming from Poland and tainted with Catholic ideas. The actual fact is that Epifanii did as many or more translations from Latin secular works as from the Greek fathers, and his school seems to have stressed Latin, not Greek, judging by the dictionaries compiled by Slavinetskii and Satanovskii. No comparable Greek dictionary has survived, and certainly it would have been as rare and necessary in Moscow as a Latin dictionary. The main source of the confusion seems to be the stories spread about his ideas in the 1680s and 1690s, when Patriarch Ioakim used his reputation as a weapon against his "latinizing" opponents in the eucharistic controversy, circulating texts purporting to record conversations of his with Simeon Polotskii in 1672–1673 in which he affirmed the correctness of "Greek" faith and learning.[8] These texts are too late and too polemical to be trustworthy, and do not constitute serious evidence.

Much better evidence purports to come from his own pen, in a quotation in a 1900 article on Epifanii by Ivan Rotar. Rotar quoted a paragraph ostensibly from the autograph manuscript of his sermons that says that the author earlier had been ensnared by the charms of Latin writers, but later in life turned to the solid faith of the Greeks. The manuscript, Synodal Library 597, in the State Historical Museum, does indeed contain Epifanii's sermons, one in holograph, but neither on the folio cited by Rotar (77v) nor anywhere else does it contain this paragraph. The quotation adduced by Rotar is actually a quotation from a 1680s tract against the "latinizers" by Evfimii Chudovskii, in which Evfimii attributed the words to Epifanii years after the latter's death on the authority of his own memory.[9] In fact, MS Sin. 597 shows precisely the opposite, for the text contains quotations in Latin, including some from Latin fathers (John Cassian, Gregory the Great, Peter Damian; naturally, Greek fathers are more common) and his marginal notes refer to Greek patristic works by Latin titles. Clearly Epifanii was using the Western printed texts of Greek fathers rather than Byzantine manuscripts, as he did with his printed translations. The handwriting in the Greek quotations is not that of seventeenth-century Greek scribes, but that taught in Western European schools, a humanist Greek hand. He also used a variety of classical writers, citing Plutarch and Plato's *Phaedo* in a sermon on the death of a monk, and referring elsewhere to Pythagoras and the story of Marcus Cato.[10] Finally, although the sermon cited incorrectly by Rotar is on the subject of learning, including Greek and Latin learning, it does not contrast the two: Epifanii merely notes in praise of Greek learning that it is admired in the Latin countries as well as on its native soil, and in the course of the sermon is mainly concerned to defend learning in general against ignorance, not Greek learning over Latin.[11]

Epifanii transmitted the practice of using Catholic and Orthodox Ukrainian writers to his follower Evfimii Chudovskii. Evfimii used in his own writings Peter Mohyla, Haliatovs'kyi, and Baranovych, as well as the church history of Cesare Baronio (in Polish translation), a classic of Counter-Reformation historiography. Just like Epifanii, Evfimii combined these interests with translations of Greek writing, those of archimandrite Meletios Syrigos (1585–1663) and Patriarch Dositheos of Jerusalem, for example. Moreover, Syrigos made extensive use of Latin authors and was the principal Greek supporter of Mohyla's catechism. Dositheos also made use of Latin authors and concepts, and until the condemnation of John Karyophylles in 1692 directed his fire mostly at Protestant influence among the Orthodox, not Catholic influence. Among the Greeks as well, there was no pure anti-Latin movement, but rather the use of Latin learning to defend Orthodoxy and to support a culture like the Kievan. The translations from Greek authors were made after 1675, but from the beginning Epifanii and Evfimii differed from Simeon Polotskii only in their style of translation. This was marked by a very self-conscious literalism, apparently designed to reflect their conception of the unity of Orthodox faith and teaching. Both Epifanii and Evfimii tried to reproduce the Greek text as literally as possible, even when this decision rendered it hard to understand. It is not clear, however, that contemporaries regarded Epifanii's literalism as opposed to Simeon's "Latin" orientation, for the 1674 project to retranslate the Bible in this manner fell under the supervision and patronage of Metropolitan Pavel, who was Simeon's patron as well. (The project was never completed because of the deaths of both Pavel and Epifanii in 1675–1676). Epifanii's literalist style of translation was based on the same emphasis on the importance of learning that Simeon Polotskii would show, and it was just as much of an innovation as Simeon's writings or the poetry of the Printing Office. Epifanii and Evfimii were in no sense obscurantists opposed to learning.[12]

Although Epifanii was primarily a scholar, he was an important preacher as well, and his sermons form the largest part of his original writings. For whatever reason, however, he never printed the sermons, and their audience was relatively narrow, as far as can be deduced from the evidence of the sermons themselves. His audience included the court, for the sermon *Slovo na prorochitsu Anna* contains a direct address to Tsar Aleksei and Patriarch Nikon, and the text was therefore part of a court ceremony, as was probably also the case with two or three others in the collection.[13] However, the great majority of his sermons must have been delivered at the Chudov Monastery to the monks and to his pupils, for the Latin and Greek quotations were certainly meaningless to any other audience, and the Slavic style seems far too complex for a parish church. This monastic audience does not imply isolation from the world, for the Chudov Monastery was anything but isolated. Situated only a few yards from the tsar's palace in the Kremlin, the monks were intimately involved in the life of the tsar's family and the great boyars of the Russian state. Furthermore, the content of the sermons is not monastic: only two of some thirty sermons touch on monastic life, and one is on the death of a monk and actually treats death, not monasticism. The other sermon (*Slovo k monakhom*, "A Homily to the Monks") is the only one to treat monasticism. The monastery is a house of tears, but unlike the world, the tears are for sins, not for honor, the treasures of silver and gold, and wealth. The true monk values *smirenie, pravda, tselomudrie, muzhestvo, razum* (humility, truth, continence, strength, reason). There are bad monks as well: "Those monks who, neglecting the restraint useful to the soul and widening their bellies with delicate foods, feed themselves [insatiably?], despising the poverty that becomes monks; they strive for the acquisition of perishable wealth that is harmful to the soul." He exhorts his listeners to get rid of pride and let humility into their souls, to rid themselves of hatred of their brothers and to replace it with love. Humility and obedience are the keys to salvation. Even to monks he stressed the sins of pride and avarice, which are his primary targets in sermons directed at laymen as well.[14] Other sermons addressed issues that were those that affected laymen, not monks. The apparent contradiction between his sermons' intended audience (the learned monks of the Chudov Monastery) and their nonmonastic content is apparent only on the surface. The close involvement of the Chudov monks with the court as advisors and confessors meant that the monks had to deal with essentially laymen's problems, and Epifanii in his sermons provided them with guidance. The large part played by the monastery in court ritual also suggests that the tsar and his court may well have been present at many of the sermons.

Epifanii's sermons were of three types: on moral themes, against heresy, and on the basic tenets of Orthodox faith, the last type chiefly to be delivered on important holidays. The first group were by far the most numerous and the others were both less numerous and less noteworthy, especially the explications of Orthodox faith. Here he dealt only with the most basic Christian notions (for example, the meaning of Christ's resurrection) and all that was new was the Baroque rhetoric and the continual appeal to learning to buttress his arguments, which included citing his authorities in the original language, even Latin.

The sermons against Old Belief and other heresies are far more significant, giving his predictably negative reaction as well as the reasons for that reaction, which reveal his ideas on the church and on the role of learning in religion. He spoke against Old Belief three times, twice presenting a moral condemnation of the movement and once speaking on the role of learning. The attack was not on their opinions of the change in ritual or any other supposedly basic point of contention but on their moral attitudes, particularly on their disobedience to the church, a grave moral defect in the eyes of Epifanii. This disobedience in turn arose from the sin of pride, a sin that occupied a central place in his version of the Christian conception of man's nature. In one sermon, "Against the Disobedient to the Church" (*Na nepokorniki tserkvi*), the church personified says, "Certain schismatics, rebels, seekers of glory, vain men have appeared who do not obey me their mother and do not obey their holy shepherds the bishops." Epifanii went on to comment that they were unlearned as well, knowing neither grammar, rhetoric, philosophy, or theology, yet "they dare to interpret, or rather to debauch, divine writings according to their own ignorance." But disobedience is their main sin, for their teachers are not sanctioned by the church, and even women preach among them. There is no salvation outside the Orthodox church, and they should return to it. The third sermon against Old Belief is the sermon on learning, *Liudie sediashche vo tme videvshe svet velii* ("The people which sat in darkness saw great light" [Matt. 4:16]). The sermon is a reply to Nikita Pustosviat's charge in his 1665 petition that Nikon's defense of his correction of the books, the *Skrizhal'*, asserted that God was darkness. Epifanii does not name the petition explicitly, but he argues light and darkness are not names of God, neither essential nor hypostatic (*estestvena ni ipostasna*), and that God is neither light nor darkness but the bringer of light. Nikita's position is thus irrelevant and a misunderstanding. The rest of the sermon goes on to defend Greek learning and by implication the Greek church and the patriarchs at the 1666–1667 council, both attacked by the Old Belief. "In the present times there are many men who hate, blinded by the murky darkness of hate, who love the murk of ignorance, do not love the bright rays of learning, hate those who are illuminated by it, envy those who are illuminated by it, and strive, dark men, to destroy it with a cloud of zeal, flattery, and treachery (Oh speeches of hypocrisy) and (Oh great disorder) to drive it away." Men must love truth, like Pythagoras and other pagan Greeks, like the Persians, and not imitate Marcus Cato who forbade his son to learn Greek out of hate of Hellenic learning. Epifanii saw the Old Belief as the product of pride, disobedience, and ignorance.[15] He certainly did not see it as the result either of blind ritualism or Russian nationalism.

The Old Believers were not the only objects of his exhortations, for he also attacked beliefs that were not held by any known sect of the time. He spoke against the notion that God would forgive sin even if the sinner did not confess to a priest (the argument being that God knows sincere repentance), and against the notion that a virtuous life with good deeds counted more for salvation than accurate knowledge of the dogmas of the Orthodox church. Epifanii preached against extreme asceticism, and it is probable that here the enemy was the *kapitonovtsy*, the followers of Kapiton.[16]

Epifanii's sermons on moral themes represent a sharp break with Russian homiletic texts of the sixteenth century, as well as the ideas of the Zealots. They do show striking continuity with the religious poetry of the Printing Office school. The predominant themes of Metropolitan Daniil in the sixteenth century—the need to maintain monastic discipline, harmony, moderation, and sexual restraint among laymen—are all absent. Epifanii barely mentions sexual sins or the drunkenness that concerned Antonii Podol'skii only a generation earlier, and then solely in the infrequent catalogs of the possible sins that might be committed. The ordinary sins of daily life, drunkenness, gluttony, and sexual misconduct, are never singled out for special attention and consequently hardly appear in the sermons. Pride (*gordost'*) and avarice (*srebroliubie*, literally love of silver) are the chief objects of his wrath. The main virtues are humility (*smirenie*), charity (*nishcheliubie*, literally love of the poor), and generosity (*shchedrota*). The selection of these sins as the main threats to man's salvation does not merely result from transplanting the worldview of the Kiev Academy to Moscow any more than the same selection by Khvorostinin meant such a mechanical borrowing from Ukrainian poets.[17]

Epifanii's emphasis on humility and charity did not imply that these were the only virtues he praised: the sermon on the prophetess Hannah was largely devoted to the praise of virtuous widowhood, and he occasionally mentions *tselomudrie* (chastity) and *vozderzhanie* (restraint, usually of the passions). However, in most cases when he touched on moral themes in passing, or when he devoted his sermon to morality, it was humility and charity that he called on his audience to cultivate. The sermon on the text *I potshchavsia izide i priiam ego razuiasia* ("And he made haste, and came down, and received him joyfully" [Luke 19:6]) is an explanation of the story of Zacchaeus, interpreting the lesson to be the importance of hospitality to strangers (*strannoliubie*), a virtue that is part of charity, and shows that Christ can turn an evil house into a good. That is, he puts "in place of untruth, truth, in place of impiety, piety, in place of niggardliness, abundance, in place of lack of mercy, mercy, in place of greed, generosity, in place of acquisitiveness, spending, in place of avarice, love of the poor, of the lack of alms, abundant almsgiving." Epifanii frequently talks about love (*milost'*) and finds that the way to Christian love is to cast out pride and to practice charity, so that his praise of love for one's fellow man is essentially a more general way of talking about humility and charity. The same theme comes into the sermons indirectly as well, as in *Ashche kto khoshchet po mne iti, da otverzhetsia sebe* ("Whosoever will come after me, let him deny himself" [Mark 8:34]) which is mainly about the need to reject worldliness, and attacks the attachment to wealth and honors, the main aspects of the world that lead men away from God. He lists other sins of the world: "much homosexuality, much adultery, much fornication, much drunkenness, much flattery [?], much murder, much avarice, much greed, much bearing of false witness, much untruth, many other numberless sins loathesome to God." A sermon that exhorts the audience to seek the kingdom of God, *Ishchite zhe pervoe tsarstva Bozhiia, i pravda ego* ("Seek ye first the kingdom of God, and his right-eousness" [Matt. 6:33]) also instructs the Christian who would seek that kingdom to cease the search for earthly wealth if he would find God. Over and over, Epifanii made it absolutely clear that the sins that threat-en mens' souls above all are pride and avarice.[18]

Epifanii also tried to provide his audience with some notion of how to improve their lives. The basis was of course correct faith and obedience to the Orthodox church, but he merely stated this requirement and did not elaborate on it except in attacking heresy. He did elaborate a pro-gram of prayer and repentance, not an organized program of specific devotions, but rather repeated calls to prayer and the demand for inward renewal, not merely external observance of God's commands. (Some of these sermons may have been designed for Lent.) Epifanii devotes much space to advice on how to overcome temptation, advising courage, pa-tience, and steadfast virtue in *Bdite i molites', da ne vnidite v iskushenie* (text from Psalm 106). In the sermon on the text *Vem zhe iako greshnikov* ("For we know them as sinners" [John 9:24]) he reminds the congregation that God hears the prayers only of the just, not the hypocritical prayers of sinners, and finally in *Bdite i molites'* (text from Matt. 27) he presents a full account of prayer, founded on compunction of the heart and combined with love, and judges it essential for a Christian life of humility and charity.[19]

Epifanii shared the concern of the Zealots of Piety for the moral state of the priesthood, and he devoted two of his sermons to their edification, both called "A Sermon to Priests" (*Slovo k iereem*). The first, beginning "*Sushchim Gospoda vsederzhitelia angelom*" exhorts the priests to avoid sin and remember that they must be worthy of the "Great Bishop" (*velikii arkhierei*), Christ. The priest must lead his flock, and himself remain a virtuous man if he is to be worthy of Christ. The second sermon on this topic, beginning "*Veleglasnyi prorok Bozhii Isaia*," is even more explicit. The priest needs a true Christian heart, "not proud but humble, not high in wisdom but humble in wisdom, not having earthly things but desiring heavenly things, not crooked but straight, not avaricious but loving the poor, not cruel but soft, not stone, but of linen." He must teach with love and meekness and try to heal in himself and others the diseases of the soul: "For the disease of the soul is the hatred loathsome to God, it is the envy that brings harm, it is the pride harmful to the mind, it is the [illegible] evil avarice, it is the untruth harmful to brotherhood, it is all-destroying slander, it is the insult to one's family, harmful to the soul. . . ." The priest must fight his own and others' sin, for the church is the only road to salvation.[20] The priesthood was thus one of the main instruments by which his moral concerns were to be brought to the individual Christian, perhaps especially important since his own preaching was necessarily rather remote. The emphasis on the moral reformation of the priesthood is reminiscent of the Zealots, and at the same time provides another link with Nikon, whom he supported to some extent in 1660. Epifanii does not, however, display the emphasis on the church hierarchy characteristic of Nikon and Ioakim except when the issue of heresy arises: then he demands obedience to the bishops. The differences are best explained by the situation of the various sermons, for his biography suggests that he remained in the good graces of the church as well as of the tsar.

Epifanii's sermons depict a worldview that was similar in its moral teaching to that of Khvorostinin or the Printing Office poets. He was also close to Nikon in his lack of interest in the cults of the saints. His one panegyric on a saint was to Iakov Borovitskii, the patron of Nikon's Iverskii Monastery that was also the exception to the patriarch's radical de-emphasis of the cults of saints. The content of his sermons meant a break, however, with the ideas of the Zealots, as did his evident loyalty to Nikon still displayed in 1660. This loyalty could last only so long, for Epifanii remained active long after his patron's downfall.

F. M. Rtishchev

In spite of his retired life and his rather difficult prose, Epifanii Slavinetskii had an effect on the world around him. This influence is manifest in the text of the life of the boyar F. M. Rtishchev, Epifanii's principal patron. This life, compiled after Rtishchev's death, is the closest we can get to a picture of the audience not only of Epifanii, but of his successor Simeon Polotskii as well, and further describes the immediate circle of both men at court.

Rtishchev's was an ancient family, though not of boyar rank. The six-teenth-century Rtishchevs were landholders on the southern frontier of the Russian state, and in 1627 F. M. Rtishchev's father, Mikhail Alekseevich, held only the rank of *likhvinskii dvorianin* (literally, gentleman of Likhvin, a small town on the steppe frontier), and rose to *moskovskii dvorianin* (gentleman of Moscow) only in 1629. He fought in the Smolensk War (1632–1634) and had married into a Smolensk family, whose lands by this time were under Polish rule. Mikhail reached the lower fringe of boyar rank in 1640 with the court title of *striapchii* (a sort of adjutant to the tsar), but it was his son, Fedor Mikhailovich, the subject of the life, that made the real career. Already in September 1645, only a few months after the accession of Tsar Aleksei Mikhailovich, the twenty-year-old F. M. Rtishchev already was a *striapchii* like his father. The life tells us that God wanted to glorify this pious youth, so by order of the tsar "this meek youth was taken into the Tsar's household, and because of his virtuous life he was honored with the service of chamberlain (*postel'nichii*)." This rank he achieved in 1648, at the age of twenty-three, and from then on he was a key figure at the Russian court.[21] Rtishchev founded a monastery on the Sparrow Hills southwest of Moscow, the Andreevskii Monastery, and had mainly Ukrainian monks brought there; Epifanii was intended to be one of their number but in fact spent his time in the Kremlin Chudov Monastery, so that Rtishchev patronized two centers of Ukrainian religious culture in the Russian capital. His court career, however, was not neglected. He accompanied the tsar in 1654 on campaign against Poland, and was involved in the negotiations with the nobles of Polish Lithuania, going on to head the Lithuanian chancellery (*Litovskii prikaz*), the Russian administration of the grand duchy of Lithuania in the years that Russia occupied the territory. In 1656 he entered the duma as an *okol'nichii* like his father, but never held boyar rank. In the late 1650s he went on to hold position in two court financial offices, the Palace Court Chancellery (*Dvortsovyi sudnyi prikaz*) and the Chancellery of the Great Palace (*Prikaz bol'shogo dvortsa*), two offices that nearly cost him his life. Both offices involved administration and justice in the palace, which meant not only the palace in the narrow sense, but also the many artisan and commercial districts of Moscow that were the property of the palace and paid rent and taxes to it. The Chancellery of the Great Palace also was an important part of the treasury, overseeing a number of other financial offices as well as its share of the revenue. As the Polish war dragged on, the government began to devalue the currency, producing massive hardship for the population of the capital, and in 1662 the mob streamed out of the city and besieged the tsar's suburban palace of Kolomenskoe, demanding punishment for Rtishchev (the "Copper Revolt"). According to the life, Rtishchev was so frightened that he nearly died, and found a priest to confess him. The revolt was suppressed, however, with aid of the foreign mercenary troops serving the Russian tsar, and Rtishchev remained in office until 1664, when he was given the post of tutor (*d'iadka*) to the tsarevich Aleksei Alekseevich, in association with Simeon Polotskii. Aleksei died in 1670, and Rtishchev followed him in 1673, at the age of forty-eight, only three years before the tsar himself. F. M. Rtishchev was a typical "new man" and courtier of the reign of Aleksei Mikhailovich, combining administrative and court positions and relying on the tsar's favor. In the early years of the reign he was close to the powerful favorite boyar B. I. Morozov (died 1661). He was friendly with Nikon during his patriarchate, but quarreled with him when Nikon broke with the tsar in 1658 (apparently the association was renewed in 1662), and he was on good terms with both Ordin-Nashchokin and B. M. Khitrovo in the 1660s.[22]

Rtishchev had the perfect court career, marred only by the "Copper Revolt" of 1662. The life compiled in the 1680s, however, paints a rather different picture. The Rtishchev of the life is noted mainly for his piety and his virtue, a virtue that is precisely what Epifanii and Simeon Polotskii were advocating, a life of humility and generosity toward the poor and unfortunate. According to the life, Rtishchev used to remonstrate quietly with Morozov when he thought the favorite's judgment was in error, though other courtiers were not courageous enough to do so. Since Rtishchev had the perfect love of God that casteth out fear, he reproved Morozov quietly and without uproar (*tikhoobrazno i bezmiatezhno*). His meekness also distinguished him from Patriarch Nikon, whose wrathfulness and rages caused him to err as well as to make enemies; here again Rtishchev was not afraid to point out Nikon's errors to him. When attacked by the mob or by slander, he put his trust in God and the tsar's knowledge of his virtue, and used patience rather than anger to justify his conduct. During wartime he took care of prisoners, ransomed captives, and protected merchants caught in the midst of the conflict. At home in Moscow he was moved by the sufferings of the poor to give alms and to build a hospital for the indigent. When he went to sell one of his villages, he lowered the price so that the new owner would not want to exact more from his former serfs, and he even freed his house serfs at his death. Needless to say, he brought up his charge, the tsarevich Aleksei, with great care and love, yet was so humble that when the tsar offered him full boyar rank, he protested his unworthiness and refused. Evidently his affection for the tsarevich was widely known, for shortly after Aleksei's death a nun of the Novodevichii Convent who had been one of his own servant women had visions of the dead tsarevich calling him to heaven.[23]

This ideal biography seems to contradict the record of the excessively successful courtier of real life, but for the men of the seventeenth century there was no contradiction. The circumstances of court were a given fact, and everyone knew that it was a place where a man could be praised for simply speaking his mind. In these circumstances the correct path for the Christian was humility, a virtue that both kept him from sin, for it restrained his ambition, and give him a certain moral authority at court, so that the humble courtier could restrain the excesses of others. For the successful courtier of lower noble origin like Rtishchev, these ideas were even more relevant, for his cultivation of humility warded off criticism by the aristocrats at court. The same religious ideal gave guidance in dealing with social inferiors as well, especially in a time of social unrest. The rebels of 1662 might accuse him of avarice and cruelty, but his charity toward the poor and unfortunate would absolve him before God. Rtishchev's life as described by his biographer exemplified all the ideas that had been current since Khvorostinin's time and came to fruition in the sermons of Epifanii Slavinetskii and Simeon Polotskii.

Simeon Polotskii

The culmination of the religious culture of the Russian court and boyar aristocracy in the seventeenth century was the work of Simeon Polotskii. His own obscure beginnings did not suggest that such brilliant success would be in his future. Simeon was born Samuil Emel'ianovich Petrovskii-Sitnianovich in 1629 in the town of Polotsk in northeastern Belorussia in the Polish-Lithuanian commonwealth. The young Sitnianovich apparently came from a well-off urban family, for his letters to his brother in 1667 are in Polish and the brother seems to have held responsible administrative positions in Minsk at that time.[24] In the years of Sitnianovich's youth the Orthodox townsmen of Polotsk were fighting an uphill battle against the Union. The Jesuits had founded a college in the town in 1580, and the killing of the Uniate bishop of Polotsk, Iosafat Kuntsevich, in nearby Vitebsk in 1623 was only the high point of decades of struggle. The relegalization of Orthodoxy in Poland in 1632 awarded the diocese of Polotsk to the Union, and in all Belorussia only the bishopric of Mstislavl' in the southeast was left to Orthodoxy. Rome's influence emanated from the Uniate metropolitan of Kiev, usually resident in Wilno or Novgorodok, as well as from the Uniate academy in Wilno. Unlike those in the Ukraine, noblemen in Belorussia were Catholic or Protestant, and Orthodoxy thus lacked lay patrons. Even worse, the Orthodox presses and lay brotherhoods in the towns that were still active around 1600 had fallen into decline by the 1640s. There were virtually no Orthodox cultural institutions left in the grand duchy of Lithuania in Sitnianovich's youth, and therefore he went to the Kiev Academy in the late 1640s and the Jesuit college in Wilno in 1650–1654. The apparent victory of Catholicism in Polotsk, however, was illusory. In western Belorussia, the population gradually gave in, but in the eastern towns of Polotsk, Vitebsk, Mogilev and Mstislavl', Orthodoxy remained strong among much of the urban and rural population. This was so much the case that in 1651 the hegumen Afinogen Kryzhanovskii of the Voskresenskii Monastery in Disna (near Polotsk) came to Moscow to plead for help against the Union, asserting that he had the support of the town magistrates of Polotsk. Kryzhanovskii was a somewhat dubious figure, and may have been exaggerating if not simply lying, but it does seem that Orthodoxy was stronger in eastern Belorussia, including among townsmen. The young Sitnianovich grew up in an area where the Orthodox faith survived among the laity of towns and villages but had increasingly suffered from Catholic repression.[25]

Like that of everyone else in the Polish state, Sitnianovich's life was turned around by the Khmel'nyts'kyi revolt, with the resultant Russo-Polish war and near-collapse of Poland. The Russian armies took Polotsk and Vitebsk in 1654, both long coveted by the tsars. The Orthodox clergy of the commonwealth, though presumably happy with the destruction of the Union, was not particularly enthusiastic about the Russian tsar or the possibility of subjection of their church to Moscow in place of Constantinople. They also remained politically loyal to the king of Poland in the early years of the war. In 1654–1656 the Orthodox clergy in the Ukraine and Belorussia seem to have been hostile to both hetman and tsar, and began to show signs of a shift only late in 1657, perhaps because of the apparently hopeless position of the Polish king, Jan Kazimierz. The death of the pro-Polish Orthodox metropolitan of Kiev, Syl'vestr Kosiv (1647–1657) may have helped as well. By 1658 most of them were opposed to the Hadiach Treaty in which Hetman Vyhovs'kyi tried to take the Ukraine back to Poland. The young Sitnianovich's reaction to all these events can be traced in his early poetry, and it parallels the political evolution of his colleagues. In 1653 he wrote (or copied) a panegyric to Metropolitan Syl'vestr. In 1654 he was presumably still in Wilno, which the Russian army captured only the following year. The early poem by the young Sitnianovich attacking the king of Sweden for his invasion of Poland in 1655 reflects this period. In any case, in 1656 at age twenty-seven, Samuil Sitnianovich entered the Orthodox Monastery of the Epiphany in Polotsk, taking the name Simeon, as he is better known. His next poems already show the shift in political views, for he greets the tsar on his return from the siege of Riga and on the capture of Dorpat, both events of the autumn of 1656. Another poem of the same year on Tsar Aleksei's abortive candidacy for the Polish throne shows that Simeon clearly wished for Russian victory in the war. The Russian success had religious consequences, and a poem of 22 June 1657 greeted the new Orthodox bishop of Polotsk and Vitebsk, Kallist.[26]

The cossack upheaval in the Ukraine and the Russian army in Belorussia swept Catholicism from the eastern lands of the commonwealth, both tsar and hetman showing particular hostility to the union. Orthodox townsmen frequently helped and supported the Russian armies, and the tsar tried to conciliate the nobility of the grand duchy by offering to preserve their political privileges and even the Catholic (Latin rite) church west of the Berezina River. The union, however, was to be extirpated, and urban mobs and the Russian armies carried out the expulsion of the Uniates and destruction of the union with a will. On this issue Tsar Aleksei as well was adamant. In this atmosphere of militantly restored Orthodoxy, Simeon spent eight years teaching the Orthodox youth of Polotsk.[27] For the newly restored Orthodoxy, the collapse of Polish authority and the expulsion of the Uniates did not mean the abandonment of the culture they had learned in the Kiev Academy and in the Polish schools; but that culture was put to quite different purposes. In both Polotsk and Kiev, the new learning was not conceived as Catholic ideology but merely as learning, a breach in the wall of confessionalism that was to prove basic to the cultural changes of the era in Russia as well. Simeon's *Stisi kraesoglasnii, glagolanii v leto 1660* already exemplified this process, for they were written to be delivered by the pupils of the Polotsk school to Tsar Aleksei. In them the poet praises the tsar for his defense of Orthodoxy and his greatness as a tsar. The form of the verse is that learned by the Orthodox from Polish poetry, but the content is praise of the absolute Orthodox tsar. The same is true of all of Simeon's occasional verse for the tsar. Perhaps Simeon would have been happy to stay in Orthodox Polotsk as part of the Russian state, but that was not to be. Poland's peace of Oliwa with Sweden in 1660 allowed the state to recover its strength, and in 1661 Polish armies recaptured Wilno and Mogilev, the most important towns of the region. Russia began to negotiate a peace, and the fighting dropped off sharply, but it was clear that Aleksei would not retain Belorussia. In 1664 Polish forces were skirmishing near Vitebsk, and about that time Simeon departed for Moscow never to return. His birthplace was surrendered without a shot to Poland as part of the truce of Andrusovo (30 January 1667). Simeon's departure for Moscow was not an isolated act, for the revival of Polish fortunes in the war combined with increasing anarchy at home (the Lubomirski revolt of 1663–1666) seems to have been the causes of general shift in the attitude of a part of the Ukrainian-Belorussian Orthodox clergy toward even closer identification with Russia. The learned Lazar Baranovych, bishop of Chernigov and a correspondent of Simeon, emerged as the chief spokesman of the pro-Russian party among the clergy.[28]

His early letters to Kiev reveal some dissatisfaction with the provinciality of the Moscow milieu, but Simeon quickly became involved in frenetic activity that did not cease until his death. In 1665 he was given space in the Zaikonospasskii Monastery in the Kitaigorod to open a small Latin school. The four known students at the beginning included Sil'vester Medvedev, later Simeon's principal follower and a major publicist, at that time a secretary of the Privy Chancellery; two subsecretaries of the palace administration; and a choirboy. He seems to have acquired a patron in the person of Paisios Ligarides, the Greek metropolitan of Gaza, then in Moscow on the affairs of the Greek church and heavily involved in the actions of tsar and church against Nikon and the Old Belief. Other and more important patrons among the clergy were the Serbian metropolitan Feodosii, then resident in Moscow; Pitirim, the metropolitan of Novgorod and later patriarch; Ilarion, the metropolitan of Riazan'; Lavrentii, the metropolitan of Kazan' (1667–1672); and, most important of all, Pavel, the former archimandrite of the Chudov Monastery and metropolitan Sarskii and Podonskii (Krutitskii, 1664–1675). Pavel was also a patron of Epifanii Slavinetskii.[29]

Simeon's attitude to the deposition of Nikon is not known, but in spite of his connections with Ligarides he was closer to Pavel, the Krutitskii metropolitan, who refused to sign the condemnation of Nikon. As a whole the Ukrainian clergy seems to have been sympathetic to the fallen patriarch. Lazar Baranovych was present at the council and said nothing in his defense, but expressed his sympathies for Nikon in correspondence. In spite of his apparent lack of enthusiasm for Nikon's deposition, Simeon soon rose to a pre-eminence in Russian religious life that he would keep until his death. When the 1666–1667 church council brought the final break with Avvakum, he was chosen to present the church's defense of its position against the Old Believers in the volume *Zhezl pravleniia* (*The Staff of Governance*). He was chosen by the tsar to be the instructor to the heir, Tsarevich Aleksei, and after the heir's untimely death in 1670, he went on to teach the new heir and future tsar, Fyodor Alekseevich. He became the major cultural force at court, bombarding it with endless panegyrics in verse, sermons for state occasions, and plays for the court theater that began in 1672. All the while he continued to write verse and numerous theological tracts and translations, acquiring Russian followers in Sil'vester Medvedev, Karion Istomin, and others. At the end of his life he put all this in order, collecting his adages and didactic verse in the *Vertograd mnogotsvetnyi* and the panegyrics in the *Rifmologion*. Two volumes of sermons were printed in the "Upper Typography," which Simeon controlled, but they saw the light only after his death, the *Obed dushevnyi* in 1681 and the *Vecheria dushevnaia* in 1683. Neither of the two volumes gives any indication of the audience, but the manuscripts of both works survive, and in the manuscript of the *Vecheria* there are notes describing the occasion of some sermons. Mostly these notes refer either to the tsar and court or to the Zaikonospasskii Monastery, where Simeon spent most of his time.[30]

Simeon's court circle also included certain boyars, for example F. M. Rtishchev and especially Boris Matveevich Khitrovo, who as head of the armory also was in charge of the icon painters. Many of the monk's poems were presented to him. In 1674–1676 three events threatened to reverse Simeon's favor: the election of Ioakim as Patriarch and the deaths in rapid succession of Metropolitan Pavel and Tsar Aleksei. The reign of Tsar Fyodor did bring something of a conservative reaction against the court theater, but the favor of the new tsar ensured that Simeon could flourish, and in 1679 he was able to set up his own printing press, the "Upper Typography," the only printing press in Moscow not under the power of Patriarch Ioakim. Furthermore, the reaction extended to the Greek clergy in Moscow, which could not please Ioakim. Only in 1681 did Ioakim succeed in reestablishing relations with the Greeks, after an unsuccessful attempt in 1678. Simeon enjoyed the favor of somewhat lesser figures such as the brothers Aleksei and Mikhail Likhachev and boyars such as princes M. G. and G. G. Romodanovskii, the latter an important general. He retained a powerful patron as well in Khitrovo until 1680, when both patron and client died.[31] Simeon Polotskii was the principal cultural and religious force among the court elite of Russia for sixteen crucial years (1664–1680), the last years of Old Russia and the eve of Peter's reforms.[32]

Recent scholarship has not only been able to appreciate better the aesthetics and ideology in Simeon's work, but it suggests a different understanding of Simeon's relationship to national culture. Simeon was explicitly and implicitly debating clearly Russian religious issues—the Old Belief and the problem of the tsar's role and authority, which had little or no analogy in Belorussia and the Ukraine—and so the older conception of him as simply an exotic foreign importation cannot be sustained. This is not to say that his cultural roots were irrelevant, for he viewed Russian problems through the prism of ideas formed in his youth in Polotsk, Wilno, and Kiev. He took from this youth the combination of militant Orthodoxy and a culture heavily permeated with Polish reading and ideas. He did not accept all these ideas uncritically. A striking aspect of Simeon's worldview was his intense monarchism, an ideology foreign to the Polish republic of the nobles, even to townsmen and to the Orthodox. Perhaps it was his experience in the years of revolt and war after 1648 that brought him to admire strong monarchs.[33] Simeon's response to the Kiev Academy was clearly not just one of passive absorption, for he seems to have rejected the intense loyalty of the academy to the Polish state. The Kiev Academy had been the work of Mohyla and the Orthodox nobility of the Ukraine, and as such its leadership was willing to flirt with Rome, if not with the existing Uniate church. After 1648 that option was closed, but in the hetmanate the new nobility, composed of nobles and the cossack officers, remained sympathetic to the idea of noble rights and privileges, including a self-government that ill accorded with Russian absolutism. The religious culture of the hetmanate responded to this situation, being essentially concerned with learned disputes with Catholic theologians and sermons directed at the unruly, rebellious, and often pro-Russian masses. The audience and problems of Ukrainian religious writers after 1648 were radically different from Simeon's, and it is not surprising that although he read their works, corresponded with them, and offered his friendship and patronage, he retained a basically different orientation. He was happy advising the heirs to an absolute monarchy, not the citizens of the often anarchic hetmanate, and made no move to return to Kiev. Simeon's patron was the tsar, not the hetman.

This was clearly a political and cultural-religious choice, for in spite of the uproar and destruction of those years the Kievan religious writers continued to publish.[34] Ioannykyi Haliatovs'kyi, the first of the important Ukrainian preachers, published his pioneering *Kliuch razumeniia* in 1659, with two more editions in 1662 and 1663. Lazar Baranovych published vast tomes of sermons in 1666 and 1674, and Antonii Radyvylovs'kyi one in 1676. This activity all took place in spite of continued anarchy in the Ukraine (the so-called *Ruina*), which lasted until the end of the wars with Turkey in 1681. Simeon's continued good relations with his Ukrainian counterparts, especially Baranovych, did not result in sermons that duplicated his Ukrainian friends' homilies. To be sure, the Ukrainians were concerned with the evils of pride and avarice, like Simeon and Epifanii Slavinetskii, but they more frequently castigated drunkenness, and mentioned sexual sins almost as often as pride and greed. Their chief concern, however, seems to have been love of power and injustice, a natural concern in the anarchic situation of the hetmanate. In addition, the most sophisticated preachers (Haliatovs'kyi and later St. Dmitrii of Rostov) also produced numerous contributions to the miracle cults: throughout the century Ukrainian presses issued fat volumes of miracles of the Kiev Monastery of the Caves, of the Mother of God, and of other cults. The Ukrainians were also much more positive about monastic asceticism, mentioning and recommending it frequently, and praising virginity with great enthusiasm. The positive attitude toward monasticism goes along with great concern for the church as an institution. Haliatovs'kyi wrote his book for the use of the parish clergy, and spent a great deal of time exhorting members of the priesthood to a better life, crucial if they were to influence the population. The emphasis on the church and monasticism was natural for the Ukrainians in other respects, for the church was still staffed by the elite (unlike Russia), very wealthy by local standards, highly educated, and a crucial part of the social structure of the newly established hetmanate. Simeon, however, was not as much concerned with the parish clergy, and the Ukrainian views on this point were closer to those of the Zealots.[35]

Simeon's Ukrainian education did not prevent him from preaching on themes that were important in Russia, in his choices following in the footsteps of Khvorostinin, the Printing Office poets, and Epifanii Slavinetskii. Naturally many of his sermons were devoted merely to explaining the religious significance of certain festivals, such as his sermon on the festival of the birth of the Mother of God. Most sermons, however, especially those in the *Obed dushevnyi*, stressed the evils of sin and the need for a virtuous life, and that meant above all the avoidance of avarice and pride and the cultivation of humility and generosity. The importance of such ideas to Simeon was noted by Robinson in his commentary on Simeon's use of the parable of Lazarus, and he correctly observes that the interpretation here is entirely in accord with Simeon's acceptance of the existing social hierarchy; that is, he merely wants the rich to act in accord with their duty to the poor, rather than seeing them as the object of damnation. Simeon was indeed no social revolutionary nor even a strict moralist, and his language and style dealing with this issue reflect this moderation. His call is to repentance, and to avoid the snares of the world and attain the kingdom of heaven, but he insists on this point with great consistency. The solution to the moral dilemma posed by wealth is quite simple to Simeon, and that is the giving of alms (*milostynia*). On riches he says:

All mortal sins are from wealth. The pride in Nebuchadnezzar was from wealth, the avarice in Judas was for the sake of wealth, the uncleanness among the Sodomites was from wealth, envy is about wealth, according to the parable (Prov. 28, Luke 16): the envious man strives to enrich himself but does not know that the merciful man possesses it [wealth], gluttony and drunkenness in the rich man in the Gospel are from wealth. The rich are wrathful, like the impious Haman at Mordecai and the whole people of Israel. Sloth is usual among the rich [and "as the door turneth upon his hinges, so doth the slothful upon his bed"] (Prov. 26:14).

But Simeon's desire is to convince the rich to use their wealth properly, for charity, for then it is not harmful to their salvation. "Gold is harmless to salvation if one does not serve it, but rules it, giving it away abundantly and willingly, distributing it to the beggars and the poor, spending it on holy and divine things, like the temples of God and church vestments, on holy monasteries, on schools for the young, orphanages, and similar things."[36] The basis of virtue, according to Simeon, even more than almsgiving, is humility, and he stresses this idea especially in Lenten sermons. Commenting on the text, "whosoever will be great among you, shall be your minister" (Mark 10:43), he explains that Christ here

teaches us that the humble virtues are to be placed in our hearts as the hard and immovable foundation of all virtues, for according to the words of St. John Chrysostom, every man who has placed humility [in his heart] places all other things without fail, preaching that if it is taken away, even if you rise high to dwell to heaven itself, all will be taken away together and at the end the evil ones will fall (Homilies on Matt. 5, chapter 5, homily 15).[37]

His sermons for festivals in the *Vecheria* reveal some of the specific applications of his moral ideas to the lives of the hierarchy, parish clergy, monks, and various kinds of laymen, as well as his views of miracle cults, the Old Belief, and other religious issues. This is not surprising, as many of these sermons were written for occasions where such people were in the audience, as we know from his notes in the manuscript. He did not record all the occasions, but those that he did are revealing. He preached before the tsar himself on St. Elijah's day (23 July) 1672 and wrote a sermon for the tsar's confessor Andrei Savinov in the same year. One sermon he delivered in the Church of the Holy Spirit near the Prechistenskii Gates, a region where many boyars lived. Similarly the two exemplary funeral sermons were written for Archimandrite Amvrosii of the Bogoiavlenskii Monastery in the Kitaigorod district of Moscow, also an aristocratic area, as the sermons indicate. They are for the burial of an "honorable" man and woman. The largest number of the sermons written for others were intended for his patron, Metropolitan Pavel Sarskii and Podonskii, who often conducted services for the tsar. The context shows. In his sermon on St. Filipp the metropolitan of Moscow, St. Filipp's humility (*smirenie*) is singled out for praise, in this case referring to his actions as hegumen of the Solovetskii Monastery and metropolitan, for Simeon the good courtier only indirectly mentions his execution by Ivan the Terrible. Pride is the characteristic sin of the rich and powerful, together with avarice, but also of heretics, and of rebellious peasants as well. In demanding humility of the poor the message is clear that they are to obey their superiors, but in demanding humility of the rich several things are involved. On the one hand humility goes along with charity in defining humane treatment of the lower orders, but on the other hand humility is necessary in the dealings of the rich with one another. Simeon does not seem to regard obedience to the tsar as mandated by the need for humility, and in general does not in the sermons preach the necessity of political obedience by the nobility. Perhaps he was just avoiding the issue, but in any case humility is required for the exercise of office and for relations among courtiers, not primarily for relations with the Tsar.[38]

Simeon followed earlier Russian religious writers in what he avoided or downplayed. Drunkenness scarcely appears in the sermons, for example, and sexual sins appear only in certain contexts. In his sermons he occasionally praises virtuous widowhood, and even virginity in the sermon on St. Catherine, and there is probably more attention to sexual restraint in Simeon than in Epifanii Slavinetskii, but he rarely brings up the question in more general contexts, as do the Ukrainian preachers. The role of sexuality in morality was closely tied to monasticism, and Simeon's views here seem equally ambiguous, for in his sermon on St. Sergii of Radonezh he holds out monasticism as the example of the perfect life, interpreted in a moral sense as showing humility and passionlessness. In general he is respectful of the monastic tradition in the sermons, yet in his unpublished verses on monks in the *Vertograd mnogotsvetnyi* he briefly sketches the ideal but goes on to a long catalog of the sins of the monks of his day, a view that seems to have been generally shared. Monks, according to the poem, ride about in carriages and drink themselves into oblivion, have mistresses, and completely ignore the vow of poverty. He calls on them to return to the ancient ideals, but neither here nor in the sermons does he seem very sanguine about the prospect.[39]

Simeon deviated noticeably from the Ukrainian preachers on the issue of miracles and icons. Naturally Simeon reaffirmed the church's teaching on miracles, but in practice he avoided the subject when the opportunity presented itself. His sermons on the saints, many of whom (Sts. Peter and Aleksei, the metropolitans of Moscow, and St. Feodosii Pecherskii) had miracle cults, do not dwell on the miracles if they mention them at all. The numerous sermons on the archetype of all miracle-working icons, the Savior Not-created-by-hands (*Spas nerukotvornyi*), do not contradict this pattern, for they were delivered to honor the patron image of the

Zaikonospasski Monastery, where Simeon had his school. The sermons on the feast days of the important miracle-working icons of the Russian state, the Vladimir, Kazan', and Tikhvin icons, use the occasion to praise the virtues of the Mother of God more than the miracles associated with the icons: "Pure are the heavens, which accept no strange imagining, pure is the sun, pure is the moon, pure is fire, pure is air, pure are the saints, pure are the angels, but purer than these is the most blessed Virgin. . . . And the most spotless Virgin never was aroused by improper passion, neither was she darkened by the dark smoke of sin."[40] Simeon defends the devotion to icons, but by restating the classic position of St. John Damascene on the subject, that icons are merely an image, a reflection of the divine, and thus are only a means to come closer to God. The emphasis on the actual icon, not on the miracle cult that may be associated with it, put him in harmony with the church's policy since Nikon's time, and serves as a commentary on it.[41] Simeon's position in this manner followed the whole thrust of his teaching, in the sermons and elsewhere, that religion had to be based on knowledge, on learning that included a thorough command of Latin, Greek, and Slavonic, as well as secular learning. This observation is often made in the literature, but its implications are not always drawn out as fully as is necessary. A learned faith, in his mind, necessarily implied a faith based on the authority of the church that downgraded popular miracle cults as much as it excluded popular amusements. It imposed on the lower orders the duty of passive obedience, but it also imposed on the nobility and clergy the duty not only to live a virtuous life but also to acquire an education sufficient to inform their faith. Indeed learning was supposed to directly lead to moral improvement, as Simeon's verse insists upon: "Nature only gives us things to live on, / Philosophy teaches us to live well / The former we have in common with beasts, / The latter makes us like angels." Or: "Philosophy corrects their [those of the rich] mores." Or: "Wisdom pleases me, I will live with her, / And I will not think of wealth."

This type of statement never appears in the sermons, which present good morals as strictly the result of correct and deep faith. It might seem that Simeon was preaching two doctrines, philosophy for the learned and faith for the unlearned, but that is probably greater consistency than he possessed; the unpublished poems have many testimonies to the importance of faith.[42]

The equation of philosophy and religion here is a cliché of post-Renaissance European thought. In the specific context of Russia in the 1670s, however, it had somewhat larger implications, making secular learning acceptable in a society still fundamentally religious. The insistence on the moral benefits of such philosophy gave it a religious function analogous to that of the sermons. It prepared the church, or least those elements in it that were influenced by Simeon, for the next phase in Russian culture, the beginnings of secular rationalism in the

Petrine age. While Simeon strove to make his own age more deeply religious through his learning, he unwittingly prepared the elite of Russian society for secularization.[43]

Simeon Polotskii's Enemies

Simeon Polotskii's death in 1680 did not mark the end of his influence. The two books of sermons, the verse Psalter, and the new edition of the story of Barlaam and Josaphat circulated even in provincial Russia. The tsar ordered even obscure Siberian monasteries supplied with the sermons, and within a few years of Simeon's death they appeared among the very few books in the library of the Kalmykovy, a merchant family of Nizhnii Novgorod. Better yet, they were consciously imitated in 1683–1687 by a priest in the town of Orel-gorodok in the vast Stroganov domain in the Urals. This anonymous priest left a vast collection of sermons called the *Statir*, which seems to have aroused the wrath of his parishioners, although the Stroganovs themselves protected him.[44] All this occurred despite the increasing controversy surrounding his name in the 1680s with the eruption of a eucharistic debate that pitted the Ukrainian church and Simeon's Russian associates against Patriarch Ioakim.

This is not the place to examine this controversy in detail, but a brief description of this epilogue to Simeon's life will serve to clarify his position. The controversy did not touch the nature of the eucharist itself but rather revolved around the precise moment in the mass when the bread and wine changed into the body and blood of Christ. The Catholic church taught that the moment occurred when the priest pronounced the words of institution (Matt. 26:26–28, "Take, eat; this is my body. . . . Drink ye all of it; For this is my blood. . . .") while the Orthodox position was that it was the priest's prayer (the *epiklesis*) that effected the change. Patriarch Ioakim asserted that the position of the Ukrainians and of Sil'vestr Medvedev, Simeon Polotskii's best pupil and his successor in Russia, was the Catholic position and contrary to Orthodox faith. Ioakim was at the same time locked in a struggle with the metropolitan of Kiev, trying to force the Ukrainian church to recognize the Moscow patriarch and not the patriarch of Constantinople as its immediate superior, and historians have suspected, probably correctly, that the real issue here was one of ecclesiastical politics. It was precisely at this time that Simeon was accused of "Latin" sympathies and orientation, while Epifanii Slavinetskii was proclaimed the champion of an exclusive "Greek" learning. The author of this bit of historical falsification was probably Epifanii's old pupil Evfimii Chudovskii, the editor of his manuscripts, his fellow monk of the Chudov Monastery, and in the 1680s a close ally of Ioakim (also formerly a Chudov monk). Ioakim was not a particularly well-educated man, and he needed educated men around him to produce the vast polemical works that came out under his name—two long attacks on the Old Believer Nikita "Pustosviat" and one on Medvedev (the *Osten*). Evfimii provided this service along with Karion Istomin (died 1717), who in the 1670s was a follower of Simeon but who later switched sides.[45]

Ioakim, however, did not merely attack Simeon's and Medvedev's eucharistic theology, but also tried to provide an alternative moral teaching and type of sermon to those of Simeon. Ioakim himself probably wrote little if anything of these sermons, but a number of manuscripts contain sermons written by Evfimii and Karion for Ioakim and the last patriarch, Adrian (1690–1702).[46] The contents reflect very clearly the priorities of Ioakim and Adrian, for they include a sermon in praise of the eucharist and enjoining the faithful to come to church in the proper spirit of humility before God and the church. The inclusion of the lives of metropolitans Filipp and Aleksei reflects Ioakim's concern for the authority of the church. These concerns are spelled out by a sermon for the Russian army delivered on the feast of St. Aleksei (17 March, presumably 1689), probably written for Ioakim by Evfimii. The text is a long attack on the sins of the age, and they are quite different from what Epifanii or Simeon conceived them to be. The primary evil is heresy, and the heretics have upset the good order and morals of the Orthodox community, bringing drunkenness and gluttony, gambling, and mutual injuries among the people. Drunkenness seems to the author the chief private sin, but far worse than this is disobedience to the authority of the church: in the old days there was no discussion of theology, but now the heretics have led everyone to talk about it. The faithful must mend their ways, they must continue to pray for the dead, to observe the fasts, to abstain from eating unclean animals, they must not shave their beards or smoke tobacco. All these things are now subject to question, for everyone (*iako blagorodnii, tako i prostii liudi*) drinks and smokes at will, sleeps through church services, and says that there is no use in the church's rituals (*chin v terkvi*), in praying for the souls of the departed, or calling on the saints. Since the heretics have undermined obedience to the church, sexual license, gambling, dancing, and the eating of meat on fast days have spread everywhere. Presumably the heretics alluded to (but never named) are the Old Believers and Sil'vestr Medvedev. The explicit conservatism of this sermon is paralleled by Evfimii's homily on the miracle of St. Michael the Archangel in Chonae, the event commemorated in the name of the Chudov (Miracle) Monastery. In contrast to Simeon's use of such events as an excuse to moralize, Evfimii dwells on the miracle, narrating it in tedious detail and affirming at the end the importance of asceticism, of mortification of the flesh—that is, he reaffirms the monastic ideal in all its purity.[47]

Finally, Evfimii Chudovskii put a new twist onto the old theme of both his teacher Epifanii and his enemy Simeon, that is, charity. Probably between 1675 and 1682 he compiled an entire "Sermon on Charity" (*Slovo o milosti*), which to a large extent repeated the arguments for the need for charity in the form of almsgiving. The new element, however, was a concrete proposal for the establishment of almshouses under the control of the church, with detailed plans of just how to do this. Not surprisingly, the fervent enemy of the Latins borrowed here from the most famous of the Polish Jesuits, Piotr Skarga, who had actually set up such charitable institutions in Krakow a century before. As in the case of Skarga, this implied not only an improvement in the life of at least some of the poor, but also a clericalization of charity. While Epifanii and Simeon appealed to the individual, Evfimii appealed to the church and the tsar. Already in 1673 the church had taken some measures, and Tsar Fyodor followed suit in 1682.[48]

Throughout the 1680s the patriarch's struggle was not particularly successful, for the regent Sophia and the favorite Golitsyn were Medvedev's patrons. He did score some victories, for in 1686 the Ukrainian church accepted the overlordship of the Moscow patriarch, though later events would make this victory largely empty. He also succeeded in sidetracking Medvedev's 1682 plan for a Moscow academy on the Kiev model. In 1687 he established the Slavo-Greco-Latin Academy under the control of the Greek Leikhudes brothers, who had arrived in Moscow two years before. The "Greek" quality of this institution was limited to the nationality of the directors and instruction in the language, however, for the Leikhudes had been educated in Padua.[49] Whatever Ioakim intended, the academy inevitably taught its Russian pupils a variant of the same culture predominant in Kiev. Ioakim's victory seemed to come in 1689. His own differences with Sophia led him to ally with the young Peter, and support him in his coup d'etat and proclamation of his decision to rule in his own right. In return Peter rewarded his ally, and Ioakim got his victim: Medvedev was tried for heresy and executed early in 1690, only a few months after Sophia's fall. Ioakim himself scarcely outlived his antagonist and died at the end of the same year, to be replaced by Adrian, who proved to be the last patriarch of Old Russia. Ultimately Medvedev was to be the victor, for after 1700 Peter's cultivation of Ukrainian prelates was to bring an even more "Latinized" Orthodoxy into the Russian church.[50]

The sermons of the seventeenth century, of Epifanii Slavinetskii, Simeon Polotskii, and the others, provide the clearest insight into the quality of religious thought and life in that era as well as into the social and political context of religion. The seventeenth century was not only the century of the absorption and adaptation of Ukrainian Baroque style in Russian literature, but also of the didacticism that was the content accompanying that style. Many of the concerns of Kiev were remote in Moscow and vice-versa: the preachers in Moscow preached mainly to the court, the tsar, his family, the boyars, and the clergy of the capital, not to the masses. The preachers' concerns were those of the audience, that is, how to preserve a virtuous life in the face of the moral temptations of court life and great wealth, the temptations of avarice and pride. This concern was both moral and social, and more than a mere instrument of social control, for court life in Russia had new dimensions. The beginnings of absolute rule and the final establishment of serfdom in 1649 created new moral dilemmas. The obvious sincere concern with moral issues was sparked by these new phenomena, and the traditional morality offered only imperfect answers. In the course of the century, with the decline of monasticism and the increasing restrictions on the popular miracle cults, preaching seemed to be stepping in to provide the needed religious guidance. For a short time at the end of the century, from about 1650 to 1690, preaching seems to have filled the gap, as Simeon Polotskii first acquired fame and favor at court and then spread his message by the printed word even to the Volga and the Urals. However, the even greater changes that were afoot quickly relegated Simeon to relative obscurity, eclipsed as he was not only by later preachers but by the full brilliance of European secular culture. In a sense, he contributed to his own demise, for the emphasis on learning and on morality produced a religion ultimately very close to a secular ethics. For the time, however, Epifanii Slavinetskii and Simeon Polotskii represented the mainstream of religion in Russia, and both used their talents and influence to try to form a religious consciousness that valued humility and generosity toward the poor above all.

Conclusion

Peter the Great did not come to the throne in August 1689 of a country possessing a simple, organic religious culture, slightly affected only by "Western" influence, as tradition would have it. The previous two centuries were periods of continuous change, gathering speed after 1645. The starting point of these changes was the decline of the authority and central importance of monasticism, a decline that is visible after about 1530.

This decline had the effect of leaving the church without a central focus of leadership over the laity, and the church tried to solve the problem by various attempts to strengthen the role of the bishops, not with entire success. At the same time, the boyar aristocracy seems to have withdrawn from even the limited role in religious life that it played before, into a world that was largely political and ever more centered on the court. The vacuum left by these changes was filled, as it were, by the miracle cults. Earlier Russians had admired and venerated living monastic saints, had gone to them for advice, and recorded their deeds in written lives, copied and recopied through the years after their death. In the sixteenth and early seventeenth centuries new living saints were few and far between, and Russians preferred to visit the tombs of older saints, usually placed in monastery churches, where in the presence of the holy relics cures were effected. The Russians who made these pilgrimages were not the boyars but the townspeople and the peasantry, with a sprinkling of lesser nobles. The shrines were a manifestation of popular religious sentiment (how widespread we cannot say) that was recorded and admired by the upper classes, a sort of myth of social harmony and unity, as well as a means for the monasteries to hold on to their authority. The attitude of the church to the shrines was somewhat ambiguous, favorable in principle, but always on the lookout for questionable cults.

In the seventeenth century these patterns began to break down. The Time of Troubles seems here to have been a watershed, calling into question the previous religious value system. The new social and political situation, growing autocracy and serfdom, prompted the changes. Soon after the election of Tsar Michael in 1613, some noblemen and chancellery secretaries began to turn to Ukrainian Orthodox writers for guidance, looking for both new form and new content. The situation of the Ukrainians was quite different from that of Khvorostinin or the Printing Office poets, and considerable adaptation was necessary to make the Ukrainian learning relevant, but by midcentury Russian religious writers, in the establishment and out of it, were generally familiar with Ukrainian religious writings. The Russian innovators did not find all of it relevant, especially the large mass of confessional polemics. The Russian writers emphasized moral problems much more than their Ukrainian models, and in particular the sins of pride and greed.

After the accession of Tsar Aleksei in 1645, the pace of change quickened. The changes came in two waves, first the ascendancy of the Zealots of Piety and Nikon (1645–1658), and then changes in the religious culture of the court. At first, the young tsar and his confessor, Stefan Vonifat'ev, the leader of the Zealots, tried to improve the quality of religious life at the parish level, reforming liturgical practices, requiring preaching, and outlawing popular festivals. Nikon continued this program but shifted the emphasis sharply toward raising the status of the clergy—in his mind the bishops and himself, not the parish priests. Nikon's downfall opened the way for a thorough reorganization of the religious culture of the court, which put preaching at the center of religious observance. This aim was accomplished in large part by the learned monks of the Kiev Academy, Epifanii Slavinetskii and Simeon Polotskii. From Epifanii's arrival in 1649 until Simeon's death in 1680, both were de facto the court preachers at the Russian court. They spread the knowledge of Latin and Western literature as well, adding to the Ukrainian religious literature some of the Latin culture of Baroque Europe. Their sermons were among their most important contributions, for these were an attempt to bring Orthodoxy and its moral teaching to the elite, the court society, in a new form. The sermons had a new content as well, for they were not merely tired summaries of traditional Orthodox Christian teachings. They followed in the tracks of Khvorostinin and the Printing Office poets. Epifanii also stressed the sins of pride and greed, contrasting them to the virtues of humility and charity (or more literally, love of the poor). Simeon followed this emphasis and, in this, underlined the fundamental unity of thoughts between the two. This unity of thought paralleled a unity of culture, for both of them were products of the Baroque Latin world of the Kiev Academy. The distinction between "Latins" and "Grecophiles" did not arise until the next generation, in the 1680s. Something that Epifanii and Simeon did not take from the Ukrainian church or the Baroque Latin world farther west was a thorough indifference to the miracle cults. In this they paralleled the Russian church's policy from Nikon's time onward, which sharply restricted the number of festivals for the saints and exerted increasing control over local cults, in large part out of fear that the Old Belief provoked any uncontrolled manifestations of popular religion. By 1680 the religious culture of Russia's elite revolved around moral problems, not monasticism or miracles. The basis for Peter's secularization of Russian culture had been laid.

The role of these changes as necessary antecedents to the Petrine reforms suggests some of their larger implications for Russian history. First it suggests that the crucial factor in the importance of "influence" of the West was what the Russians wanted from the West. They chose what they wanted and rejected the rest. The contact with Italy in the period 1470–1520 was quite extensive in a way, for Milanese architects built almost the whole of the Kremlin complex, walls, churches, and palaces (the latter later altered), and Maksim Grek brought to Russia at least the philological side of Renaissance culture. The effect of all this was minimal, however, and Maksim's work was simply absorbed into the existing religious world. From the late sixteenth century on, Moscow maintained a flourishing "German" quarter of Protestant Northern Europeans, which included Germans, Dutch, Scottish, and English inhabitants, and the effect of these settlers (outside the military realm) was almost nil. Their largest contribution was the provision of actors for the plays of the court theater of the 1670s, a theater created under the guidance of the Polish-trained Belorussian monk Simeon Polotskii. For it was Kiev hundreds of miles to the southwest, not the Germans down the street, that attracted the Russians, and this in spite of traditionally greater tolerance of Protestants over Catholics and suspicion of the purity of Ukrainian Orthodoxy under Catholic rule. When the Russians turned to Kiev, they also selected what they wanted. The miracle cults that flourished in the Ukraine and were celebrated by its preachers evoked no response, nor did the confessional polemics or the particular moral emphases of Ukrainian preachers. Through Kiev the Russians also came to know an increasing quantity of Polish writings as well as Western European works in Polish translation, but again, the Russians were selective.

In large part this was the result of differences in circumstance and practice. Central and Eastern European miracle cults during the Counter Reformation were major phenomena, and in both Poland and the Habsburg lands nobles were enthusiastic participants, judging from the surviving records. Russian boyars were uninterested, the church grew cautious after 1653, and so the literature of Counter-Reformation miracle cults had no impact. Preaching was different, and here through Kiev the preachers of Poland and Catholic Europe had an impact, particularly in matters of form and in the role of preaching in religious life.

The second larger implication is that the evolution of religion (and therefore of culture as a whole) in Russia in these centuries led the country down a road that rapidly converged with that of Western Europe. Both Reformation and Counter Reformation had resulted in an enormous increase in the role of preaching among Protestants and Catholics, so that the Orthodox church, at least in Moscow if not the provinces, grew much more similar to the Christian churches of the West, in practice if not in dogma. These preachers were speaking to the Russian court and landholding class, and their impact was entirely on that elite, not on the masses. This was not a small contribution, for in recasting Orthodoxy along largely moral lines, the preachers brought the Russian boyars very close to the culture of virtue that Otto Brunner characterized as the hallmark of European noble culture in the early modern era.[1] The notion of virtue in the sermons was also an individual notion, for the whole purpose of the sermon was to move the individual listener, not the community or the state, to a better life. Differences remained, for the Russian preachers stressed humility and charity, not justice and restraint, but they also had moved beyond asceticism to a morality designed for action in the world. In this way they created a foundation for the future. The evolution of religious life and thought inside Russia brought the country up to the gate of Europe. Peter opened it.

Appendix: The Manuscripts of Epifanii Slavinetskii's Sermons

At the present there are five known copies of the sermons of Epifanii Slavinetskii. The most important is GIM, Synodal Collection, Sin. 597, written in Epifanii's own handwriting on ff. 90–97v. There are altogether six different hands in the manuscript, including Epifanii's, all of them Ukrainian cursive (*skoropis'*) of the seventeenth century. There are also marginal corrections in the hand of Evfimii Chudovskii. The sermons, thirty in number, were written on separate sheets of paper of uneven size and later sewn together. The watermarks on ff. 20, 37, and 107 confirm the date, as they are similar to those known from the 1670s and 1680s (coat of arms of Amsterdam). Another manuscript in the Synodal collection (Sin. IV) contains some of the same sermons as Sin. 597, and is mostly of later date, although two sermons are from Epifanii's hand.[1]

Recently A. S. Eleonskaia has discovered a manuscript of the end of the seventeenth century, also in GIM (Barsov collection 459) containing copies of twenty-one sermons also in Sin. 597 and the "Slovo o milosti." A fourth manuscript is MS 290П/145 in the Central Scientific Library of the Ukrainian Academy of Sciences in Kiev. The text is written in Russian (not Ukrainian) *ustav* (uncial) with a contemporary inscription stating that it was presented by Patriarch Ioakim but not giving the name of the person to whom it was presented. It came to the academy from the library of the Kiev Monastery of the Caves, and it is possible that this or some other Ukrainian monastery was given the manuscript in the 1680s, at the time when Ioakim was trying to use Epifanii's legacy against Medvedev. It contains forty-one sermons attributed to Epifanii, as well as patristic homilies, a dialogue on the eucharist that is also found in the *Osten,* a tract attributed to Epifanii on certain grammatical questions in the creed, and a list of Epifanii's writings. The title page attributes all forty-one sermons to Epifanii, although there is no independent confirmation of eleven of them (the others are in Sin. 597). The hand is late seventeenth century, and it closely resembles those such as Sin. 221, which clearly came from the patriarchal scriptorium.[2] I examined Sin. 597, Sin. IV, and the Kiev manuscript, but not MS Barsov 459 or the collection of Epifanii's sermons among the sermons of Afanasii of Khomogory in the Archangel collection of the library of the Academy of Sciences in Leningrad. Afanasii's preaching career began in the 1680s, so these are apparently late copies as well.[3]

Notes

Introduction

1. There is no account of the evolution of the historiography of the Russian church. Some useful pages are to be found, however, in Georgii Florovskii, *Puti russkogo bogosloviia*, 3d ed. (Paris, 1983), the principal work on the history of theology in the past two centuries.
2. Metropolitan Makarii (Bulgakov), *Istoriia russkoi tserkvi*, vols. 1–12 (St. Petersburg, 1877–1891); cf. 10:224–32; 11:212–22; 12:9, 114–18, 218–26. Golubinskii also never completed his monumental church history, which stops in the mid-sixteenth century. His main work was E. E. Golubinskii, *Istoriia russkoi tserkvi*, 4 vols. (Moscow, 1883–1916) and idem, *K nashei polemike s staroobriadtsami* (Moscow, 1905). Cf. Florovskii, *Puti*, 372–73.
3. D. S. Likhachev, *Chelovek v literature drevnei Rusi*, 2d ed. (Moscow, 1970); and his *Razvitie russkoi literatury X–XVII vekov: Epokhi i stil'* (Leningrad, 1973).
4. A. N. Robinson, *Bor'ba idei v russkoi literature XVII v.* (Moscow, 1974); A. S. Eleonskaia, *Russkaia publitsistika vtoroi poloviny XVII v.* (Moscow, 1978); and A. N. Robinson, ed., *Russkaia staropechatnaia literatura (XVI-pervaia chetvert' XVIII v.): Simeon Polotskii i ego knigoizdatel'skaia deiatel'nost'* (Moscow, 1982).
5. G. P. Fetdotov, *Sviatye drevnei Rusi*, 3d ed. (Paris, 1985), 176–77, 187–90.
6. Further impulses (less well studied) came from the Greeks of the Ottoman empire and the Venetian possessions, who were not carriers of "traditional Byzantinism" but of the culture of the University of Padua. Padua was the alma mater of almost all important Greek scholars from Theophilus Corydaleus (c. 1574–1646) to lesser folk like the Leikhudes brothers who came to Russia in 1685.

Chapter 1

1. Gerhard Podskalsky, *Christentum und theologische Literatur in der Kiever Rus' (988–1237)* (Munich, 1982), 50; Ia. N. Shchapov, *Gosudarstvo i tserkov' drevnei*

Rusi X–XIII vv. (Moscow, 1989); V. O. Kliuchevskii, *Drevnerusskie zhitiia sviatykh kak istoricheskii istochnik* (Moscow, 1871; reprint, Moscow, 1988), 58–65 (including the very doubtful exception of Bishop Arkadii [died 1163], whose life in sixteenth-century manuscripts seemed to Kliuchevskii archaic in style); G. Iu. Filippovskii, "Zhitie Leontiia˙ Rostovskogo," in *Slovar' knizhnikov i knizhnosti drevnei Rusi, vyp. 1. (XI–pervaia polovina XIV v.)*, ed. D. S. Likhachev (Leningrad, 1987), 159–61; L. A. Dmitriev, "Zhitie Varlaam a Khutynskogo," in ibid., 138–42; and Richard D. Bosley, "The Saints of Novgorod: À propos of A. S. Chorošev's Book on the Church in Medieval Novgorod," *Jahrbücher für Geschichte Osteuropas* 32 (1984): 1–15. The lives of the saints are the principal source for the role of monks and others in the church, though chronicles provide some information. The church historians of the nineteenth century were especially interested in the history of the hierarchy, so that the monastic character of the church comes through less clearly than in primary sources: Metropolitan Makarii [Bulgakov], *Istoriia russkoi tserkvi;* Golubinskii, *Istoriia,* and, in that tradition, A. V. Kartashev, *Ocherki po istorii russkoi tserkvi,* 2 vols. (Paris, 1959).

2. Metropolitan Kiprian, "Zhitie . . . Petra," in *Stepennaia kniga, PSRL,* 21: 321–32; "Zhitie . . . Aleksiia," in "Voskresenskaia letopis'," *PSRL,* 8:26–28; and N. Shliakov, "Zhitie sv. Aleksiia mitropolita moskovskogo v pakhomievskoi redaktsii," *IORIaS* 19 (1914): 85–152; Kliuchevskii, *Drevnerusskie,* 74–77, 82–88, 134–40; Nikolai Barsukov, *Istochniki russkoi agiografii,* Izdaniia obshchestva liubitelei drevnei pis'mennosti 81, (St. Petersburg, 1882), 27–32, 431–50; Golubinskii, *Istoriia,* 2, pt. 1:116–20, 188–90, 405–9, 495–99, 544–45, 558. Shchapov, *Gosudarstvo i tserkov',* 76–123, demonstrates that the legal powers of bishops consisted of jurisdiction over clergy and family disputes. When the lives of the Novgorod archbishops come to be written down in the fifteenth century, the authors rely for their information entirely on the chronicles and the Kievan *Paterik,* which demonstrates that in earlier times the lives of the archbishops were not considered important. The other important saintly bishop, St. Stefan of Perm' (died 1396) was primarily a missionary.

   The literary silence of the metropolitans and bishops of the fourteenth century is even more marked than in the Kievan period, for Metropolitan Ilarion, Bishop Kirill of Turov, and Bishop Serapion of Vladimir did at least compose sermons.

3. D. Abramovich, ed., *Das Paterikon des Kiever Höhlenklosters,* Slavische Propyläen 2 (Munich, 1964); and L. A. Ol'shevskaia, "Paterik Kievo-Pecherskii," in Likhachev, *Slovar',* vyp. 1:308–13. The pattern of life of the monks of the Kiev Monastery of the Caves thus continued the pattern shown by the late Byzantine holy man, and advisor and miracle worker: Peter Brown, "The Rise and Function of the Holy Man in Late Antiquity," *Journal of Roman Studies* 61 (1971): 80–101.

4. Ludolf Müller, ed., *Die Legenden des heiligen Sergij von Radonež,* Slavische Propyläen 17 (Munich, 1967), XXXI–XXXII, 91–97, 101–7, 118–32; G. M. Prokhorov, *Povest' o Mitiae: Rus' i Vizantiia v epokhu Kulikovskoi bitvy* (Leningrad, 1978); John Meyendorff, *Byzantium and the Rise of Russia* (Cambridge, 1981), 132–36, 214–17; Igor Smolitsch, *Russisches Mönchtum: Entstehung, Entwicklung, und Wesen 988–1917,* Das östliche Christentum, Abhandlungen, n.s., nos. 10/11 (Würzburg, 1953), 79.

5. Shchapov, *Gosudarstvo i tserkov'*, 131–48; Paul Bushkovitch, "The Limits of Hesychasm: Some Notes on Monastic Spirituality in Russia 1350–1500," *Forschungen zur osteuropäischen Geschichte*, 38 (Berlin, 1986): 97–109, I. Mansvetov, *Tserkovnyi ustav (tipik), ego obrazovanie i sud'ba v grecheskoi i russkoi tserkvi* (Moscow, 1895), 265–94; L. V. Betin, "Ob arkhitekturnoi kompozitsii drevnerusskikh vysokikh ikonostasov," and "Istoricheskie osnovy drevnerusskogo vysokogo ikonostasa," both in *Drevnerusskoe iskusstvo: Khudozhestvennaia kul'tura Moskvy i prilezhashchikh k nei kniazhestv XIV–XVI vv.* (Moscow, 1970), 41–56 and 57–72. In Russia a distinction was made between the monks, or black clergy, and the rest—parish priests, deacons, and other clergy, all called white clergy.
6. Dm. Tschizewskij, ed., *Pachomij Logofet: Werke im Auswahl*, Nachdruck der Ausgabe von V. Jablonskij, Slavische Propyläen 1 (Munich, 1963), I–LXIII; Bushkovitch, "Hesychasm."
7. A. P. Kadlubovskii, ed., "Zhitie prepodobnogo Pafnutiia Borovskogo, pisannoe Vassianom Saninym," *Sbornik istoriko-filologicheskogo obshchestva pri Institute im. kn. Bezborodko* 2 (1899): 98–149.
8. G. P. Fedotov, *Sviatye drevnei Rusi*, (3d ed. Paris, 1985), 187–90; Likhachev, *Razvitie russkoi literatury*, 124–37; Ia. S. Lur'e, *Ideologicheskaia bor'ba v russkoi publitstistike kontsa XV–nachala XVI veka* (Moscow and Leningrad, 1960).
9. Recently A. I. Pliguzov has questioned this traditional assessment of monastic wealth, showing that the proportion of one-third comes from an English source that is not necessarily reliable. However, his attempt to suggest that the monasteries owned a much lower proportion of the land in the sixteenth century is unconvincing. His main argument is retrospective. At the end of the seventeenth century (using Vodarskii's figures) the church owned about 20 percent of the peasantry, and as Pliguzov correctly notes, the church had slowly acquired more land in the previous two centuries. However, he fails to take into account that the Russia of 1550 did not include Siberia and the southern border, both of which were settled intensively only after about 1590, and where church landholding was extremely small. Church land was concentrated in the center of the Russian state, south of the taiga and north of the steppe, in the sixteenth and seventeenth century the area of old settlement and developed agriculture and trade. Vodarskii's figures show that in the central area in 1678 the church owned 21 percent of the peasantry (29 percent in the northwest), but in the southern black-earth region, the northern part of the newly settled steppe lands, only 10 percent. Furthermore, in the oldest settled parts of the central area (Moscow, Vladimir, Rostov, Suzdal' districts) the proportion of ecclesiastical serfs to secular varied from 27 up to 46 percent (this in Rostov) of the peasantry. Since we know so little about demographic and economic changes in central Russia from the sixteenth century to the seventeenth, there is no reason to object to the figure of one-third for the sixteenth century, pending further investigation. See A. I. Pliguzov, "O razmerakh tserkovnogo zemlevladeniia v Rossii XVI v.," *Istoriia SSSR*, 1988, no. 2:157–63; Ia. E. Vodarskii, *Naselenie Rossii v kontse XVI–nachale XVIII veka* (Moscow, 1977), 221–23, 227.
10. Iosif Volotskii, *Prosvetitel'* (Kazan', 1855); A. A. Zimin and Ia. S. Lur'e, eds., *Poslaniia Iosifa Volotskogo* (Moscow and Leningrad, 1959).
11. Nil Sorskii, *Predanie i ustav*, ed. M. S. Borovkova-Maikova, Pamiatniki drevnei pis'mennosti i iskusstva, 179 (St. Petersburg, 1912). On Nil and the

Josephites, see Lur'e, *Ideologicheskaia bor'ba*, 316–37 and 449–81; Fairy von Lilienfeld, *Nil Sorskii und seine Schriften: Der Bruch der Tradition im Russland Ivans III,* Quellen und Untersuchungen zur Konfessionskunde der Orthodoxie (Berlin, 1963); Edgar Hösch, *Orthodoxie und Häresie im alten Russland,* Schriften zur Geistesgeschichte des östlichen Europas 7 (Wiesbaden, 1975); and David Goldfrank, "New and Old Perspectives on Iosif Volotsky's Monastic Rules," *Slavic Review* 34 (June 1975): 279–301. Recently Donald Ostrowski has shown that there is legitimate doubt that the landholding issue was fully debated (if at all) at the 1503 council, and may have matured only in the 1530s. His further conclusion, that there were no parties disputing the landholding issue, is not convincing, though he does show that actual secularization was not discussed, at least before about 1550. Indeed, not secularization but the restriction on the growth of monastic landholding was the issue, though Soviet historians use the term *sekuliarizatsiia* for both: see, for example, S. M. Troitskii, "Sekuliarizatsiia v Rossii," *Sovetskaia istoricheskaia entsiklopediia,* 12 (Moscow, 1969), 712–13. On the other hand, both Josephites and nonpossessors use a general moral vocabulary that suggests the belief that landholding was either good or bad. In the latter case, the conclusion that someone contemplated more far-reaching measures is natural. Ostrowski also fails to take into account the consequences of Nil's preference for hermitage. See Donald Ostrowski, "Church Polemics and Monastic Land Acquisition in Sixteenth Century Muscovy," *Slavonic and East European Review* 64 (July 1986): 355–79.

12. On Vassian, see Lur'e, *Ideologicheskaia bor'ba,* and N. A. Kazakova, *Ocherki po istorii russkoi obshchestvennoi mysli, pervaia tret' XVI veka* (Leningrad, 1970), 87–154; N. A. Kazakova, *Vassian Patrikeev i ego sochineniia* (Moscow and Leningrad, 1960), 36–138, with Vassian's writings, 223–81; and E. Hösch, 129–38.

13. On Maksim's life see Jack Haney, *From Italy to Muscovy: The Life and Works of Maxim the Greek* (Munich, 1973); Elie Denissoff, *Maxime le Grec et l'occident* (Paris and Louvain, 1943); V. S. Ikonnikov, *Maksim Grek i ego vremia,* 2d ed. (Kiev, 1915); V. F. Rzhiga, "Opyty po istorii russkoi publitsistiki XVI v.: Maksim Grek kak publitsist," *TODRL* 1 (1934): 5–120; Kazakova, *Ocherki,* 155–243; Bernhard Schulze, *Maksim Grek als Theologe,* Orientalia Christiana Analecta 167 (Rome, 1963); N. V. Sinitsyna, *Maksim Grek v Rossii* (Leningrad, 1977); D. M. Bulanin, *Perevody i poslaniia Maksima Greka* (Leningrad, 1984); N. N. Pokrovskii, ed., *Sudnye spiski Maksima Greka i Isaka Sobaki* (Moscow, 1971). Literature on the Greek church in this era is sparse. See George A. Maloney, *A History of Orthodox Theology since 1453* (Belmont, Mass., 1976), 89–161; Steven Runciman, *The Great Church in Captivity* (Cambridge, 1968); Gerhard Podskalsky, *Griechische Theologie in der Zeit der Türkenherrschaft (1453–1821): Die Orthodoxie im Spannungsfeld der nachreformatorischen Konfessionen des Westens* (Munich, 1988); and N. F. Kapterev, *Kharakter otnoshenii Rossii k pravoslavnomu vostoku v XVI i XVII stoletiiakh,* 2d ed. (Sergiev Posad, 1914).

14. Maksim Grek, *Sochineniia,* 3 vols. (Kazan', 1860–1894; 2d ed., 1894–1897), vol. 1 (2d ed.), 19–32; vol. 2 (1st ed.), 5–52, 89–184, 260–76, 290–94, 319–37, 346–57, 394–415; Sinitsyna, *Maksim Grek,* 229–33; Podskalsky, *Griechische Theologie,* 89–97. Historians have usually seen the source of Maksim's troubles with Metropolitan Daniil in the Greek's views on monastic

landholding. This issue did not even come up directly in the two trials, and the concentration on this dispute by historians has overshadowed Maksim's own very clear statement to the contrary.

15. "Zhitie i podvizi i otchasti chiudes prepodobnogo ottsa nashego Zosimy . . . i Savatiia," *Velikie Minei-chet'i,* Moscow, April 1912, 502–95.

16. [Savva Chernyi], "Zhitie i prebyvanie vkrattse prepodobnogo ottsa nashego igumena Iosifa," *Velikie Minei-chet'i,* St. Petersburg, September 1868, 453–99; Ia. S. Lur'e, "Zhitie Iosifa Volotskogo," in D. S. Likhachev, ed., *Slovar' knizhnikov i knizhnosti drevnei Rusi,* vyp. 2 (vtoraia polovina XIV–XVI v.), 2 vols. (Leningrad, 1988), 1:273–76.

17. "Skazanie v krattse o prepodobnem starttse Danile Pereiaslavskom," in *Stepennaia kniga, PSRL,* 21:615–26; Kliuchevskii, *Drevnerusskie,* 282–83; Nancy Shields Kollmann, *Kinship and Politics: The Making of the Muscovite Political System 1345–1547* (Stanford, Calif., 1987), 203; A. A. Zimin, *Formirovanie boiarskoi aristokratii v Rossii vo vtoroi polovine XV–pervoi treti XVI v.* (Moscow, 1988), 172–74. Vasilii Andreevich Cheliadnin was the recipient of one of Joseph Volotskii's epistles: Zimin and Lur'e, *Poslaniia Iosifa Volotskogo,* 227–28.

18. "Skazanie," 624–25; Kollman, *Kinship,* 238; Zimin, *Formirovanie,* 157–58.

19. V. Zhmakin, *Mitropolit Daniil i ego sochineniia, ChOIDR,* 1881, no. 1:1–256; 1881, no. 2:257–281, 650–58, 677–86, appendix: 39–46.

20. S. M. Kashtanov, *Finansy srednevekovoi Rusi* (Moscow, 1988), 6–21.

21. Kashtanov, *Finansy,* 92–136; D. E. Kozhanchikov, ed., *Stoglav* (St. Petersburg, 1863), 275–76.

22. Jack Edward Kollmann, Jr., "The *Stoglav* Council and Parish Priests," *Russian History/Histoire russe* 7 (1980): 65–91. Golubinskii, *Istoriia,* 2, pt. 2:42–46, 52–54, 57–58, asserts that the tithers had disciplinary functions earlier but cites no evidence for this statement. See A. S. Pavlov, ed., *Pamiatniki drevnerusskogo kanonicheskogo prava, RIB* 6, pt. 1 (St. Petersburg, 1880), 83–102; *AAE,* 1, no. 54:40 (1455); *Akty sotsial'no-ekonomicheskoi istorii Severo-vostoka Rusi kontsa XIV–nachala XVI v.,* (Moscow, 1952), 1:426–27; I. Pokrovskii, *Russkie eparkhii v XVI–XIX vv., ikh otkrytie, sostav i predely* 2 vols. (Kazan', 1897–1913), 1:53, 68–80, 126–55; *AI,* 1, no. 298:541–44.

23. Kozhanchikov, *Stoglav,* 179–221. The land elders were the heads of local government that were established in the 1550s to replace the traditional feeding (*kormlenie*) system.

24. Ibid., 43–45, 47–50, 54–55, 57, 165–72.

25. Kashtanov, *Finansy,* 114–26.

26. Ibid., 130–35; Kozhanchikov, *Stoglav,* 206–7.

27. *DAI,* vol. 1 (St. Petersburg, 1846), no. 28 (27–30), no. 32 (33–34), no. 43 (57–60); Paul Bushkovitch, "The Epiphany Ceremony of the Russian Court in the Sixteenth and Seventeenth Centuries," *Russian Review* 49 (1990): 1–18. The Palm Sunday ceremony, in which the tsar walked through the Kremlin and Red Square leading the metropolitan seated on a horse, was first noted in 1548, and also was designed to show the tsar's respect for the metropolitan, though it does not seem to have the implication of rejection of popular ritual in the Epiphany ceremony: Robert O. Crummey, "Court Spectacles in Seventeenth Century Russia: Illusion and Reality," in *Essays in Honor of A. A. Zimin,* ed. Daniel Waugh (Columbus, Ohio, 1985), 130–58.

28. Kozhanchikov, *Stoglav,* 135–37, 140–42. The condemnations also include

rather obscure popular prophets, noblemen (*deti boiarskie*) who gamble rather than go to church, and those who read astrological books, so the deviations from Christian practice condemned by the council clearly were not confined to the peasantry: Ibid., 137–39.

29. *AAE*, 1, nos. 241, 247, 248, 360 (257–61, 269–70, 439–42); *Akty Kholmogorskoi i Ustiuzhskoi eparkhii*, part 1: 1500–1699, *RIB* 12 (St. Petersburg, 1894), 132–38; V. N. Bochkarev, *Stoglav i istoriia sobora 1551 goda* (Iukhnov, 1906), 141–48.

30. "Ukaznaia kniga zemskogo prikaza," Zimin, ed., *Pamiatniki russkogo prava*, 6 vols. (Moscow, 1952–1959), 5:327–425, esp. 340, 342, 359–60, 384, 399; Antonio Possevino, "Moscovia," in *Historiae Ruthenicae scriptores exteri*, ed. A. Starczewski, 2 vols. (Berlin and St. Petersburg, 1841–1842), 2:279. See also my chapter 3 ("The Church in the Seventeenth Century"). These popular rituals disappeared only with the collectivization of agriculture in 1929–1934.

31. A. A. Zimin, *I. S. Peresvetov i ego sovremenniki* (Moscow, 1958), 71–91; idem, *Reformy Ivana Groznogo* (Moscow, 1960), 263–64, 375–88; R. G. Skrynnikov, *Nachalo Oprichniny*, Uchenye zapiski Leningradskogo gos. pedagogicheskogo instituta im. A. I. Gertsena 294 (Leningrad, 1966), 86–89, 203–8.

32. O. M. Bodianskii, "Moskovskie sobory na eretikov XVI veka," *ChOIDR*, 1847, god 3, no. 3, pt. 2:1–30; Zimin, *Peresvetov*, 153–214; *AAE*, 1, no. 239 (249–56); Artemii, "Poslaniia startsa Artemiia XVI veka," *RIB* 4 (St. Petersburg, 1878), 1201–1448; Zinovii Otenskii, *Istiny pokazanie* (Kazan', 1863); Urban, Wacław, "Kosy, Teodozy," *Polski słownik biograficzny*, 14 (Wrocław, 1968–69), 369; S. Kot, *Ideologia polityczna i społeczna braci polskich zwanych arianami* (Warsaw, 1932); idem, "Szymon Budny: Der grösste Häretiker Litauens im 16. Jahrhundert," in *Studien zur älteren Geschichte Osteuropas* 1, Wiener Archiv für Geschichte des Slaventums und Osteuropas 2 (1956), 63–118; Marceli Kosman, *Reformacja i kontrreformacja w Wielkim Ksiestwie Litewskim w swietle propagandy wyznaniowej* (Wrocław, 1973), 63–103.

Zinovii Otenskii's works present a textual problem of their own: see Nancy Yanoshak, "A Fontological Analysis of the Major Works Attributed to Zinovii Otenskii" (Ph.D. diss., Georgetown University, 1981).

33. S. A. Belokurov, ed., "Zhitie prep. Iosifa volokolamskogo," *ChOIDR*, 1903, no. 3:15–20, 24, 30, 37–42; D. S. Likhachev, "Zabytyi serbskii pisatel' pervoi poloviny XVI v. Anikita Lev Filolog," in *Gorski Vijenac: A Garland of Essays Offered to Prof. E. M. Hill*, ed. R. Auty, L. R. Lewitter, and A. P. Vlasto (Cambridge, 1970), 215–19; Lur'e, "Iosifa Volotskogo Zhitie"; and R. P. Dmitrieva, "Lev Filolog," in Likhachev, ed., *Slovar'*, vyp. 2, 2:3–6.

34. [Varlaam], "Povest' o Nifonte, episkope Novgorodskim," in *Pamiatniki starinnoi russkoi literatury*, 4 vols. (St. Petersburg, 1860–1862), 4:1–9; R. P. Dmitrieva, "Vasilii," in *Slovar'*, vyp. 2, 1:112–16; Kliuchevskii, *Drevnerusskie*, 252; *Stepennaia kniga, PSRL*, 21:191.

35. Kapterev, *Kharakter*, 34–60. A. Ia. Shpakov, *Gosudarstvo i tserkov' v ikh vzaimnykh otnosheniiakh v Moskovskom gosudarstve*, 2 vols. (Kiev and Odessa, 1904–1912); and V. I. Buganov, M. P. Lukichev, and N. M. Rogozhin, eds., *Posol'skaia kniga po sviaziam Rossii s Gretsiei (pravoslavnymi ierarkhami i monastyriami) 1588–1592 gg.* (Moscow, 1988).

36. "Povest' ob Antonii Rimlianine," in *Pamiatniki starinnoi russkoi literatury*,

1:263–70; E. A. Fet, "Zhitie Antoniia Rimlianina," in Likhachev, ed., *Slovar'*, vyp. 2, 1:245–47.

37. "Zhitie . . . Fillipa mitropolita moskovskogo," Vat. Slav. 30; Ihor Sevčenko, "A Neglected Byzantine Source of Muscovite Political Ideology," in *The Structure of Russian History*, ed. Michael Cherniavsky (New York, 1970), 80–107; Kliuchevskii, *Drevnerusskie*, 311–12; E. E. Golubinskii, *Istoriia Kanonizatsii sviatykh v russkoi tserkvi, ChOIDR*, 1903, no. 1:231; and Paul Bushkovitch, "The Life of Metropolitan Filipp: Tsar and Metropolitan in the Sixteenth Century," *California Slavic Studies* (forthcoming).

38. G. N. Moiseeva, "Zhitie Novgorodskogo arkhiepiskopa Serapiona," *TODRL* 21 (1965): 147–65; R. P. Dmitrieva, "Zhitie novgorodskogo arkhiepiskopa Serapiona kak publitsisticheskoe proizvedenie XVI v.," *TODRL* 41 (1988): 364–74.

39. Another example of the absence of Josephite domination was the council decisions of 1580 and 1584 further restricting monastic privilege. Even if the church was united behind the monasteries (which does not seem to be the case), it did not convince the tsar and his government: Kashtanov, *Finansy*, 221–30; E. I. Kolycheva, *Agrarnyi stroi Rossii XVI veka* (Moscow, 1987), 119–68; R. G. Skrynnikov, *Rossiia nakanune "Smutnogo vremeni"* (Moscow, 1980), 23–26.

Chapter 2

1. Kollmann, *Kinship*, presents the thesis that the pre-1547 Grand Prince was a referee among powerful clans. Additional evidence from the side of political ideology is supplied in Bushkovitch, "National Consciousness" and "Epiphany." R. G. Skrynnikov's description of the period 1584–1604 as one of competition among powerful boyar clans and factions is found in his *Rossiia nakanune "Smutnogo vremeni."* On the lesser landholders, see most recently V. B. Kobrin, *Vlast' i sobstvennost' v srednevekovoi Rossii (XV–XVI vv.)* (Moscow, 1985).

2. A. K. Leont'ev, *Obrazovanie prikaznoi sistemy upravleniia v Russkom gosudarstve* (Moscow, 1961); Richard Hellie, *Enserfment and Military Change in Muscovy* (Chicago, 1971); Kollmann, *Kinship*; Zimin, *Formirovanie*; Paul Bushkovitch, "The Formation of a National Consciousness in Early Modern Russia," *Harvard Ukrainian Studies* 10 (1986): 355–76.

3. On the elite, see S. B. Veselovskii, *Issledovaniia po istorii klassa sluzhilikh zemlevladel'tsev* (Moscow, 1969); A. A. Zimin, "Sostav Boiarskoi dumy v XV–XVI vekakh," in *Arkheograficheskii ezhegodnik za 1957 g.* (Moscow, 1958), 41–87; idem, "Feodal'naia znat' Tverskogo i Riazanskogo velikikh kniazhestv i moskovskoe boiarstvo kontsa XV–pervoi tret'i XV v.," *Istoriia SSSR*, 1973, no. 3:124–42; idem, "Suzdal'skie i rostovskie kniaz'ia vo vtoroi polovine XV–pervoi tret'i XVI v.," *Vspomogatel'nye istoricheskie distsipliny* 7 (1976): 56–69; idem, "Kniazheskaia znat' i formirovanie sostava Boiarskoi dumy vo vtoroi polovine XV–pervoi tret'i XVI v.," *Istoricheskie zapiski* 103 (1979): 195–241; idem, *Formirovanie*; Kobrin, *Vlast' i sobstvennost' v srednevekovoi Rossii*, esp. 48–160; Gustave Alef, "Reflections on the Boyar Duma in the Reign of Ivan III," *Slavonic and East European Review* 45 (1967): 76–123; Gustave Alef, "The

Crisis of the Muscovite Aristocracy: A Factor in the Growth of Monarchical Power," *Forschungen zur osteuropäischen Geschichte* 15 (1970): 15–58; Hartmut Rüss, *Adel und Adelsoppositionen im Moskauer Staat,* Quellen und Studien zur Geschichte des östlichen Europas 7 (Wiesbaden, 1975); A. M. Kleimola, "Patterns of Duma Recruitment, 1505–1550," in Waugh, *Essays,* 232–58; M. E. Bychkova, *Sostav klassa feodalov Rossii v XVI v.* (Moscow, 1986); Kollmann, *Kinship.* The older work of V. O. Kliuchevskii, *Boiarskaia duma drevnei Rusi,* 4th ed. (St. Petersburg, 1909), is based on late and scanty original sources: cf. S. O. Shmidt, *Rossiiskoe gosudarstvo v seredine XVI stoletiia* (Moscow, 1984), 112–19.

4. Veselovskii, *Issledovaniia,* 87; Kollmann, *Kinship,* 40–41. These complex distinctions in rank are found in official documents of the time emanating from the various offices, but in unofficial texts the aristocrats of whatever rank are usually referred to as "boyars" or even "dignitaries" (*vel'mozhi*). This is the usage, for example, in the lives of saints throughout the sixteenth and seventeenth centuries.

5. The reason for this lay in the lack of functional differentiation in Russian society. There simply was no distinction between the landholding class and the army, as Russia maintained a mass light-cavalry army up to the middle of the seventeenth century. This was necessary to compete with the mass light-cavalry armies of its principal opponents, Poland and the Tatars, and to prevent the Tatar raids it had to be mobilized every summer on the southern border. As there was no functional distinction between soldier and provincial landholder in the lower ranks, so there was little distinction at the top between aristocrat, general, provincial governor, diplomat, and adviser to the prince. The same men did all these things.

6. The origins of the system are somewhat obscure. Zimin (*Formirovanie,* 296–305) found little evidence before the early sixteenth century, and Kollmann seems to agree: *Kinship,* 26, 67–70. The classic studies are A. I. Markevich, *O mestnichestve* (Kiev, 1879), and *Istoriia mestnichestva v Moskovskom gosudarstve v XV–XVI veke* (Odessa, 1888).

7. Abramovych, *Paterikon,* 1–5, 34; Shchapov, *Gosudarstvo i tserkov',* 131–63; Peter Charanis, "The Monk in Byzantine Society," *Dumbarton Oaks Papers* 25 (1971): 76–77; John Philip Thomas, *Private Religious Foundations in the Byzantine Empire,* Dumbarton Oaks Studies 24 (Washington, D.C., 1987); Jean Meyendorff, *Introduction à l'étude de Grégoire Palamas,* Patristica sorboniensia 3 (Paris, 1959). Among other Christian societies, medieval Western Europe also saw widespread entrance into monasteries by noblemen, a fact noted in basic handbooks such as R. W. Southern, *Western Society and the Church in the Middle Ages* (Harmondsworth, 1970).

8. Müller, *Legenden,* 33–36; Tschizewskij, *Pachomij: Werke,* xx–xxi, xxv–xxvi, xxxiii–xxxvi.

9. Kadlubovskii, ed., Vassian Sanin, "Zhitie . . . Pafnutiia," 122–23, 130–31, 133–36; [Savva Chernyi], "Zhitie . . . Iosifa," 465, 469–72, 475–76, 493–97; Zimin, *Formirovanie,* 76, 214, 219; idem, *Krupnaia feodal'naia votchina i sotsial'no-politicheskaia bor'ba v Rossii (konets XV–XVI v.)* (Moscow, 1977), 107, 113, 115, 172; Kollman, *Kinship,* 218. A *stol'nik* ranked below an *okol'nichii.* By the seventeenth century the ranks of *dumnyi d'iak* (court secretary) and *dumnyi dvorianin* (court gentryman) came ahead of that of table assistant.

10. Zimin, *Krupnaia feodal'naia votchina*, 105–65; idem, *Formirovanie*, 56–58; Kollmann, *Kinship*, 241. The documentary record of the monastery's acquisition of land is in the second volume of *Akty feodal'nogo zemlevladeniia i khoziaistva*, 2 vols. (Moscow, 1951–1956). Dionisii Zvenigorodskii's genealogical interests are noted in Bychkova, *Sostav*, 39–44, 74–77.

11. N. Nikol'skii, *Kirillo-Belozerskii monastyr' i ego ustroistvo do vtoroi chetverti XVII veka (1397–1625)*, vol. 1, pts. 1–2 (St. Petersburg, 1897–1910), pt. 2:12–22, 177–86; A. I. Kopanev, *Istoriia zemlevladeniia Belozerskogo kraia XV–XVI vv.* (Moscow and Leningrad, 1951), 86–141.

12. Nikol'skii, *Kirillo-Belozerskii monastyr*, pt. 1, XLV–LVIII. The boyars may have initially followed the tsar, for Ivan IV was the single greatest contributor to the monastery. Tsars Fyodor and Boris Godunov continued the practice, but on a much reduced scale. Their contributions indeed may not have been terribly significant, for the tsars and their families gave to many monasteries.

13. P. M. Stroev, *Spiski ierarkhov i nastoiatelei monastyrei Rossiiskoi tserkvi* (St. Petersburg, 1877), 55; *PSRL*, 13:165, 250, 374, 378–381, 403, 405. Afanasii appears in the genealogies in neither Zimin, *Formirovanie*, 38, 42, nor Kollmann, *Kinship*, 224–25.

14. "Kormovaia kniga Kirillo-Belozerskogo monastyria," *Zapiski otdeleniia russkoi i slavianskoi arkheologii imp. Russkogo arkheologicheskogo obshchestva* 1 (1851): 46–105; D. S. Likhachev and Ia. S. Lur'e, "Poslanie v Kirillo-Belozerskii Monastyr' (1573)" in *Poslaniia Ivana Groznogo* (Moscow and Leningrad, 1951), 162–92; R. G. Skrynnikov, *Oprichnyi terror* (Leningrad, 1969), 20, 137–39; Kollmann, *Kinship*, 240; Zimin, *Formirovanie*, 133, 146; idem, *Reformy*, 410. The church still stands, an example of a curiously archaic style for 1554: see G. Bocharov and V. Vygolov, *Vologda, Kirillov, Ferapontovo, Belozersk*, 3d ed. (Moscow, 1979), 169–70, 197, ill. 78; and I. A. Kochetkov, O. V. Lelekova and S. S. Pod"iapol'skii, *Kirillo-Belozerskii monastyr'* (Leningrad, 1979), 34, 119, ills. 14, 25, 27. Bocharov and Vygolov mistakenly believe Vorotynskii to have been exiled, but confuse him with his brother Mikhail who died on his way to prison in the monastery in 1573: A. A. Zimin, *V kanun groznykh potriasenii* (Moscow, 1986), 10–11.

15. A. V. Gorskii, "Istoricheskoe opisanie sviatoi Troitse-Sergievy Lavry," *ChOIDR*, 1879, no. 2:79–101. For the histories of these clans, see the works of Zimin, Alef, and Kollmann cited in n. 3 and the following sources: V. I. Buganov, ed. *Razriadnaia kniga 1475–1598 gg.* (Moscow, 1966); S. R. Mordvinova and A. L. Stanislavskii, eds., *Boiarskie spiski poslednei chetverti XVI–nachala XVII vv. i rospis' russkogo voiska 1604 g.*, 2 pts. (Moscow, 1979); Kobrin, *Vlast'*, 91 (Durovs); and Iu. G. Alekseev, *Agrarnaia i sotsial'naia istoriia severo-vostochnoi Rusi XV–XVI vv.: Pereiaslavskii uezd* (Moscow and Leningrad, 1966), 160 (Stogovs). *Okol'nichii* was an honorific rank just below boyar in dignity.

16. Skrynnikov, *Nachalo*, 78, 113, 154; idem, *Terror*, 92–94; A. A. Novosel'skii et al., eds. *Akty Russkogo gosudarstva 1505–1526 gg.* (Moscow, 1975); and *Akty sotsial'no-ekonomicheskoi istorii severo-vostochnoi Rusi*, vol. 1, passim. This general pattern also appears to hold for the Simonov Monastery near Moscow, judging from L. I. Ivina, *Krupnaia votchina severo-vostochnoi Rusi kontsa XIV–pervoi poloviny XVI v.* (Leningrad, 1979). Ivina studied the accumulation of land in the monastery's possession, but land donations were often given by

monks, who do not seem to come from princely, boyar, or other elite families, save for a few political cases.

17. A. A. Zimin, *Rossiia na poroge novogo vremeni (Ocherki politicheskoi istorii Rossii
pervoi tret'i XVI v.)* (Moscow, 1972), 223–30. Smolitsch, *Russisches Mönchtum*,
82, n. 1, is misleading in describing Russian monks as nobles, for he groups
lesser local landholders with the handful of aristocrats.

18. Stroev, *Spiski*, 82, 332, 442, 452; Zimin, *Formirovanie*, 48–49, 53; Kollmann,
Kinship, 50, 139–45, 222–24; Ia. S. Lur'e, "Vassian," in Likhachev, ed., *Slovar'*, vyp. 2, 1:117–18.

19. On Daniil, see Zimin, *Krupnaia . . . votchina*, 164, n. 352. On Filipp
"Zhitie . . . Filippa," Vat. slav. 30; Leonid, ep. dmitrovskii, *Zhizn' sviatogo
Filippa, mitropolita Moskovskogo i vseia Rossii* (Moscow, 1861); and Bushkovitch, "Life." For Filipp's life and family, see A. A. Zimin, *Oprichnina Ivana
Groznogo* (Moscow, 1964), chap. 5 ("Mitropolit Filipp i oprichnina"), esp.
221–25, 239–57; idem, *Formirovanie*, 176, 178, 180–81; and Veselovskii,
Issledovaniia, 143–46, ("In general the Kolychevs, who greatly multiplied in
the sixteenth century, got themselves an important position not so much by
their good family and wealth but by their number," 144). The elder (boyar
and *okol'nichii* line) of the Kolychevs is described in Kollmann, *Kinship*, 212–
13. Fillip's uncle I. I. Umnoi-Kolychev is not the same person as the monk of
the same name mentioned by Ivan IV (*Poslaniia*, 173).

20. I. E. Zabelin, *Domashnii byt Russkogo naroda v XVI i XVII st.*, 2 vols. (Moscow,
1872), 1:313–72.

21. The palace itself gives hints as to the nature of the religious life of the court.
The best general view is again Zabelin, *Domashnii*, 1:108–312. The lost
frescoes of the palace of Ivan IV's time also contain important clues. The
icon-painter Simon Ushakov's seventeenth-century description preserves
the iconography for us, which reveals the themes of the Gold Room: the just
and warlike rulers of the Old Testament (Joshua) and the saintly princes of
Russia (St. Vladimir or Vladimir Monomakh, who receives the Byzantine
regalia). This is a religion that emphasizes the virtuous ruler, a religion of
public and monarchical virtue with specific reference to the "Tale of the
Vladimir Princes." See O. I. Podobedova, *Moskovskaia shkola zhivopisi pri Ivane
IV: Raboty v Moskovskom Kremle 40–70-kh godov XVI v.* (Moscow, 1972), 59–68,
193–98 (illustrations). The metropolitans of Moscow received the rank of
patriarch in 1589.

22. Bushkovitch, "Epiphany Ceremony"; and Zabelin, *Domashnii*, 1:335–42.
This ceremony was quite different from the Epiphany ceremony at the late
Byzantine court, which centered on the presentation (*prokypsis*) of the em-
peror on a platform to the nobility and clergy, who venerated him. See
Pseudo-Kodinos, *Traité des offices*, ed. Jean Verpeaux, Le monde byzantin 1
(Paris, 1966), 189–221, 226–27, 240–41; August Heisenberg, "Aus der
Geschichte und Literatur der Palaiologenzeit," *Sitzungsberichte der Bayerischen
Akademie der Wissenschaften: Philosophisch-philologische und historische Klasse* 10
(1920): 85–89, reprinted in August Heisenberg, *Quellen und Studien zur
spätbyzantinischen Geschichte* (London, 1973).

23. Makarii, *Istoriia*, 8:66–67, asserted that the ceremony was known only from
the time of Ivan IV, which is confirmed by Crummey, who also confirms a
Novgorod origin for the ritual: Crummey, "Court Spectacles." Again the
Byzantine ceremony, called the *peripatos*, was quite different, as the patriarch

walked in the procession after the emperor, and nowhere was he led on a donkey by the emperor. Pseudo-Kodinos, *Traité*, 224–26; Heisenberg, "Palaiologenzeit," 82–85; and Georg Ostrogorsky, "Zum Stratordienst des Herrschers in der byzantinisch-Slawischen Welt," in *Byzanz und die Welt der Slawen* (Darmstadt, 1974), 101–21. It should be noted that the Byzantine ceremonies, both at Epiphany and Palm Sunday, underlined the glory and dignity of the emperor, whereas the Russian ceremonies had the metropolitan as their focal point.

24. N. A. Kazakova and Ia. S. Lur'e, *Antifeodal'nye ereticheskie dvizheniia na Rusi XIV–nachala XVI v.* (Moscow and Leningrad, 1955), 109–32, 147–70; Kollman, *Kinship*, 47–48. The heretic Kuritsyns were not related to the Kamenskii-Kuritsyns, a minor (no duma ranks) branch of the Ratshich-Akinfovich line.

25. V. Malinin, *Starets Eleazarova monastyria Filofei i ego poslaniia* (Kiev, 1901), supplement, 26–47, 49–56; G. M. Prokhorov, "Poslaniia Nila Sorskogo," *TODRL* 29 (1974): 125–43; Lur'e, *Ideologicheskaia bor'ba*, 295–96; Kazakova, *Ocherki po istorii russkoi obshchestvennoi mysli;* N. A. Kazakova, ed., *Vassian Patrikeev i ego sochineniia* (Moscow and Leningrad, 1960); Zimin, *Formirovanie*, 31–34; Kollman, *Kinship*, 117, 136, 140, 155, 196, 225.

26. A. A. Zimin and Ia. S. Lur'e, eds., *Poslaniia Iosifa Volotskogo* (Moscow and Leningrad, 1959), 179–83, 187–229; Lur'e, *Ideologicheskaia bor'ba*, 204–84; A. A. Zimin, *Rossiia na rubezhe XV–XVI stoletii* (Moscow, 1982), 82–85, 197–232; idem, *Formirovanie*, 172–74, 273; and Kollmann, *Kinship*, 87, 203, 210. In genealogical books B. V. Kutuzov was called *okol'nichii* but is not listed in the service records: Zimin, *Krupnaia . . . votchina*, 41; and idem, *Formirovanie*, 258–60.

27. V. F. Rzhiga, "Boiarin-zapadnik XVI v. (F. I. Karpov)," *Uchenye zapiski instituta istorii RANION* 4 (1929): 39–48; E. N. Kimeeva, "'Poslanie mitropolitu Daniilu' Fedora Karpova," *TODRL* 9 (1953): 220–34; A. A. Zimin, "Obshchestvenno-politcheskie vzgliady F. I. Karpova," *TODRL* 12 (1956): 160–73; V. G. Druzhinin, "Neskol'ko neizvestnykh literaturnykh pamiatnikov iz sbornika XVI-go veka," *LZAK za 1908 g.* 21 (1909): 1–117, esp. 106–13; Zimin, *Peresvetov*, 50, 52–54, 153–56, 158; idem, *Formirovanie*, 74, 91, 264–66; and Kollmann, *Kinship*, 208–9, 217.

28. Zimin, *Formirovanie*, 240; Kollmann, *Kinship*, 220–21. Vasilii Mikhailov Tuchkov wrote in 1537 what became the standard version of the life of St. Mikhail Klopskii, but he never held high rank: "Vasilii [Tuchkov] the author of the life of Mikhail Klopskii . . . never occupied outstanding service posts, never got into the duma . . ." (Veselovskii, *Issledovaniia*, 207). As Riazan' *dvoretskii*, he was majordomo of the palace for the formerly independent principality of Riazan'. He was also general in the left-hand regiment in 1543. See Buganov, *Razriadnaia kniga*, 104; L. Dmitriev, ed., *Povest' o zhitii Mikhaila Klopskogo* (Moscow and Leningrad, 1958), 73–86, 141–67; L. A. Dmitriev, "Tuchkov Vasilii Mikhailovich," in Likhachev, ed., *Slovar'*, vyp. 2, 2:446–48.

29. Maksim Grek, *Sochineniia*, 1:258–73 (Bulow), 278–301 (Karpov), 364–65 (Bulow), 406–24 (Bulow); 2:346–57 (Ivan IV), 357–67 (Makarii), 367–76 (Daniil as ex-metropolitan), 379–82 (Sil'vestr), 382–86 (Aleksei), 386–88 (Grigorii "the deacon"), 388–94 (Prince Dmitrii [Andreevich, son of prince Andrei Uglitskii?]), 415–20 (prince Petr Shuiskii), 420–21 (Mikhail Vas-

il'evich Petrovich [Shuiskii?]), 421–24 ("brother Grigorii"), 424–25 ("Lord and brother Georgii"); Ikonnikov, *Maksim,* 228–45, 272–73, 392, 459–60; Sinitsyna, *Maksim,* 76–93; Bulanin, *Perevody,* 55–57, 191–202. The Greek version of the letter to Prince P. I. Shuiskii is in Kh. Loparev, "Zametka o sochineniiakh prep. Maksima Greka," *Bibliograficheskaia letopis'* 3 (1917): 50–70. On Prince P. I. Shuiskii, see Zimin, *Formirovanie,* 72; idem, *Reformy,* 260, 268, 412; idem, *Oprichnina,* 107–8; and Kollmann, *Kinship,* 235–36. On Bulow, see H. Raab, "Über die Beziehungen Bartholomäus Ghotans und Nicolaus Bulows zum Gennadij-Kreis in Novgorod," *Wissenschaftliche Zeitschrift der Universität Rostock: Gesellschafts- und sprachwissenschaftliche Reihe* 8 (1958–1959): 419–22; and Norbert Angermann, "Neues über Nicolaus Bulow und sein Wirken im Moskauer Russland," *Jahrbücher für Geschichte Osteuropas,* n.s., 17 (1969): 408–19. On Karpov, see my n. 26.

30. A. L. Shapiro, ed., *Agrarnaia istoriia Severo-zapadnoi Rossii: Vtoraia polovina XV–nachalo XVI v.* (Leningrad, 1971); idem, *Agrarnaia istoriia Severo-zapadnoi Rossii: Novgorodskie piatiny* (Leningrad, 1974); idem, *Agrarnaia istoriia Severo-zapadnoi Rossii: Sever, Pskov, Obshchie itogi razvitiia Severo-zapada* (Leningrad, 1978); Carsten Goehrke, *Die Wüstungen in der Moskauer Rus',* Quellen und Studien zur Geschichte des östlichen Europas 1 (Wiesbaden, 1968); and Kolycheva, *Agrarnyi stroi Rossii XVI veka.* All of these works stress the general prosperity of Russian agriculture until about 1560.

31. Zhmakin, *Daniil, ChOIDR,* 1881, no. 2:470–501, 560–615, appendix: 14–32. Daniil did not address his sermons to laywomen, who were largely under the authority of husbands and fathers.

32. A. S. Orlov, ed., *Domostroi po konshinskomu spisku i podobnym,* pts. 1–2 (Moscow, 1908), provides the text. See A. S. Orlov, *Domostroi: Issledovanie* (Moscow, 1917); Zimin, *Peresvetov,* 41–70, with a review of the older literature. A critical approach to Sil'vestr's political role is provided by Antony Grobovsky, *The "Chosen Council" of Ivan IV: A Reinterpretation* (Brooklyn, N.Y., 1969): and A. Grobovskii, *Ivan Groznyi i Sil'vestr (Istoriia odnogo mifa)* (London, 1987), who observes (71, n. 56) that it is difficult to take the *Domostroi* as the views of Sil'vestr. See also Carolyn Johnston Pouncy, "The Origins of the *Domostroi*: A study in Manuscript History," *Russian Review* 46 (1987): 357–74. Pouncy concludes that the work is a sixteenth-century text not by Sil'vestr and that it is directed at laymen (not clergy) of the lesser landholding class (not merchants).

33. Orlov, *Domostroi,* pt. 2:5–19, 24–25.

34. Prince Telepnev-Obolenskii Nemoi's library given to the Iosifo-Volokolamskii monastery is an example. The Golovins seem to have had a library at midcentury: Shmidt, *Rossiiskoe gosudarstvo,* 88, and M. I. Slukhovskii, *Bibliotechnoe delo v Rossii do XVIII veka* (Moscow, 1968), 71–76. There is little evidence of writing by members of the elite on religious subjects after 1550. It did occur: Prince Andrei Kurbskii's works written in Lithuania are an example, though they may be as much a response to the Orthodox milieu of Lithuania as to anything else: Inge Auerbach, *Andrej Michajlovič Kurbskij: Leben in osteuropäischen Adelsgesellschaften des 16 Jahrhunderts* (Munich, 1985).

35. A verbal loyalty to Josephism survived until the end of the century. In 1584–1585 Bishop Leonid of Riazan' complained to Tsar Fyodor that Bishop Evfimii of Rostov had caused him grave dishonor by asserting at a banquet

that he was not a Josephite: *AI,* 1, no. 216:410–11. Both bishops were soon deposed: perhaps they were merely troublemakers. Stroev, *Spiski,* 332, 415.

Chapter 3

1. Since Golubinskii's history never got beyond the sixteenth century, the standard histories of the church in this period are Makarii, *Istoriia,* and Kartashev, *Ocherki.* Neither are fully satisfactory.
2. Makarii, *Istoriia,* 11:10–19; Dmitrii Skvortsov, *Dionisii Zobninovskii, arkhimandrit Troitse-Sergievskoi Lavry* (Tver', 1890), esp. 207–35, 252–38; Simon Azar'in and Ivan Nasedka, *Zhitie i podvigi prep. ottsa nashego Dionisiia, arkhimandrita Troitskogo Sergieva monastyria* (Moscow, 1808); and N. F. Kapterev, "Snosheniia Ierusalimskikh patriarkhov s russkim pravitel'stvom s poloviny XVI do kontsa XVIII stoletiia," *Pravoslavnyi Palestinskii sbornik* 15, no. 1, (1895): 27–115. On Filaret: S. P-v, "Filaret," *Russkii biograficheskii slovar',* vol. Faber-Tsiavlovskii (St. Petersburg, 1901), 94–103; J. L. H. Keep, "The Regime of Filaret 1619–1633," *Slavonic and East European Review* 38 (1959–1960): 334–60; E. D. Stashevskii, *Ocherki po istorii tsarstvovaniia Mikhaila Fedorovicha,* vol. 1 (Kiev, 1913); and Bushkovitch, "Epiphany."
3. Kartashev, *Ocherki,* 2:96–99; Makarii, *Istoriia,* 11:23–33; and V. P. Kolosova and V. I. Krekoten', eds., *Ukrains'ka poeziia: Kinets' XVI–pochatok XVII st.* (Kiev, 1978), 118–19; this passage forms part of a polemical text in verse of the late sixteenth century, discussed in detail in chapter 6.
4. "Prenie litovskogo protopopa Lavrentiia Zizaniia . . . ," in N. Tikhonravov, ed., *Letopisi russkoi literatury i drevnostei,* vol. 2 (Moscow, 1859), sec. 2:80–100; *Katekhizis Lavrentiia Zizaniia,* Pamiatniki drevnei pis'mennosti 17 (St. Petersburg, 1878); K. V. Kharlampovich, *Malorossiiskoe vliianie na velikorusskuiu tserkovnuiu zhizn',* vol. 1 (Kazan', 1914), 103–13; Lavrentii Zyzanii, *Hramatyka slovens'ka,* ed. V. V. Nimchuk (Kiev, 1980); Cyrillus Tranquillus Stavroveckij, *"Perlo mnohocennoje" (Černěhov 1646),* ed. Hartmut Trunte, Bausteine zur Geschichte der Literatur bei den Slaven 22/1–22/2, 2 vols. (Cologne and Vienna, 1984–1985), 2:136–38, 171–73; and [Kirill Trankvillion Stavrovetskij], *Evangelie uchitel'noe* (Rakhmanov, 1619). Kharlampovich noted that Zizanii's and other Ukrainian works continued to circulate in Russia, a fact demonstrated by later research: K. M. Asafov, T. N. Protas'eva, and M. N. Tikhomirov, "Zapisi na knigakh staroi pechati XVI–XVII vekov," in *Arkheograficheskii ezhegodnik za 1961 god* (Moscow, 1962), 276–344, esp. 288, 291–93, 307, etc. Thus only the Zizanii incident really suggests differences between Filaret and Ukrainian Orthodoxy. Given his patronage of Nasedka (see chapter 6), perhaps the picture of Filaret as a xenophobic conservative should be revised: all that can be proved is a hostility to Catholicism shared in most cases by the Ukrainians.
5. M. Hrushevs'kyi, *Istoriia Ukrainy-Rusy,* 10 vols. (Reprint New York, 1954–1958), 6:444–564, 7:402–25; Ia. D. Isaievych, *Bratstva ta ikh rol' v rozvytku ukrains'koi kul'tury XVI–XVIII st.* (Kiev, 1966): Ia. D. Isaevich, *Preemniki pervopechatnika* (Moscow, 1981); and A. I. Anushkin, *Na zare knigopechataniia v Litve* (Vilnius, 1970); B. N. Floria, "Drevnerusskie traditsii i bor'ba vostochnoslavianskikh narodov za vossoedinenie," in *Drevnerusskoe nasledie i istoricheskie sud'by vostochnogo slavianstva,* ed. V. T. Pashuto, B. N. Floria, and

A. L. Khoroshkevich (Moscow, 1982), 151–238; and Frank E. Sysyn, *Between Poland and the Ukraine: The Dilemma of Adam Kysil, 1600–1653* (Cambridge, Mass., 1985).

6. Russia also had contact in the first half of the century with Orthodox Greeks from the Ottoman Empire. Less is known about these relations, and they seem to have been less important than those with the Ukraine, but they never ceased. The Greeks played a role in Ukrainian Orthodox affairs and thus had indirect contact with Russia as well. See Kapterev, *Kharakter*; B. L. Fonkich, *Grechesko-russkie kul'turnye sviazi v XV–XVII vv.* (Moscow, 1977); Steven Runciman, *Great Church*; Maloney, *History*; Gunnar Hering, *Oekumenisches Patriarchat und europäische Politik, 1620–1638*, Veröffentlichungen des Instituts für Europäische Geschichte Mainz 45 (Wiesbaden, 1968); and Peter Meienberger, *Johann Rudolf Schmid zum Schwarzenhorn als kaiserlicher Resident in Konstantinopel in den Jahren 1629–1643: Ein Beitrag zur Geschichte der diplomatischen Beziehungen zwischen Österreich und der Türkei in der ersten Hälfte des 17. Jahrhunderts*, Geist und Werk der Zeiten 37 (Frankfurt, 1973), 206–20.

7. In Russian the term Old Believers is considered rude, but as the English equivalent has caught on, it will be used here. On the terminology of the seventeenth century and later, see V. S. Rumiantseva, *Narodnoe antitserkovnoe dvizhenie v Rossii v XVII veke* (Moscow, 1986), 3–5.

8. The schism remained a live issue in the Russian church into the twentieth century and much of the basic literature is at least in part polemical. Even N. F. Kapterev, the most important prerevolutionary writer on the subject (and whose career suffered because his views were too objective for the church authorities in the 1880s), was still concerned to a large extent with the truth or falsity of charges of the 1660s. See N. F. Kapterev, *Patriarkh Nikon i Tsar' Aleksei Mikhailovich*, 2 vols. (Sergiev Posad, 1909–1912). Some more recent treatments are Pierre Pascal, *Avvakum et les débuts du raskol*, 2d ed., Etudes sur l'histoire, l'économie, et la sociologie des pays slaves 8 (Paris, 1963); Sergei Zen'kovskii, *Russkii raskol staroobriadchestva* (Munich, 1970); and in a less traditional vein, Michael Cherniavsky, "The Old Believers and the New Religion," *Slavic Review* 25 (1966): 1–39; and the work of A. N. Robinson and V. S. Rumiantseva.

9. N. V. Rozhdestvenskii, ed., "K istorii bor'by s tserkovnymi besporiadkami, otgoloskami iazychestva i porokami v russkom bytu XVII v.," *ChOIDR*, 1902, no. 2, pt. 4:1–31, esp. 22–23. On *mnogoglasie*, see Johann von Gardner, *System und Wesen des russichen Kirchengesangs*, Schriften zur Geistesgeschichte des östlichen Europas 12 (Wiesbaden, 1976), and idem, *Gesang der russisch-orthodoxen Kirche*, Schriften zur Geistesgeschichte des östlichen Europas 17 (Wiesbaden, 1987), 15–22; and N. D. Uspenskii, *Drevnerusskoe pevcheskoe iskusstvo* (Moscow, 1965).

10. Rozhdestvenskii, "K istorii," 24–26. It should be noted that these customs are recognizably the same as those of peasants and more traditional urban people as late as the early twentieth century. The Zealots' campaigns against these customs, like the tsars', were obviously unsuccessful. See Bushkovitch, "Epiphany."

11. Patriarch Ioasaf's letter is in *AAE*, 3, no. 264:401–5. It gives the motivation for the letter as the various troubles of Russia and the defeats at the hands of the unfaithful (the Smolensk War of 1632–1634) rather than any petition. The similarity of wording and the address to the Moscow clergy suggests that

perhaps an identical petition came from Moscow. On Iosif, see N. V. Ponyrko, "Iosif," in "Issledovatel'skie materialy dlia 'Slovaria knizhnikov i knizhnosti drevnei Rusi,'" *TODRL* 40 (1985): 111–14; Iosif, *Poucheniia* (Moscow, 1642); and *AAE*, 4, no. 327: 487–89. Iosif's homilies are reworkings of traditional texts and focus neither on the concerns of the Zealots in the 1640s nor the later concerns of Epifanii Slavinetskii and Simeon Polotskii.

12. Mohyla's catechism was the result of the 1642 Council of Iasi in Moldavia, called to condemn the errors of Patriarch Cyrill Lukaris, whose theology had been influenced by Calvinism. The Mohyla catechism contained a number of formulations that edged very close to the Catholic version, though a council in Constantinople in 1643 and Patriarch Nektarios of Jerusalem approved it. It was printed in Moscow in 1649 and remained a standard also among the Greeks until 1672. The Greek hierarchy in the decades after Lukaris seems to have been so concerned with crypto-Calvinist error that it was tolerant of colleagues who flirted with Catholicism. Patriarch Adrian had it reprinted in Moscow as late as 1696. See Runciman, *Great Church*, 340–51; Podskalsky, *Griechische Theologie*, 207–13, 233–36; and the text in *Sobranie kratkiia nauki ob artikulakh very* (Moscow, 1649).

13. As the title suggests, Nafanail included Zakharii Kopystens'kyi's book of the same title as well (for discussion on him and his work, see chapter 6). See also Rumiantseva, *Narodnoe*, 42–65; and V. S. Rumiantseva, "Kruzhok Stefana Vnifant'eva," in *Obshchestvo i gosudarstvo feodal'noi Rossii* (Moscow, 1975), 178–88; idem, *Narodnoe*, 31–65; *Kniga o vere* (Moscow, 1648); E. I. Kaluzhniatskii, "Igumena Nafanaila 'Kniga o vere', ee istochniki i znacheniia v istorii iuzhno-russkoi polemicheskoi literatury," *ChOIDR*, 1886, no. 4, pt. 2:1–36; Hans Peter Niess, *Kirche in Russland zwischen Tradition und Glaube*, Kirche im Osten 13, (Göttingen, 1977); and S. A. Belokurov, "Moskovskii Pechatnyi dvor v 1649 godu," *ChOIDR*, 1887, no. 4, pt. 4: 1–32; and P. N. Nikolaevskii, "Moskovskii Pechatnyi dvor pri Patriarkhe Nikone," *Khrist'ianskoe chtenie*, 1890, nos. 1–2; 1891, nos. 1–2.

14. For the Moscow revolt, see most recently E. V. Chistiakova, *Gorodskie vosstaniia v Rossii v pervoi polovine XVII veka (30-40-e gody)*, (Voronezh, 1975), 62–106; S. V. Bakhrushin, "Moskovskoie Vosstanie 1648 g.," in *Nauchnye trudy*, ed. A. A. Zimin et al., 4 vols. (Moscow, 1952–1955), 2:46–91; P. P. Smirnov, *Posadskie liudi i ikh klassovaia bor'ba do serediny XVII veka*, 2 vols. (Moscow and Leningrad, 1947–1948), 2:158–95. The assembly's documents are found in *SGGD*, 3, no. 129:438–39; A. N. Zertsalov, "Novye dannye o Zemskom sobore 1648–1649 gg.," *ChOIDR*, 1887, no. 3, pt. 4:1–80; P. P. Smirnov, "Neskol'ko dokumentov k istorii Sobornogo Ulozheniia i Zemskogo Sobora 1648–1649 godov," *ChOIDR*, 1913, no. 4, pt. 4:1–20; and the text of the code itself: M. N. Tikhomirov and P. P. Epifanov, eds. *Sobornoe Ulozhenie 1649 g.* (Moscow, 1961), chaps. 13 (on the Monastery Office), 17, arts. 42–44 (prohibition of sale of noble estates to the church) and 19, arts. 1–9, 20 (confiscation of church and boyar tax-exempt property in towns).

15. S. A. Belokurov, "Deianie Moskovskogo tserkovnogo sobora 1649 goda," *ChOIDR*, 1894, no. 4, pt. 3:29–52; and idem, *Materialy po Russkoi istorii* (Moscow, 1888), 455–56.

16. M. Gorchakov, *Monastyrskii prikaz (1649–1725)* (St. Petersburg, 1868), 11–101.

17. A. A. Zimin, ed., *Pamiatniki russkogo prava*, 8 vols. (Moscow, 1952–1961),

5:384; Bushkovitch, "Epiphany"; and Golubinskii, *Istoriia Kanonizatsii*, 229–38.

18. The tsar's request for the learned monks of 14 May 1649 is in *SGGD*, 3, no. 136:449–50. Kharlampovich, *Malorossiiskoe*, 119–46; V. O. Eingorn, *O snosheniiakh Malorossiiskogo dukhovenstva s Moskovskim pravitel'stvom v tsarstvovanie Alekseia Mikhailovicha, ChOIDR*, 1893, no. 2, pt. 4:1–370; 1894, no. 3, pt. 3:371–570; 1898, no. 4, pt. 3:570–794; 1899, no. 1, pt. 4:795–922; 1899, no. 2, pt. 4:933–1104. Kapterev and many other historians saw Vonifat'ev's loyalties to the Greeks as primary and the invitation to the Kievan monks as resulting from a need for Greek translators, not from interest in Kievan writings or culture, to him merely "Latinism": Kapterev, *Patriarkh Nikon*, 1:18–22, 36–51. The Zealots, however, were clearly knowledgeable about Kievan writings, as were many Russian religious writers of the early seventeenth century (see chapter 6). In reality there was no contradiction, for the Ukrainian church was subject to the patriarch of Constantinople and maintained close ties with the Greeks, who were in turn as involved in Latin culture almost as much as the Ukrainians. On the situation in the Ukraine and the Academy, see Hrushevs'kyi, *Istoriia*, 8, pt. 2:83–101; Frank E. Sysyn, *Between Poland and the Ukraine*; S. T. Golubev, *Kievskii Mitropolit Petr Mogila i ego spodvizhniki*, 2 vols. (Kiev, 1883–1898); Aleksander Jabłonowski, *Akademia Kijowsko-Mohilańska* (Cracow, 1900); Z. I. Khyzhniak, *Kyivo-Mohylians'ka Akademiia* (Kiev, 1981); "The Kiev Mohyla Academy," *Harvard Ukrainian Studies*, 8, nos. 1–2 (1984); and Ambroise Jobert, *De Luther à Mohila: La Pologne dans la crise de la chretienté 1517–1648*, Collection historique de l'institut d'études slaves 21 (Paris, 1974). The hetmanate was the part of the Ukraine east of the Dniepr River subject to the hetman, the leader of the Ukrainian cossacks.

19. A. S. Belokurov, "Arsenii Sukhanov," *ChOIDR*, 1891, no. 1, pt. 3:1–328; 1892, no. 2, pt. 3:329–440; Arsenii Sukhanov, "Proskinitarii Arseniia Sukhanova," *Pravoslavnyi Palestinskii sbornik* 7, no. 3 (1889): 1–390; Kapterev, "Snosheniia," 125–54. Paisios also established good relations with the future patriarch Nikon on this visit.

20. Belokurov, "Deianie," 48–49, publishing a document from the tsar's *tainyi prikaz* (privy chancellery). N. Gibbenet, *Istoricheskoe issledovanie o dele Patriarkha Nikona*, 2 vols. (St. Petersburg, 1882–1884), 2:470–72 (Iosif's *sobornoe ulozhenie*) and *AAE*, 4, no. 327:487–89.

21. Makarii, *Istoriia*, 11:176–79. Some attempts to advance these goals remained. See, for example, Metropolitan Iona of Rostov's rescript to his clergy of August 1652: *AI*, 4, no. 62:172–77.

22. Kapterev, *Patriarkh Nikon*, 1:106–36; A. N. Robinson, ed., *Zhizneopisaniia Avvakuma i Epifaniia: Issledovaniia i teksty* (Moscow, 1963), 146; N. I. Subbotin, *Materialy dlia istorii raskola za pervoe vremia ego sushchestvovanie*, 9 vols. (Moscow, 1875–1895), 1:20–26 (Avvakum's letter of 14 September 1653 to Vonifat'ev), 17–78 (Neronov's letters and petitions). The documentary evidence for the earliest phase of the split (1653–1658) is quite sparse. The only contemporary confirmation of Avvakum's account of Nikon's rescript is the printed *Psaltir'* of 11 February 1653, which lacked the traditional supplementary articles justifying the old practices. Even this evidence does not, strictly speaking, confirm the existence and contents of the rescript. Avvakum's 1653 letter, mentioned earlier, comes from contemporary archival sources,

but informs the reader only of Nikon's persecution of him but not its cause. Neronov's letters, from an eighteenth-century miscellany, are also mainly about his sufferings at Nikon's hands. His petition to the tsar of 27 February 1654 (Subbotin, *Materialy*, 1:51–70) is the first mention of the substance of the dispute, confirmed otherwise only in the 11 February 1653 *Psaltir'* (indirectly) and in contemporary accounts of the councils found in printed books, the *Skrizhal'* (1655–1656) and the 1655 *Sluzhebnik*. The "Zhitie Grigoriia Neronova" (in Subbotin, *Materialy* 1:243–305) was composed after Neronov's death (1670), and says virtually nothing about the disputes of 1653–1656, merely mentioning Neronov's exile to Vologda in very vague terms, suggesting unjust persecution but not revealing the cause. The history of the central events of the schism are very imperfectly known, with many mysterious episodes such as the visit of the Greek metropolitan of Naupaktos and Arta, Gabriel Vlasios, between October 1652 and February 1653, precisely the eve of the split. Metropolitan Gabriel's mission seems to have been theological and cultural rather than financial, but his discussions with Nikon remain unknown: Kapterev, "Snosheniia," 167–71. See also the recent review of the problem in Paul Meyendorff, "The Liturgical Reforms of Nikon" (Ph.D. diss., University of Notre Dame, 1987), 5–10.

23. Of the two accounts, that in the *Skrizhal'* is the fuller and more formal, comprising a separate text on the council. The 1655 *Sluzhebnik* describes the 1654 council in the preface (ff. 1–39), going on to briefly describe the 1655 council. The *Sluzhebnik* was published on 31 August 1655, while the *Skrizhal'* had a more complex printing history. It was begun in October 1655, but not completed until 6 June 1656, the delay apparently caused by Nikon's desire to receive supplementary support from Constantinople. The *Sluzhebnik* is thus the earliest dated source for the 1654 council, and it is the less informative of the two. While Nikon's opening speech is almost identical in the two accounts, the *Sluzhebnik* summarizes the supporting conciliar documents of 1589 and 1593, while the text in the *Skrizhal'* quotes them at greater length. The *Skrizhal'* also added the six specific liturgical issues, absent in the *Sluzhebnik*. It should be noted here that none of the many writers to deal with these events has produced (or given evidence of searching for) archival confirmation of these councils and their proceedings, though the Privy Chancellery (for one) seems to have kept records of other councils. The account presented here, like that of previous historians, may not be at all accurate, for the two accounts are highly polemical documents. The absence of any mention of the dispute over the sign of the cross is particularly suspicious. See *Sluzhebnik* (Moscow, 1655), 1–20; and *Skrizhal'* (Moscow, 1655–1656), "O imeni Boga nashego Iisusa Khrista," ff. 1–59 (numbered separately; usually the eleventh article in the book, ff. 486–515 in the modern penciled folio numbers in the Lenin Library copy microfilmed in the Center for Research Libraries, Chicago). The latter account carries a date, 7162 (1653–1654), on f. 515. See Kapterev, *Patriarkh Nikon*, 1:136–40. Paul Meyendorff, "The Liturgical Reforms of Nikon" (Ph.D. diss., University of Notre Dame, 1987), 10–19 uses Subbotin's publication of an undated manuscript that parallels the account in the *Skrizhal'*. He does not seem to notice either here or in his earlier account of the 1654 council that the sources do not wholly support the traditional chronology of events.

24. Karl Christian Felmy, *Die Deutung der göttlichen Liturgie in der russischen The-*

ologie, Arbeiten zur Kirchengeschichte 54 (Berlin and New York, 1984), 15–
111.

25. The Assembly decision is in *SGGD*, 3, no. 157:481–89. See also S. M. Solov'ev, *Istoriia Rossii s drevneishikh vremen*, 15 vols. (Moscow, 1960–1966),
5:587–629; Hrushevs'kyi, *Istoriia*, 9:609–12, 642–50, 728–965; Ludwik
Kubala, *Wojna moskiewska r. 1654–1655*, Szkice historyczne, serja 3 (Warsaw,
1910). Needless to say, these events receive quite different interpretation in
these classics of the respective national historiographies, as well as by subsequent historians.

26. Eingorn speculated that the involvement of Nikon in relations with the
Ukrainian church, largely handled otherwise by the tsar's emissary B. M.
Khitrovo, may have been one of the factors leading to the split between
Nikon and Aleksei a few months later. Eingorn, "O Snosheniiakh," 119, n.
99; Georg von Rauch, "Moskau und der Westen im Spiegel der sch-
wedischen diplomatischen Berichte der Jahre 1651–1655," *Archiv für
Kulturgeschichte* 34 (1952): 63.

27. Solov'ev, *Istoriia*, 5:629–31; Gibbenet, *Istoricheskoe*, 2:473–76; Kapterev, *Patriarkh Nikon*, 1:152–55; and Rumiantseva, *Narodnoe*, 93–106. The icon in
question was one of the Savior *Nerukotvornyi* (i.e., the Greek *acheiropoeton*,
uncreated by hands) that belonged to a townsman.

28. The account of the 1655 council in the preface to the *Sluzhebnik* describes the
business of the council as collecting Greek and Slavic manuscripts so as to
produce a corrected *Sluzebnik*—that is, the text that the preface introduces.
However, Paul of Aleppo gives a quite different account of both the inspiration of the council and its agenda. He claims that the idea was that of his
father Makarios, the patriarch of Antioch, and that various liturgical issues
were discussed, all on the initiative of Makarios. See "Puteshestvie antiokhiiskogo patriarkha Makariia v Rossiiu v polovine XVII veka, opisannoe
ego synom, arkhidiakonom Pavlom Aleppskim," trans. G. Murkos, *ChOIDR*,
1896, no. 4, pt. 2:1–156; 1897, no. 4, pt. 3:1–202; 1898, no. 3, pt. 3:1–208;
1898, no. 4, pt. 2:1–195; see 1898, no. 3, pt. 3:170–71. Kapterev believed
Paul of Aleppo to be a more reliable source, as the *Sluzhebnik* account maintains that a letter from Paisios of Jerusalem was read at the council, while in
fact it arrived in Moscow two months later. The letter was actually the work
of the archimandrite Meletios Syrigos, a supporter of Mohyla at the 1642
church council at Iasi: Kapterev, *Patriarkh Nikon*, 1:159; and Podskalsky,
Griechische Theologie, 211.

29. Subbotin, *Materialy* 1:124–33, is the record of the 1656 council's decisions,
the only council known from published documents of the time. (Subbotin
found it in the Synodal Rolls, now in the State Historical Museum, GIM. The
document is undated, but since it assumes Neronov's presence it must be
from 1656, as he was in exile for the councils of 1654 and 1655.) The only
other known contemporary account of the council is in the "Vopros velikogo
gosudaria sviateishego Nikona," *Skrizhal'*, ff. 1–7v (modern numbers 422–
428v). The two are not fully compatible, for the Synodal Rolls document
condemns Neronov for believing that the ancient Greek and Slavic books do
not help salvation and for rebellion against church authority. The "Vopros,"
however, concerns only the making of the sign of the cross. On the other
hand, the "Vopros" does not try to provide a complete account of the council
of 1656, and forms an introduction to the next four chapters of the book

(works of Damascene Studite, etc.) on the correct way of making the sign of the cross. Kapterev, *Patriarkh Nikon,* 1:193–95 accepted the account in the *Skrizhal'* as valid.

30. Nikon seems to have supported this war with the same enthusiasm that he showed for the Polish War. The Swedish ambassadors Bjelke, Essen, and Krusenstiern (who all hated Nikon and held him responsible for the war) reported in October 1657 that he was the main person in the Russian state behind the war: "Die rechte causa impulsiva undt der ratt so das gantze wark treibet, das ist des Patriarchen grausamme und listige natur die Ihn zu allen mitteln reitzet, durch welche Er dominatum Ecclesiasticum stabilire." Supposedly he flattered the tsar into agreeing to the war, his real purpose being to be able to use the army to support his church reforms in the face of popular discontent. The Swedes interpreted the real purpose of the reform to be the establishment of the power of the church over the state. G. V. Forsten, "Snosheniia Shvetsii s Rossiei vo vtoroi polovine XVII veka (1648–1700)," *ZMNP* 316 (April 1898): 324–25.

31. Pokrovskii, *Russkie eparkhii,* 1:237–38, 247–54; and Subbotin, *Materialy* 1:9–13 with 1656 date. Streshnev brought up the Kolomna incident as a charge against Nikon in 1662: Gibbenet, *Istoricheskoe,* 2:532. The metropolitanate of Krutitsy (Krutitsy was a district of Moscow) was the inheritor of the eparchy of Sarai and the Don, the Orthodox eparchy within the Golden Horde. From 1461 its bishops had their seat in Krutitsy, a district within Moscow, and functioned as assistants to the Russian metropolitans. In 1589 their rank was raised to metropolitan, under the patriarch of Moscow. Formally they remained metropolitans "of Sarai and the Don" (*Sarskii* and *Podonskii*) but were often called "of Krutitsy" (*Krutitskii*). See N. A. Solov'ev, "Saraiskaia i Krutitskaia eparkhiia," *ChOIDR* 1894, no. 3, pt. 1:1–226.

32. Kapterev, *Patriarkh Nikon,* 1:394–431. The earliest documents are a letter of Nikon to the tsar in July 1658, apologizing for his departure to the monastery without the tsar's permission, and a deposition of Trubetskoi of 15 February 1660, describing the events in the Dormition Cathderal on 10 July 1658: *Delo o Patriarkhe Nikone* (St. Petersburg, 1897), no. 1, 6:1–2, 15–16. A similar deposition from the same day by *stol'nik* Andrei Matiushkin confirms the incident with Khitrovo and Meshcherskii: Gibbenet, *Istoricheskoe,* 1:178–79. These three documents were prepared for the church council of 1660 that was to depose Nikon officially. In June 1662, Nikon wrote in justification of his actions to Paisios, metropolitan of Gaza, that he had objected to the power of laymen, the tsar's officials, to judge and administer the church (a reference to the Monastery Office), and only then recounted the story of Khitrovo's insult: Gibbenet, *Istoricheskoe,* 1:222–27. The most extensive account of the incident from Nikon's side comes in a letter of 8 February 1666 (the eve of his final deposition), where the same causes were given: at first the tsar was in harmony with the church but "then he gradually grew proud and haughty [*nacha pomalu gorditisia i vysitisia*] and when we said, 'stop!', [he] began to interfere with his power in the affairs of the patriarchate and control our court." Here the Khitrovo incident was also recounted in fullest detail. Cf. *Zapiski otdeleniia russkoi i slavianskoi arkheologii imp. Russkogo arkheologicheskogo obshchestva* (St. Petersburg, 1861), 2:510–30, esp. 513. Nikon cited the Khitrovo incident at the council of 1666–1667: Gibbenet, *Istoricheskoe,* 2:1008–9, 1013. All of these documents ultimately come from

the archive of the tsar's Privy Chancellery, which kept the evidence for the councils that were to try to depose Nikon officially. On Trubetskoi, see Robert O. Crummey, *Aristocrats and Servitors: The Boyar Elite in Russia 1613–1689* (Princeton, 1983), 100, 186, and on Teimuraz in Moscow, N. T. Nakashidze, *Gruzino-russkie politicheskie otnosheniia v pervoi polovine XVII veke* (Tbilisi, 1968), 182–89.

33. *AAE*, 3, nos. 211–12:309–11, no. 225:335–36.

34. Nikon also mobilized supplies and soldiers for the army: *Zapiski*, 2:591–93. Gorchakov's study of the Monastery Office (based solely on published administrative documents) records Nikon's opposition expressed after 1658, but nothing of his relationship to administrative practice in 1652–1658: Gorchakov, *Monastyrskii prikaz*, 89–95. The basic works on the Privy Chancellery give the impression that Tsar Aleksei, not Nikon, was in charge of the state. See I. A. Gurliand, *Prikaz velikogo gosudaria tainykh del* (Iaroslavl', 1902); and A. I. Zaozerskii, *Tsarskaia votchina XVII veka*, 2d ed. (Moscow, 1937), 234–306. Other records, such as those of the *Razriad*, reveal the same picture. The only example of Nikon's involvement in government known to me is his rescript of 16 August 1655, to the Banditry Office (*Razboinyi prikaz*), ordering it not to punish bandits and thieves who repented of their crimes to the church: *Polnoe sobranie zakonov Rossiiskoi imperii*, vol. 1, no. 163 (St. Petersburg, 1830), 355–56. This action of Nikon's was brought up later by Streshnev in his questions to Paisios. Tsar Aleksei's policy on this issue fluctuated considerably during his reign, and it is hard to see Nikon's rescript as a major infraction. The issue did concern the church as well as the state.

35. Kapterev, *Patriarkh Nikon*, 2:122–208; and *Delo*, nos. 117–23, 429–38. A better example of Nikon's views on the dignity of the patriarchate is suggested by his translation of the relics of Metropolitan Filipp to Moscow in 1652. However, Tsar Aleksei supported this act fully, even writing an epistle to the relics in March 1652, begging the saint's forgiveness for his predecessor's (Ivan IV's) misdeeds: *SGGD*, 3, no. 147:471–72. At Nikon's trial at the 1666 council, however, Aleksei adduced Nikon's statement in a letter to Patriarch Dionysios of Constantinople that Ivan had unjustly mistreated Filipp as a dishonor to the memory of his ancestor: Gibbenet, *Istoricheskoe*, 2:1012. Nikon claimed in 1663 that before he agreed to be patriarch he told the tsar that he would imitate Filipp in reproving any actions of the tsar contrary to "holy commands," and Aleksei agreed. See Valerie Tumins and George Vernadsky, eds., *Patriarch Nikon on Church and State: Nikon's "Refutation"* (Berlin, New York, and Amsterdam, 1982), 636. The *Zhitie* of Filipp stresses the metropolitan's right to reprove the tsar for his political acts (not an issue with Nikon, it seems) and to be judged by clerics alone. The latter was clearly an issue, but only after 1658: Bushkovitch, "Filipp." Eingorn's belief that Nikon's correspondence with Ukrainian churchmen offended Khitrovo and contributed to the break with the tsar is only speculation.

36. *Delo*, no. 3, 3–5; Gibbenet, *Istoricheskoe*, 1:167–72.

37. Kapterev, *Patriarkh Nikon*, 2:256–68; Gibbenet, *Istoricheskoe*, 1:180–220, 2:495–96. *Delo*, nos. 5–27, 12–111. The Greek prelates did not constitute a particularly high-level delegation, for the most senior members seem to have been the archbishops Parthenios of Thebes and Kyrillos of Chios.

38. Gibbenet, *Istoricheskoe*, 2:518–50. On Paisios, a highly dubious character, see G. Vorob'ev, "Paisii Ligarid," *Russkii biograficheskii slovar'*, vol. Pavel–Petr (Il-

eika), 118–22; V. Grumel, "Ligarides, Paisios," *Dictionnaire de théologie catholique,* no. 9, 1:749–57; Harry Hionides, *Paisius Ligarides* (New York, 1972); Podskalsky, *Griechische Theologie,* 251–58; and Ligarides' history of the 1666–1667 council in William Palmer, *The Patriarch and the Tsar,* 6 vols. (London, 1871–1876), 3:1–311. Ligarides was born in a Greek (but Catholic) family in Crete and educated in Rome, but about 1640 managed to get himself accepted as Orthodox, with the secret mission of bringing about church union. In 1652 Paisios, the patriarch of Jerusalem, made him metropolitan of Gaza.

39. Tumins and Vernadsky, *Patriarch Nikon,* 408–9. Paisios responded in turn by reviewing the council of 1660 at the tsar's request and finding Nikon mostly in the wrong, in particular rejecting his argument that he had not left the patriarchal dignity, only the office. See Kapterev, *Patriarkh Nikon,* 2:268–93; Gibbenet, *Istoricheskoe,* 2:585–89.

40. Nikon's appearance in Moscow: Gibbenet, *Istoricheskoe,* 2:736–59, and *Delo,* nos. 31–43, 121–246. Correspondence with the Greeks and decision of deposition: Gibbenet, *Istoricheskoe,* 2:561–85, 640–736, 759–73, 776–84, 796–850, 854–908, 910–63, 981–97, and *Delo,* nos. 49–77, 270–314. The story of the Greeks' participation in these events is poorly known and almost entirely from the Russian side. Some idea can be found in Kapterev, *Patriarkh Nikon,* 2:323–65, Runciman, *Great Church,* 320–27. On Nektarios, see V. Grumel, "Nectaire," *Dictionnaire de théologie catholique,* 11, no. 1:50–58; "Nektarios," *Thrēskeutikē kai ethikē enkyklopaideia,* 12 vols. (Athens, 1962–1968), 9:396–97; Podskalsky, *Griechische Theologie,* 244–48; and his anti-Catholic tract, *Confutatio imperii Papae in ecclesiam* (Iasi, 1682; reprint, London, 1702). Though a frequent anti-Catholic polemicist, Nektarios had approved Mohyla's catechism in 1662.

41. Gibbenet, *Istoricheskoe,* 2:997–1099 (the whole trial); esp. 1002–18; 1019 (quotation); and 1099 (final quotation); and Kapterev, *Patriarkh Nikon,* 2:209–55. Ligarides presumably still thought of himself as Catholic, but had little contact with Rome by this time. Kapterev and other Russian church historians, concerned about the correctness of the council's decisions, have stressed his character and presumed Catholicism, but what role did it play? There is no evidence that he was still in contact with Rome or following its dictates, nor is it clear what Rome would have to gain from helping to depose Nikon. In trying to interfere in such quarrels among the Greeks in the seventeenth century, Rome supported pro-Catholic Greeks, but who could Rome support in Russia? After the council (September 1668) Ligarides claimed that he was furthering the cause of union. The statement came, however, in a letter to a Catholic correspondent inquiring on behalf of the papal nuncio in Warsaw about Ligarides' doings in Moscow. If Ligarides had been following Rome's orders to further the Uniate cause, the nuncio in Warsaw should have known about them. In 1673 the Roman Congregatio de propaganda fide, supposedly Paisios's bosses, prepared a memo from the information of Vidoni, the then-nuncio in Poland, in which Paisios's claim to have helped the cause of union is noted, but the example has to do with attempting to change the Russian attitude to baptism, not Nikon. Rome does not seem to have been in control. See Emile Legrand, *Bibliothèque hellénique du XVIIe siècle,* 5 vols. (Paris, 1894–1903), 4:8–61, esp. 53–54, 59–61. The Greeks' attitude to Ligarides seems to have been ambiguous, a clear condemnation coming only after the 1666–1667 council. Podskalsky gives the im-

pression that the chief enemy of the Greek hierarchy was the crypto-Calvinism of Lukaris and his follower John Karyophylles (c. 1600–c. 1693), officially condemned in 1692, and only after this did Dositheos of Jerusalem turn the main attention of the church against Catholic influence: Podskalsky, *Griechische Theologie*, 181, 236–42, 282–94.

42. Pavel was a priest in his early life, then a monk in the Novospasskii Monastery and archimandrite of the Chudov Monastery (1659–1664), after which he was Sarskii and Podonskii (Krutitskii) metropolitan until his death in 1675. He was also Simeon Polotskii's patron. Ioasaf II had been archimandrite of the Trinity–St. Sergii Monastery from 1656 until he was chosen patriarch. Vs. Sreznevskii, "Pavel," *Russkii biograficheskii slovar'*, vol. Pavel–Petr (Ileika), 73–75; N. A. Solov'ev, "Saraiskaia," 84–91; N. B., "Ioasaf II," *Russkii biograficheskii slovar'*, vol. Ibak–Kliucharev, 296–98; O. A. Belobrova, "Ioasaf II," in "Materialy," 40, 97–99; and Kapterev, "Snosheniia," 187–270.

43. K. V. Bazilevich, *Denezhnaia reforma Alekseia Mikhailovicha i vosstanie v Moskve v 1662 g.* (Moscow and Leningrad, 1936); V. I. Buganov, *Moskovskoe vosstanie 1662 g.* (Moscow, 1964).

44. Ivan Rumiantsev, *Nikita Konstantinov Dobrynin ("Pustosviat")* (Sergiev Posad, 1916), dopolnenie, 248–326; Subbotin, *Materialy*, 4:179–223.

45. Rumiantseva, *Narodnoe*, 143–87.

46. N. Subbotin, ed., *Deianiia moskovskikh soborov 1666 i 1667 godov* (Moscow, 1893), 16–16v.; Robinson, *Zhizneopisaniia*, 167–68; Kapterev, *Patriarkh Nikon*, 2:336–420. Simeon Polotskii refuted the petitions of Lazar' and Nikita in his *Zhezl pravleniia* (Moscow, 1668). Avvakum here defends the Old Believer position on the sign of the cross. While the Orthodox declared the proper gesture to require three fingers (thumb, index, and middle fingers, symbolizing the Trinity), the Old Believers used the index and middle fingers (symbolizing the dual nature of Christ). They also held together the thumb and last two fingers of the hand folded to symbolize the Trinity. Thus they actually used five fingers, though the greater importance of the two gave rise to the popular description of the Old Believer custom as two fingers.

47. Pascal, *Avvakum*, 388–463; L. E. Ankudinova, "Sotsial'nyi sostav pervykh raskol'nikov," *Vestnik LGU, Seriia istorii, iazyka i literatury* 3, no. 14 (1956): 56–68; A. I. Mazunin, ed., *Povest' o boiaryne Morozovoi* (Leningrad, 1979); and Rumiantseva, *Narodnoe*, 141–43.

48. I. Ia. Syrtsov, *Vozmushchenie solovetskikh monakhov-staroobriadtsev v XVII v.* (Kostroma, 1889); N. A. Barsukov, *Solovetskoe vosstanie 1668–1676 gg.* (Petrozavodsk, 1954); and E. Barsov, ed., "Akty otnosiashchiesia k istorii Solovetskogo bunta," *ChOIDR*, 1883, no. 4, pt. 5:1–92.

49. Pascal, *Avvakum*, 532–54; and Rumiantseva, *Narodnoe*, 186. Ioakim (Savelov, 1620–1690) came from a landholding family and became a monk in 1655, enjoying the patronage of both Nikon and F. M. Rtishchev. Archimandrite of the Chudov Monastery in 1664–1673, he became metropolitan of Novgorod in 1673 and patriarch in the following year. On Ioakim, see "Ioakim," *Russkii biograficheskii slovar'*, vol. Ibak–Kliucharev, 174–77; N. Barsukov, ed., *Zhitie i zaveshchanie sviateishego patriarkha moskovskogo Ioakima*, Izdania Obshchestva liubitelei drevnei pis'mennosti 47 (St. Petersburg, 1879); P. A. Smirnov, "Ioakim patriarkh Moskovskii," *Chteniia obshchestva liubitelei dukhovnogo pros-*

veshcheniia, 1879, no. 2:192–230; 1879, no. 4:417–36; 1880, no. 5:556–602; 1881, no. 4:469–529; 1888, no. 5:575–605; and A. P. Barsukov, "Vserossiiskii Patriarkh Ioakim Savelov," *Pamiatniki drevnei pis'mennosti* 83 (St. Petersburg, 1891), appendix 6, 1–15.

50. Nikon benefited little from his forgiveness, for he died on the way home from exile in September 1681. Kapterev, "Snosheniia," 236, 240–48; Kartashev, *Ocherki*, 2:233.

51. *PSZ*, 2, no. 711, p. 784.

52. Pokrovskii, *Russkie eparkhii*, 1:285–90, 314–86; and T. B. Solov'eva, "O vzaimootnosheniiakh tsarskoi vlasti i patriarshestva po zemel'nomu i finansovomu voprosam vo vtoroi polovine XVII v. v Rossii," *Vestnik moskovskogo universiteta: Seriia istoriia* 5 (1978): 60–72. Solov'eva sees Ioakim as largely successful in defense of church property and tax privileges.

53. On the recognition of saints, see chapter 4. Nikolai Vinogradskii, *Tserkovnyi sobor v Moskve 1682 goda* (Smolensk, 1899); Mansvetov, *Tserkovny ustav (Tipik)*, 323–69; K. Nikol'skii, *Materialy dlia istorii ispravleniia bogosluzhebnykh knig: Ob ispravlenii ustava tserkovnogo v 1682 godu i mesiachnykh minei v 1689–1691 gg.*, Pamiatniki drevnei pis'mennosti 115 (St. Petersburg, 1896). Many of the demotions were of festivals of the discovery of relics of saints whose day of birth or death was celebrated elsewhere in the year (e.g., Tsarevich Dmitrii).

54. In the early years of Sophia's regency, Ioakim and his chief spokesman, the monk Evfimii of the Chudov Monastery, began to attack one Sil'vestr Medvedev, the chief Russian pupil of Simeon Polotskii. The charge was that Medvedev, influenced by the Latin atmosphere of Kiev through his teacher Simeon, was preaching a Catholic view of transubstantiation, specifically that he took the Catholic view of when in the mass transubstantiation took place. The dispute continued unresolved through the 1680s, complicated by the disputes about what kind of school to found in Moscow. Simeon and Sil'vestr wanted a school modeled on the Ukrainian schools, with their Jesuit curriculum and emphasis on learning Latin. Ioakim claimed that Medvedev was smuggling in papist teachings, and succeded in founding a rival, headed by the Leikhudes brothers, two Greeks. As an issue of national culture this dispute was more than a little specious, for the Leikhudes had been educated at Padua in exactly the same culture as Simeon in Kiev. Their school had essentially the same curriculum and emphasized Latin almost as much as Medvedev's proposal. The important thing to Ioakim in these rather obscure disputes was that the "Latin" option was allied to the court, in this case to Sophia's court and the cultural tastes of her favorite, V. V. Golitsyn. Ioakim preferred a school beholden to him and reflecting the religious culture of the Balkan Greeks. Toward the end of Sophia's reign he was in the ascendant, for not only did he get his school on his terms but he was able to bring the metropolitanate of Kiev under his control (1687). The young Peter's coup d'etat of 1689 gave him his chance, and Medvedev was quickly arrested, convicted of heresy, and beheaded in January 1690. Ioakim's support of Peter against Sophia was profoundedly short-sighted, however, for Peter proved to be the most powerful enemy the supporters of Nikon and Ioakim could have had. See I. P. Kozlovskii, "Sil'vestr Medvedev," *Kievskie universitetskie izvestiia* 35 (February 1895): 1–49; 35 (March 1895): 50–90; 35 (May 1895): 91–130; A. A. Prozorovskii, "Sil'vestr Medvedev," *ChOIDR*, 1896, no.

2, pt. 4:1–148; 1896, no. 3, pt. 4:149–378; 1896, no. 4, pt. 3:379–606; A. V. Florovskii, "Chudovskii monakh Evfimii," *Slavia* 19 (1949–1950): 100–52; M. Smentsovskii, *Brat'ia Likhudy: Opyt issledovaniia iz istorii tserkovnogo prosveshcheniia i tserkovnoi zhizni kontsa XVII i nachala XVIII vekov* (St. Petersburg, 1899); and S. K. Smirnov, *Istoriia moskovskoi Slaviano-greko-latinskoi akademii* (Moscow, 1855).

Chapter 4

1. Fedotov, *Sviatye*, 187–90; Ia. S. Lur'e, ed., *Istoki russkoi belletristiki* (Leningrad, 1970), 387–449; and Likhachev, *Razvitie*, 127–37.
2. Kliuchevskii, *Drevnerusskie*; Golubinskii, *Istoriia Kanonizatsii*, esp. 11–39; and V. Vasil'ev, *Istoriia kanonizatsii russkikh sviatykh*, ChOIDR, 1893, no. 3, pt. 3:1–256. Recent literature continues to follow Golubinskii very closely, such as A. S. Khoroshev, *Politicheskaia istoriia russkoi kanonizatisii (XI–XVI vv.)* (Moscow, 1986). Fedotov noted that Golubinskii's emphasis on miracles as primary evidence for sainthood was incorrect: Fedotov, *Sviatye*, 11–17.
3. Golubinskii, *Istoriia Kanonizatsii*, 43–49; Khoroshev, *Politicheskaia*, 13–36; Andrzej Poppe, "O vremeni zarozhdeniia kul'ta Borisa i Gleba," *Russia Medievalis* 1 (1973): 6–29; Gail Lenhoff, *The Martyred Princes Boris and Gleb: A Socio-cultural Study of the Cult and the Texts*, UCLA Slavic Studies 19 (Columbus, Ohio, 1989); and Podskalsky, *Christentum*, 106–16. As noted by Podskalsky (118), the Kievan texts that praised St. Vladimir specifically noted the absence of miracles at his tomb and quoted St. John Chrysostom to the effect that actions, not miracles, make a man holy. This would seem to imply some criteria, but the texts are literary-liturgical compositions, not official documents. In the West as well, the church tried to keep the holy life of a saint as the center of attention, while for the layman the essential point was the direct experience of the supernatural. Cf. Andre Vauchez, *La sainteté en occident aux derniers siècles du Moyen Age d'après les procès de canonisation et les documents hagiographiques*, Bibliothèque des écoles françaises d'Athènes et de Rome 241 (Rome, 1981), 43.
4. The Russian church recognized the validity of these relics as well as those of other Pechera monks only in 1762. See Golubinskii, *Istoriia Kanonizatsii*, 50–53, 59–60, 202; Khoroshev, *Politicheskaia*, 36–46, who stresses the central role of Sviatopolk; Podskalsky, *Christentum*, 54; O. V. Tvorogov, "Zhitie Antoniia Pecherskogo," in Likhachev, *Slovar'*, vyp. 1:135–36; and the definitive study of R. D. Bosley, "A History of the Veneration of SS. Theodosij and Antonij" (Ph.D. diss., Yale University, 1980), 146–67.
5. The Greek church as well seems to have lacked a strict canonization procedure. Most saints seem to have gradually appeared in liturgical books, and only in controversial cases (like that of St. Gregory Palamas) was a council called to adjudicate the matter. After 1453 formal decisions of the patriarch and church hierarchy were more common (or perhaps simply better recorded). Hans-Georg Beck, *Kirche und theologische Literatur im Byzantinischen Reich* (Munich, 1959), 274–75; Ruth Macrides, "Saints and Sainthood in the Early Palaiologan Period," in *The Byzantine Saint*, University of Birmingham Fourteenth Spring Symposium of Byzantine Studies, ed. Sergei Hackel (Studies Supplementary to Sobornost 5) (1981), 67–87. Cf. also Paul Mag-

dalino, "The Byzantine Holy Man in the Twelfth Century," ibid., 51–66; and Golubinskii, *Istoriia Kanonizatsii*, 385–405.

6. Golubinskii, *Istoriia Kanonizatsii*, 67, 542, 382–83; Khoroshev, *Politicheskaia*, 98; Macrides, "Sainthood," 87, n. 135; John Meyendorff, *Byzantium*, 156; F. Miklošich and J. Müller, *Acta et diplomata graeca medii aevi*, 6 vols. (Vienna, 1860–1890), 1:191.

7. Kiprian's life was included in the Book of Degrees and is published there: *PSRL*, 21:321–32, esp. 330.

8. Voskresenskaia chronicle, *PSRL*, 8:121; A. A. Zimin, ed., *Ioasafovskaia letopis'* (Moscow, 1957), 42; *AI*, 1, no. 43:87, the letter of Metropolitan Iona (to the Lithuanian state and church). Khoroshev suggests that the canonization took place at a church council in 1447, but then goes on to state that "The lack of any indication of the presence of the canonization question in the agenda of the council can be explained by the poor organization of the procedures [*deloproizvodsto*] of canonization of that era" (*Politicheskaia*, 122). Another, more probable, explanation is that canonization was not discussed and did not take place in 1447.

9. Golubinskii, *Istoriia Kanonizatsii*, 85–92.

10. "Voskresenskaia letopis'," *PSRL*, 8:150 [1463]; *Ioasafovskaia letopis'*, 53–54 [1463]; "Sofiiskaia vtoraia letopis'," *PSRL*, 6:186–87 [1467]; L'vov Chronicle, *PSRL*, 20:277–78 [1467]; Book of Degrees, *PSRL*, 21:306–14; *Velikie Minei-chet'i*, St. Petersburg, September 1868, 1255–82; Kliuchevskii, *Drevnerusskie*, 172–73; Khoroshev, 155–57; Barsukov, *Istochniki*, 597–600; N. I. Se-rebrianskii, "Drevnerusskie kniazheskie zhitiia," *ChOIDR*, 1915, no. 3:1–296, cf. 229–32; L. A. Dmitriev, "Zhitie Fedora iaroslavskogo," in Likhachev, *Slovar'*, vyp. 1:179–81. Prince Fedor appeared in the first printed service books, in 1602 and 1610, so he seems to have been recognized as a saint without difficulty: Golubinskii, *Istoriia Kanonizatsii*, 229; and *Ustav* (*Oko tserkovnoe*) (Moscow, 1610), 287–90.

11. "Voskresenskaia letopis'," *PSRL*, 8:269; Zimin, *Rossiia na poroge*, 256–57; Golubinskii, *Istoriia Kanonizatsii*, 83, 100; G. Z. Kuntsevich, "Podlinnyi spisok o novykh chudotvortsakh," *IORIaS* 15 (1910): 252–57; Zimin relied on MS GBL Undol'skii 310 (not listed by Barsukov) for his information on the events of 1523.

12. Kliuchevskii, *Drevnerusskie*, 289–90; Barsukov, *Istochniki*, 340–43; and M. D. Kagan, "Zhitie Makariia Koliazinskogo," in Likhachev, ed., *Slovar'*, vyp. 2, 1:293–96.

13. Golubinskii, *Istoriia Kanonizatsii*, 86, 152, 557; Barsukov, *Istochniki*, 146–48 (all seventeenth century): Kliuchevskii, *Drevnerusskie*, 282–83; the life of Daniil was included in the Book of Degrees, *PSRL*, 21:615–26, cf. 624; O. A. Belobrova, "Zhitie Daniila Pereiaslavskogo," in Likhachev, ed., *Slovar'*, vyp. 2, 1:257–59.

14. Golubinskii, *Istoriia Kanonizatsii*, 87–88, citing MS (now GBL) Trinity 654. Cf. Arsenii and Ilarii, "Opisanie slavianskikh rukopisei biblioteki Troitse-Sergievoi Lavry," *ChOIDR*, 1878, no. 4:179, 233–34; Barsukov, *Istochniki*, 233–36; and A. V. Gorskii and K. I. Nevostruev, *Opisanie slavianskikh rukopisei Moskovskoi sinodal'noi biblioteki*, 5 vols. (Moscow, 1855–1917), 2, pt. 3: 132–33. This manuscript (Syn. 234) is a seventeenth-century miscellany that follows the tale of the discovery of Iakov's relics with miracles going up to 1582. Kliuchevskii accepted the authenticity of these documents in the tale,

but gave no reason for doing so: Kliuchevskii, *Drevnerusskie*, 425. In 1572 there was still skepticism about Iakov, for the Second Novgorod Chronicle recorded that Archbishop Leonid of Novgorod again investigated the miracles, and again found them to be real: "Novgorodskaia tret'ia letopis'," *PSRL*, 3:168. Golubinskii's assertion, *Istoriia Kanonizatsii*, (114) that the 1572 incident immediately produced a national festival is without proof. His own list of festivals in the printed liturgical books of the seventeenth century shows a festival for Iakov from 1610 and for Andrei of Smolensk from 1602: Golubinskii, *Istoriia Kanonizatsii*, 230, 235.

15. N. M. Karamzin, *Istoriia gosudarstva Rossiiskogo*, 6th ed., 12 vols. (St. Petersburg, 1851–1853), 9:51–52, and "Primechaniia," 27–29; *AAE*, 1, no. 213:203–4; Golubinskii, *Istoriia Kanonizatsii*, 99–100; Vasil'ev, *Istoriia kanonizatsii*, 155–83; Kuntsevich, "Podlinnyi spisok"; N. I. Serebrianskii, "Drevnerusskie . . . zhitiia," *ChOIDR*, 1915, no. 3; *Povest' o Petre i Fevronii*, ed. R. P. Dmitrieva (Leningrad, 1979); O. A. Belobrova, "Zhitie Prokopiia Ustiuzhskogo," in Likhachev, ed., *Slovar'*, vyp. 2, 1:322–24.

16. Mikhail Klopskii and Konstantin of Murom were omitted in 1602 and 1633, but present in the others. Makarii of Kaliazin and Zosima and Savvatii Solovetskii had only local festivals in the *Ustav* of 1641: Nikol'skii, *Materialy*, 8.

17. Kliuchevskii, *Drevnerusskie*, 248, 266–67; R. P. Dmitrieva, "Vasilii," in Likhachev, ed., *Slovar'*, vyp. 2, 1:112–16; idem, "Markell," in Likhachev, ed., *Slovar'*, vyp. 2, 2:103–4; Golubinskii, *Istoriia Kanonizatsii*, 54–56, 227–36.

18. Kozhanchikov, *Stoglav*, 36–38.

19. Pokrovskii, *Sudnye spiski*, 125–39; S. O. Shmidt, *Stanovlenie rossiiskogo samoderzhavstva* (Moscow, 1973), 152–56.

20. Kliuchevskii, *Drevnerusskie*, 240–41, 460–63; Golubinskii, *Istoriia Kanonizatsii*, 103–7, 227–36; Vasil'ev, *Istoriia kanonizatsii*, 183–99; Kozhanchikov, *Stoglav*, 130; Ia. S. Lur'e, "Zhitie Iony," in Likhachev, ed., *Slovar'*, vyp. 2, 1:270–73, where Lur'e notes the existence of another manuscript of the Kliuchevskii version in the collection of the Solovetskii Monastery in the Public Library, Leningrad.

21. Barsukov, *Istochniki*, 238–39; Kliuchevskii, *Drevnerusskie*, 250–64; R. P. Dmitrieva, "Vasilii," in Likhachev, ed., *Slovar'*, vyp. 2, 1:112–16; V. I. Okhotnikov, "Zhitie Evfrosina," ibid., 262–64; L. V. Sokolova, "Roman", ibid., vyp. 2, 2:311–13, who prefers a date for Efrem's life of 1545–1554.

22. Kozhanchikov, *Stoglav*, 37–38.

23. Dmitriev, *Povest' o zhitii Mikhaila Klopskogo*, 85–86, citing the "Sofiiskaia vtoraia letopis'," *PSRL*, 6:301.

24. Lur'e, *Ideologicheskaia bor'ba*, 322–23; "Sudnoe delo Vassiana Patrikeeva," in Kazakova, *Vassian*, 297–98; Pokrovskii, *Sudnye spiski*, 111–13.

25. Pokrovskii, *Sudnye spiski*, 113.

26. Kozhanchikov, *Stoglav*, 44–45, 47–50, 54, 57, 114–16, 165–213. It might be objected that the criticism of monastic shortcomings was a commonplace of medieval Christian societies, East and West. In this specific case, however, the criticism was new and unique, for all the controversy about monasticism in the years roughly 1480–1530 yielded nothing of this type. Vassian Patrikeev, for example, stuck to the issue of monastic landholding, and does not seem to have found other faults in the monastic life of Josephite monasteries or others: Vassian Patrikeev, "Slovo otvetno," in Kazakova, *Vassian*, 254–71.

27. The notice on Peter of the Horde's local festival comes from a late Volokolamsk Monastery service book, and that of Iakov of Borovichi is merely a chronicle notice of miracles. Antonii Siiskii (died 1556) was more recent and substantial as a spiritual figure. One version of his life was written by Tsarevich Ivan Ivanovich, but the fact of establishment of a local festival is unclear. Efrem of Novyi Torzhok (died 1053) was a semilegendary figure whose very late life asserts that Metropolitan Dionisii established a local festival in his honor in the years 1584–1587. In the 1641 *Ustav* his festival was made optional: Nikol'skii, *Materialy,* 22–23. Only Antonii Siiskii's local festival seems based on hard evidence. Golubinskii, *Istoriia Kanonizatsii,* 110–11, 113–14, 117, 230–31, 234; *Ustav,* 1610, ff. 349–351v, 447–448, 556v–557v, 754–757v; *PSRL,* 3:168; Kliuchevskii, *Drevnerusskie,* 38–43, 300–3, 335–36, 425–26; Barsukov, *Istochniki,* 51-55, 233–36, 195–97, 453–56; Charles J. Halperin, "A Chingissid Saint of the Russian Orthodox Church: The Life of Peter, tsarevich of the Horde," *Canadian-American Slavic Studies* 9 (1975): 324–35; R. P. Dmitrieva, "Povesti o Petre tsareviche ordynskom," Likhachev, ed., *Slovar',* vyp. 2, 2:256–59; and L. A. Dmitriev, "Zhitie Antoniia Siiskogo," ibid., vyp. 2, 1:247–48.

28. Golubinskii, *Istoriia Kanonizatsii,* 230, 235; and *Ustav,* 1610, ff. 320v–324v, 543–546v, 813–816.

29. *Ustav,* 1610, 310v–311v, 312–318, 376v–378v, 417–419v, 430–436v, 577v–581v, 617–618, 689v–694, 801–802; Golubinskii, *Istoriia Kanonizatsii,* 81, 85, 153, 230, 232, 234, 239; Barsukov, *Istochniki,* 398–400, 502–8, 591–92; Kliuchevskii, *Drevnerusskie,* 268–69, 289–91, 353; V. A. Kuchkin, *Povesti o Mikhaile Tverskom* (Moscow, 1974); and Moiseeva, "Zhitie . . . Serapiona." There are also the three saints included in the "1549" list that appear in the 1602 book, Archbishop Evfimii (II) Viazhitskii of Novgorod, Stefan of Perm', and Evfimii of Suzdal' (see previous discussion). There is little concrete evidence for the time of their recognition, but their presence in the "1549" list, apparently a propaganda document, and the 1602 book points to the second half of the sixteenth century. G. M. Prokhorov notes that Stefan was recognized for a national festival only in the seventeenth century, but cites no source: G. M. Prokhorov, "Stefan," in Likhachev, ed., *Slovar',* vyp. 2, 2:411–16.

30. Zimin, *Reformy,* 275–77, stressed centralization, while Skrynnikov, *Ivan Grozny* (Moscow, 1975), 32, and Golubinskii, *Istoriia,* vol. 2, pt. 1:772–73, stressed the church's need for greater prestige. Kartashev, *Ocherki,* 1:432–33, noted both aspects.

31. S. F. Platonov, *Ocherki po istorii Smuty,* 3d ed. (St. Petersburg, 1910), 352–57, 364–68.

32. *AAE,* 2, no. 222:379–80; "written according to form and propriety, as for other saints." Golubinskii, *Istoriia Kanonizatsii,* 232, 236, 240. Kornilii is a good example of the internal contradiction in Golubinskii's conception of the recognition of saints. On p. 120 of *Istoriia Kanonizatsii* he asserted that Kornilii was recognized only for a local feast day, while on page 236 he noted that Kornilii had been approved for a national festival but did not appear in the seventeenth-century printed service books.

33. *Pis'ma russkikh gosudarei,* vol. 1, *1526–1658* (Moscow, 1848), no. 18, pp. 27–28. Tsar Michael went on a pilgrimage to the monastery after Filaret's recognition of the cult. This monastery became a great pilgrimage site, and also

the site of a great fair, later moved to Nizhnii Novgorod to become Russia's greatest fair by the early nineteenth century. The festival occurs in all service books after 1619. Golubinskii, *Istoriia Kanonizatsii*, 234, 241, 251.

34. For example, the Trinity Monastery was under the jurisdiction of the *Prikaz Bol'shogo Dvortsa*, a privilege for the monks because they were thus under the administration and courts of the tsar's treasury, not those of local officials. For the monastery's status, see the act of 1616 in *AI*, 3, no. 69:63–64. The 1627 confirmation: *AAE*, 3, no. 173:256–57. On the bureaucratization of the church, see Keep, "Regime of Filaret."

35. *AI*, 4, no. 20, and *AAE*, 4, no. 323:482–84. Although in the interests of the monks, such arrangements reduced the jurisdiction of the patriarch, something that would later arouse Nikon's ire.

36. *AAE*, 3, no. 168:254–47. The festival of the Robe of the Lord, however, does not appear in the *Ustav* of 1633, only in the *Sviattsy* of 1646: *Ustav* (*Oko tserkovnoe*) (Moscow, 1633), f. 443v (10 July); and *Sviattsy* (Moscow, 1646), ff. 293v–295 (10 July).

37. On Adrian, see Golubinskii, *Istoriia Kanonizatsii*, 130, 154–55, and *AI*, 3, no. 141:230. On Daniil see *AAE*, 4, no. 330:492–93. Neither Adrian nor Daniil ever acquired national celebrations: Golubinskii, *Istoriia Kanonizatsii*, 231–32, 240.

38. *Skrizhal'*, ff. 1–59. The discussions at the 1682 church council suggest that the command was obeyed.

39. Golubinskii, *Istoriia Kanonizatsii*, 236, 241–42, 253; *Ustav*, 1610, ff. 239–865; *Ustav*, 1633, ff. 185–479; and *Sviattsy*, 1646.

40. Subbotin, *Deianiia*, 8–8v, 27v–28v. Another text of the council decisions is to be found in Subbotin, *Materialy*, vol. 3 (Moscow, 1874). I have interpreted *khodiat v mire*, "going in the world/community," as begging. The life of the holy fools seems to be exactly like that of the holy fools of the mid-nineteenth century, begging from town to town and staying in the palaces and houses of the wealthy.

41. O. A. Belobrova, "Anny Kashinskoi zhitie," "Issledovatel'skie materialy," 39, 186–87; Kuchkin, *Povesti*, 269–72; V. Undol'skii, "Uchenye trudy Epifaniia Slavinetskogo," *ChOIDR*, 1846, no. 4:69–72.

42. "Moskovskii sobor o zhitii Velikoi Kniagini Anny Kashinskoi," *ChOIDR*, 1871, no. 4, pt. 1:45–50, 56–57; N. I. Kostomarov, "Tserkovno-istoricheskaia kritika v XVII veke," *Vestnik Evropy*, 1870, no. 4:479–506; I. Ia. Kunkin, "Gorod Kashin: Materialy dlia ego istorii," *ChOIDR*, 1905, no. 3, pt. 1:52–67; Golubinskii, *Istoriia Kanonizatsii*, 159–69. Vasil'ev thought that the real reason lay with Old Belief, in part because the Old Belief naturally rejected the findings of the council and in part because of the complications surrounding the gesture of blessing. Vasil'ev's point is that the making of the sign of the cross and the gesture of blessing were frequently confused (especially on icons, which led to the repainting of innumerable icons of St. Nicholas after 1667), and that the council was afraid to sanction a gesture that might appear to support the Old Belief position on the sign of the cross. The text tells us only that the main concern of the church was the exclusive right of the church hierarchy to decide matters of faith and worship, rejecting any outside disagreement as uncanonical. The issue of authority in such pronouncements was indeed a central point of contention between the church and the Old Belief, and in this sense the existence of the schism did influence the council. At the same time the councils repeated the insistence

on a properly written life of a saint that goes back at least to the councils of 1547–1551 and was standard in disputed cases. Vasil'ev, *Istoriia kanonizatsii,* 238–43.

43. "Moskovskii sobor," 54–55. In 1909 the Holy Synod restored sanctity to Anna of Kashin.

44. The main issue was Tsar Fedor's proposal to expand greatly the number of Russian bishops (from seventeen to seventy). The church fell far short of the tsar's wishes, only agreeing to four new eparchies and rejecting entirely his proposal to put all bishops, new and old, under the authority of the patriarch and metropolitans.

45. Vinogradskii, *Tserkovnyi,* 38–78, 176–85, supplement, 56–57; Mansvetov, *Tserkovnyi ustav,* 323–56; K. Nikol'skii, *Materialy,* 52; and Golubinskii, *Istoriia Kanonizatsii,* 169, 243–56.

46. Vladimir Borisov, *Opisanie goroda Shui i ego okrestnostei* (Moscow, 1851), prilozhenie, nos. 86–87, pp. 422–27.

47. Borisov, *Opisanie,* nos. 89–93, pp. 430–38, and nos. 44–45, pp. 337–40. In number 46 the editor has misinterpreted the date: 23 November 7178 is 1669, not 1670, since the year began in September.

48. Information on the local cults of Suzdal' comes from Ananii Fedorov, a local clergyman who produced a history of the town in 1754, later edited and amplified for publication by Ia. A. Solov'ev, a local historian. Most information on local cults comes from such sources, this one being among the best (the authors used local church archives and quote documents in full rather than merely summarizing them). Ananii Fedorov [and Ia. A. Solov'ev], "Istoricheskoe sobranie o bogospasaemom grade Suzdale," *Vremennik moskovskogo obshchestva istorii i drevnostei rossiiskikh* 22, pt. 2 (1855): 1–212. See esp. 117–53, 182–88. Golubinskii, *Istoriia Kanonizatsii,* 115, 143–45, 549, 553–54.

49. Arkadii was claimed to be the monastic pupil of the better-known Efrem of Novyi Torzhok, who appeared in the service books from 1610 to 1648, after which he was excluded: Golubinskii, *Istoriia Kanonizatsii,* 117–18, 231, 239, 317, 549.

50. Like so many of the local cults, however, it did not die here. In the eighteenth century the Church of the Savior in the Savior Monastery was rebuilt in stone at some expense by a local merchant, Timofei Filat'ev Bubkov, and a story was compiled (or at least copied) of the relics and icon of the saint. At some point, apparently in the eighteenth century too, a small convent was built in the town in honor of Arkadii, even though he was not officially a saint of the Russian church and did not appear in service books. (Filaret of Chernigov did include him in his mammoth collection of the lives of the saints in 1855.) The convent was still flourishing in the late nineteenth century. See I. P. Vinogradov, *Istoricheskii ocherk goroda Viaz'my s drevneishikh vremen do XVII v.* (Moscow, 1890). Vinogradov was the unusual local historian, who used and cited archival material, in this case Pitirim's report in the papers of the Sarskii and Podonskii (Krutitskii) metropolitan, then in the Rumiantsev museum (now Lenin Library).

Chapter 5

1. Miracle cults are a good example of the utility of studies of Western European religious phenomena for the history of Orthodoxy in Russia. In spite of

the differences in dogma, spirituality, and institutions, the main branches of Christianity (other than Protestant churches) display rather similar types of devotion to the relics of saints. The types of miracles, even if they appear at somewhat different times, are the same: miracles of healing and of power. The comparison also allows the historian to see differences that are significant, as we shall see. For a basis, see Peter Brown, *The Cult of the Saints* (Chicago, 1981); Benedicta Ward, *Miracles and the Medieval Mind,* rev. ed. (Aldershot, U.K., 1987), 33–87; Pierre-André Sigal, *L'homme et le miracle dans la France mediévale (XIe–XIIe siecle)* (Paris, 1985), 293–96, 299–304; and Thomas Head, *Hagiography and the Cult of Saints: The Diocese of Orleans 800–1200* (Cambridge, 1990).

2. Byzantium also cannot have influenced Russia in the matter of miracles, for it seems to have displayed a quite different pattern. From the beginning public miracles ran parallel to the healing cults, and continued to do so until the end of the Byzantine empire. There is no equivalent to Ward or Sigal's work for Byzantium, but a comparison of the early miracles of St. Demetrius of Thessalonica with those of Serrai, Constantinople (Patriarch Athanasios), and Anatolia (all fourteenth century) seems not to reveal an evolutionary pattern as in Western Europe. The first two parts of the miracles of St. Demetrius record primarily some very public miracles involving the preservation of the city from various disasters, while the third book (tenth century) records healing miracles. The objects of the latter miracles seem to be largely from the upper classes. The Serrai miracles were primarily miracles of power, while the Anatolian were a mixture of miracles of power and cures. (The Serrai miracles may reflect thirteenth-century material, though the text seems to be from the fourteenth.) The miracles of Patriarch Athanasios I at his shrine in Constantinople are healing miracles, and all the healed are peasants and humble folk, save two palace officials. See "Miracula S. Demetrii Thessalonicensis," *Patrologia graeca* (Paris, 1864), 116, 1203–1398, which records miracles of the seventh to tenth centuries; Maximilian Treu, ed., *Theodori Pediasimi eiusque amicorum quae existant* (Potsdam, 1899), 17–25; A. Papadopulo-Kerameus, *Sbornik istochnikov po istorii Trapezundskoi Imperii,* vol. 1, *Zapiski istoriko-filologicheskogo fakul'teta imp. S.-Petersburgskogo universiteta* 44 (St. Petersburg, 1897); Speros Vryonis, *The Decline of Hellenism in Medieval Asia Minor and the Process of Islamization from the Eleventh through the Fifteenth Century* (Berkeley, 1971), 36–42; and Alice-Mary M. Talbot, *Faith Healing in Late Byzantium: The Posthumous Miracles of the Patriarch Athanasios I of Constantinople by Theoktistos the Stoudite,* The Archbishop Iakovos Library of Ecclesiastical and Historical Sources 8 (Brookline, Mass., 1983).

3. M. V. Kukushkina, *Monastyrskie biblioteki russkogo Severa: Ocherki po istorii knizhnoi kul'tury XVI–XVII v.* (Leningrad, 1977), gives some idea of the production and distribution of saints' lives: some were sold to peasant pilgrims, but this does not seem to have been the main market. Not only were the miracle stories written and compiled by the literate elite, they also described the cures of a rather restricted part of the population, particularly of the peasantry. Peasants cured at the shrines usually came from larger villages or those near towns, and we do not even know what proportion of even these peasants visited the shrines. No presently known sources exist that could unambiguously reveal the beliefs and values of the greater part of the rural

population. Even from the eighteenth century there are very few sources that would permit the historian to examine the religious mind of even one Russian peasant, in the manner that Carlo Ginzburg could examine his Friulian miller or Alain Lottin his weaver of Lille. The case of the Siberian peasant A. L. Sakalov, arrested in 1760 for schismatic beliefs, seems to be the closest analogy to these cases from Western Europe. Sakalov was not in fact an Old Believer, but had some heterodox views of his own. See N. N. Pokrovskii, "Ispoved' altaiskogo krest'ianina," *Pamiatniki kul'tury—novye otkrytiia 1978* (Leningrad, 1979), 49–57. The Old Believer polemicists, though most were "popular" writers in that they wrote for nonelite audiences, did not come from the greater body of the peasantry nor may we assume that they spoke for them. See Carlo Ginzburg, *The Cheese and the Worms: The Cosmos of a Sixteenth-Century Miller*, trans. John and Anne Tedeschi (New York, 1982); Alain Lottin, *Chavatte, ouvrier lillois: Un contemporain de Louis XIV* (Paris, 1979); and Peter Burke, *Popular Culture in Early Modern Europe* (New York, 1978).

4. Dmitrij Tschizewskij, ed., *Das Paterikon des Kiever Höhlenklosters*, repr. D. Abramovych edition of 1931, Slavische Propyläen 2 (Munich, 1964), 128–33. The Vladimir icon first came to the city in the time of Andrei Bogoliubskii as a frankly political and dynastic cult. See Ellen Hurwitz, *Prince Andrej Bogoljubskij: The Man and the Myth*, Studia historica et philologica 12, sectio slavica 4 (Florence, 1980), 54–59; and I. L. Zhuchkova, "Skazanie o chudesakh ikony bogomateri," in Likhachev, ed., *Slovar',* vyp. 1:416–18. The story of the icon's repulse of Tamerlane is found first in the chronicles, e.g., "Sofiiskaia vtoraia letopis'," *PSRL*, 6:124–28; and "Voskresenskaia letopis'," *PSRL*, 8:65–68. Later on (sixteenth century) a "Skazanie ob ikone Vladimirskoi Bozhiei Materi" was composed using this and other sources: see I. L. Zhuchkova, "Povest' o Temir-Aksake," and "Skazanie o ikone bogomateri vladimirskoi," in Likhachev, ed., *Slovar'*, vyp. 2, 2:283–87 and 360–62. The story of the Znamenie is found in *Pamiatniki starinnoi russkoi literatury* 1:241–42, and see L. A. Dmitriev, "Skazanie o bitve novgorodtsev s suzdal'tsami," in Likhachev, ed., *Slovar'*, vyp. 2, 2:347–51. The Tikhvin ikon is discussed by R. P. Dmitrieva, "Skazanie o ikone bogomateri Tikhvinskoi," in Likhachev, ed., *Slovar'*, vyp. 2, 2:365–67.

5. Müller, *Die Legenden des Heiligen Sergij*, pt. 1:68.

6. Ibid., pt. 2:87–100; and *Zhitie i sluzhby sv. Sergeia* (Moscow, 1646), 143–59. This role is in accord with the role of the shrine at the Trinity Monastery in court ritual, in which it was an object of a yearly pilgrimage by the whole court, dynasty, boyars, and servants.

7. "Zhitie pr. Kirilla," in Tschizewskij, *Pachomij: Werke*, xlviii–lx.

8. "Voskresenskaia letopis'," *PSRL*, 8:158–68 [1471], 185–99 [1478], 206–7 [1480], 253–57 [1514], 269 [1522]; A. A. Zimin, ed., *Ioasafovskaia letopis'* (Moscow, 1957), 62–73 [1471], 98–117 [1478], 120–22 [1480], 161–65 [1514]. On these chronicles, see Zimin, *Rossiia na poroge*, 37–41.

9. These miracle stories appended to the lives of saints form the basis of the ensuing analysis of the miracle cults. Most manuscript copies made in the sixteenth through eighteenth centuries of the lives of saints, as well as most tales of miraculous icons, contain such an appendix, and since the number of individual manuscript copies of the life of a particular saint is often large (up to a hundred copies), the number of copies of the appendix is also large. This

chapter makes no pretense to exhaust the manuscripts for even one saint's life, in any case a lifetime's work. It only attempts to give a reading of the evidence, based on published and unpublished texts of the lives, relying on the work of previous editors in some cases and on inspection of the manuscripts in others. In the manuscripts and publications I have seen I do not think there are major problems with the transmission of the miracle stories, and impressionistic evidence suggests that these appendices are more uniform than the lives of the saints, which often exist in several redactions. In an attempt to narrow the limitless field of miracle stories, those chosen here represent as fully as possible the cults of the main saints and miraculous icons of the Russian state, with some local cults as well, so as to get the broadest possible pattern. One feature of these sources should be noted, however: they only measure devotion and pilgrimage to miracle-working objects, but not devotion or pilgrimage with the simpler aim of prayer at a holy site. The two existed in this and later periods, as the chronicles and the *dvortsovye razriady* (palace service records) reveal for the family of the tsar and the court, which annually made a pilgrimage to the Trinity–St. Sergii Monastery for the festival of St. Sergii on 25 September. Numerous other sources, including the saints' lives, mention this practice, but do not permit conclusions about its extent.

10. *Velikie Minei-chet'i,* April (Moscow, 1912), 502–601; and A. A. Savich, *Solovetskaia votchina XV–XVII vv.* (Perm', 1927), 23–93. The regional character of the Solovetskii cult precluded noblemen, as there was no land in the north other than monastery and crown land.

11. "Nikonovskaia letopis'," *PSRL,* 12:190–92 [1479], 13, 37–43 [1522], 152–54 [1547 fire], 155–223 [Kazan' campaigns], 295 [1558], 345–64 [1563]; *Stepennaia kniga, PSRL,* 21:554–55 [1479] 597–604 [1522], 636–38 [1547 fire], 638–51 [Kazan' campaigns], 658–59 [1558], 662 [1563]; "Istoriia o Kazanskom tsarstve," *PSRL,* 19:62–63, 141–43, 422–24. The Book of Degrees also included many miracle stories that were not included in the chronicles, even the Nikon chronicle. See B. M. Kloss, *Nikonovskii svod i russkie letopisi XVI–XVII vv.* (Moscow, 1980): T. F. Volkova, "Kazanskaia istoriia," in Likhachev, ed., *Slovar',* vyp. 2, 2:450–58.

12. Moscow University Library (MGU), MS 5M183, ff. 18–206v, and V. Mansikka, ed., *Zhitie Aleksandra Nevskogo,* Pamiatniki drevnei pis'mennosti i iskusstva 180 (St. Petersburg, 1913), 107–16, 177–200, texts: 26–31, 49-124. The text of the life of Aleksandr Nevskii in MGU MS 5M183 (a MS of the late seventeenth–early eighteenth century) is the version of Iona Dumin compiled in 1591 but with additional miracles: E. I. Koniukhova, *Slaviano-russkie rukopisi XIII–XVIII vv. Nauchnoi biblioteki im. A. M. Gor'kogo Moskovskogo gosudarstvennogo universiteta* (Moscow, 1964), 76–77. On the textual history, see D. M. Bulanin, "Iona Dumin," in Likhachev, ed., *Slovar',* vyp. 2, 1:430–32. The life of Savva is the work of Varlaam-Vasilii of Pskov (see chapter 4).

13. Andreas Kappeler, *Russlands erste Nationalitäten: Das Zarenreich und die Völker der mittleren Wolga von 16. bis 19. Jahrhundert,* Beiträge zur Geschichte Osteuropas 14 (Cologne, 1982), 94–120, 137–48.

14. MGU MS 5Qi 186, ff. 96–196v, a seventeenth-century miscellany: Koniukhova, *Slaviano-russkie rukopisi,* 75–76. Gurii and Varsonofii were recognized as saints with a national feast day only in the *Ustav* of 1610: Golubinskii, *Istoriia Kanonizatsii,* 230; and *Ustav,* 1610, 320v–324v; and N. F.

Droblenkova, "Germogen," in Likhachev, ed., *Slovar'*, vyp. 2, 1:153–63. This seems to be another case of flattering the provinces by including local saints made under pressure of the Troubles.

15. [Germogen], *Tvoreniia sviateishego Germogena Patriarkha moskovskogo i vseia Rossii* (Moscow, 1912), 1–34. This cult acquired a national festival only in 1633 for 8 July (commemorating the icon's appearance) and in 1646 for 22 October (commemorating the icon's role in the 1612 victory over the Poles). *Ustav*, 1610, ff. 771–777; *Ustav*, 1633, ff. 242–242v; 441v–442; *Sviattsy*, 1646, ff. 54–54v, and *sub die* 8 July.

16. I. I. Kuznetsov, "Sviatye blazhennye Vasilii i Ioann Khrista radi moskovskie chudotvortsy, *Zapiski moskovskogo arkheologicheskogo instituta*" 8 (1910): 57–72; A. M. Panchenko, "Zhitie Vasiliia Blazhennogo," in Likhachev, ed., *Slovar'*, vyp. 2, 1:250–51; "Novyi letopisets," *PSRL*, 14:38; and *Ustav*, 1610, 813–16.

17. Houghton Library, Harvard University, Kilgour Collection F, *Kniga zhitie Zosimy i Savvatiia chudotvortsev*, ff. 245–347, esp. ff. 257–284v, 287v–300v, 302–307, 325–334v, and 338v–347. The history of the text of the life itself is unclear in several points, but seems to consist of a number of purely stylistic reworkings of the basic text of Spiridon-Savva from 1503: R. P. Dmitrieva, "Zhitie Zosimy i Savvatiia solovetskikh," in Likhachev, ed., *Slovar'*, vyp. 2, 1:264–67. See also N. E. Nosov, *Stanovlenie soslovno-predstavitel'nogo gosudarstva v Rossii* (Leningrad, 1969), 240–83.

18. After the Troubles the icon was not returned to Kazan' but placed in the Church of the Mother of God on Red Square by Pozharskii. The church was in Pozharskii's own parish. Pozharskii decorated the icon at Tsar Michael's wish in 1625: "Novyi letopisets," *PSRL*, 14:132–33. However, the *Ustav* of 1610 does not show a festival for 8 July, and the 1633 *Ustav* does not show one for the battle on 22 October. Only in 1646 does the *Sviattsy* show both (see n. 15).

19. Avraamii Palitsyn, *Skazanie Avraamiia Palitsyna*, ed. E. V. Kolosova and O. A. Derzhavina (Moscow and Leningrad, 1955); "Inoe skazanie," "Povest' o videnii . . ." [by Terentii], "Povest' o chudesnykh videniiakh v Nizhnem Novgorode i Vladimire," "Povest' i videnii mnikhu Varlaamu," in *Pamiatniki drevnei russkoi pis'mennosti otnosiashchiesia k smutnomu vremeni, RIB* 13, ed. S. F. Platonov (St. Petersburg, 1891), 1–144, 177–86, 235–48; "Novyi letopisets," *PSRL*, 14:123–26, 132–33; the story of the Tikhvin siege in the "Novgorodskaia tret'ia letopis'," *PSRL*, 3:267–73; and Bushkovitch, "National Consciousness."

20. The story is found in *Dvortsovye razriady*, 5 vols. (St. Petersburg, 1850–1855), 2:767–822, esp. 803 and 809. The two men are identified from N. N. Golitsyn, *Ukazatel' k Dvortsovym razriadam* (St. Petersburg, 1912). See also "Novyi letopisets," *PSRL*, 14:151–52; "Inoe skazanie," in Platonov, *Pamiatniki*, 137–38; and S. N. Gukhman, "'Dokumental'noe' skazanie o dare Shakha Abbasa Rossii," *TODRL* 28 (1974): 255–70. There is also an unpublished variant of this story by Semen Shakhovskoi: Edward Keenan, *The Kurbskii-Groznyi Apocrypha* (Cambridge, Mass., 1971), 143.

21. Golubinskii, *Istoriia Kanonizatsii*, 230; *Zhitie i sluzhba sv. Savvy Storozhevskogo* (Moscow, 1646), 40v–55, esp. 47v–49, 50v, 51v; Dmitrieva, "Markell," *Pistsovye knigi Moskovskogo gosudarstva*, ed. N. V. Kalachov, pt. 1, *Pistsovye knigi XVI veka*, otdel 1, ed. N. V. Kalachov, (St. Petersburg, 1872), 23, 177, 228, 673; and Crummey, *Aristocrats*, 183, 186, 192. The Savvo-Storozhevskii

Monastery, and presumably its miracle cult, enjoyed the patronage of Tsar Aleksei Mikhailovich, another reason for the publication of the *Zhitie*. As Rtishchev was the tutor of Tsarevich Aleksei, and a favorite of Tsar Aleksei, the glorification of Rtishchev also served the tsar's ends. See Gurliand, *Prikaz*, 205–9, who points out that the Privy Chancellery took care of the monastery after 1654. The discovery of St. Savva's relics in 1652 undoubtedly was part of this patronage: Golubinskii, *Istoriia Kanonizatsii*, 547.

22. As the Volga basin was more thickly populated, and trade with Western Europe shifted to St. Petersburg, Nizhnii Novgorod replaced Yaroslavl' as the most prosperous of the Volga towns. The famous Nizhnii Novgorod fair was founded at the nearby Makar'ev Monastery only in the mid-seventeenth century and became Russia's leading fair only in the late eighteenth century. The city's important church buildings are mainly from the very end of the seventeenth century onward. On all this, see Paul Bushkovitch, *The Merchants of Moscow 1580–1650* (Cambridge and New York, 1980), 30, 95–101, 106–8.

23. MGU MS 5M183, ff. 422–431v, and A. A. Turilov, "Maloizvestnye pamiatniki iaroslavskoi literatury XIV–nachala XVIII v. (Skazaniia o iaroslavskikh ikonakh)," in *Arkheograficheskii ezhegodnik za 1974 g.* (Moscow, 1975), 168–74. Koniukhova's catalog omits the story of the Tolgskii ikon. The story of the Vladimir icon takes up only ff. 386–422, followed by the present story: Koniukhova, *Slaviano-russkie rukopisi*, 77.

24. I. V. Bazhenov, ed., "Skazanie o chudesakh kostromskoi Fedorovskoi ikony Bogomateri," *Vestnik istorii i arkheologii* 19 (St. Petersburg, 1909): 187–260. The social group that came to the shrine is thus quite similar to the group that was involved in opposition to the religious reforms after 1645. In 1652 the Kostroma townspeople objected to the attempts to suppress the old popular rituals, and in 1666 some evidence of religious dissent surfaced in the town's nearby villages. See Rumiantseva, *Narodnoe*, 86–90, 138–40. Rumiantseva's evidence for the social radius of Old Belief in the 1660s and 1670s suggests a close correspondence with the social radius of the miracle cults, that is, townspeople, clergy, and peasants from the nearby (or larger) villages. It is difficult not to see the rise of Old Belief among such groups as a cause of the decline of the miracle cults, especially because of the coincidence in time (c. 1640–1660).

These icon cults did not acquire any festival recognized in the printed service books, not even in the 1646 *Sviattsy*.

25. K. A. Dokuchaev-Baskov, "Skazanie o chudesakh ot obraza prep. Makariia Zheltovodskogo i Unzhenskogo v Kargopol'skoi Khergozerskoi pustyni," *ChOIDR* 1902, no. 3, pt 4:1–34.

26. A. I. Nikol'skii, "Pamiatnik i obrazets narodnogo iazyka i slovesnosti Severodvinskoi oblasti," *IORIaS* 17 (1912): 98, and see also A. Orlov, "Narodnye predaniia o sviatyniakh russkogo Severa," *ChOIDR*, 1913, no. 1, pt. 3:47–55. If *trapeza* does refer to the altar area of the church, the incident underlines the uniqueness of the events: women are not usually permitted into the altar area of an Orthodox church.

The village was not a remote and isolated agricultural settlement but a trading village on the important artery formed by the Northern Dvina River. In the seventeenth century it seems to have been a center of the rural iron industry, and later became known for its painted woodwork, the earliest physical examples of which date from the eighteenth century. After 1676 it belonged to the Solovetskii Monastery. See A. Ts. Merzon and Iu. A. Tikhonov, *Rynok Ustiuga Velikogo* (Moscow, 1960), 156, 209, 211, 432–33, 507–8; K. N. Serbina, *Krest'ianskaia zhelezodelatel'naia promyshlennost' severo-zapadnoi Rossii XVI– pervoi poloviny XIX v.* (Leningrad, 1971), 138, 141, 144, 226; S. K. Zhegalova, *Russkaia narodnaia zhivopis'* (Moscow, 1975); and O. V. Kruglova, *Narodnaia rospis' Severnoi Dviny* (Moscow, 1987).

27. The story was quite well known in the North, as the early eighteenth-century Vologda chronicle testifies. It mentions the story (under the year 1627!) among the very few northern miracle stories it describes. See the "Vologodskaia letopis'," *PSRL*, 37:175–76. On the more extreme popular ascetic movements, see Rumiantseva, *Narodnoe*, 66–93.

28. The Ozhegovs' role appears in a court case of 1686 in *Akty kholmogorskoi i ustiuzhskoi eparkhii*, pt. 2, *RIB* 14 (St. Petersburg, 1894), 1153–1226. Nikol'skii, "Pamiatnik," 87–96, 100–104. The relatively large number of seventeenth-century manuscripts extant containing a local legend of this sort suggests considerable popularity of the miracles in the North. See Orlov, "Narodnye," *ChOIDR*, 1913, no. 1, pt. 3:47–55.

29. Ivan Timofeev, *Vremennik*, ed. O. A. Derzhavina (Moscow and Leningrad, 1951); Ivan Khvorostinin, "Povest'," and Semen Shakhovskoi, "Povesti," in Platonov, *Pamiatniki*, 525–58, 837–76; Fyodor Griboedov, *Istoriia o tsariakh i velikikh kniaziakh zemli Russkoi*, Pamiatniki drevnei pis'mennosti 121 (St. Petersburg, 1896); "Letopistsy poslednei chetverti XVII veka," *PSRL*, 31; and E. V. Chistiakova and A. P. Bogdanov, *"Da budet potomkam iavleno": Ocherki o russkikh istorikakh vtoroi poloviny XVII veka i ikh trudakh* (Moscow, 1988), 37–40.

30. S. O. Shmidt, "K istorii monastyrskoi kolonizatsii XVII v. (Povest' o nachale Oranskogo monastyria)," *Voprosy istorii religii i ateizma* 12 (1964): 305–9. This is the same V. P. Sheremetev with whom Avvakum came into conflict over the question of the shaving of beards. Cf. Robinson, *Zhizneopisaniia*, 144; Crummey, *Aristocrats*, 46, 119, 185.

31. The earlier stories of conflict between monks and peasants are much more veiled and usually pit the living saint against the peasantry. Cf. I. U. Budovnits, *Monastyri na Rusi i bor'ba s nimi krest'ian v XIV–XVI vv.* (Moscow, 1966).

32. N. F. Droblenkova, "Zhitie Sergiia Radonezhskogo," in Likhachev, ed., *Slovar'*, 2, 2:330–36; Simon Azarin, *Kniga o chudesakh pr. Sergiia*, Pamiatniki drevnei pis'mennosti i iskusstva 70 (St. Petersburg, 1888), iv–vi, 1–20. On Azarin, see also E. N. Klitina, "Simon Azarin (Novye dannye po maloizuchennym istochnikam)," *TODRL* 34 (1977): 298–312; and O. A. Belobrova and E. N. Klitina, "Simon Azarin," and "Issledovatel'skie materialy," 40, 161–62.

33. Monastery servants, *monastyrskie slugi*, were a socially heterogeneous group, some merely servants, some petty landholders whose descendants later took their place in the eighteenth-century gentry.

34. *Zhitie i sluzhby sv. Sergiia*, 143–59.

35. Azarin, *Kniga*, 6–7, and A. S. Zernova, *Knigi kirillovskoi pechati, izdannye v Moskve v XVI–XVII vekakh* (Moscow, 1958), 64.

36. Gorskii, "Istoricheskoe," *ChOIDR*, 1878, no. 4:1–204; 1879, no. 2:1–117.

37. The healing miracles in Azarin's text were the standard ones, except that a few aristocrats were cured, including two members of the Saltykov family,

Mikhail Mikhailovich (of boyar rank, died 1671) and the daughter of the boyar Lavrentii Dmitrievich (died 1659/1660). Azarin, *Kniga,* 40–41, 48–51, 61–63, 93–96, 128–29; Crummey, *Aristocrats,* 179–80, 183–84, 187. V. I. Nagoi and N. I. Sheremetev were not of duma rank but belonged to clans whose elder members usually were.

38. Azarin, *Kniga,* 123–28. Some of the land at issue was urban property, implying that the monks were objecting to losses during the town reforms, the *posadskoe stroenie* of the 1640s. A *volost'* was a subdivision of an *uezd,* and normally included only a few villages.

39. Filipp was first recognized as a saint in the service books of 1646: Golubinskii, *Istoriia Kanonizatsii,* 231, and see my chapter 4.

40. The icon was used earlier in 1648 to cure Tsar Aleksei of an illness, and was one of the varieties of Greek icons of the Mother of God popular in Russia from midcentury on. The Iviron had been a Georgian monastery founded on Mount Athos in the eleventh century, but by this period was largely Greek and also one of the richest of the Athonite monasteries. Nikon ordered printed in 1658 a collection of tales about the Iverskii Monastery (as it was called) on Lake Valdai entitled *The Imagined Paradise—Rai myslennyi* (Iverskii Monastery, 1658)—which included a story, *O sviashchennoi obiteli Ivirskoi i o chestnei ikone Portaitskoi,* that was a Slavic translation and adaptation of a Greek legend of the late sixteenth century published by J. B. Bury, "Iviron and Our Lady of the Gate," *Hermathena* 10 (1899): 71–99. See D. M. Bulanin, "Skazanie o ikone bogomateri Iverskoi," in Likhachev, ed., *Slovar',* vyp. 2, 2:362–65. The Slavic version is an adaptation that omits a few details and in one place adds some lines that add more miracles to the story. Most of the rest of the book is taken up with a Bulgarian story in praise of the (Bulgarian) Zograf Monastery on Athos, in which miracles both help the monks preserve their faith against the Latins and increase their wealth, and with some other stories about the Iverskii Monastery in Russia. The monastery's other publication was a collection of hymns known in Slavic as *Fikara,* a collection known in Greek and Balkan Slavic monasteries as well. Extensively copied, it is little studied. See Georgi Dancev, "Les copies slaves du 'Recueil de prières du moine Tikara, considéré à tort jusqu'à présent comme l'oeuvre de Demetrios Cantacuzène," *Palaeobulgarica/Starobulgaristika* 4 (1980): 25–39. The Balkan atmosphere of the monastery's publications contrasts sharply with the traditional view that it was "Lithuanian" in inspiration because of the (presumed) origins of the monks. On the building of the monastery and its productive activities, see S. I. Sivak, "Ivan Isaev—stroitel' Iverskogo monastyria," in *Pamiatniki kul'tury—novye otkrytiia 1979* (Leningrad, 1980), 456–58; E. V. Kondrat'eva, "Novye dannye o deiatel'nosti keramicheskoi masterskoi Valdaiskogo monastyria," in *Pamiatniki kul'tury—novye otkrytiia 1980* (Leningrad, 1981), 465–77.

41. *Rai myslennyi,* 65v–68.

42. Golubinskii, *Istoriia Kanonizatsii,* 87–89, 113–14, 230, and see my chapter 4.

43. *Rai myslennyi,* 61v–62v. Nikon earlier reported a vision at the monastery (pillars of fire) in a letter to Tsar Aleksei of 27 February 1654: *Pis'ma russkikh gosudarei,* 1:302–3, no. 384.

44. [Archimandrite Leonid] *Istoricheskoe opisanie stavropigial'nogo Voskresenskogo monastyria Novyi Ierusalim imenuemogo,* ChOIDR, 1874, no. 1, pt. 1:1–124; 1874, no. 2, pt. 1:125–366; 1875, no. 1, pt. 1:367–464; 1875, no. 2, pt.

1:465–544; 1875, no. 3, pt. 1:545–767; and M. A. Il'in, *Kamennaia letopis' moskovskoi Rusi* (Moscow, 1966), 176–204. Nikon actually built a third monastery, the Monastery of the Cross (Krestnyi Monastery) on an island in Lake Onega in 1656–1660, which contained a wooden cross filled with small relics of various saints that came to be an object of pilgrimage and worship. However, Nikon paid much less attention to the Krestnyi Monastery, and so little has been written about it that information from architectural historians is hard to come by. Nikon preferred to live in the Monastery of the New Jerusalem, and seems to have chosen it precisely because it represented his notion of the perfect monastic community better than any other, including the Iverskii Monastery. He was buried there and his biographer Shusherin was a monk of that monastery, clearly considering that he was continuing his teacher's traditions in the appropriate place. This was his major effort, not the remote Krestnyi Monastery.

45. Epifanii in *Rai myslennyi*, 1–30 (second pagination). For the identification see Sil'vestr Medvedev, "Oglavlenie knig, kto ikh slozhil," ed. V. Undol'skii, *ChOIDR*, 1846, no. 3, pt. 4:21; and Undol'skii, "Uchenye trudy Epifaniia Slavinetskogo," *ChOIDR*, 1846, no. 4, pt. 4:69.

46. Later we shall see how Simeon Polotskii dealt with the miraculous icons of the Mother of God in the same manner.

47. In exile after 1667 Nikon himself worked miraculous cures, and indeed while he was still alive in 1673–1676. In exile Nikon was trying to prove that he still had God's approval as rightful patriarch, and the cures had the same function as the shrine of St. Filipp he had established in the Assumption Cathedral, to demonstrate the dignity of the patriarchate. Filipp had returned to an older use of miracles, but transferred them from holy monk to holy bishop. The miracles are recorded in an appendix occasionally added to Shusherin's life of Nikon: S. A. Belokurov, ed., "Dela sviat. Nikona patriarkha, pache zhe reshchi chudesa vrachebnaia," *ChOIDR*, 1887, no. 1, pt. 5:81–114.

48. Ioannikii Galiatovskii, *Nebo novoe*, originally L'vov, 1665, excerpts in Ioanykii Haliatovs'kyi, *Kliuch rozuminnia*, ed. I. P. Chepiha (Kiev, 1985), 242–343; A. I. Sobolevskii, *Perevodnaia literatura Moskovskoi Rusi XIV–XVII vekov* (St. Petersburg, 1903), 222–224. A later example of such compilations is a manuscript of 1716, the *Kniga solntse presvetloe* in the Moscow University Library, a sort of personal collection of Marian and other miracles. In spite of the date, it is compiled almost exclusively from seventeenth-century (and earlier) material, including the *Nebo novoe*. The manuscript, MGU 293, belonged to the watchman in the Kremlin Annunciation Cathedral, and has the text on ff. 7–190v. The manuscript also includes the story of the Krasnoborsk miracles (528–38) and various lives of saints. Similar purposes were achieved by the 1677 translation ordered by Tsar Aleksei of the medieval collection of exempła called *Speculum magnum*, reedited and published by Joannes Maior, S. J., of Arras in Douai in 1603. Maior's text was in turn translated into Polish in 1621, and the Russians worked from this version. The work was widely copied, with 159 manuscripts known in 1965, and has Marian stories similar to those in the *Zvezda*. O. A. Derzhavina, *"Velikoe zertsalo" i ego sud'ba na russkoi pochve* (Moscow, 1965), 29.

49. The eighteenth-century church followed the mildly enlightened policy of the post-Petrine state and suppressed a number of local cults as pure super-

stition, but the peasants, townspeople, and the provincial gentry retained loyalty to both recognized and unrecognized cults. After the Napoleonic wars the increasing conservatism of church and state brought a revival and even new cults for the first time in over a century. St. Mitrofan of Voronezh in 1831 was the first, but the most famous was St. Tikhon Zadonskii in 1861, the year of peasant emancipation. Over all these cults lay a heavy air of official inspiration and political motivation, the desire to keep the peasantry and lower orders in general obedient to the Orthodox tsar. The response of the liberal gentry and intelligentsia was Repin's painting *The Procession of the Cross in Kursk Gubernia* (1887), a portrayal of police-sponsored superstition, but on this issue Repin's inchoate radicalism was even echoed in the writings of such a conservative critic of the church establishment as the writer Leskov. The manipulation of miracle cults became such an embarrassment that by the turn of the century even the arch-reactionary Pobedonostsev balked at the recognition of the cult of St. Serafim Sarovskii. The result of this use of the cults in the nineteenth century was that historians, secular and ecclesiastical, did not take them seriously as a historical problem, and they were left to local antiquaries, if they were studied at all. The occasional remarks of historians were usually dismissive, even when they had spent some time on reading and analyzing the sources, as in the case of Kliuchevskii. See Paul Bushkovitch, "V. O. Kliuchevskii as Historian of Religion and the Church," in "Kliuchevskii's Russia: Critical Studies," ed. Marc Raeff, *Canadian-American Slavic Studies* 20 (1986): 357–66.

Chapter 6

1. On serfdom, see V. I. Koretskii, *Zakreposhchenie krest'ian i klassovaia bor'ba v Rossii vo vtoroi polovine XVI veka,* (Moscow, 1970), and idem, *Formirovanie krepostnogo prava i pervaia krest'ianskaia voina v Rossii* (Moscow, 1975), summing up Soviet views, and Hellie, *Enserfment,* for an alternative conception. On the gentry petitions, see Hans-Joachim Torke, *Die staatsbedingte Gesellschaft im Moskauer Reich* (Leiden, 1974), 103–18, and the petitions themselves in P. P. Smirnov, ed., "Chelobitnye dvorian i detei boiarskikh vsekh gorodov v pervoi polovine XVII v.," *ChOIDR* 1915, no. 3, pt. 1:1–73.

2. See Crummey, *Aristocrats,* and my chapter 2. The role of the central administration ("bureaucracy") in this process is a matter of some dispute. See N. F. Demidova, "Biurokratizatsiia gosudarstvennogo apparata absoliutizma v XVII–XVIII vv.," in *Absoliutizm v Rossii,* ed. N. M. Druzhinin (Moscow, 1964), 206–42; N. F. Demidova, *Sluzhilaia biurokratiia v Rossii XVII v. i ee rol' v formirovanii absoliutizma* (Moscow, 1987); Bořivoj Plavšic, "Seventeenth-Century Chancelleries and Their Staffs," in *Russian Officialdom: The Bureaucratization of Russian Society from the Seventeenth to the Twentieth Century* ed. Walter M. Pintner and Don K. Rowney (Chapel Hill, N.C., 1980), 19–45; Hans-Joachim Torke, "Gab es im Moskauer Reich des 17. Jahrhunderts eine Bürokratie?" *Forschungen zur osteuropäischen Geschichte* 38 (Berlin, 1986): 276–98; and Peter Brown, "Early Modern Bureaucracy: The Evolution of the Chancellery System from Ivan III to Peter the Great, 1478–1717" (Ph.D. diss., University of Chicago, 1978). Torke's skepticism about the utility of the term

bureaucracy seems to me well taken, but the controversies of this sort illuminate our basic ignorance of seventeenth-century administration.

3. The private chapels imitated those of the tsar in the Kremlin: Crummey, *Aristocrats*, 150–57. On the military changes, see John Keep, *Soldiers of the Tsar: Army and Society in Russia 1462–1874* (Oxford, 1985), 13–92; Hellie, *Enserfment*, and A. V. Chernov, *Vooruzhennye sily russkogo gosudarstva v XVI–XVII vv.* (Moscow, 1954). Noble landholding in the seventeenth century has not been extensively studied but see A. A. Novosel'skii, *Votchinnik i ego khoziaistvo v XVII veke* (Moscow and Leningrad, 1929); D. I. Petrikeev, *Krupnoe krepostnoe khoziaistvo XVII v.* (Leningrad, 1967), on the Morozov estates; V. M. Vorob'ev and A. Ia. Degtiarev, *Russkoe feodal'noe zemlevladenie ot "Smutnogo vremeni" do kanuna petrovskikh reform* (Leningrad, 1986), on the Novgorod area; Iu. A. Tikhonov, *Pomeshchich'i krest'iane v Rossii: feodal'naia renta v XVII–nachale XVIII v.* (Moscow, 1974); Vodarskii, *Naselenie,* and idem, *Dvorianskoe zemlevladenie v Rossii v XVII–pervoi polovine XIX v.* (Moscow, 1988).

4. Bushkovitch, "National Consciousness"; Iov, "Povest' o chestnem zhitii tsaria i velikogo kniazia Fedora Ivanovicha vseia Russii," *PSRL,* 14:1–22; and G. P. Enin, "Iov," in Likhachev, ed., *Slovar',* vyp. 2, 2:415–20.

5. *Zhitie i podvizi i otchasti chiudese . . . Filippa mitropolita moskovskogo i vseia Rusii,* Vat. Slav. 30, ff. 1–56v. This is a seventeenth-century *poluustav* copy of the more common of the two redactions of the life. See Bushkovich, "Life"; Kliuchevskii, *Drevnerusskie,* 311–12; Barsukov, *Istochniki,* 566–75; and Dmitrieva, "Zhitie Filippa," in Likhachev, ed., *Slovar',* vyp. 2, 1, 342–44.

6. Platonov, *Ocherki;* R. G. Skrynnikov, *Rossiia v nachale XVII v.: Smuta* (Moscow, 1988); Bushkovitch, "National Consciousness"; and Palitsyn, *Skazanie . . . Palitsyna.* Palitsyn combines this moralism quite comfortably with endless miracle stories. Only later did the moral writers start to deemphasize miracles.

7. In the case of Prince Semen Shakhovskoi (died 1654), the reaction was so strong that he began to try to conceive of human action in nonreligious terms, making him an exceptional case in all respects: Bushkovitch, "National Consciousness," 372–73; V. K. Ziborov, "Ob avtore tak nazyvaemoi povesti Katyreva-Rostovskogo," *Istochnikovedenie literatury Drevnei Rusi* (Leningrad, 1980), 244–50; and more generally, see Keenan, *Apocrypha,* 33–35, 180–86, 201–4. Unlike Khvorostinin (to be discussed), Shakhovskoi came from a rather obscure lesser noble family. One prince Ivan Shakhovskoi, presumably his father, was a minor military commander in 1586 at Belev, and governor at Toropets in 1594 and 1595: Buganov, *Razriadnaia kniga,* 366, 484, 492.

8. The princes Khvorostinin came from the Iaroslavl' line of princes, rulers of the Iaroslavl' principality annexed by Moscow in 1463. They were thus very distant relatives of Shakhovskoi and of the Iaroslavl' saints, princes Fedor and his sons. The author's grandfather, Prince Ivan Mikhailovich Khvorostinin (died 1564), fathered four sons, including Andrei, who were in the *Oprichnina.* One of them was the author's uncle, Prince Dmitrii Ivanovich Khvorostinin, who became a boyar in November 1584, also a supporter of Boris and an important general. Dmitrii seems to have died about 1590. His son, Ivan Dmitrievich, became an *okol'nichii* in 1603 and died in 1614, leading a revolt against Vasilii Shuiskii while governor of Astrakhan'. Zimin,

Oprichnina, 107, 154–55, 365, 432, 467, 469, 473, 477; idem, *V kanun,* 72, 78, 84, 121, 138, 149, 187, 193, 216, 284; Crummey, *Aristocrats,* 180; Platanov, *Ocherki,* 313; idem, *Drevnerusskie skazaniia i povesti o Smutnom vremeni XVII veka, Sochineniia* (St. Petersburg, 1913), 2:230–40; Keenan, *Apocrypha,* 31–33; and E. P. Semenova, "I. A. Khvorostinin i ego 'Slovesa dnei,'" *TODRL* 34 (1979): 286–97.

9. Platonov, *Pamiatniki,* 531–33.
10. Ibid., 536–38; and Semenova, "Khvorostinin," 297.
11. Platonov, *Pamiatniki,* 550.
12. Renate Lachmann, ed., *Die Makarij-Rhetorik ("Knigi sut' ritoriki dvoi po tonku v voprosech spisany"),* Slavistische Forschungen 27, no. 1, Rhetorica Slavica 1 (Cologne and Vienna, 1980). The Ukrainian grammars of Slavic, those of Lavrentii Zizanii (*Grammatika slovenska,* Wilno, 1596) and Meletii Smotrytskii, (*Grammatiki slovenskiia pravilnoe sintagma,* Ev'e, 1619) both concluded with short sections on versification. Smotrytskii's work was republished in Moscow in 1648.
13. Antonii Podol'skii may have been Nasedka's principal antagonist in this controversy, but he too had a mixture of conservative and innovative tendencies. Like Nasedka, Antonii wrote verse but apparently fairly traditional in content: V. K. Bylinin, "Stikhotvornye 'Predisloviia mnogorazlichna' v rukopisiakh pervoi poloviny XVII v.," *Zapiski otdela rukopisei GBL* 44 (Moscow, 1983): 16–17. Also like Nasedka, his other religious writings were fairly conservative. In his sermons he presents drunkenness as the chief sin to be avoided, not the issues that concerned most of the innovative religious writers of the century. He adapted the Ukrainian Baroque style to a quite traditional content. See Antonii Podol'skii, "O p'ianstve," and "O tsarstve nebesnom," *Pravoslavnyi sobesednik,* 1862, no. 1:283–88, 369–85; 1864, no. 1:108–26, 227–46. Antonii seems to have been a Russian of the petty nobility and a *pod"iachii* (undersecretary) of the *Razriad,* but with connections with the Printing Office through his former superior Efim Grigor'evich Telepnev, who moved in 1620 to head the Printing Office from the *Razriad.* See A. Pokrovskii, "K biografii Antoniia Podol'skogo," *ChOIDR,* 1912, no. 2, pt. 3:33–38; and A. M. Panchenko, "Podol'skii Antonii," "Issledovatel'skie Materialy," 40, 152–55. He was not alone in his attitudes, for Archbishop Nektarii of Tobol'sk (1636–1640), previously a monk of the Nilovo-Stolbenskii Monastery, shared the same interest in the new rhetoric and the special concern with drunkenness. Nektarii seems also to have been a monastic traditionalist. See E. K. Romodanovskaia, *Russkaia literatura v Sibiri pervoi poloviny XVII v.* (Novosibirsk, 1973), 55–65.
14. It in turn was one of the components of the *Kirillova kniga* (Moscow, 1644) and the *Kniga o vere,* collections of mostly Ukrainian polemical works against Protestantism and Catholicism. These collections were later among the chief devotional readings of the Old Believers.
15. Baptism was a subject of special concern, for the Catholic missionary Orsini, who passed through Russia returning from Persia, reported that the different ritual of baptism was one of the chief Russian objections to the Catholic faith. E. Shmurlo, *Rimskaia Kuriia na russkom pravoslavnom vostoke v 1609–1654 godakh* (Prague, 1928), 78; G. V. Forsten, "Snosheniia Danii s Rossiei v tsarstvovanie Khristiana IV," *ZhMNP* 280 (April 1892): 331–34.
16. A. Shilov, "Ivan Nasedka," *Russkii biograficheskii slovar',* Naake-Nakenskii–

Nikolai Nikolaevich Starshii (St. Petersburg, 1914), 105–10; Aleksandr Golubtsov, "Pamiatniki preniia o vere," *ChOIDR*, 1892, no. 2, pt. 2:1–350, but esp. 111–54, 169–80, 232–40, 263–308, 315–49; and Rumiantseva, *Narodnoe*, 44–50, 94.

17. Zizanii (died by 1621) was a teacher in the Orthodox fraternities of L'vov and Wilno and the brother of Lavrentii Zizanii. Panchenko treats Nasedka as a complete traditionalist, calling him an *ortodoksal'nyi nachetchik, ravno nepriiaznennyi i k ukrainskomy bogosloviiu, i k grecheskim "shataniiam"*: A. M. Panchenko, *Russkaia stikhotvornaia kul'tura XVII veka* (Leningrad, 1973), 32. This is the traditional interpretation in the scholarly literature, evidently based on the Trankvillion episode, but the content of the *Kirillova kniga* alone is enough to refute this view: he cannot be hostile to Ukrainian theology yet extensively publish it at the same time. Furthermore, Trankvillion had already been condemned in the Ukraine, and the Russians were merely following along. This episode, as well as the condemnation in Moscow of Lavrentii Zizanii's catechism, which also occurred in 1627, gave occasion to a decree of the tsar and patriarch forbidding "Lithuanian" books in Russia. This decree is normally cited to show the hostility of the Russian church to Ukrainian religious writings, although it was pointed out seventy years ago by the main authority on Ukrainian-Russian ecclesiastical relations that it was not enforced by the 1630s—or after, it should be added. See Kharlampovich, *Malorossiiskoe vliianie*, 103–13. Rumiantseva interprets the contents of the *Kirillova kniga* as quite innovative, looking forward to the Vonifat'ev circle, which would make Nasedka even less a traditionalist.

18. The offending memorandum is in Golubtsov, "Pamiatniki prenii," 158–65. See also V. I. Gal'tsov, "Svedeniia o S. I. Shakhovskom v opisi arkhiva Posol'skogo prikaza 1673 g.," in *Arkheograficheskii ezhegodnik za 1976 g.* (Moscow, 1977), 79–81.

19. Platonov, *Drevnerusskie skazaniia*, 230–57. Panchenko simply replaces the notion of secret Catholicism with that of secret Arianism. See Panchenko, *Russkaia stikhotvornaia*, 27–29.

20. Platonov, *Pamiatniki*, 525–26, where Khvorostinin uses the expression in the title to his historical tale.

21. The texts are published in S. F. Platonov, V. I. Savva, and V. G. Druzhinin, eds., "Vnov' otkrytye polemicheskie sochinenia XVII veka protiv eretikov," *LZAK za 1905 g.* 18 (1907): 1–177. Platonov's reasons for attributing the anti-Protestant tract to Katyrev-Rostovskii are that the manuscript he used was in the possession of a nobleman of the Uglich district, whereas Khvorostinin's was a Iaroslavl' family (the neighboring district!), and the remark by the author that he was miraculously cured by divine grace after the tsar's own physicians had given up on him, whereas Khvorostinin was often under suspicion or worse at court. This first reason is simply trivial: many manuscripts known to be written or copied in one part of Russia have turned up in distant parts, and nothing of this sort can be concluded merely on the basis of the possession of the manuscript. The second reason is equally specious, for Khvorostinin was as often in the tsar's good graces as in his bad graces. There is no good reason to reject the clear use of Khvorostinin's "signature" "Duks Ivan" in the manuscript. Finally, the recent confirmation that Katyrev-Rostovskii's tale of the Smuta is only a very slight adaptation of Shakhovskoi's tale suggests that Katyrev-Rostovskii was not a

writer of importance, if even a writer at all. See M. V. Kukushkina, "Semen Shakhovskoi—avtor Povesti o Smute," in *Pamiatniki kul'tury—novye otkrytiia 1974 g.* (Moscow, 1975), 75–78. The Ukrainian poems from which Khvorostinin worked are in Kolosova and Krekoten', *Ukrains'ka,* 71–136.

22. Platonov, Savva, and Druzhinin, "Predislovie . . . o vospitanie chad," 33–37, "K chitateliu," 38–39, "Povest' ili vozglashenie," 40–80, "Povest' sleznaia o Listriskom . . . sobore," 81–106.

23. All of the manuscripts date from the early seventeenth century, before 1630, and thus from Khvorostinin's lifetime, and all come from Ukrainian monasteries, the *Skarga* from a small monastery near Putivl', the second section from the library of the Kievo-Mikhailovskii Monastery, and the third from a small monastery near Vol'nitsa Zagorovskaia in Volhynia. Kolosova, and Krekoten', *Ukrains'ka,* 71–88 (*Skarga*), 89–114 (Kievo-Mikhailovskii), and 115–36 (Zagorovskii).

24. The Ukrainian anti-Latin polemics probably date from before 1596, and represent a response to the spread of Protestantism, Catholicism, and Polish culture among their ecclesiastical and secular elite, especially after the Lublin Union between Poland and Lithuania in 1569: Kolosova and Krekoten', *Ukrains'ka,* 25–55.

25. Ivan Vyshenskii, *Sochineniia,* ed. I. P. Eremin (Moscow and Leningrad, 1955).

26. This attitude in the Ukraine was to wane after 1620, when the Orthodox hierarchy was restored with Greek help and the metropolitan of Kiev, Peter Mohyla, founded the Kievan Academy, an attempt to duplicate the aristocratic Catholic culture of Poland on the basis of Orthodox faith. In Khvorostinin's lifetime, however, the defense of Ukrainian-Belorussian Orthodoxy meant to a large extent the defense of a religion of provincial nobles and peasants and their impoverished clergy, a defense that naturally stressed the humility and apostolic poverty of that clergy against Roman wealth and pride.

27. Platonov, Savva, and Druzhinin, "Vnov' otkrytye," 49–74, follows Kolosova and Krekoten', *Ukrains'ka,* 71–84, but Platonov, Savva, and Druzhinin, 74–77 follows not Kolosova, 84–88 (the end of the Kievo-Mihailovskii section), but Kolosova, 131–32 (in the Zagorovskii section). He omitted most of the parts of the "Kievo-Mikhailovskii" section that praises monasticism and virginity and attacks the Arians: Kolosova, 93–99, 109, 110–13. It is also possible that he only knew the *Skarga* and the "Zagorovskii" section, as the complete complex seems to have been separated early. Khvorostinin did not entertain any secret sympathies for the Arians, for he stated in the verse preface to the whole: *Ariivo i Savelievo uchenie proklinaiu,* "I curse the teaching of Arius and Sabellius." Platonov, Savva, and Druzhinin, "Vnov' otkrytye," 42. The line occurs in the first of Khvorostinin's prefaces. He may have considered the issues in this section irrelevant or of secondary interest. There were no Arians in Russia, and in the early seventeenth century no one any longer doubted the divinity of Christ.

28. Platonov, Savva, and Druzhinin, "Vnov' otkrytye," 44–47.

29. Ibid., 33–37. The text of the preface is sometimes found in manuscripts separately. The remarks on the works against Florence and various Protestants show Khvorostinin to be the author of the verse anti-Protestant tract

discussed subsequently. This essentially moral polemic against Catholicism is a change from the earlier tradition of polemic, which concentrated more on the dogmatic issues. This was the case with Maksim Grek: Sinitsyna, *Maksim Grek,* 75–87.

30. The 1619 version of Kopystens'kyi's is Zakharii Kopystenskii, *Kniga o vere, Arkhiv Iugo-zapadnoi Rossii,* pt. 1, vol. 8, vyp. 1 (Kiev, 1914), 59–179. Zakharii was archimandrite of the Kievo-Pecherskii Monastery from 1624 to his death in 1627, thus succeeding Elisei Pletenets'kyi in this citadel of Orthodoxy in the Ukraine.

The tract on images adapted by Khvorostinin was relatively popular in Russia, for there exists another adaptation made in Novgorod in 1639 with a verse preface identifying the author (in an acrostic) as Pop Stefan. The editor suggested Pop Stefan was Stefan Vonifatiev, but this was clearly the only Stefan he could think of. Vonifatiev did not, as far as we know, write verse. A more likely author is the priest Stefan Gorchak, a relatively prolific poet of the 1630s and 1640s. See "Zametka ob odnoi staropechatnoi knige," *ChOIDR,* 1880, no. 1:1–10, and Panchenko, *Russkaia stikhotvornaia,* 49–50, 68–71. Ivan Nasedka also used both parts for his *Izlozhenie na liutory* of 1622–1623 and again for his *Kirillova kniga* (Moscow, 1644), a collection of Patristic, Greek, and Ukrainian-Belorussian tracts in defense of Orthodoxy as well as on general theological issues. On Nasedka's writings and adaptations, see also Hans Peter Niess, *Kirche in Russland zwischen Tradition und Glaube,* Kirche im Osten 13 (Göttingen, 1977), 131. The tract appeared again in Nafanail's *Kniga o vere.* On Nafanail's identity, see Niess, 54–59, who displays perhaps more skepticism than is called for.

31. Platonov, Savva, and Druzhinin, "Vnov' otkrytye," 117–77. On the tradition of critique of Protestant belief, see D. Tsvetaev, "Protestantsvo i protestanty v Rossii do epokhi preobrazovanii," *ChOIDR,* 1889, no. 4:1–328; 1890, 1, pt. 2: 329–782, esp. 512–696; Ludolf Müller, *Die Kritik des Protestantismus in der russischen Theologie von 16. bis zum 18. Jahrhundert,* Abhandlungen der Akademie der Wissenschaften und Literatur Mainz 1 (Mainz, 1951); and Valerie Tumins, ed., *Tsar Ivan IV's Reply to Jan Rokyta* (The Hague and Paris, 1971).

32. L. N. Maikov, *Ocherki iz istorii russkoi literatury XVII i XVIII stoletii* (St. Petersburg, 1889), 1–162, was an early study. Strictly speaking the verse is presyllabic, as the lines have varied numbers of syllables. Isosyllabic verse seems to have begun with Simeon Polotskii.

33. I. F. Golubev claimed that a poem found in a miscellany in a Kalinin (Tver') library was the work of Prince Semen Shakhovskoi. The clue in the poem (line 271) gives the author's name as a *"shestichislennyi kamen' dragii"* ("six-numbered," that is, six-lettered precious stone), which Golubev interpreted to mean Simeon, the son of Jacob, on the basis of the Biblical reference in Exod. 28:15–21 and 39:12, to the twelve stones for each of the twelve tribes of Israel. However, in the Septuagint, and therefore the Slavic Bible, none of the stones in either language has six letters. The reference must be to the twelve stones mentioned in Revelation 21:20, where one of the stones is, in Greek, *hyacinthos,* giving Slavic *iakinf.* There is only one word that both means a precious stone and has six letters: *iakinf* (which is also a Christian name): I. I. Sreznevskii, *Slovar' drevnerusskogo iazyka,* 3 vols. (reprint,

Moscow, 1989), 1, pt. 1:11. The Byzantine exegete of Revelations known in Russia, Andrew of Caesaria, identified the *hyacinthos* in the text with St. Simon. This suggests Shakhovskoi as a possibility, though it cannot be excluded that the author's Christian name was Iakinf. The text also refers to the addressee as the son of Michael (line 281), which Golubev believes to be Prince Dmitrii Mikhailovich Pozharskii, as the addressee's great victories against the enemies of Russia are mentioned. The language of the poem is very general, however, and could refer to a number of great boyars whose fathers bore the name Michael: some passages seem more appropriate to the tsar himself, though at the time of Shakhovskoi's presumed death in 1654 Tsar Aleksei Mikhailovich's victories had bearly begun. On the whole, the poem consists of praise of the valor and generosity of the addressee, and asks for his favor. See I. F. Golubev, "Dva neizvestnykh stikhotvornykh poslanii pervoi poloviny XVII veka," *TODRL* 17 (1961): 391–413, and Keenan, *Apocrypha*, 203, who reproduces the poem as Shakhovskoi's on 172–77. Panchenko expressed skepticism on this attribution in V. P. Adrianova-Peretts and A. M. Panchenko, *Russkaia sillabicheskaia poeziia XVII–XVIII vv.* (Leningrad, 1970), 362–63, and put the title with the attribution to Shakhovskoi in brackets (43).

On Tatishchev, who wrote in the 1640s, and Ziuzin, see Bylinin, "Stikhotvornye 'Predisloviia,'" 11–12; Crummey, *Aristocrats,* 181, 206–7; and Panchenko, *Russkaia stikhotvornaia,* 42–43, 246–47. Rogov also joined Nasedka in the debates with the Danes, but fell afoul of Nikon (then metropolitan of Novgorod) in 1649. He was in favor again by 1650, and died shortly thereafter: A. Shilov, "Rogov, Mikhail Stefanovich," in *Russkii biograficheskii slovar',* vol. Reitern–Rol'tsberg, 281–82. On Samsonov see also Veselovskii, *D'iaki,* 462. From 1631 Samsonov was a *d'iak* of the Patriarchal Palace Office. Veselovskii had no data on Romanchukov.

34. Illustrations of this mood are in the poem by the "six-lettered precious stone" (Adrianova-Peretts and Panchenko, *Russkaia,* 43–55), and the works of Savvatii in L. S. Sheptaev, "Stikhi spravshchika Savvatiia," *TODRL* 21 (1965): 5–28 esp. 12–16, 22–24: no. 1 (to Prokofiev), no. 2 (to the head of the Printing Office, Prince A. M. L'vov), and no. 6 (to the Tsar's confessor Nikita). On I. N. Romanov-Kasha, see Crummey, *Aristocrats,* 114, 178; and Platonov, *Ocherki,* 234, 279, 341, 395, 431, 439, 531.

35. Later on the boyar Prince M. Iu. Tatishchev (1620–1701) addressed the tsar in similar terms, as did Simeon Polotskii. This appears to be a rather late work, as the tsar is unnamed but seems to be Aleksei, and the verse is a petition for high rank, which he was awarded only in 1684. Sheptaev, "Savvatiia," no. 7, pp. 25–28; Kh. Loparev, "Opisanie rukopisi Moskovskogo Chudova Monastyria No. 57–359," *ChOIDR,* 1886, no. 3, pt. 5:8–9 (Savvatii to Ivan Nikitich Romanov).

36. Panchenko, *Russkaia Stikhotvornaia,* 244–45, 248–52; and Golubev, "Dva neizvestnykh," 404–7. On M. N. Odoevskii, see Crummey, *Aristocrats,* 120, 139.

37. Loparev, "Opisanie," 3–5; Panchenko, *Russkaia Stikhotvornaia,* 253–55, 244–46, 268–69.

38. Panchenko, *Russkaia Stikhotvornaia,* 248–52, 244–46, 267.

39. Once again, this was not merely a case of borrowing from foreign sources.

Ukrainian religious writings of the early seventeenth century concerned with morality rather than dogma or confessional polemic, such as Stavrovetskii's *Evangelie uchitel'noe*, of 1619, contain precisely such a complete catalog of sins.

40. For these reasons, amounting to a breakdown of the medieval genre, the text's editor maintains that it is not "really" a *zhitie* and therefore should be titled *Povest' ob Ulianii Osor'inoi*. Perhaps, but in the manuscripts it is the Life of Iuliana of Murom, or Iuliana Lazarevskaia (of Lazarevo, the village she owned and where she was buried), and however correct the notion that the text is not "really" a *zhitie*, that title for such a text precisely captures its transitional nature. See M. O. Skripil', "'Povest' ob Ulianii Osor'inoi' (Kommentarii i teksty)", *TODRL* 7 (1948): 256–323, esp. 256–57. Julia Alissandratos argues, on the other hand, that Iuliana was really a saint since the word *sviataia* is used of her, and that the genre is the traditional life of the saint. The first argument misunderstands sainthood in Russia, as we have seen. The second seriously underestimates the originality of the religious content of the life, with its unusual emphasis on charity. Alissandratos examined only the formal structure of the work, finding it to be very conventional, in my mind incorrectly. The content is certainly not traditional. Julia Alissandratos, "New Approaches to the Problem of Identifying the Genre of the Life of Julijana Lazarevskaja," *Cyrillomethodianum* 7 (1983):235–44.

41. Later on she expressed a desire to enter a convent, which her husband refused, but they agreed to refrain from sexual intercourse. This decision is in keeping with Iuliana's perfection but does not detract from the main theme of the life, charity and mercy. Even Russian monastic lives rarely mention sexual temptation in spite of the long monastic tradition of condemnation of women and insistence on celibacy: on the antifeminine tradition, see L. V. Titova, *Beseda ottsa s synom o zhenskoi zlobe* (Novosibirsk, 1987), 114–55. This absence of sexual themes is in contrast to canon law and penitential literature, which is full of the subject, as is to be expected: Eve Levin, *Sex and Society in the World of the Orthodox Slavs, 900–1700* (Ithaca, N.Y., 1989). Levin's concentration on canonical and penitential writings tends to overemphasize the role of sexuality in (particularly Russian) Orthodox ethical teachings, as does her use of often rather heterodox popular and semipopular tales rather than the main monastic lives.

42. Skripil', "Povest," 277, 279, 281–82.

43. Ibid., 279.

44. Ibid., 279–81.

45. It is difficult to detect any greater emphasis on either pride or greed, as opposed to the situation in Western Europe, where the emphasis in early medieval Europe on pride gave way to an emphasis on avarice. In early modern Western Europe the emphasis was on sexual sins and on avarice, while pride came only sixth in the amount of attention for Catholic preachers. Papal court preachers stressed luxury and avarice, followed by ambition (not pride, apparently). See Lester K. Little, "Pride Goes before Avarice: Social Change and the Vices in Latin Christendom," *American Historical Review* 76 (1971): 16–49; John W. O'Malley, *Praise and Blame in Renaissance Rome: Rhetoric, Doctrine, and Reform in the Sacred Orators of the Papal Court, c.*

1450–1521 (Durham, N.C., 1979), 187–91; and Jean Delumeau, *La péché et la peur: La culpablisation en Occident (XIII–XVIII siècles)* (Paris, 1983), 470–97.

Chapter 7

1. The few references to these sermons tell us only that they had a great effect on the audience and that the Ukrainian preachers (Slavinetskii) complained of their unlearned character. See Robinson, *Bor'ba idei*, 254–56.

2. Here the collection merely continues a main theme of Khvorostinin and Nasedka, as well as that of the short collection of tracts in defense of icons published in Moscow in 1642, *Sbornik o pochitanie ikon* (Moscow, 1642). The collection thus fitted in well with the printed service books of the 1640s, which contain the largest number of saints' festivals in pre-Petrine Russia (see chapter 4).

3. The reception of the writings of St. John Chrysostom among the Orthodox Slavs in the Middle Ages is a subject of considerable significance for the history of religion, but one that is immensely complex. The practice of excerpting the texts and then using them in liturgical books, menologies, and various collections of short devotional works makes the problem of simply indentifying the translations, their sources, and subsequent histories virtually impossible without a major scholarly effort. Preliminary work has shown, for example, that only six of his homilies were translated in full before the fourteenth century, when the Greek anthology of his homilies known as the *Margarit* was translated in full. The most widely copied texts, however, remained in the collections of real and spurious excerpts, the *Zlatoust* and the *Izmaragd*. It seems to be the case that St. John Chrysostom, at least by the time of the hesychasts, came to be used (or viewed) as primarily an ascetic writer, whose works formed part of the normal readings in Russian monasteries. The Zealots, by contrast, were more interested in the full text of St. John, which had the result of providing an image of his teaching that was not one of strict asceticism but more moderate and suitable for lay audiences. A. Arkhangel'skii, "K izucheniiu drevnerusskoi literatury: Tvoreniia ottsov tserkvi v drevnerusskoi pis'mennosti," *ZhNMP* 258 (July 1888): 1–49; (August 1888): 203–95, esp. 203–32; E. E. Granstrem, "Ioann Zlatoust v drevnei russkoi i iuzhnoslavianskoi pis'mennosti (XI–XIV vv.)," *TODRL* 35 (1980): 345–75; and E. E. Granstrem, "Ioann Zlatoust v drevnei russkoi i iuzhnoslavianskoi pis'mennosti (XI–XIV vv.)," *TODRL* 29 (1974): 186–93.

4. *Patrologia Graeca* 49 (Paris, 1859) ("De poenitentia"): 283–300, 323–36, and 35 (Paris, 1857) ("De pauperum amore"), 857–909. In all these cases the Slavic translation of the 1647 volume is extremely close to the Greek, apart from minor textual variants.

5. M. P. Alekseev, "Erazm Rotterdamskii v russkom perevode XVII v.," in *Slavianskaia filologiia 1: Sbornik statei, posviashchennyi IV Mezhdunarodnomu s"ezdu slavistov* (Moscow, 1958), 275–336, esp. 290–92, 308–22; N. A. Kazakova, "Russkii perevod XVII v. truda Blau 'Theatrum orbis terrarum sive Atlas Novus,'" *Vspomogatel'nye istoricheskie distsipliny* 17 (1985): 161–78; and V. V. Nimchuk, ed., *Leksykon latyns'kyi E. Slavynets'koho, Leksykon sloveno-latyns'kyi E. Slavynets'koho ta A. Korets'koho-Satanovs'koho* (Kiev, 1973). The Latin dictionary was compiled first in 1642, presumably in Kiev, then reworked in Moscow in

1650. The Slavic Latin dictionary is undated, but was compiled in Moscow when Satanovskii was in Moscow, thus 1649–1653. Satanovskii also translated Meffreth's *Hortulus reginae,* a collection of late fifteenth-century Catholic sermons for the tsar. On Evfimii Chudovskii, see Florovskii, "Chudovskii inok," 103–7. A. P. Bogdanov, following earlier conclusions of Kapterev, asserts that there was no such school in the Chudov Monastery: A. P. Bogdanov, "K polemike kontsa 60-kh–nachala 80-kh godov XVII v. ob organizatsii vysshego uchebnogo zavedeniia v Rossii," in *Issledovaniia po istochnikovedeniiu istorii SSSR XIII–XVIII vv.,* ed. V. I. Buganov, (Moscow, 1986), 191, 208.

6. For court ceremonies at the Chudov Monastery, see *Vykhody gosudarei tsarei i velikikh kniazei Mikhaila Fedorovicha, Alekseia Mikhailovicha, i Fedora Alekseevicha* (Moscow, 1844), e.g., 230 (6 September 1650), 238 (17 February 1651), 332 (20 May 1660), 366 (2–3 November 1661), and 513 (20 May 1669). The archimandrites are listed in Stroev, *Spiski,* 162–63. The monastery church of the Miracle of St. Michael the Archangel (festival 6 September) is not to be confused with the Cathedral of St. Michael the Archangel (festival 8 November), the burial place of the ruling dynasty. Ceremonies at the Cathedral of St. Michael consisted mainly of prayers for the ancestors of the tsar. (The Romanovs were related by marriage to the previous Riurikovich rulers of Russia, the original Moscow dynasty.) The monastery, destroyed in the 1930s, was roughly on the site now occupied by the Palace of Congresses, while the Archangel Cathedral still stands.

7. On Epifanii, see V. Pevnitskii, "Epifanii Slavinetskii, odin iz glavnykh deiatelei russkoi dukhovnoi literatury," *Trudy Kievskoi dukhovnoi akademii,* 1861, no. 8:405–38, no. 10:135–82; Ivan Rotar, "Epifanii Slavinetskii, literaturnyi deiatel' XVII v.," *Kievskaia starina* 71 (October 1900): 1–38, (November 1900): 189–217, (December 1900): 347–400; A. S. Eleonskaia, *Russkaia oratorskaia proza v literaturnom protsesse XVII veka* (Moscow, 1990), 55–85; Alekseev, "Erazm"; and Nimchuk, *Leksykon,* 5–58.

8. The two stories in question are an account in the *Osten,* a polemical work of about 1690 normally attributed to Evfimii Chudovskii, and one including a conversation with the Moldavian scholar and diplomat Nikolai Milescu-Spafarii (c. 1635–1708). See *Osten* (Kazan', 1863); and I. F. Golubev, "Vstrecha Simeona Polotskogo, Epifaniia Slavinetskogo, i Paisiia Ligarida s Nikolaem Spafariem i ikh beseda," *TODRL* 26 (1971): 294–301. The notion of Epifanii as the leader of a "grecophile" party persists in modern handbooks such as the recent Pushkin House history of Russian literature. See the chapter by A. M. Panchenko, "Literatura 'perekhodnogo veka'," in N. I. Prutskov, ed., *Istoriia russkoi literatury,* 4 vols. (Leningrad, 1980–1983), 1:291–407, esp. 334–35, where the idea is repeated, with the additional notion that the "Latins" (Simeon Polotskii) represented an early rationalism that Epifanii and the "Grecophiles" opposed. Panchenko also asserts here that Epifanii's thought was formed before the influence of Mohyla was dominant in Kiev, an assertion for which there is no biographical evidence.

9. Rotar, "Epifanii," 9; Smentsovskii, *Brat'ia Likhudy,* appendix, XXIII. Evfimii's tract, *"Rassuzhdenie"* (Smentsovskii, VI–XXVI) is clearly a work of the 1680s, referring among others things to Tsar Aleksei as the previous tsar. This is a clearly polemical work, for in it Evfimii misuses a quotation from Epifanii's sermon on learning (Sin. 597, ff. 76–81) against the Old Belief to buttress

his argument. Evfimii took the quotation (Smentsovskii, XXI–XXII, featuring the passage on Marcus Cato) out of context, thus falsifying the message of Epifanii's sermon (see subsequent discussion). On the tract, see Bogdanov, "K polemike," 195–99.

10. State Historical Museum (GIM), Moscow, Synodal Collection, Sin. 597, ff. 14v (John Cassian), 33 (Gregory the Great, "Homilies on the Gospels," chap. 4, quoted in Latin), 104v (Peter Damian and Plutarch), 79 (Plato), 80 (Pythagoras and Marcus Cato). I owe the observation on Sin. 597's Greek hand to B. L. Fonkich. Eleonskaia also notes Epifanii's positive attitude to classical learning as well as to "Latin" authors: Eleonskaia, *Russkaia oratorskaia*, 72–73.

11. The opponent of Epifanii in the sermon is Nikita Pustosviat, whose petition of 1665 raised the issue of learning in general and learning of the Greek language and religious tradition in general. The sermon has a clue relating it to Nikita's petition in its discussion of the names of God, an issue brought up by Nikita in attacking the use of quotations from Pseudo-Dionysius in the *Skrizhal'* (see my n. 15). This clue thus dates the sermon to about 1665–1666, the period immediately after the petition. Neither Simeon Polotskii nor other "Latins" were the opponents of Epifanii in this sermon. The life of the boyar Rtishchev, the *Zhitie milostivogo muzha Fedora, zvaniem Rtishcheva*, also contributed to this legend, as it stresses that Epifanii was learned in the "Slavic and Greek tongues and others," ignoring his Latin dictionary and translations of Latin secular works as well as his knowledge of the Latin fathers. However, this is also a text of the 1680s and edited by Evfimii Chudovskii, Epifanii's erstwhile pupil, but in the 1680s Ioakim's ally and an opponent of the "Latins" in the eucharistic controversy. Evfimii knew that Epifanii had no preference for Greek over Latin learning, for his marginal notes are found on Sin. 597, but he clearly chose to bend the truth to defend his and Patriarch Ioakim's views. The life of Rtishchev also conceals Rtishchev's friendship with Simeon Polotskii when Rtishchev and Simeon were tutors to the then Tsarevich Aleksei. See I. Kozlovskii, "F. M. Rtishchev: Istoriko-biograficheskoe issledovanie," *Kievskie universitetskie izvestiia* 46 (January 1906): 1–52; (February 1906): 53–100; (June 1906): 101–132; (November 1906): 133–52; (December 1906): 153–201 (text on pp. 155–68).

12. Ol'ga Strakhova, "Problema 'Nestandartnogo' perevoda sv. pisaniia v Moskovskoi Rusi," *California Slavic Studies* (forthcoming); T. A. Isachenko-Lisovaia, "O perevodcheskoi deiatel'nosti Evfimiia Chudovskogo," in *Khristianstvo i tserkov' v Rossii feodal'nogo perioda (Materialy)*, ed. N. N. Pokrovskii (Novosibirsk, 1989), 194–210; and Florovskii, "Chudovskii inok," 110–12, 140–44. Bogdanov, in his eagerness to defend Simeon and his followers from the charge of being merely "Westernizers," correctly sees their central concern with education, but falls into the equal error of interpreting Epifanii and especially Evfimii and Patriarch Ioakim as obscurantist traditionalists. As we have seen, this was not the case, for this view depends too heavily on Rotar's error and Evfimii's writings from after 1680: Bogdanov, "K polemike." The Greeks as well were no obscurantists, and began to oppose learning per se only well into the eighteenth century in reaction to European rationalism: Podskalsky, *Griechische Theologie*, 329–85.

13. Sin. 597, ff. 90–97v. This is also the one sermon that was written in Epifanii's own hand.

14. *Slovo k monakhom*, GIM, Sin. 597, ff. 13–16v, 14v: "monasi sii, izhe du-

shepoleznoe vozderzhanie prenebregshe, i chrevesa svoia razshyrivshe slastnimi pishchami chrevone[nasytno?] pitaiutsia, ubozhestvo monakholepoe prezrevshe v priobreteni bogatsv tlennykh dushevrednykh ustremliaiutsia." The other sermon, *Pomiani iako smert' ne zamedlit,* GIM, Sin. 597, ff. 104–107v, is also the one with the references to Plutarch and Plato.

15. "Against the Disobedient to the Church" (*Na nepokorniki tserkvi*), TsNB, Kiev, MS. 290II/145, ff. 677–697; "Obretaiutsia zhe netsii raskolnitsi, miatezhnitsi, slavoliubtsi, tshcheslavtsi, nepokaraiushchiisia mne materi svoei i ne slushaiushchii pastyrei svoikh sviashchennykh arkhiereev" "derziut bozhestvennaa pisaniia po svoemu nevezhestvu tolkovati pache zhe reku razvrashchati," 679, 680–81; "The words of the Lord are pure words, as silver tried in a furnace of earth" (*Slovesa gospodnia, slovesa chista serebro razhdeneno, iskusheno zemli,* Psalm 12:6), GIM, Moscow, Sin. 597, ff. 82–85v; and Liudie, f. 79: "Po nyneshnykh vremenei vezde obretaiutsia mnozi nenavistnii chelovetsi mrachnoiu nenavisti tmoiu oslepleni, izhe vozliubivshe mrak nevedeniia iasnyia ucheniia luchi ne liubiat, teiu ozariaiushchia nenavidiat, teiu ozariaiushchimsia zavidiat, i tuiu temnii rveniia, lesti, kovarstva, o glagolaniia litsemeriia oblakom razrushati, i o velie buistvo i prognati usilstvuiut." The Kiev manuscript also contains a sermon on ff. 641–658 on the text "And there appeared a great wonder in heaven, a woman clothed with the sun, and the moon under her feet, and upon her head a crown of twelve stars" (*I znamenie velie iavisia na nebesi, zhena oblechena v solntse i luna pod nogama eia i na glave eia venets ot zvezd dvanadesiati,* Rev. 12:1). This sermon is here attributed to Epifanii and attacks Old Belief. The style is somewhat unusual for him, but the arguments are the same as in the other sermons of the subject and seem to have been inspired if not written by him. Nikita Pustosviat's petition containing the relevant passage is in Rumiantsev, *Nikita,* 338–42, appendix, 250–51.

16. The sermons on confession and asceticism are *Pokaitesia, priblizhisia bo tsarstvo nebesnoe, Khleb nas nasushchnyi dazhd' nam dnes,* and probably *Egda postites', ne budete iako zhe litsemeri,* GIM, Sin. 597, ff. 37–40v, 21–24v, and 98–101v. This last sermon continues the themes of the previous two, but unlike them contains no direct reference to heresy. It may not be specifically directed against heretical ideas, but it does reinforce the condemnation of extreme asceticism.

17. Before the 1650s very few sermons were printed in the Ukraine, and most were written for public ceremonies only partly ecclesiastical, such as the burial of various bishops, which had political overtones. The only compendia of ordinary homiletic texts, besides translations of the fathers, were the *uchitel'nye evangelia,* Gospel readings interspersed with short sermons that tried to cover all the possible human failings and thus show no especial selectivity. The Ukrainian sermons that were coming off the presses after Epifanii came to Moscow do not show his emphasis on pride and avarice—not surprising in view of the quite different social and religious context of the Ukraine. See, for example, Kirill Trankvillion Stavrovets'kyi [Cyrillus Stavroveckij], *Evangelie uchitel'noe* (Rakhmanov, 1619), and many other examples of sermons. Recently Eve Levin has shown that dealing with sexual sins was largely the preserve of the parish priest at confession, and that the penalties were mild in Russia compared with those normal among Balkan Orthodox Slavs or Western Catholics: Levin, *Sex and Society.*

18. GIM, Sin. 597, ff. 25–28v: "vmesto nepravdi pravda, vmesto zlochestiia

blagochestie, vmesto skupstva obilie, vmesto nemiloserdiia miloserdie, vmesto likhoimstva shchedrota, vmesto voskhishcheniia rastocheniia, vmesto srebroliubiia nishcheliubie, lisheniia milostini obilnaia milostini" (25); 116–119v; 33–36v: "Mnogo muzhelozhstva, mnogo preliubodeianiia, mnogo bluda, mnogo piianstva, mnogo laskeserdstva, mnogo chelovekoubiistva, mnogo srebroliubiia, mnogo likhoimstva, mnogo lzhesvidel'stva, mnogo nepravdi, mnogo inikh bezchislennikh grekhov bogomerzkikh" (34; this catalog of sins includes a rare reference to sexual sins); 41–44v.

19. GIM, Sin. 597, ff. 29–32v, 72–75v, and 124–127v.

20. GIM, Sin. 597, ff. 45–50v; 116–119v: "[serdtse] ne gordelivoe no smirennoe, ne vysokomudroe, no smirennomudroe, ne zemnykh imushchee no nebesnykh zhelaiushchee, ne kosvennoe no pravoe, ne srebroliubivoe no nishcheliubivoe, ne zhestokoe no miagkoe, ne kamennoe no plotianoe" (116), "nedug zhe dushevnyi est' bogomerzkaia nenavist', est' vredonosnaia zavist', est' umovrednaia gordost', est' [illegible] zlobnoe srebroliubie, est' bratovrednaia nepravda, est' vsepagubnaia kleveta, est' dushevrednaia blizhnikh obida . . ." (116v).

21. The elder Rtishchev achieved duma rank in 1650 as an *okol'nichii* and served as the director of the New Quarter (*Novaia Chet'*), a lesser financial office in 1651. In 1651 he entered a monastery, an unusual step for a duma member but perhaps not for a man of his original milieu in Likhvin. He outlived his son and died in 1677. Kozlovskii, "Rtishchev," 13–15, 29; Crummey, *Aristocrats*, 152, 189.

22. Both Ordin-Nashchokin and Khitrovo were "new men" as well, promoted from families previously not of duma rank and somewhat isolated among the aristocrats. All three were also considerably more intellectual than the average duma aristocrat, with Ordin-Nashchokin's theories on Russia's foreign policy and Khitrovo's patronage of religious art. Ordin-Nashchokin and Khitrovo got along with Rtishchev but not with one another. Kozlovskii, "Rtishchev," 31–69, 77–79, 102–10; Crummey, *Aristocrats*, 100–101, 151, 156, 160–61.

23. "Zhitie milostivogo muzha Fedora zvaniem Rtishcheva"; Kozlovskii, "Rtishchev," 155–68.

24. Peter A. Rolland, "'Dulce est et fumos videre Patriae'—Four Letters by Simiaon Polacki," *Harvard Ukrainian Studies* 9 (1985): 166–81. The letters also reveal Simeon's militant Orthodoxy and his brother's Catholicism. Evidently the family was divided in its loyalties, for in the 1637 canonization processus on Iosaphat Kuntsevich, the Uniate martyr, one Gabriel Sitnianowicz, described as "bonus unitus," testified to Iosafat's miraculous cure of his mother. The mother embraced the union as a result, but apparently her husband, Gabriel's father, did not, for nothing is said of him but that he was a "consul" of Polotsk. See Athanasius G. Welykyj, ed., *S. Josaphat Hieromartyri Documenta Romana Beatificationis et Canonizationis*, 3 vols., Analecta Ordinis S. Basilii Magni, sec. III, ser. II (Rome, 1952–1967), 2:279–80. Sitnianovich was an unusual name, and in a small town like Polotsk it is unlikely that two members of the local elite would bear it and be unrelated. The story also reveals an internal religious conflict in the family similar to that revealed by Simeon's 1667 letters.

25. Kosman, *Reformacja*, 249–50; Floria, "Drevnerusskie traditsii," in Pashuto,

Floria, and Khoroshkevich, eds., *Drevnerusskoe nasledie*, 233; L. S. Abet-sedarskii, *Belorussiia i Rossiia XVI–XVII vv.* (Minsk, 1978), 126–29; and *Vossoedinenie Ukrainy s Rossiei*, 3 vols. (Moscow, 1954), 3, no. 12:21–24. Simeon himself claimed in a satirical poem of 1661 that Afinogen was not a hegumen and had claimed many titles falsely. This is a clearly hostile source that cannot easily be verified, but it may be that Afinogen was used precisely because he could easily be disclaimed. See Peter A. Rolland, "Three Early Satires by Simeon Polotsky," *Slavonic and East European Review* 63 (1985):1–20, esp. 12–20. The religious and cultural situation of the Orthodox is best revealed, however, by the diary of Afanasii Fillipovich, a hegumen of Brest (died 1648) who spent much of his time in the 1630s and 1640s petitioning the king of Poland for redress of grievances. His struggle was wholly unsuccessful, and he was finally murdered in reprisal for alleged support of the Khmel'nyts'kyi revolt in September 1648. Although Belorussia's most militant spokesman of Orthodoxy, his culture was largely Polish: he wrote in a Slavonic that was heavily polonized, and even presented Tsar Michael with a description of the sufferings of the Orthodox in 1638 written in Latin verse! See Afanasii Fillipovich, *Diariush*, *RIB* 4 (St. Petersburg, 1878), 49–156.

26. Eingorn, *O snosheniiakh*, 51–97, 101–2, 121; Sysyn, *Between Poland*, 127–28; Peter Allen Rolland, "Aspects of Simeon Polockij's Early Verse (1648–1663)" (Ph.D. diss., Indiana University, 1978), 167–72, 175–84. Simeon praised Tsar Aleksei's construction of an Orthodox church in Dünaburg (Daugavpils): Rolland, "Aspects," 167. Over the years A. N. Robinson has attempted to prove that Simeon was a Uniate monk of the Basilian order. He adduces the inscription on one of Simeon's books where he described himself as a monk "of the Order of St. Basil" (*ordinis S. Basilii*), as well as the remark in the Curlander Jakob Reitenfels' 1680 account of Russia that Simeon was a "Basilian monk." V. K. Bylinin also defends the notion that Simeon became a Uniate Basilian monk in Wilno in 1650–1653, presumably remaining one secretly after 1656. His grounds for this position are the text of a Catholic Easter play in a manuscript (GIM Synodal collection 731) containing some early writings of Simeon's. See N. P. Kiselev, "O moskovskom knigopechatanii XVII veka," in *Kniga: Issledovaniia i materialy* (Moscow, 1960), 2:166; A. N. Robinson, "Simeon Polotskii i russkii literaturnyi protsess," 8, and V. K. Bylinin, "Neizuchennaia shkol'naia p'esa Simeona Polotskogo," in Robinson, *Russkaia staropechatnaia . . . Simeon*, 311, Robinson, *Bor'ba idei*, 49.

Robinson and Bylinin's interpretation of the term *Basilian* in this context is based on a misunderstanding. Basilian was the common Western term for Orthodox monks long before the Uniate Basilian order was formed in the wake of the 1596 Union of Brest. In 1525 Johannes Faber described Russian monks as living "under the rule of Basil the Great," and in 1577 the emperor's ambassador Cobenzl wrote of the monks of the Trinity–St. Sergii Monastery as "of the order of St. Basil" (*ordinis D. Basilii*), the same phrase Slavinetskii used three-quarters of a century later: Starczewski, ed., *Scriptores*, I. Faber, 7, II, Cobenzl, 15. These examples could be multiplied for Russian and Greek monks as well. A contemporary Catholic encyclopedia even gives as the first meaning of Basilian the following: "Erroneous term for monks of the Greek rite that arose in the Latin Middle Ages from the assumption that they lived under the 'rule' of St. Basil as the monks of the

West under the rule of St. Benedict." *Lexikon für Theologie und Kirche,* 10 vols.
(Freiburg, 1957–1965), 2:37. Furthermore, the orthodox monks of Belorussia and the Ukraine seem to have regularly described themselves as
being of the "order of St. Basil," as is the case of Epifanii Slavinetskii and the
militant defender of Belorussian Orthodoxy, Afanasii Fillipovich: Nimchuk,
ed., *Leksykon,* 23, where the title page of Epifanii's Latin dictionary, inscribed
"Moschovia, 1650," describes him as "Ordinis S. Basilii magni"; for Fillipovich, see my n. 25. Bylinin's school play proves nothing, as he cannot
prove that Simeon wrote it, and did not merely copy another's work for
reference or as a school exercise. Other manuscripts of Simeon, such as
TsGADA f. 381, no. 1791, contain numerous exercises of this sort, such as
"Arithmetica" (ff. 187–192) or "Philosophia moralis" (ff. 199–202), and copies of various Catholic theological disputations, none of them on topics at
issue with the Orthodox church. On ff. 17–177 is a "Rhetorica practica," a
compilation of examples and texts, some apparently original, some not. He
states on f. 17 "composita per me Samuelem Piotrowski Sitnianowicz, anno
dni. 1653; incepta 20 martii" and on f. 170 "Finitum Ao. 1653, Julii 22."
From the dates this compilation clearly comes from the Wilno period, but
includes (ff. 45–45v) a homily for the festival of St. Silvester, which is a
panegyric to the Orthodox metropolitan of Kiev, Syl'vestr Kosiv. Finally, the
1667 letters to his brother show him to be militantly Orthodox. They also
show his association with Teodosii Baevs'kyi, one of the politically pro-Polish
(but Orthodox) Mohylan party in the Ukrainian-Belorussian church:
Rolland, "'Dulce,'" 172–76, 178–79; and Sysyn, *Between Poland,* 127–28.

27. Simeon did not get along well with the new (Russian-appointed) Orthodox
bishop of Polotsk, Kallist Zhitoraiskii (bishop, 1657–1663), who imprisoned
Simeon in April 1659. Simeon called Kallikst a wolf, not a shepherd:
Rolland, "Aspects," 175, and "Satires," 15–16.

28. The history of Orthodoxy in Belorussia is not nearly as well known as it is in
the Ukraine for these years, but it seems to have roughly followed the
patterns in the Ukraine. See Sysyn, *Between Poland,* 89–90; Anushkin, *Na
zare;* Abetsedarskii, *Belorussiia,* 95–207; and Eingorn, *O snosheniiakh,* 99–
240. On the war the best account is A. N. Mal'tsev, *Rossiia i Belorussiia v
seredine XVII veka* (Moscow, 1974), esp. 135–77.

29. I. Tatarskii, *Simeon Polotskii, ego zhizn' i deiatel'nost'* (Moscow, 1886), 99–110.
Bogdanov asserts, citing Prozorovskii, that the school was closed in 1668, but
Prozorovskii only says that records of payments cease in that year, which may
have been merely transferred to another office. Prozorovskii actually believed that the school continued, perhaps to Simeon's death. Bogdanov, "K
polemike," 191, 208; Prozorovskii, "Medvedev," 63–69, 74.

30. Tatarskii, *Simeon Polotskii,* 110–52, 293–96; Eingorn, *O snosheniiakh,* 387–88;
A. S. Eleonskaia, "Rabota Simeona Polotskogo nad podgotovkoi k pechati
knig 'Obed dushevnyi' i 'Vecheria dushevnaia,'" in Robinson, *Russkaia staropechatnaia . . . Simeon,* 184–85.

31. V. P. Grebeniuk, "'Rifmologion' Simeona Polotskogo (Istoriia sozdaniia,
struktura, idei)," in Robinson, *Russkaia staropechatnaia . . . Simeon,* 280, 284;
L. A. Chernaia, "Verkhniaia tipografiia Simeona Polotskogo," in ibid., 46–
59; Kapterev, "Snosheniia," 236–37; Crummey, *Aristocrats,* 46–48, 192, 201,
206. Khitrovo's importance is clear in the reports of diplomats, such as the

Danes: G. V. Forsten, "Datskie diplomaty pri moskovskom dvore vo vtoroi polovine XVII veka," *ZhMNP* 355 (September 1904): 157.

32. Simeon's significance has the been the subject of considerable debate over the years, a debate still relevant to our understanding of him and his period. Nineteenth-century scholars were unsympathetic to Baroque aesthetics, which they found "unoriginal," and to "Polish" influence, which they saw as intrinsically hostile to Russian culture. Maikov and Tatarskii's pioneering studies advanced the view that colors all but the most recent work, that he was an unoriginal transmitter of Kievan religious culture, which they described in the terms usual to their age as "dead scholasticism." They held that both the poetry and sermons of Simeon, like those of the Ukrainian writers, were essentially empty of meaning, merely repeating the banalities of Christian faith in an "abstract" and "artificial" manner. The historic importance of his work in Russia thus lay solely in his teaching of Latin and the conveyance of knowledge about "Western" culture. O. I. Bilets'kyi and I. P. Eremin retained this framework after the revolution in their studies of the poetry and plays, but their detailed analysis of the verse succeeded in conveying a more accurate picture of his ideas and cultural background. Of the early scholars, only V. Popov looked at Simeon's religion with an open mind and noted that his sermons were not nearly as "abstract" as they seemed, but in fact addressed many real concerns of the seventeenth century. However, Popov was not an established scholar; he wrote the book as a master's dissertation in theology but left the seminary to pursue a career as inspector of village schools in his native Viatka province, like so many Russians of his generation preferring to serve the people in obscurity rather than follow a career as a scholar. Popov's sensitivity to the social issues made his work unassimilable in the philological climate of the time, and Simeon Polotskii had to wait until A. N. Robinson made clear his importance as the most articulate representative of the new culture of the seventeenth-century court and elite. Maikov, "Simeon Polotskii," in *Ocherki*; Tatarskii, *Simeon Polotskii*; V. Popov, *Simeon Polotskii kak propovednik* (Moscow, 1886); Oleksandr Bilets'kyi, *Zibrannia prats'*, vols. 1–5 (Kiev, 1965–1966), esp. 1:371–449; I. P. Eremin, "Poeticheskii stil' Simeona Polotskogo," *TODRL* 6 (1948): 125–53; Simeon Polotskii, *Izbrannye sochineniia*, ed. I. P. Eremin (Moscow and Leningrad, 1953), 223–60; Robinson, *Bor'ba idei*; Eleonskaia, *Russkaia publitsistika*; Anthony Hippesley, *The Poetic Style of Simeon Polotsky*, Birmingham Slavonic Monographs 16 (Birmingham, 1985); and David Ladner, "Simeon Polockij's Metrical Psalter: Context and Pattern" (Ph.D. diss., Yale University, 1976). Bilets'kyi and Ryszard Łuzny have discussed his relationship with Polish and Ukrainian writers, but mainly in the realm of poetry. See Ryszard Łuzny, *Pisarze kręgu Akademii Kijowsko-Mohilańskiej a literatura polska*, Zeszyty naukowe uniwersytetu Jagiellońskiego 142, Prace historycznoliterackie 11 (Cracow, 1966).

33. Eleonskaia, *Russkaia oratorskaia*, 86–115; and Simeon Polotskii, *Orel Rossiiskii*, Pamiatniki drevnei pis'mennosti 133 (St. Petersburg, 1915). Some useful reflections on the philosophical basis of Simeon's poltical views can be found in the recently published posthumous work of A. S. Lappo-Danilevskii, *Istoriia Russkoi obshchestvennoi mysli i kul'tury XVII–XVIII vv.* (Moscow, 1990), 131–36.

34. The interpretations of the Ukrainian religious writers of the seventeenth century have evolved as have those of Simeon Polotskii. The normal view, formed over a century ago, also presents them as mechanical copyists of Polish models, irrelevant to the life of their time and purveyors of a "scholastic" culture. See N. F. Sumtsov, *K istorii iuzhnorusskoi literatury semnadtsatogo stoletiia, Lazar' Baranovich* (Khar'kov, 1884); idem, "Ioannikii Galiatovskii (K istorii iuzhnorusskoi literatury semnadtsatogo veka)," *Kievskaia starina* 8 (January 1884): 1–20, (February 1884): 183–204, (March 1884): 371–90, (April 1884): 565–88; idem, "Innokentii Gizel': K istorii iuzhnorusskoi literatury XVII v.," *Kievskaia starina* 10 (October 1884): 183–226; idem, "O literaturnykh nravakh iuzhnorusskikh pisatelei," *IORIaS*, 11 (1906): 259–80; and Mikhailo Vozniak, *Istoriia ukrains'koi literatury*, vols. 1–3 (L'vov, 1920–1924), esp. 2:298–355. The differences between the Ukrainian and Polish preachers of the time cannot be treated here, but examination of Polish preachers, such as Piotr Skarga (*Kazania sejmowe*, Cracow, 1597) or Szymon Starowolski (*Swiatnica pańska*, Cracow, 1645) reveals numerous differences from both Ukrainian and Russian preachers. Skarga stressed the need for harmony and obedience in society, whereas Starowolski insisted on the dignity and power of the priesthood, a theme absent in Ukrainian sermons. Recently V. I. Krekoten' has broken new ground with a study of the exempla in the sermons of Antonii Radyvylovs'kyi, where he concludes that the sermons emphasized the sins of love of power, lack of meekness in both masters and servants, and the need for gentleness and justice on the part of rulers. Unlike Skarga, however, he did not stress obedience. He also notes that the traditional views of these sermons as imitations of Polish style were based on generalizing the views of Feofan Prokopovich and lack of close study of the texts: see V. I. Krekoten', *Opovidannia Antoniia Radyvylovs'koho* (Kiev, 1983), 11–55, 183–200; and Antonii's works: Antonii Radivilovskii, *Ogorodok Marii bogoroditsy* (Kiev, 1676); and idem, *Venets Khristov* (Kiev, 1688). Ukrainian sermons are generally neglected, but see on stylistic matters also Michael Berndt, *Die Predigt Dimitrij Tuptalos: Studien zur ukrainischen und russischen Barockpredigt* (Frankfurt/Main, 1975).

35. Galiatovskii, *Kliuch razumeniia* pt. 1:54–67, and passim; Innokentii Gizel', *Mir s Bogom cheloveku* (Kiev, 1669); and Lazar' Baranovich, *Mech dukhovnyi* (Kiev, 1666). The Ukrainians had long been the proponents of miracle cults, perhaps because of the need to show signs of God's favor toward Orthodoxy. Zakharii Kopystens'kyi used miracles this way in his 1621–1622 defense of Orthodoxy against the union: *Palinodiia, RIB* 4 (St. Petersburg, 1878), 313–1200, esp. 841–57. Ukrainian compilations of miracle stories from the first half of the seventeenth century primarily recorded miracles of this type, such as those recorded by Metropolitan Petr Mohyla himself: "Skazaniia Petra Mogily o chudesnkyh i zamechatel'nykh iavleniiakh v tserkvi pravoslavnoi," ed. S. Golubev, in *Arkhiv Iugo-zapadnoi Rusi*, pt. 1, vol. 7 (Kiev, 1887), 49–132. During his metropolitanate lavish accounts of the cults were published, beginning with Athanasiusz Kalnofoyski, *Teraturgima* (Kiev, 1638), a description of the miracles in the Kiev Monastery of the Caves; Kalnofoyski and Hilarion Denisowicz, *Parergon cudów świętych obraza przeczystej Bogarodzice w monastyrze Kupiatickim* (Kiev, 1638). Haliatovs'kyi too produced a collection of miracles of the Mother of God, including ones occurring in Catholic territory, called *Nebo novoe* (L'vov, 1665), and later

editions in L'vov and Chernigov. Krekoten''s study of Antonii Radyvylovs'kyi's exempla reveals a similar preoccupation with miracles, not so much healing miracles at shrines but the direct intervention of the divine in human life. Krekoten', *Opovidannia*, 95–100.

36. Charity does not mean giving money to the church or even the monasteries, and in this he again deviates from his Ukrainian teachers, who mention these forms of charity as often as the Christian's personal alms. Humility is a somewhat more complex notion, and here Simeon's difficulty in fitting the moral dilemmas of his time into the traditional Christian ideas seems to come into play.

37. Simeon Polotskii, *Obed dushevnyi* (Moscow, 1681), "Slovo 1 v nedeliu 26 po soshestviiu sviatogo dukha," 425v–431v, 426: "vsi gresi smertnii iz bogatstva byvaiut. Gordost' v Navukhodonosore iz bogatstva, lakomstvo vo Iude bogatstva dlia, nechistota v sodomianekh ot bogatstva, zavist' o bogatstvakh, po pritochniku: podvizaetsia obogatitisia muzh zavidliv, i ne vest' iako milostivyi obladaet im. Chrevobesie i piianstvo v bogatom evangel'skom ot bogatstva. Gnevlivi bogatii iako Aman nechestivyi na Mardokheia i na ves' rod izrailskii. 'Lenost' obychno byvaet v bogatykh izhe iako dver' na stezhai: tako na lozhakh si obrashchaiutsia.'" "Slovo 1 v nedeliu 7 po soshestviiu sviatogo dukha," 134–140, 137v–138: "bezvredno est' spaseniiu zlato, asche kto ne rabotaet emu, no gospodstvuet, razdaia neskudno i blagokhotno, rastochaia nishchim i bednym, istroshsia na sviataia i bozhestvennaia: iako na khramy bozhiia i utvari tserkovnyia, na obiteli sviatyia, na uchilishcha iunykh, na siropitalishcha, i tym podobnyia." "Slovo 1 v nedeliu 5 sviatyia maslenitsy," 623v–628v, 624: "smirennyia dobrodeteli pouchaet ny, da to iako tverdoe i nepodvizhnoe vsekh dobrodetelei osnovanie, v serdtsakh nashikh polozheno budet, ponezhe po slovesi sviatogo Ioanna Zlatoustogo vsiak polozhiv smirenie, bezbedstvenno vsia inaia vozlagaet, nazidaia, tomu zhe otiatu byvshu, ashche dazhed' samogo nebese prebyvaniia vysotoiu vzydeshi, kupno vsia otemliutsia, i vkonets zleishii otpadaiut." On the style of the *Obed*, see Johannes Langsch, *Die Predigten der 'Coena Spiritualis' von Simeon Polockij*, Veröffentlichungen des Slavischen Instituts an der Friedrich-Wilhelm-Universität Berlin 26 (Berlin, 1940).

38. Gorskii and Nevostruev, *Opisanie*, 2, pt. 3:212–13. Amvrosii held the office 1675–1685, so the sermons thus date from 1675–1680: Stroev, *Spiski*, 176. Simeon Polotskii, *Vecheria dushevnaia* (Moscow, 1683), 14–20v, and *Obed*, 372–78 (cf. Robinson, *Bor'ba idei*, 256–59, 274–77), *Obed*, 48–59; *Vecheria*, 123v–131, 152–159v (Metropolitan Peter of Moscow), 209v–216v (St. Filipp). Sil'vestr Medvedev tried to soften what mild criticism of the tsar the sermon contained but was unsuccessful, for Simeon printed his original text. See Eleonskaia, "Rabota", in Robinson, *Russkaia staropechatnaia . . . Simeon*, 188–89; and idem, *Russkaia oratorskaia*, 119–20. Simeon's play for the court theater, *Tragediia o Navukhodonosore*, presents the image of the proud tyrant defeated by faith and humility. Cf. Simeon Polotskii, *Izbrannye*, 189–204.

39. *Vecheria*, ff. 108–115v (St. Catherine), 274–280v (St. Evdokiia); State Historical Museum (GIM), Synodal Collection, MS 285, *Venets very kafolicheskoi*, ff. 402–408 (pride and greed), 408–410 (sex); *Vecheria*, ff. 55–64v (St. Sergii Radonezhskii), 131v–139 (St. Savva Storozhevskii); and Simeon Polotskii, *Izbrannye*, 8–10. The poems in this collection contain the same moral teachings as the sermons. See L. I. Sazonova, "'Vertograd mnogotsvetnyi' Sim-

eona Polotskogo (Evoliutsiia khudozhestvennogo zamysla)," in Robinson, *Russkaia staropechatnaia . . . Simeon*, 203–58, esp. 210–15.

40. "Chista sut' nebesa, iazhe nikoego strannogo voobrazheniia priemliut, chisto solntse, chista luna, chist ogn', chist vozdukh, chisti svetii, chisti angeli, no pache vsekh sikh chista preblagoslovennaia deva . . . neporochnaia zhe deva nikogdazhe strastiiu bezchinnoiu vozmutisia, nikogdazhe temnym sogresheniia dymom pomrachisia." "Slovo 2 v den' iavleniia ikony prechistyia Bogoroditsy imenuemye kazanskiia," *Vecheria*, 381v.

41. *Vecheria*, ff. 442–449 (miracles: sermon on the Dormition), 152–159v (Peter), 266v–274 (Aleksei), 304v–310v (Feodosii), 317v–324 (Vladimir icon), 345–361 (Tikhvin icon), 375–389 (Kazan' icon), 455–474 (Savior Uncreated by hands), 492v–500v (the theology of icons: sermon on the translation of the icon of the Savior Not-created-by-hands, one of seven: 455–500v). Eleonskaia, "Rabota," in Robinson, *Russkaia staropechatnaia . . . Simeon*, 184–85.

42. For Simeon's views on education, see Eleonskaia, *Russkaia publitsistika*, 147–73; the poem "Filosofiia" in Simeon Polotskii, *Izbrannye*, 68–71; and also ibid., 73–74, 75, and *Vecheria*, prilozhenie, 1–7v.

43. Essentially Avvakum grasped this point, and in his attacks on the church's new concern with learning (of which Simeon was only the most brilliant example) and his praise of simplicity, he found the chink in the armor. Simeon clearly thought that on the whole, learning—both philological and philosophical—was necessary to faith, and believed that the introduction of the learning that he represented would buttress faith in Russia. Eventually, by Peter's time, the church agreed with him, but the nobility used that learning to forge a culture that was not irreligious but secular, and in this sense Avvakum was proved right. Avvakum's stubborn resistance to church authority also revealed a latent contradiction in Simeon's religion, that between the general call to moral improvement and the elite nature of the education he demanded. How were the simple people to understand that they should abandon the traditional popular entertainments if they had to learn Latin to do so? Obviously they were merely to obey their more learned superiors, and indeed this was the approach the church would take: the Old Believers were accused mainly of ignorance in polemics through the next two hundred years, and the people were simply commanded to obey their more learned superiors. Thus, in spite of the surface abstract universalism of Simeon's sermons, they, together with those of Epifanii Slavinetskii, mark the beginning of the fundamental split in culture, religious and otherwise, that marked Russia in the centuries from Peter onward.

44. Eleonskaia, *Russkaia oratorskaia*, 165–98. The *Statir* remains unpublished, though excerpts were published in *Dukhovnaia beseda* (1858), and see also I. Malyshevskii, "Russkii prikhodskii sviashchennik—propovednik XVII v.," *Trudy Kievskoi dukhovnoi akademii*, 1861, no. 4:385–466; P. T. Alekseev, "'Statir' (Opisanie anonimnoi rukopisi XVII veka)," in *Arkheograficheskii ezhegodnik za 1964* (Moscow, 1965), 92–101; Romodanovskaia, *Russkaia literatura*, 12; N. A. Baklanova, *Torgovo-promyshlennaia deiatel'nost' Kalmykovykh vo vtoroi polovine XVII v.* (Moscow, 1959), 189. Some sense of the circulation of books can be found in N. A. Baklanova, "Russkii chitatel' XVII veka," *Drevnerusskaia literatura i ee sviazi s novym vremenem*, (Moscow, 1967), 156–93; and S. P. Luppov, *Kniga v Rossii v XVII veke* (Leningrad, 1970), esp. 110, 168.

Simeon's sermons were not found in the northern monastic libraries according to M. V. Kukushkina, *Monastyrskie*, 152.

45. Smirnov, "Ioakim"; Barsukov, *Ioakima*; and on Evfimii, see S. N. Brailovskii, "Ocherki iz istorii prosveshcheniia v Moskovskoi Rusi v XVII veke: Chudovskii inok Evfimii," Moscow, 1890 (originally *Chteniia obshchesva liubitelei dukhovnogo prosveshcheniia*, 1890, kn. 2, no. 9); and Florovskii, "Chudovskii inok."

46. One good example is Sin. 221, a miscellany compiled for Adrian in the 1690s but containing sermons written for occasions in the 1680s. It opens with 155 folios copied from the *Evangelie uchitel'noe* of the previously condemned Ukrainian theologian Kirill Trankvillion Stavrovetskii. The excerpts copied here call for repentance of sin and attack all possible sins, save in the last sermon, which singles out drunkenness and sexual license. For Sin. 221, see Gorskii and Nevostruev, *Opisanie*, 2, pt. 3:252–66. The watermarks confirm the dating to the 1690s. The appearance of Stavrovetskii in a manuscript of works designed by Evfimii Chudovskii for the patriarchs and reflecting their views suggests that the idea that Ioakim and Evfimii were wholly "anti-Ukrainian" and "anti-Latin" may need some revision.

47. GIM, Synodal Collection, Sin. MS 221, ff. 187–205 (Aleksei), 294–396 (Filipp), 206–225v ("Bez very nevozmozhno ugoditi Bogu," dated 1687), 397–416 ("Slovo na byvshee chudo v Kolassaekh frigiiskikh, ezhe v Khonekh ot vseslavnogo arkhistratiga Mikhaila," by Evfimii). Karion Zaulonskii's theological tract, "Imia novoe," in GIM, Synodal Collection, Sin. MS 471, ff. 1–56, is dedicated to Ioakim and dated 1686. See A. P. Bogdanov, ed., *Pamiatniki obshchestvenno-politicheskoi mysli v Rossii kontsa XVII veka: Literaturnye panegiriki*, 2 vols. (Moscow, 1983), 2:268–69. It also reflects the same concerns as these sermons, for this dull disquisition on the name of Christ emphasizes not Christ as son of God or moral teacher but Christ as dogmatic teacher, tsar, and prophet, a parallel to Evfimii's sermons.

48. S. N. Brailovskii, ed., *Slovo Chudovskogo inoka Evfimiia o milosti*, Pamiatniki drevnei pis'mennosti 101 (St. Petersburg, 1894); Eleonskaia, *Russkaia oratorskaia*, 148–64.

49. Padua was the birthplace of the philosophy of Theophilus Corydaleus, who advocated a neo-Aristotelianism that went back to Pomponazzi. Corydaleus's teachings dominated all Greek schools after about 1650. Cléobule Tsourkas, *Les débuts de l'enseignement philosophique et de la libre pensée dans les Balkans: La vie et l'oeuvre de Théophile Corydalée (1570–1646)*, Institute for Balkan Studies, Publication 95 (Thessalonika, 1967); Smirnov, *Istoriia*; Smentsovskii, *Brat'ia Likhudy*; Podskalsky, *Griechische Theologie*, 14, 194–99, 276–81; and Bogdanov, "K polemike."

50. When Adrian died in 1702, Peter simply failed to replace him. Stefan Iavorskii, a former professor at the Kiev Academy and since 1700 metropolitan of Riazan', was made conservator of the patriarchate until 1719, when Peter abolished the patriarchate entirely. He put the church under the Holy Synod, a board of bishops, abbots, and civil servants headed by a layman, the *Ober-procuror* of the Most Holy Synod. Under Iavorskii's influence a sort of Baroque semi-Catholic spirituality became predominant in the Russian church, lasting until midcentury. In his last years Peter was closer to Feofan Prokopovich, another Ukrainian from the Kiev Academy but hostile

to Iavorskii's vision of the church and his type of spirituality. Metropolitan of Novgorod from 1711, Feofan carried out Peter's will in the church until his own death in 1736. In Prokopovich Peter also found a preacher, though of a different stamp from the seventeenth-century preachers: Prokopovich was the court preacher par excellence, always ready for state occasions and preaching a morality more in tune with the secularized culture that was the result of Peter's reforms.

Conclusion

1. Otto Brunner, *Adeliges Landleben und europäischer Geist: Leben und Werk Wolf Helmhards von Hohberg 1612–1688* (Salzburg, 1949), 61–138.

Appendix

1. A. N. Protas'eva, *Opisanie rukopisei Sinodal'nogo sobraniia (ne voshedshikh v opisanie A. V. Gorskogo i K. I. Nevostrueva),* 2 vols. (Moscow, 1970–1973), 2:107.
2. Eleonskaia, *Russkaia oratorskaia,* 61–63; N. I. Petrov, *Opisanie rukopisnykh sobranii, nakhodiashchikhsia v gorode Kieve, ChOIDR,* 1897, no. 1, pt. 2:98–99.
3. MS Archangel Spiritual Seminar 306: V. Veriuzhskii, *Afanasii, arkhiepiskop Kholmogorskii* (St. Petersburg, 1908): 29–30.

Bibliography

AAE   Akty arkheograficheskoi kommissii
AI   Akty istoricheskie
ChOIDR   Chteniia v obshchestve istorii i drevnostei rossiiskikh
DAI   Dopolneniia k aktam istoricheskim
GBL   Gosudarstvennaia biblioteka im. Lenina
GIM   Gosudarstvennyi istoricheskii muzei
IORIaS   Izvestiia otdela russkogo iazyka i slovesnosti
LZAK   Letopis' zaniatii arkheograficheskoi kommissii
PSRL   Polnoe sobranie russkikh letopisei
RIB   Russkaia istoricheskaia biblioteka
SGGD   Sobranie gosudarstvennykh gramot i dogovorov
TODRL   Trudy otdela drevnerusskoi literatury
TsNB   Tsentral'na naukova biblioteka Akademii nauk Ukrains'koi RSR
ZhMNP   Zhurnal Ministerstva narodnogo prosveshcheniia

Manuscript Sources

State Historical Museum, Moscow, Manuscript Division, Synodal collection

No. IV.4: *Sbornik,* late seventeenth century in various hands, both cursive and *poluustav.*

No. 221: *Sbornik,* late seventeenth century, *poluustav,* possibly connected with Patriarch Ioakim.

No. 285: Simeon Polotskii, "Venets very kafolicheskia" (ff. 1–324v); "Kniga kratkikh voprosov" (ff. 325–477); late seventeenth century, *poluustav.*

No. 346, "Shchit very," late seventeenth century, *poluustav.*

No. 471: Karion Zaulonskii, "Imia novoe," 1686, ff. 1–75, *poluustav* turning into cursive.

No. 597: *Sobranie raznykh pouchenii.* Ff. 1–131v, in Ukrainian cursive, late seventeenth century. The sermons of Epifanii Slavinetskii, in various hands including his own (ff. 90–97v).

No. 716: *Sbornik,* 1690s, *poluustav,* includes "Zhitie Fedora Rtishcheva" (ff. 1–36v), and "Slovo o milosti" (37–74) attributed to Evfimii Chudovskii.

Moscow University Library, Division of Manuscripts and Rare Books
9: *Sbornik XVIII v.,* includes a number of earlier miracle stories.
293: *Sbornik,* early eighteenth century, includes *Kniga solntse presvetloe* (ff. 1–348v).
5Qi 8085: *Sbornik zhitii XVIII v.*
5Qi 186: *Sbornik: Kazanskii zhitiinik,* seventeenth century, *poluustav,* includes "Povest' o iavlenii chudotvornyia ikony . . . Marii izhe v Kazani" (ff. 56–95v) and "Zhitie Guriia i Varsonofiia" (ff. 96–196v).
5M 183: *Sbornik zhitii skazanii i slov kontsa XVII–nachala XVIII v.,* includes "Povest' o chudesakh vladimirskoi ikony" (ff. 362–384v), "Povest' o Temire-Aksake" (ff. 386–422), "Chiudo Tolgskoi ikony Bogoroditsy" and related stories (ff. 422–431v), "Zhitie i chudesa sv. Guriia i Varsonofiia kazanskikh" (ff. 584–620).

Central State Archive of Ancient Documents (TsGADA), Moscow
fund 381, Moscow Synodal Typography, no. 1791: holograph miscellany of Simeon Polotskii, 513 ff.

Central Scientific Library of the Academy of Sciences of the Ukrainian SSR, Manuscript Division, Kiev
290П/145: *Slovesa sochinennaia ieromonakhom Epifaniem Slavinetskim,* late seventeenth century, *ustav.*

Bibliotheca apostolica vaticana, Manuscript Division
Vat. Slav. 30: *Zhitie i podvizi i otchasti chiudese . . . Filippa mitropolita moskovskogo i vseia Rusi,* late seventeenth century, *poluustav.*

Houghton Library, Harvard University, Kilgour Collection
F: *Kniga zhitie Zosimy i Savatiia chudotvortsev,* (late ?) seventeenth century, *poluustav.*

British Library, Manuscript Division
Harl. 3373: *Sbornik,* includes (ff. 15–162v) "Zhitie Zosimy i Savvatiia," c. 1700, cursive.

Primary Sources (published)

Abramovych, D., ed. *Das Paterikon des Kiever Höhlenklosters,* ed. Dmitrij Tschizewskij. Slavische Propyläen 2. Munich, 1964.
Adrianova-Peretts, V. P., and A. M. Panchenko, eds. *Russkaia sillabicheskaia poeziia XVII–XVIII vv.* Leningrad, 1970.
Akty feodal'nogo zemlevladeniia i khoziaistva. 2 vols. Moscow, 1951–1956.
Akty kholmogorskoi i ustiuzhskoi eparkhii. RIB 12 and 14. St. Petersburg, 1894.
Akty sotsial'no-ekonomicheskoi istorii Severo-vostochnoi Rusi kontsa XIV–nachala XVI v. 3 vols. Moscow, 1952–1964.
Antonii Podol'skii. "O p'ianstve," and "O tsarstve nebesnom." *Pravoslavnyi sobesednik,* 1862, no. 1:283–88, 369–85; 1864, no. 1:108–26, 227–46.

Antonii Radivilovskii. *Ogorodok Marii bogoroditsy.* Kiev, 1676.

———. *Venets Khristov.* Kiev, 1688.

Azarin, Simon. *Kniga o chudesakh pr. Sergiia.* Pamiatniki drevnei pis'mennosti i iskusstva 70. St. Petersburg, 1888.

Baranovich, Lazar'. *Mech dukhovnyi.* Kiev, 1666.

Barskov, Ia. L., ed. "Pamiatniki pervykh let Russkogo staroobriadchestva." *LZAK za 1911 g.* (1912): 1–424.

Barsov, E., ed. "Akty otnosiashchiesia k istorii Solovetskogo bunta." *ChOIDR*, 1883, no. 4, pt. 5:1–92.

Barsukov, N., ed. *Zhitie i zaveshchanie sviateishego patriarkha moskovskogo Ioakima.* Izdaniia Obshchestva liubitelei drevnei pis'mennosti 47. St. Petersburg, 1879.

Bazhenov, I. V., ed. "Skazanie o chudesakh kostromskoi Fedorovskoi ikony Bog-materi." *Vestnik istorii i arkheologii* 19 (St. Petersburg, 1909): 187–260.

Belokurov, S. A. "Deianie Moskovskogo tserkovnogo sobora 1649 goda." *ChOIDR*, 1894, no. 4, pt. 3:29–52.

———, ed. "Dela sviat. Nikona patriarkha, pache zhe reshchi chudesa vracheb-naia." *ChOIDR*, 1887, no. 1, pt. 5:81–114.

———, ed., "Zhitie prep. Iosifa volokolamskogo." *ChOIDR*, 1903, no. 3:1–47.

Bodianskii, O. M. "Moskovskie sobory na eretikov XVI veka." *ChOIDR*, 1847, god 3, no. 3, pt. 2:1–30.

Bogdanov, A. P., ed. *Pamiatniki obshchestvenno-politicheskoi mysli v Rossii kontsa XVII veka: Literaturnye panegiriki.* 2 vols. Moscow, 1983.

Brailovskii, S. N., ed. *Slovo Chudovskogo inoka Evfimiia o milosti.* Pamiatniki drevnei pis'mennosti 101. St. Petersburg, 1894.

Buganov, V. I., ed. *Razriadnaia kniga 1475–1598 gg.* Moscow, 1966.

Buganov, V. I., M. P. Lukichev, and N. M. Rogozhin, eds. *Posol'skaia kniga po sviaziam Rossii s Gretsiei (pravoslavnymi ierarkhami i monastyriami) 1588–1592 gg.* Moscow, 1988.

Bury, J. B. "Iviron and Our Lady of the Gate." *Hermathena* 10 (1899): 71–99.

Bylinin, V. K. "Stikhotvornye 'Predisloviia mnogorazlichna' v rukopisiakh pervoi poloviny XVII v.." *Zapiski otdela rukopisei GBL* 44 (Moscow, 1983): 5–38.

Delo o Patriarkhe Nikone. St. Petersburg, 1897.

Derzhavina, O. A. *"Velikoe zertsalo" i ego sud'ba na russkoi pochve.* Moscow, 1965.

Dimitrii Rostovskii. *Runo oroshennoe.* Chernigov, 1683.

Dmitriev, L. A., ed. *Povest' o zhitii Mikhaila Klopskogo.* Moscow and Leningrad, 1958.

Dmitrieva, R. P., ed. *Povest' o Petre i Fevronii.* Leningrad, 1979.

Dokuchaev-Baskov, K. A. "Skazanie o chudesakh ot obraza prep. Makariia Zheltovodskogo i Unzhenskogo v Kargopol'skoi Khergozerskoi pustyni." *ChOIDR*, 1902, no. 3, pt. 4:1–34.

Druzhinin, V. G. "Neskol'ko neizvestnykh literaturnykh pamiatnikov iz sbornika XVI-go veka," *LZAK za 1908 g.* 21 (1909): 1–117.

Dvortsovye razriady. 5 vols. St. Petersburg, 1850–1855.

Eingorn, V. O. "Rechi proiznesennye Ioannikiem Galiatovskim v Moskve v 1670 g." *ChOIDR*, 1895, no. 4, pt. 2:1–13.

[Epifanii Slavinetskii]. "Skazanie ot bozhestvennykh pisanii, iako o sviatykh v nebese sushchikh, nedostoit molitisia nam, da ostaviatsia im grekhi. " *Treb-nik,* ff. 1–16v (295–310v). Moscow, 1677.

Fedorov, Ananii, [and Ia. A. Solov'ev]. "Istoricheskoe sobranie o bogospasaemom grade Suzdale." *Vremennik moskovskogo obshchestva istorii i drevnoste rossiiskikh* 22, pt. 2 (1855): 1–212.

Fillipovich, Afanasii. *Diariush. RIB* 4, 49–156. St. Petersburg, 1878.

Galiatovskii, Ioannikii. *Kliuch razumeniia.* L'vov, 1663.

———. *Nebo novoe.* L'vov, 1665.

See also Haliatovs'kyi.

[Germogen]. *Tvoreniia sviateishego Germogena Patriarkha moskovskogo i vseia Rossii.* Moscow, 1912.

Gizel', Innokentii. *Mir s Bogom cheloveku.* Kiev, 1669.

Golitsyn, N. N. *Ukazatel' k Dvortsovym razriadam.* St. Petersburg, 1912.

Golubtsov, Aleksandr, ed. "Chinovnik novgorodskogo sofiiskogo sobora." *ChOIDR,* 1899, no. 2, pt. 1:1–272.

———. "Pamiatniki preniia o vere." *ChOIDR,* 1892, no. 2, pt. 2:1–350.

Griboedov, Fedor. *Istoriia o tsariakh i velikikh kniaziakh zemli Russkoi.* Pamiatniki drevnei pis'mennosti 121. St. Petersburg, 1896.

Haliatovs'kyi, Ioanykii. *Kliuch rozuminnia,* ed. I. P. Chepiha. Kiev, 1985.

See also Galiatovskii.

Iosif. *Poucheniia.* Moscow, 1642.

Iosif Volotskii. *Prosvetitel'.* Kazan', 1855.

Iov. "Povest' o chestnom zhitii tsaria i velikogo kniazia Fedora Ivanovicha vseia Russii." *PSRL,* vol. 14, 1–22. St. Petersburg, 1910.

"Istoriia o Kazanskom tsarstve." *PSRL,* vol. 19, ed. G. Z. Kuntsevich. St. Petersburg, 1903.

Ivan Vyshenskii. *Sochineniia,* ed. I. P. Eremin. Moscow and Leningrad, 1955.

John Chrysostom. "De pauperum amore." *Patrologia graeca,* vol. 35, 857–909. Paris, 1857.

———. "De poenitentia." *Patrologia graeca,* vol. 49, 283–300. Paris, 1859.

Kadlubovskii, A. P., ed. "Zhitie prepodobnogo Pafnutiia Borovskogo, pisannoe Vassianom Saninym." *Sbornik istoriko-filologicheskogo obshchestva pri Institute im. kn. Bezborodko* 2 (1899): 98–149.

Kalachov, N. V., ed. *Pistsovye knigi Moskovskogo gosudarstva,* pt. 1, *Pistsovye knigi XVI veka.* 2 vols. St. Petersburg, 1872–1877.

Kalnofoyski, Atanasiusz. *Teraturgima.* Kiev, 1638.

Kalnofoyski, Atanasiusz, and Hilarion Denisowicz. *Parergon cudów świętych obraza przeczystej Bogarodzice w monastyrze Kupiatickim.* Kiev, 1638.

Katekhizis Lavrentiia Zizaniia. Pamiatniki drevnei pis'mennosti 17. St. Petersburg, 1878.

Kazakova, N. A., ed. *Vassian Patrikeev i ego sochineniia.* Moscow and Leningrad, 1960.

Kirillova kniga. Moscow, 1644.

Kniga o vere. Moscow, 1648.

Kolosova, V. P., and V. I. Krekoten', eds. *Ukrains'ka poeziia: Kinets XVI–pochatok XVII st.* Kiev, 1978.

Kopystenskii, Zakharii. *Kniga o vere. Arkhiv Iugozapadnoi Rossii,* pt. 1, vol. 8, vyp. 1, 59–179. Kiev, 1914.

———. *Palinodiia. RIB* 4, 313–1200. St. Petersburg, 1878.

"Kormovaia kniga Kirillo-Belozerskogo monastyria." *Zapiski otdeleniia russkoi i slavianskoi arkheologii Russkogo arkheologicheskogo obshchestva* 1 (1851): 46–105.

Kozhanchikov, D. E., ed. *Stoglav.* St. Petersburg, 1863.

Kuchkin, V. A. *Povesti o Mikhaile Tverskom.* Moscow, 1974.

Kuntsevich, G. "Podlinnyi spisok o novykh chudotvortsakh." *IORIaS* 15 (1910): 252–57.

Kuznetsov, I. I. "Sviatye blazhennye Vasilii i Ioann Khrista radi moskovskie chudotvortsy." *Zapiski moskovskogo arkheologicheskogo instituta* 8 (1910): 1–494.

Lachmann, Renate, ed. *Die Makarij-Rhetorik ("Knigi sut' ritoriki dvoi po tonku v voprosech spisany").* Slavistische Forschungen 27, no. 1, Rhetorica Slavica 1. Cologne and Vienna, 1980.

"Letopistsy poslednei chetverti XVII veka." *PSRL,* vol. 31. Moscow, 1968.

Likhachev, D. S., and Ia. S. Lur'e. *Poslaniia Ivana Groznogo.* Moscow and Leningrad, 1951.

Loparev, Kh. "Zametka o sochineniiakh prep. Maksima Greka." *Bibliograficheskaia letopis'* 3 (1917): 50–70.

"L'vovskaia letopis'." *PSRL,* vol. 20. St. Petersburg, 1910–1914.

Maksim Grek. *Sochineniia.* 3 vols., Kazan', 1860–1894; 2d ed., Kazan', 1894–1897.

Mansikka, V., ed. *Zhitie Aleksandra Nevskogo.* Pamiatniki drevnei pis'mennosti i iskusstva 180. St. Petersburg, 1913.

Mazunin, A. I., ed. *Povest' o boiaryne Morozovoi.* Leningrad, 1979.

Medvedev, Sil'vestr. "Oglavlenie knig, kto ikh slozhil," ed. V. Undol'skii. *ChOIDR,* 1846, no. 3, pt. 4:1–30.

Miklosich, F., and J. Müller. *Acta et diplomata graeca medii aevi.* 6 vols. Vienna, 1860–1890.

"Miracula S. Demetrii Thessalonicensis." *Patrologia graeca,* vol. 116, 1203–1398. Paris, 1864.

Mohyla, Petr. "Skazaniia Petra Mogily o chudesnykh i zamechatel'nykh iavleniiakh v tserkvi pravoslavnoi," ed. S. Golubev. *Arkhiv Iugozapadnoi Rusi,* pt. 1, vol. 7, 49–132. Kiev, 1887.

———. *Sobranie kratkiia nauki ob artikulakh very.* Moscow, 1649.

Moiseeva, G. N. "Zhitie Novgorodskogo arkhiepiskopa Serapiona." *TODRL* 21 (1965): 147–65.

Mordvinova, S. R., and A. L. Stanislavskii, eds. *Boiarskie spiski poslednei chetverti XVI–nachala XVII vv. i rospis' russkogo voiska 1604 g.* 2 pts. Moscow, 1979.

"Moskovskii sobor o zhitii Velikoi Kniagini Anny Kashinskoi." *ChOIDR,* 1871, no. 4, pt. 1:45–62.

Müller, Ludolf, ed. *Die Legenden des heiligen Sergij von Radonež: Nachdruck der Ausgabe von Tichonravov mit einer Einleitung und einer Inhaltsübersicht.* Slavische Propyläen 17. Munich, 1967.

[Nasedka, Ivan, and Simon Azarin]. *Zhitie i podvigi prep. ottsa nashego Dionisiia, arkhimandrita Troitskogo Sergieva monastyria.* Moscow, 1808.

Nektarios. *Confutatio imperii Papae in ecclesiam.* Iasi, 1682; reprint, London, 1702.

Nikol'skii, A. I. "Pamiatnik i obrazets narodnogo iazyka i slovesnosti Severodvinskoi oblasti." *IORIaS* 17 (1912): 87–105.

"Nikonovskaia letopis'," *PSRL,* vols. 9–13, 14, no. 2. St. Petersburg, 1862–1918; reprint, Moscow, 1965.

Nil Sorskii, *Predanie i ustav,* ed. M. S. Borovkova-Maikova. Pamiatniki drevnei pis'mennosti i iskusstva 179. St. Petersburg, 1912.

Nimchuk, V. V., ed. *Leksykon latyns'kyi E. Slavynets'koho, Leksykon sloveno-latyns'kyi E. Slavynets'koho ta A. Korets'koho-Satanovs'koho.* Kiev, 1973.

"Novgorodskaia tret'ia letopis'". *PSRL,* vol. 3, 202–305. St. Petersburg, 1841.

Novosel'skii, A. A., et al., eds. *Akty Russkogo gosudarstva 1505–1526 gg.* Moscow, 1975.

"Novyi letopisets." *PSRL,* vol. 14, no. 1, 23–154. St. Petersburg, 1910; reprint, Moscow, 1965.

Orlov, A. "Narodnye predaniia o sviatyniakh russkogo Severa." *ChOIDR,* 1913, no. 1, pt. 3:47–55.

Orlov, A. S., ed. *Domostroi po konshinskomu spisku i podobnym.* pts. 1–2. Moscow, 1908.

Osten. Kazan', 1863.

Palitsyn, Avraamii. *Skazanie Avraamiia Palitsyna,* ed. E. V. Kolosova and O. A. Derzhavina. Moscow and Leningrad, 1955.

Palmer, William. *The Patriarch and the Tsar.* 6 vols. London, 1871–1876.

Pamiatniki starinnoi russkoi literatury, izd. gr. Grigoriem Kushelevym-Bezborodka. 4 vols. St. Petersburg, 1860–1862.

Papadopulo-Kerameus, A. *Sbornik istochnikov po istorii Trapezundskoi imperii,* vol. 1. Zapiski istoriko-filologicheskogo fakul'teta imp. S.- Peterburgskogo universiteta 44. St. Petersburg, 1897.

Pavlov, A. S., ed. *Pamiatniki drevnerusskogo kanonicheskogo prava,* pt. 1. *RIB* 6. St. Petersburg, 1880.

Pis'ma russkikh gosudarei, vol. 1, *1526–1658.* vol. 1, Moscow, 1848.

Platonov, S. F., ed. *Pamiatniki drevnei russkoi pis'mennosti otnosiashchiesia k smutnomu vremeni. RIB* 13. St. Petersburg, 1891.

Platonov, S. F., V. I. Savva, V. G. Druzhinin, eds. "Vnov' otkrytye polemicheskie sochineniia XVII veka protiv eretikov." *LZAK za 1905 g.* 18 (1907): 1–177.

Pokrovskii, N. N., ed. *Sudnye spiski Maksima Greka i Isaka Sobaki.* Moscow, 1971.

"Poslaniia startsa Artemiia XVI veka." *Pamiatniki polemicheskoi literatury v Zapadnoi Rusi. RIB* 4, 1201–1448. St. Petersburg, 1878.

"Prenie litovskogo protopopa Lavrentiia Zizaniia. . . ." In N. Tikhonravov, ed., *Letopisi russkoi literatury i drevnostei,* vol. 2, sec. 2, 80–100. Moscow, 1859.

Prolog. Moscow, 1659.

Psaltir'. Moscow, 1653.

Pseudo-Kodinos. *Traité des offices,* ed. by Jean Verpeaux. Le monde byzantin 1. Paris, 1966.

"Puteshestvie antiokhiiskogo patriarkha Makariia v Rossiiu v polovine XVII veka, opisannoe ego synom, arkhidiaknom Pavlom Aleppskim," trans. G. Murkos. *ChOIDR,* 1896, no. 4, pt. 2:1–156; 1897, no. 4, pt. 3:1–202; 1898, no. 3, pt. 3:1–208; 1898, no. 4, pt. 2:1–195.

Rai myslennyi. Iverskii Monastery, 1658.

Robinson, A. N., ed. *Zhizneopisaniia Avvakuma i Epifaniia: Issledovaniia i teksty.* Moscow, 1963.

Rozhdestvenskii, N. V., ed. "K istorii bor'by s tserkovnymi besporiadkami, otgoloskami iazychestva i porokami v russkom bytu XVII v." *ChOIDR,* 1902, no. 2, pt. 4:1–31.

Sbornik iz 71 slov. Moscow, 1647.

Sbornik o pochitanie ikon. Moscow, 1642.

Serebrianskii, N. I. "Drevnerusskie kniazheskie zhitiia." *ChOIDR,* 1915, no. 3:1–296.

Sheptaev, L. S. "Stikhi spravshchika Savvatiia." *TODRL* 21 (1965): 5–28.

Shliakov, N. "Zhitie sv. Aleksiia mitropolita moskovskogo v pakhomievskoi redaktsii." *IORIaS* 19 (1914): 85–152.

Shmidt, S. O. "K istorii monastyrskoi kolonizatsii XVII v. (Povest' o nachale Oranskogo monastyria)." *Voprosy istorii religii i ateizma* 12 (1964): 297–309.

Simeon Polotskii. *Izbrannye sochineniia,* ed. I. P. Eremin. Moscow and Leningrad, 1953.

———. *Obed dushevnyi.* Moscow, 1681.

———. *Orel Rossiiskii.* Pamiatniki drevnei pis'mennosti 133. St. Petersburg, 1915.

———. *Vecheria dushevnaia.* Moscow, 1683.

———. *Zhezl pravleniia.* Moscow, 1668.

Skarga, Piotr. *Kazania na Niedziele i Święta całego roku.* 6 vols. Leipzig, 1843.

———. *Kazania sejmowe,* ed. St. Kot. L'vov, 1926.

———. *Pisma wszystkie.* 4 vols. Warsaw, 1923–1926.

Skripil', M. O. "'Povest' ob Ulianii Osor'inoi,' (Kommentarii i teksty)." *TODRL* 6 (1948): 256–323.

Skrizhal'. Moscow, 1655–1656.

Sluzhebnik. Moscow, 1655.

Skvortsov, I. A., ed. *Dukhovenstvo Moskovskoi eparkhii v XVII veke.* Moscow, 1916.

Smirnov, P. P. "Chelobitnye dvorian i detei boiarskikh vsekh gorodov v pervoi polovine XVII v." *ChOIDR,* 1915, no. 3, pt. 1:1–73.

———. "Neskol'ko dokumentov k istorii Sobornogo Ulozheniia i Zemskogo Sobora 1648–1649 godov." *ChOIDR,* 1913, no. 4, pt. 4:1–20.

Smotryts'kyi, Meletii. *Hramatyka,* ed. V. V. Nimchuk. Kiev, 1979.

Sobranie kratkiia nauki ob artikulakh very. Moscow, 1649.

"Sofiiskaia vtoraia letopis'." *PSRL,* vol. 6, 115–358. St. Petersburg, 1853.

Starczewski, A., ed. *Historiae Ruthenicae scriptores exteri.* 2 vols. Berlin and St. Petersburg, 1841–1842.

Starowolski, Szymon. *Swiatnica pańska.* Cracow, 1645.

Stavroveckij [Stavrovetskii], Cyrillus [Kirill] Tranquillus. *"Perlo mnohocennoje" (Cerněhov 1646),* ed. Hartmut Trunte. Bausteine zur Geschichte der Literatur bei den Slaven 22/1–22/2. 2 vols. Cologne and Vienna, 1984–1985.

Stavrovetskii, Kirill. *Evangelie uchitel'noe.* Rakhmanov, 1619.

Stepennaia kniga. PSRL, vol. 21. St. Petersburg, 1908–1913.

Subbotin, N. I., ed. *Deianiia moskovskikh soborov 1666 i 1667 godov.* Moscow, 1893.

———. *Materialy dlia istorii raskola za pervoe vremia ego sushchestvovanie.* 9 vols. Moscow, 1875–1895.

Sukhanov, Arsenii. "Proskinitarii Arseniia Sukhanova." *Pravoslavnyi Palestinskii sbornik* 7, no. 3 (1889): 1–390.

Sviattsy. Moscow, 1646.

Talbot, Alice-Mary M. *Faith Healing in Late Byzantium: The Posthumous Miracles of the Patriarch Athanasios I of Constantinople by Theoktistos the Stoudite.* The Archbishop Iakovos Library of Ecclesiastical and Historical Sources 8. Brookline, Mass., 1983.

Tikhomirov, M. N., and P. P. Epifanov, eds. *Sobornoe ulozhenie 1649 g.* Moscow, 1961.

Timofeev, Ivan. *Vremennik,* ed. O. A. Derzhavina. Moscow and Leningrad, 1951.

Treu, Maximilian, ed. *Theodori Pediasimi eiusque amicorum quae existant.* Potsdam, 1899.

Tschizewskij, Dm., ed. *Pachomij Logofet: Werke im Auswahl.* Nachdruck der Ausgabe von V. Jablonskij. Slavische Propyläen 1. Munich, 1963.

Tumins, Valerie, ed. *Tsar Ivan IV's Reply to Jan Rokyta.* The Hague and Paris, 1971.

Tumins, Valerie, and George Vernadsky, eds. *Patriarch Nikon on Church and State: Nikon's "Refutation."* Berlin, New York, and Amsterdam, 1982.

Tsvetaev, D. "Protestantsvo i protestanty v Rossii do epokhi preobrazovanii." *ChOIDR,* 1889, no. 4:1–328; 1890, no. 1, pt. 2:329–782.

Ustav (Oko tserkovnoe). Moscow, 1610.

Ustav (Oko tserkovnoe). Moscow, 1633.

Velikie Minei-chet'i, sobrannye Vserossiiskim patriarkhom Makariem. September–April. St. Petersburg and Moscow, 1868–1916.

"Vologodskaia letopis'." *PSRL,* vol. 37, 160–193. Leningrad, 1982.

"Voskresenskaia letopis'." *PSRL,* vols. 7–8. St. Petersburg, 1856–1859.

Vossoedinenie Ukrainy s Rossiei. 3 vols. Moscow, 1954.

Vykhody gosudarei tsarei i velikikh kniazei Mikhaila Fedorovicha, Alekseia Mikhailovicha, i Fedora Alekseevicha. Moscow, 1844.

Welykyj, Athanasius G., ed. *S. Josaphat Hieromartyri Documenta Romana Beatificationis et Canonizationis.* 3 vols. Analecta Ordinis S. Basilii Magni, sectio III, series II. Rome, 1952–1967.

Zapiski otdeleniia russkoi i slavianskoi arkheologii imp. Russkogo arkheologicheskogo obshchestva 2. St. Petersburg, 1861.

Zertsalov, A. N. "Novye dannye o Zemskom sobore 1648–1649 gg." *ChOIDR,* 1887, no. 3, pt. 4:1–80.

Zhitie i sluzhba sv. Savvy storozhevskogo. Moscow, 1646.

Zhitie i sluzhby sv. Sergiia i Nikona. Moscow, 1646.

Zimin, A. A., ed. *Ioasafovskaia letopis'.* Moscow, 1957.

———. *Pamiatniki russkogo prava.* 8 vols. Moscow, 1952–1961.

Zimin, A. A., and Ia. S. Lur'e, eds. *Poslaniia Iosifa Volotskogo.* Moscow and Leningrad, 1959.

Zinovii Otenskii. *Istiny pokazanie.* Kazan', 1863.

Zyzanii, Lavrentii. *Hramatyka slovens'ka,* ed. V. V. Nimchuk. Kiev, 1980.

Books and Articles

Abetsedarskii, L. S. *Belorussiia i Rossiia XVI–XVII vv.* Minsk, 1978.

Alef, Gustave. "The Crisis of the Muscovite Aristocracy: A Factor in the Growth of Monarchical Power." *Forschungen zur osteuropäischen Geschichte* 15 (1970): 15–58.

———. "Reflections on the Boyar Duma in the Reign of Ivan III." *Slavonic and East European Review* 45 (1967): 76–123.

Alekseev, Iu. G. *Agrarnaia i sotsial'naia istoriia severo-vostochnoi Rusi XV–XVI vv.: Pereiaslavskii uezd.* Moscow and Leningrad, 1966.

Alekseev, M. P. "Erazm Rotterdamskii v russkom perevode XVII v." In *Slavianskaia filologiia 1: Sbornik statei, posviashchennyi IV Mezhdunarodnomu s"ezdu slavistov,* 275–336. Moscow, 1958.

Alekseev, P. T. "'Statir' (Opisanie anonimnoi rukopisi XVII veka)." In *Arkheograficheskii ezhegodnik za 1964,* 92–101. Moscow, 1965.

Alissandratos, Julia. "New Approaches to the Problem of Identifying the Genre of the Life of Julijana Lazarevskaja." *Cyrillomethodianum* 7 (1983): 235–44.

Andreev, N. E. "O dele d'iaka Viskovatogo." *Seminarium Kondakovianum* 5 (1932): 191–242.

Angermann, Norbert. "Neues über Nicolaus Bulow und sein wirken im Moskauer Russland." *Jahrbücher für Geschichte Osteuropas*, n.s. 17 (1969): 408–19.

Ankudinova, L. E. "Sotsial'nyi sostav pervykh raskol'nikov." *Vestnik LGU, Seriia istorii iazyka i literatury* 3, no. 14 (1956): 56–68.

Anushkin, A. I. *Na zare knigopechataniia v Litve*. Vilnius, 1970.

Arkhangel'skii, A. "K izucheniiu drevnerusskoi literatury: Tvoreniia ottsov tserkvi v drevnerusskoi pis'mennosti." *ZhMNP* 258 (July 1888): 1–49; (August 1888): 203–95.

[Arsenii and Ilarii]. "Opisanie slavianskikh rukopisei biblioteki Troitse-Sergievoi Lavry." *ChOIDR*, 1878, no. 2:1–352; 1878, no. 4:1–240; 1879, no. 2:1–267; 1880, no. 4:1–44.

Asafov, K. M., T. N. Protas'eva, and M. N. Tikhomirov. "Zapisi na knigakh staroi pechati XVI-XVII vekov." In *Arkheograficheskii ezhegodnik za 1961 god*, 276–344. Moscow, 1962.

Auerbach, Inge. *Andrej Michajlovič Kurbskij: Leben in osteuropäischen Adelsgesellschaften des 16 Jahrhunderts*. Munich, 1985.

Bakhrushin, S. V. *Nauchnye trudy*, 4 vols. ed. A. A. Zimin et al. Moscow, 1952–1955.

Baklanova, N. A. "Russkii chitatel' XVII veka." In *Drevnerusskaia literatura i ee sviazi s novym vremenem*, 156–193. Issledovaniia i materialy po drevnerusskoi literature 2. Moscow, 1967.

———. *Torgovo-promyshlennaia deiatel'nost' Kalmykovykh vo vtoroi polovine XVII v.* Moscow, 1959.

Barsukov, A. P. "Vserossiiskii Patriarkh Ioakim Savelov." Pamiatniki drevnei pis'mennosti 83, appendix 6, 1–15. St. Petersburg, 1891.

Barsukov, N. A. *Solovetskoe vosstanie 1668–1676 gg.* Petrozavodsk, 1954.

Barsukov, Nikolai. *Istochniki russkoi agiografii*. Izdaniia obshchestva liubitelei drevnei pis'mennosti 81. St. Petersburg, 1882.

Bazilevich, K. V. *Denezhnaia reforma Alekseia Mikhailovicha i vosstanie v Moskve v 1662 g.* Moscow and Leningrad, 1936.

Beck, Hans-Georg. *Geschichte der orthodoxen Kirche im byzantinischen Reich*. Die Kirche in ihrer Geschichte, B. 1, Lieferung D. 1. Göttingen, 1980.

———. *Kirche und Theologische Literatur im byzantinischen Reich*. Munich, 1959.

Belokurov, S. A. "Arsenii Sukhanov." *ChOIDR*, 1891, nos. 1–2, pt. 3:1–440.

———. *Materialy po Russkoi istorii*. Moscow, 1888.

———. "Moskovskii Pechatnyi dvor v 1649 godu." *ChOIDR*, 1887, no. 4, pt. 4:1–32.

Berndt, Michael. *Die Predigt Dmitrij Tuptalos: Studien zur ukrainischen und russischen Barockpredigt*. Frankfurt/Main, 1975.

Betin, L. V. "Istoricheskie osnovy drevnerusskogo vysokogo ikonostasa." In *Drevnerusskoe iskusstvo: Khudozhestvennaia kul'tura Moskvy i prilezhashchikh k nei knizazhestv XIV–XVI vv.*, 57–72. Moscow, 1970.

———. "Ob arkhitekturnoi kompozitsii drevnerusskikh vysokikh ikonostasov." in *Drevnerusskoe iskusstvo: Khudozhestvennaia kul'tura Moskvy i prilezhashchikh k nei knizazhestv XIV–XVI vv.*, 41–56. Moscow, 1970.

Bilets'kyi, Oleksandr. *Zibrannia prats'*. Vols. 1–5. Kiev, 1965–1966.

Bocharov, G., and V. Vygolov. *Vologda, Kirillov, Ferapontovo, Belozersk*. Moscow, 1979.

Bochkarev, V. N. *Stoglav i istoriia sobora 1551 goda*. Iukhnov, 1906.

Bogdanov, A. P. "K polemike kontsa 60-kh—nachala 80-kh godov XVII v. ob organizatsii vysshego uchebnogo zavedeniia v Rossii: istochnikovedcheskie zametki." In *Issledovaniia po istochnikovedeniiu Istorii SSSR XIII–XVIII vv.*, ed. V. I. Buganov, 177–209. Moscow, 1986.

Borisov, Vladimir. *Opisanie goroda Shui i ego okrestnostei*. Moscow, 1851.

Borst, Arno. *Mönche am Bodensee*. Sigmaringen, 1978.

Bosl, Karl. "Der Adelsheilige: Idealtypen und Wirklichkeit, Gesellschaft und Kultur im merowingzeitlichen Bayern des 7. und 8. Jahrhunderts." In *Speculum historiale, Festschrift J. Spoerl*, 167–187. Freiburg and Munich, 1965.

Bosley, Richard D. "A History of the Veneration of SS. Theodosij and Antonij." Ph.D. diss., Yale University, 1980.

———. "The Saints of Novgorod: À propos of A. S. Chorošev's Book on the Church in Medieval Novgorod." *Jahrbücher für Geschichte Osteuropas* 32 (1984): 1–15.

Botvinnik M. B. *Lavrentii Zizanii*. Minsk, 1973.

Brailovskii, S. "Filologicheskie trudy Epifaniia Slavinetskogo." *Russkii filologicheskii vestnik* 23 (1890): 236–67.

———. "Ocherki iz istorii prosveshcheniia v Moskovskoi Rusi v XVII veke: Chudovskii monakh Evfimii." *Chteniia obshchestva liubitelei dukhovnogo prosveshcheniia*, 1890, kn. 2, no. 9, and Moscow, 1890.

Brodovich, I. A. "E. E. Golubinski (Peskov)." *Sbornik Khar'kovskogo istoriko-filologicheskogo obshchestva* 19 (1912): 299–315.

Brown, Peter. *The Cult of the Saints*. Chicago, 1981.

———. "The Rise and Function of the Holy Man in Late Antiquity." *Journal of Roman Studies* 61 (1971): 80–101.

Brown, Peter B. "Early Modern Bureaucracy: The Evolution of the Chancellery System from Ivan III to Peter the Great, 1478–1717." Ph.D. diss., University of Chicago, 1978.

———. "Muscovite Government Bureaus." *Russian History* 10 (1983): 269–330.

Brunner, Otto. *Adeliges Landleben und europäischer Geist: Leben und Werk Wolf Heimhards von Hohberg 1612–1688*. Salzburg, 1949.

Budovnits, I. U. *Monastyri na Rusi i bor'ba s nimi krest'ian v XIV–XVI vv.* Moscow, 1966.

Buganov, V. I. *Moskovskoe vosstanie 1662 g.* Moscow, 1964.

Bulanin, D. M. *Perevody i poslaniia Maksima Greka*. Leningrad, 1984.

Burke, Peter. *Popular Culture in Early Modern Europe*. New York, 1978.

Bushkovitch, Paul. "The Epiphany Ceremony of the Russian Court in the Sixteenth and Seventeenth Centuries." *Russian Review* 49 (1990): 1–18.

———. "The Formation of a National Consciousness in Early Modern Russia." *Harvard Ukrainian Studies* 10 (1986); 355–76.

———. "The Life of Metropolitan Filipp: Tsar and Metropolitan in the Sixteenth Century." *California Slavic Studies* (forthcoming).

———. "The Limits of Hesychasm: Some Notes on Monastic Spirituality in Russia, 1350–1500." *Forschungen zur osteuropäischen Geschichte* 38 (Berlin, 1986): 97–109.

———. *The Merchants of Moscow 1580–1650*. Cambridge and New York, 1980.

———. "Orthdoxy and Old Rus' in the Thought of S. P. Shevyrev." *Forschungen zur osteuropäischen Geschichte* (forthcoming).

———. "V. O. Kliuchevskii as Historian of Religion and the Church." In "Kliuchevskii's Russia: Critical Studies," ed. Marc Raeff. *Canadian-American Slavic Studies* 20 (1986): 357–366.

Bychkova, M. E. *Sostav klassa feodalov Rossii v XVI v.* Moscow, 1986.

Bylinin, V. K. "K probleme poetiki slavianskogo barokko: 'Vertograd mnogotsvetnyi' Simeona Polotskogo." *Sovetskoe slavianovedenie* 1 (1982): 54–65.

———. "K voprosu o polemike vokrug russkogo ikonopisaniia vo vtoroi polovine XVII v: 'Beseda o pochitanii ikon sviatykh' Simeona Polotskogo." *TODRL* 38 (1985): 281–89.

Charanis, Peter. "The Monk in Byzantine Society." *Dumbarton Oaks Papers* 25 (1971): 61–84.

Cherepnin, L. V. *Zemskie sobory russkogo gosudarstva v XVI–XVII vv.* Moscow, 1978.

Cherniavsky, Michael. "The Old Believers and the New Religion." *Slavic Review* 25 (1966): 1–39.

Chernov, A. V. *Vooruzhennye sily russkogo gosudarstva v XVI–XVII vv.* Moscow, 1954.

Chistiakova, E. V. *Gorodskie vosstaniia v Rossii v pervoi polovine XVII veka (30-40-e gody)*. Voronezh, 1975.

Chistiakova, E. M. and A. P. Bogdanov. *"Da budet potomkam iavleno": Ocherki o russkikh istorikakh vtoroi poloviny XVII veka i ikh trudakh*. Moscow, 1988.

Crummey, Robert O. *Aristocrats and Servitors: The Boyar Elite in Russia 1613–1689*. Princeton, 1983.

———. "Court Spectacles in Seventeenth Century Russia: Illusion and Reality." In *Essays in Honor of A. A. Zimin*, ed. Daniel Clarke Waugh, 130–158. Columbus, Ohio, 1985.

Dancev, Georgi. "Les copies slaves du Recueil de prières du moine Tikara, considéré à tort jusqu'à présent comme l'ouevre de Demetrios Cantacuzène." *Palaeobulgarica/Starobulgaristika* 4 (1980): 25–39.

Delumeau, Jean. *Le péché et la peur: La culpabilisation en Occident (XVII–XVIII siècles)*. Paris, 1983.

Demidova, N. F. "Biurokratizatsiia gosudarstvennogo apparata absoliutizma v XVII–XVIII vv." In *Absoliutizm v Rossii*, ed. N. M. Druzhinin, 206–42. Moscow, 1964.

———. *Sluzhilaia biurokratiia v Rossii XVII v. i ee rol' v formirovanii absoliutizma*. Moscow, 1987.

Denissoff, Elie. *Maxime le Grec et l'occident*. Paris and Louvain, 1943.

Derzhavina, O. A. *"Velikoe zertsalo" i ego sud'ba na russkoi pochve*. Moscow, 1965.

Dictionnaire de théologie catholique. 15 vols. Paris, 1935–1950.

Dmitrieva, R. P. "Zhitie novgorodskogo arkhiepiskopa Serapiona kak publitsisticheskoe proizvedenie XVI v." *TODRL* 41 (1988): 364–74.

Eingorn, V. O. *O snosheniiakh Malorossiiskogo dukhovenstva s Moskovskim pravitel'stvom v tsarstvovanie Alekseia Mikhailovicha*. *ChOIDR*, 1893, no. 2, pt. 4:1–370; 1894, no. 3, pt. 3:371–570; 1898, no. 4, pt. 3:570–794; 1899, no. 1, pt. 4:795–932; 1899, no. 2, pt. 4:933–1104.

Eleonskaia, A. S. *Russkaia oratorskaia proza v literaturnom protsesse XVII veka*. Moscow, 1990.

————. *Russkaia publitsistika vtoroi poloviny XVII v.* Moscow, 1978.

Eremin, I. P. "Poeticheskii stil' Simeona Polotskogo." *TODRL* 6 (1948): 125–53.

Fedotov, G. P. *Sviatye drevnei Rusi.* 3d ed. Paris, 1985.

Felmy, Karl Christian. *Die Deutung der göttlichen Liturgie in der russischen Theologie.* Arbeiten zur Kirchengeschichte 54. Berlin and New York, 1984.

Florovskii, A. V. "Chudovskii inok Evfimii." *Slavia* 19 (1949–1950): 100–152.

Florovskii, Georgii. *Puti russkogo bogosloviia.* 3d ed. Paris, 1983.

Fonkich, B. L. *Grechesko-russkie kul'turnye sviazi v XV–XVII vv.* Moscow, 1977.

Forsten, G. V. "Datskie diplomaty pri moskovskom dvore vo vtoroi polovine XVII veka." *ZhMNP* 355 (September 1904): 110–81; 356 (November 1904): 67–101; 356 (December 1904): 291–374.

————. "Snosheniia Danii s Rossiei v tsarstvovaniie Khristiana IV." *ZhMNP* 280 (April 1892): 281–335.

————. "Snosheniia Shvetsii s Rossiei vo vtoroi polovine XVII veka (1648–1700)." *ZhMNP* 315 (February 1898): 210–77; 316 (April 1898): 321–54; 317 (May 1898): 48–103; 317 (June 1898): 311–50; 323 (June 1899): 277–339; 325 (September 1899): 47–92.

Gal'tsov, V. I. "Svedeniia o S. I. Shakovskom v opisi arkhiva Posol'skogo prikaza 1673 g." In *Arkheograficheskii ezhegodnik za 1976 g.,* 79–81. Moscow 1977.

Gardner, Johannes von. *Gesang der russisch-orthodoxen Kirche.* Schriften zur Geistesgeschichte des östlichen Europas 17. Wiesbaden, 1987.

————. *System und wesen des russischen Kirchengesanges.* Schriften zur Geistesgeschichte des östlichen Europas 12. Wiesbaden, 1976.

Gibbenet, N. *Istoricheskoe issledovanie o dele Patriarkha Nikona.* 2 vols. St. Petersburg, 1882–1884.

Ginzburg, Carlo. *The Cheese and the Worms: The Cosmos of a Sixteenth-Century Miller,* trans. John Tedeschi and Anne Tedeschi. New York, 1982.

Goehrke, Carsten. *Die Wüstungen in der Moskauer Rus'.* Quellen und Studien zur Geschichte des östlichen Europa 1. Wiesbaden, 1968.

Goldfrank, David. "New and Old Perspectives on Iosif Volotsky's Monastic Rules." *Slavic Review* 34 (June 1975): 279–301.

Golubev, I. F. "Dva neizvestnykh stikhotvornikh poslanii pervoi poloviny XVII." *TODRL* 17 (1961): 391–413.

————. "Vstrecha Simeona Polotskogo, Epifaniia Slavinetskogo, i Paisiia Ligarida s Nikolaem Spafariem i ikh beseda." *TODRL* 26 (1971): 294–301.

Golubev, S. T. *Kievskii Mitropolit Petr Mogila i ego spodvizhniki.* 2 vols. Kiev, 1883–1898.

Golubinskii, E. E. *Istoriia Kanonizatsii sviatykh v russkoi tserkvi.* *ChOIDR*, 1903, no. 1:1–600.

————. *Istoriia russkoi tserkvi.* 4 vols. Moscow, 1883–1916.

————. *K nashei polemike s staroobriadtsami.* Moscow, 1905.

Gorchakov, M. *Monastyrskii prikaz (1649–1725).* St. Petersburg, 1868.

Gordeeva, N. A., and L. P. Tarasenko. "Literaturnye istochniki dvukh ikon 1694 g. Kirilla Ulanova." *TODRL* 38 (1985): 309–25.

Gorskii, A. V. "Istoricheskoe opisanie sviatoi Troitse-Sergievy Lavry." *ChOIDR,* 1878, no. 4:1–204; 1879, no. 2:1–117.

Gorskii, A. V., and K. I. Nevostruev, *Opisanie slavianskikh rukopisei Moskovskoi sinodal'noi biblioteki.* 5 vols. Moscow, 1855–1917; reprint Monumenta linguae Slavicae dialecti veteris: Fontes et dissertationes 2. Wiesbaden, 1964.

Granstrem, E. E. "Ioann Zlatoust v drevnei russkoi i iuzhnoslavianskoi pis'mennosti (XI–XIV vv.)." *TODRL* 29 (1974): 186–93, and 35 (1980): 345–75.

Graus, František. *Volk, Herrscher, und Heiliger im Reich der Merowinger: Studien zur Hagiographie der Merowingerzeit.* Prague, 1965.

Grobovsky, Antony. *The "Chosen Council" of Ivan IV: A Reinterpretation.* Brooklyn, N.Y., 1969.

———. *Ivan Groznyi i Sil'vestr (Istoriia odnogo mifa).* London, 1987.

Gukhman, S. N. "'Dokumental'noe' skazanie o dare Shakha Abbasa Rossii." *TODRL* 28 (1974): 255–270.

Gurliand, I. A. *Prikaz velikogo gosudaria tainykh del.* Iaroslavl', 1902.

Halperin, Charles. "A Chingissid Saint of the Russian Orthodox Church: The Life of Peter, *tsarevich* of the Horde." *Canadian-American Slavic Studies* 9 (1975): 324–35.

Haney, Jack. *From Italy to Muscovy: The Life and Works of Maxim the Greek.* Humanistische Bibliothek, Reihe 1, Abhandlungen 19. Munich, 1973.

Head, Thomas. *Hagiography and the Cult of Saints: The Diocese of Orleans 800–1200.* Cambridge, 1990.

Heisenberg, August. "Aus der Geschichte und Literatur der Palaiologenzeit." *Sitzungsberichte der Bayerischen Akademie der Wissenschaften: Philosophisch-philologische und historische Klasse* 10 (1920): 1–144; reprinted in August Heisenberg, *Quellen und Studien zur spätbyzantinischen Geschichte.* London, 1973.

Hellie, Richard. *Enserfment and Military Change in Muscovy.* Chicago, 1971.

Hering, Gunnar. *Oekumenisches Patriarchat und europäische Politik 1620–1643.* Veröffentlichungen des Instituts fur Europäische Geschichte Mainz 45. Wiesbaden, 1968.

Hionides, Harry. *Paisius Ligarides.* New York, 1972.

Hippesley, Anthony. *The Poetic Style of Simeon Polotsky.* Birmingham Slavonic Monographs 16. Birmingham, 1985.

Hösch, Edgar. *Orthodoxie und Häresie in alten Russland.* Schriften zur Geistesgeschichte des östlichen Europa 8. Wiesbaden, 1975.

Hrushevs'kyi, M. *Istoriia Ukrainy-Rusy.* 10 vols. Kiev, 1913–1936; Reprint New York, 1954–1958.

Hubensteiner, Benno. *Vom Geist des Barock: Kultur und Frommigkeit im alten Bayern.* Munich, 1967.

Hurwitz, Ellen. *Prince Andrej Bogoljubskij: The Man and the Myth.* Studia historica et philologica 12, Sectio slavica 4. Florence, 1980.

Iablonskii, V. *Pakhomii Serb i ego agiograficheskie pisaniia.* St. Petersburg, 1908.

Iaremenko, P. K. *Ukrains'kyi pys'mennyk-polemist Khrystofor Filalet.* L'vov, 1974.

Ikonnikov, V. S. *Maksim Grek i ego vremia.* 2d ed. Kiev, 1915.

Il'in, M. A. *Kamennaia letopis' moskovskoi Rusi.* Moscow, 1966.

Il'inskii, F. M. "Bol'shoi katikhizis Lavrentiia Zizaniia." *Trudy kievskoi dukhovnoi akademii,* 1898, no. 2:157–80; 1898, no. 5:75–87; 1898, no. 6:229–67; 1898, no. 8:599–607; 1898, no. 10: 264–300; 1899, no. 3:393–414.

Isaievych, Ia. D. *Bratstva ta ikh rol' v rozvytku ukrains'koi kul'tury XVI–XVIII st.* Kiev, 1966.

———. *Preemniki pervopechatnika.* Moscow, 1981.

"Issledovatel'skie materialy dlia 'Slovaria knizhnikov i knizhnosti drevnei Rusi'." *TODRL* 39 (1985): 18–277.

"Issledovatel'skie materialy dlia 'Slovaria knizhnikov i knizhnosti drevnei Rusi'." *TODRL* 40 (1985): 31–189.

Ivina, L. I. *Krupnaia votchina severo-vostochnoi Rusi kontsa XIV–pervoi poloviny XVI v.* Leningrad, 1979.

Jabłonowski, Aleksander. *Akademia Kijowsko-Mohilańska.* Cracow, 1900.

Jaksche, Harald. "Slavische Handschriften in der Vatikanischen Bibliothek." *Römische Historische Mitteilungen* 5 (1961–1962): 225–31.

Jobert, Ambroise. *De Luther à Mohila: La Pologne dans la crise de la chretienté 1517–1648.* Collection historique de l'institut d'études slaves 21. Paris, 1974.

Kaluzhniatskii, E. I. "Igumena Nafanaila 'Kniga o vere', ee istochniki i znacheniia v istorii iuzhno-russkoi polemicheskoi literatury." *ChOIDR*, 1886, no. 4, pt. 2: 1–36.

Kämpfer, Frank. "Verhöre über das Entfernen von Ikonen aus den Kirchen: Ein Vorgang aus dem Moskau des Jahres 1657." In *Unser ganzes Leben Christus unserm Gott überantworten: Studien zur ostkirchlichen Spiritualität: Fairy von Lilienfeld zum 65. Geburtstag,* ed. Peter Hauptmann, Kirche im Osten 17, 295–302. Göttingen, 1982.

Kappeler, Andreas. *Russlands erste Nationalitäten: Das Zarenreich und die Völker der mittleren Wolga von 16. bis 19. Jahrhundert.* Beiträge zur Geschichte Osteuropas 14. Cologne, 1982.

Kapterev, N. F. *Kharakter otnoshenii Rossii k pravoslavnomu vostoku v XVI i XVII stoletiiakh.* 2d ed. Sergiev Posad, 1914.

———. *Patriarkh Nikon i Tsar' Aleksei Mikhailovich.* 2 vols. Sergiev Posad, 1909–1912.

———. "Snosheniia Ierusalimskikh patriarkhov s russkim pravitel'stvom s poloviny XVI do kontsa XVIII stoletiia." *Pravoslavnyi Palestinskii sbornik* 15, no. 1 (1895): 1–509.

Karamzin, N. M. *Istoriia gosudarstva Rossiiskogo.* 6th ed. 12 vols. St. Petersburg, 1851–1853.

Kartashev, A. V. *Ocherki po istorii russkoi tserkvi.* 2 vols. Paris, 1959.

Kashtanov, S. M. *Finansy srednevekovoi Rusi.* Moscow, 1988.

———. *Sotsial'no-politicheskaia istoriia Rossii kontsa XV– pervoi poloviny XVI v.* Moscow, 1967.

Kazakova, N. A. *Ocherki po istorii russkoi obshchestvennoi mysli: Pervaia tret' XVI veka.* Leningrad, 1970.

———. "Russkii perevod XVII v. truda Blau 'Theatrum orbis terrarum sive Atlas Novus.'" *Vspomogatel'nye istoricheskie distsipliny* 17 (1985): 161–79.

Kazakova, N. A., and Ia. S. Lur'e. *Antifeodal'nye ereticheskie dvizheniia na Rusi XIV–nachala XVI v.* Moscow and Leningrad, 1955.

Keenan, Edward L. *The Kurbskii-Groznyi Apocrypha: The Seventeenth-Century Genesis of the "Correspondence" Attributed to Prince A. M. Kurbskii and Tsar Ivan IV.* Cambridge, Mass., 1971.

Keep, J. H. L. "The Regime of Filaret 1619–1633." *Slavonic and East European Review* 38 (1959–1960): 334–60.

———. *Soldiers of the Tsar: Army and Society in Russia 1462–1874.* Oxford, 1985.

Kharlampovich, K. V. *Malorossiiskoe vliianie na velikorusskuiu tserkovnuiu zhizn'.* Vol. 1. Kazan', 1914.

Khoroshev, A. S. *Politicheskaia istorii russkoi kanonizatsii (XI–XVI vv.).* Moscow, 1986.

Khyzhniak, Z. I. *Kyivo-Mohylians'ka Akademiia.* Kiev, 1981.

"The Kiev Mohyla Academy." *Harvard Ukrainian Studies* 8, nos. 1–2 (1984).

Kimeeva, E. N. "'Poslanie mitropolitu Daniilu' Fedora Karpova." *TODRL* 9 (1953): 220–34.

Kiselev, N. P. "O moskovskom knigopechatanii XVII veka." *Kniga: Issledovaniia i materialy* 2, 123–86. Moscow, 1960.

Kleimola, A. M. "Patterns of Duma Recruitment, 1505–1550." In *Essays in Honor of A. A. Zimin,* ed. Daniel Clarke Waugh, 232–58. Columbus, Ohio, 1985.

Klitina, E. N. "Simon Azarin (Novye dannye po maloizuchennym istochnikam)." *TODRL* 34 (1977): 288–312.

Kliuchevskii, V. O. *Boiarskaia duma drevnei Rusi.* 4th ed. St. Petersburg, 1909.

———. *Sochineniia.* 8 vols. Moscow, 1956–1959.

———. *Drevnerusskie zhitiia sviatykh kak istoricheskii istochnik.* Moscow, 1871; reprint, Moscow, 1988.

Kloss, B. M. *Nikonovskii svod i russkie letopisi XVI–XVII vv.* Moscow, 1980.

Kobiak, N. A., and I. V. Pozdeeva. *Slaviano-russkie rukopisi XV–XVI vekov Nauchnoi biblioteki Moskovskogo unversiteta (Postupleniia 1964–1978 godov).* Moscow, 1981.

Kobrin, V. B. *Vlast' i sobstvennost' v srednevekovoi Rossii (XV–XVI vv.).* Moscow, 1985.

Kochetkov, I. A., O. V. Lelekova, and S. S. Pod"iapol'skii. *Kirillo-Belozerskii monastyr'.* Leningrad, 1979.

Kollmann, Jack Edward, Jr. "The Moscow *Stoglav* ('Hundred Chapters') Church Council of 1551." Ph.D. diss., University of Michigan, 1978.

———. "The *Stoglav* Council and Parish Priests." *Russian History/Histoire russe* 7 (1980): 65–91.

Kollmann, Nancy Shields. *Kinship and Politics: The Making of the Muscovite Political System 1345–1547.* Stanford, Calif., 1987.

Kolycheva, E. I. *Agrarnyi stroi Rossii XVI veka.* Moscow, 1987.

Kondrat'eva, E. V. "Novye dannye o deiatel'nosti keramicheskoi masterskoi Valdaiskogo monastyria." In *Pamiatniki kul'tury—novye otkrytiia 1980,* 465–77. Leningrad, 1981.

Koniukhova, E. I. *Slaviano-russkie rukopisi XIII–XVIII vv. Nauchnoi biblioteki im. A. M. Gor'kogo Moskovskogo gosudarstvennogo universiteta.* Moscow, 1964.

Kopanev, A. I. *Istoriia zemlevladeniia Belozerskogo kraia XV–XVI vv.* Moscow and Leningrad, 1951.

Koretskii, V. I. *Formirovanie krepostnogo prava i pervaia krest'ianskaia voina v Rossii.* Moscow, 1975.

———. *Zakreposhchenie krest'ian i klassovaia bor'ba v Rossii vo vtoroi polovine XVI veka.* Moscow, 1970.

Kosman, Marceli. *Reformacja i kontrreformacja w Wielkim Księstwie Litewskim w swietle propagandy wyznaniowej.* Wrocław, 1973.

Kostomarov, N. I. "Tserkovno-istoricheskaia kritika v XVII veke." *Vestnik Evropy,* 1870, no. 4:479–506.

Kot, S. *Ideologia polityczna i społeczna braci polskich zwanych arianami.* Warsaw, 1932.

———. "Szymon Budny: Der grosste Häretiker Litauens im 16. Jahrhundert." In *Studien zur älteren Geschichte Osteuropas* 1, Wiener Archiv für Geschichte des Slaventums und Osteuropas 2 (1956): 63–118.

Kozlovskii, I. "F. M. Rtishchev: istoriko-biograficheskoe issledovanie." *Kievskie universitetskie izvestiia* 46 (January 1906): 1–52; (February 1906): 53–100;

(June 1906): 101–32; (November 1906): 133–52; (December 1906): 153–201.

Kozlovskii, I. P. "Sil'vestr Medvedev." *Kievskie universitetskie izvestiia* 35 (February 1895): 1–49; 35 (March 1895): 50–90; 35 (May 1895): 91–130.

Krekoten', V. I. *Opovidannia Antoniia Radyvylovs'koho.* Kiev, 1983.

Kruglova, O. V. *Narodnaia rospis' Severnoi Dviny.* Moscow, 1987.

Kubala, Ludwik. *Wojna moskiewska r. 1654–1655.* Szkice historyczne, serja 3. Warsaw, 1910.

Kukushkina, M. V. *Monastyrskie biblioteki russkogo Severa: Ocherki po istorii knizhnoi kal'tury XVI–XVII v.* Leningrad, 1977.

————. "Semen Shakhovskoi—avtor Povesti o Smute." In *Pamiatniki kul'tury— novye otkrytiia 1974 g.*, 75–78. Moscow, 1975.

Kunkin, I. Ia. "Gorod Kashin: Materialy dlia ego istorii." *ChOIDR*, 1905, no. 3:1–82.

Ladner, David. "Simeon Polockij's Metrical Psalter: Context and Pattern." Ph.D. diss., Yale University, 1976.

Langsch, Johannes. *Die Predigten der 'Coena Spiritualis' von Simeon Polockij.* Veröffentlichungen des Slavischen Instituts an der Friedrich-Wilhelm-Universität Berlin 26. Berlin, 1940.

Lappo-Danilevskii, A. S. *Istoriia Russkoi obshchestvennoi mysli i kul'tury XVII–XVIII vv.* Moscow, 1990.

Legrand, Emile. *Bibliothèque hellénique du XVIIe siècle.* 5 vols. Paris, 1894–1903.

Lenhoff, Gail. *The Martyred Princes Boris and Gleb: A Socio-cultural Study of the Cult and the Texts.* UCLA Slavic Studies 19. Columbus, Ohio, 1989.

Leonid. *Istoricheskoe opisanie stavropigial'nogo Voskresenskogo monastyria Novyi Ierusalim imenuemogo. ChOIDR*, 1874, no. 3:1–124; 1874, no. 4:125–366; 1875, no. 1:367–464; 1875, no. 2:465–544; 1875, no. 3:545–767.

Leonid. *Zhizn' sviatogo Filippa, mitropolita Moskovskogo i vseia Rossii.* Moscow, 1861.

Leont'ev, A. K. *Obrazovanie prikaznoi sistemy upravleniia v Russkom gosudarstve.* Moscow, 1961.

Levin, Eve. *Sex and Society in the World of the Orthodox Slavs, 900–1700.* Ithaca, N.Y., 1989.

Lexikon für Theologie und Kirche. 10 vols. Freiburg, 1957–1965.

Likhachev, D. S. *Chelovek v literature drevnei Rusi.* 2d ed. Moscow, 1970.

————. *Poetika drevnerusskoi literatury.* 3rd ed. Moscow, 1979.

————. *Razvitie russkoi literatury X–XVII vekov: Epokhi i stil'.* Leningrad, 1973.

Likhachev, D. S., ed. *Slovar' knizhnikov i knizhnosti drevnei Rusi, Vyp. 1 (XI–pervaia polovina XIV v.).* Leningrad, 1987.

————. *Slovar' knizhnikov i knizhnosti drevnei Rusi, Vyp. 2 (vtoraia polovina XIV–XVI v.).* 2 vols. Leningrad, 1988.

————. "Zabytyi serbskii pisatel' pervoi poloviny XVI v. Anikita Lev Filolog." In *Gorski Vijenac: A Garland of Essays Offered to Prof. E. M. Hill,* ed. R. Auty, L. R. Lewitter, and A. P. Vlasto, 215–219. Cambridge, 1970.

Lilienfeld, Fairy von. *Nil Sorskii und seine Schriften: Der Bruch der Tradition im Russland Ivans III.* Quellen und Untersuchungen zur Konfessionskunde der Orthodoxie. Berlin, 1963.

Little, Lester K. "Pride Goes before Avarice: Social Change and the Vices in Latin Christendom." *American Historical Review* 76 (1971): 16–49.

Loparev, Kh. "Opisanie rukopisi Moskovskogo Chudova Monastyria no. 57–359." *ChOIDR*, 1886, no. 3, pt. 5:1–20.

Lottin, Alain. *Chavatte, ouvrier lillois: Un contemporain de Louis XIV.* Paris, 1979.

Łowmiański, Henryk. *Religija słowian i jej upadek.* Warsaw, 1979.

Luppov, S. P. *Kniga v Rossii v XVII veke.* Leningrad, 1970.

Lur'e, Ia. S. *Ideologicheskaia bor'ba v russkoi publitsistike kontsa XV—nachala XVI veka.* Moscow and Leningrad, 1960.

———, ed. *Istoki russkoi belletristiki.* Leningrad, 1970.

Łużny, Ryszard. *Pisarze kręgu Akademii Kijowsko-Mohilańskiej a literatura polska.* Zeszyty naukowe uniwersytetu Jagiellońskiego 142, Prace historycznoliterackie 11. Cracow, 1966.

Macrides, Ruth. "Saints and Sainthood in the Early Palaiologan Period." In *The Byzantine Saint,* University of Birmingham Fourteenth Spring Symposium of Byzantine Studies, ed. Sergei Hackel, 67–87. Studies Supplementary to Sobornost 5. Birmingham, 1981.

Magdalino, Paul. "The Byzantine Holy Man in the Twelfth Century." In *The Byzantine Saint,* ed. Sergei Hackel, 51–66. Birmingham, 1981.

Maikov, L. N. "Simeon Polotskii." In *Ocherki iz istorii russkoi literatury XVII i XVIII stoletii,* 1–162. St. Petersburg, 1889.

———. "Simon Polotskii o russkom ikonopisanii." *Bibliograf* 11 (1888): 341–50.

Mainka, R. M. *Zinovij von Oten', ein russischer Polemiker und Theologe der Mitte des 16. Jahrhunderts.* Orientalia Christiana Analecta 160. Rome, 1961.

Makarii (Bulgakov). *Istoriia russkoi tserkvi.* Vols. 1–12. St. Petersburg, 1877–1891.

Malinin, V. *Starets Eleazarova monastyria Filofei i ego poslaniia.* Kiev, 1901.

Maloney, George A. *A History of Orthodox Theology since 1453.* Belmont, Mass., 1976.

Mal'tsev, A. N. *Rossiia i Belorussiia v seredine XVII veka.* Moscow, 1974.

Malyshevskii, I. I. *Aleksandriiskii patriarkh Meletii Pigas i ego uchastie v delakh Russkoi tserkvi.* 2 vols. Kiev, 1872.

Malyshevskii, I. "Russkii prikhodskii sviashchennik—propovednik XVII v." *Trudy Kievskoi dukhovnoi akademii,* 1861, no. 4:385–466.

Mansvetov, I. *Kak u nas pravilis' tserkovnye knigi: Materialy dlia istorii knizhnoi spravy v XVII stoletii.* Moscow, 1883.

———. *Mitropolit Kiprian v ego liturgicheskoi deiatel'nosti: Istoriko-liturgicheskoe issledovanie.* Moscow, 1882.

———. *Tserkovnyi ustav (Tipik), ego obrazovanie i sud'ba v grecheskoi i russkoi tserkvi.* Moscow, 1895.

Markevich, A. I. *Istoriia mestnichestva v Moskovskom gosudarstve v XV—XVI veke.* Odessa, 1888.

———. *O mestnichestve.* Kiev, 1879.

Meienberger, Peter. *Johann Rudolf Schmid zum Schwarzenhorn als kaiserlicher Resident in Konstantinopel in den Jahren 1629–1643: Ein Beitrag zur Geschichte der diplomatischen Beziehungen zwischen Osterreich und der Türkei in der ersten Hälfte des 17. Jahrhunderts.* Geist und Werk der Zeiten 37. Frankfurt, 1973.

Meyendorff, Jean. *Introduction à l'étude de Grégoire Palamas.* Patristica sorboniensia 3. Paris, 1959.

Meyendorff, John. *Byzantium and the Rise of Russia.* Cambridge, 1981.

Meyendorff, Paul. "The Liturgical Reforms of Nikon." Ph.D. diss., University of Notre Dame, 1987.

Miliukov, P. N. *Ocherki istorii russkoi kul'tury.* 3 vols. 3d ed. St. Petersburg, 1902.

Merzon, A. Ts., and Iu. A. Tikhonov. *Rynok Ustiuga Velikogo (XVII vek).* Moscow, 1960.

Müller, Ludolf. *Die Kritik des Protestantismus in der russischen Theologie von 16. bis zum 18. Jahrhundert.* Abhandlungen der Akademie der Wissenschaften und Literatur Mainz 1. Mainz, 1951.

Nakashidze, N. T. *Gruzino-russkie politicheskie ostnosheniia v pervoi polovine XVII veka.* Tbilisi, 1968.

Niess, Hans Peter. *Kirche in Russland zwischen Tradition und Glaube.* Kirche im Osten 13. Göttingen, 1977.

Nikolaeva, T. V. *Drevnii Zvenigorod.* Moscow, 1978.

Nikolaevskii, P. N. "Moskovskii Pechatnyi dvor pri Patriarkhe Nikone." *Khristianskoe chtenie,* 1890, nos. 1–2: 114–41; nos. 9–10: 434–67; 1891, nos. 1–2.

Nikol'skii, K. *Materialy dlia istorii ispravleniia bogosluzhebnykh knig: Ob ispravleniia ustava tserkovnogo v 1682 godu i mesiachnykh minei v 1689–1691 gg.* Pamiatniki drevnei pis'mennosti 115. St. Petersburg, 1896.

Nikol'skii, N. *Kirillo-Belozerskii monastyr' i ego ustroistvo do vtoroi chetverti XVII veka (1397–1625).* Vol. 1, pts. 1–2. St. Petersburg, 1897–1910.

Nosov, N. E. *Stanovlenie soslovno-predstavitel'nogo gosudarstva v Rossii.* Leningrad, 1969.

Novosel'skii, A. A. *Votchinnik i ego khoziaistvo v XVII veke.* Moscow and Leningrad, 1929.

Obolensky, Dmitrii. "Popular Religion in Medieval Russia." *The Religious World of Russian Culture, Essays in Honor of Georges Florovsky,* vol. 2, ed. Andrew Blane, 43–54. The Hague and Paris, 1975.

Ogienko, I. I. "Propovedi Ioannikiia Galiatovskogo, iuzhno-russkogo propovednika XVII-go veka." *Sbornik kharkovskogo istoriko-filologicheskogo obshchestva,* 19 (1913):401–18.

O'Malley, John W. *Praise and Blame in Renaissance Rome: Rhetoric, Doctrine, and Reform in the Sacred Orators of the Papal Court, c. 1450–1521.* Duke Monographs in Medieval and Renaissance Studies 3. Durham, N.C., 1979.

Orlov, A. S. *Domostroi: Issledovanie.* Moscow, 1917.

Ostrogorsky, Georg. "Zum Stratordienst des Herrschers in der byzantinisch-slawischen Welt." In *Byzanz und die Welt der Slawen,* 101–21. Darmstadt, 1974.

Ostrowski, Donald. "Church Polemics and Monastic Land Acquisition in Sixteenth Century Muscovy." *Slavonic and East European Review* 64 (July 1986): 355–79.

Panchenko, A. M. *Russkaia stikhotvornaia kul'tura XVII veka.* Leningrad, 1973.

Pascal, Pierre. *Avvakum et les débuts du raskol.* 2d ed. Études sur l'histoire, l'économie et la sociologie des pays slaves 8. Paris, 1963.

Pashuto, V. T., B. N. Floria, and A. L. Khoroshkevich, eds. *Drevnerusskoe nasledie i istoricheskie sud'by vostochnogo slavianstva.* Moscow, 1982.

Perov, I. F. *Eparkhial'nye uchrezhdeniia v russkoi tserkvi v XVI–XVII vv.* Riazan', 1882.

Petrikeev, D. I. *Krupnoe krepostnoe khoziaistvo XVII v.* Leningrad, 1967.

Petrov, N. I. *Opisanie rukopisnykh sobranii, nakhodiashchikhsia v gorode Kieve.* ChOIDR, 1892, no. 1, pt. 2:1–174; 1892, no. 2, pt. 2:175–240; 1892, no. 3, pt. 2:241–321; 1897, no. 1, pt. 2:1–128; 1904, no. 1, pt. 2:1–196; 1904, no. 4, pt. 2:197–308; and vols. 1–3, Kiev and Moscow, 1891–1905.

Pevnitskii, V. "Epifanii Slavinetskii, odin iz glavnykh deiatelei russkoi dukhovnoi literatury." *Trudy Kievskoi dukhovnoi akademii*, 1861, no. 8:403–38; 1861, no. 10: 135–82.

Platonov, S. F. *Drevnerusskie skazaniia o povesti o Smutnom vremeni XVII veka, Sochineniia*. Vol. 2. St. Petersburg, 1913.

——. *Moskva i Zapad*. Leningrad, 1925.

——. *Ocherki po istorii Smuty*. 3d ed. St. Petersburg, 1910.

Plavšic, Bořivoj. "Seventeenth-Century Chancelleries and Their Staffs." In *Russian Officialdom: The Bureaucratization of Russian Society from the Seventeenth to the Twentieth Century*, ed. Walter M. Pintner and Don K. Downey, 19–45. Chapel Hill, N.C.. 1980.

Pliguzov, A. I. "O razmerakh tserkovnogo zemlevladeniia v Rossii XVI v." *Istoriia SSSR*, 1988, no. 2:157–63.

Podobedova, O. I. *Moskovskaia shkola zhivopisi pri Ivane IV: Raboty v Moskovskom Kremle 40-70-kh godov XVI v.* Moscow, 1972.

Podskalsky, Gerhard. *Christentum und theologische Literatur in der Kiever Rus' (988–1237)*. Munich, 1982.

——. *Griechische Theologie in der Zeit der Türkenherrschaft (1453–1821): Die Orthodoxie im Spannungsfeld der nachreformatorischen Konfessionen des Westens*. Munich, 1988.

Pokrovskii, A. "K biografii Antoniia Podol'skogo." *ChOIDR*, 1912, no. 2, pt. 3:33–38.

Pokrovskii, I. *Russkie eparkhii v XVI–XIX vv., ikh otkrytie, sostav i predely*. 2 vols. Kazan', 1897–1913.

Pokrovskii, N. N. "Ispoved' altaiskogo krest'ianina." In *Pamiatniki kul'tury—novye otkrytiia 1978*, 49–57. Leningrad, 1979.

——, ed. *Khristianstvo i tserkov' v Rossii feodal'nogo perioda (Materialy)*. Novosibirsk, 1989.

Popov, V. *Simeon Polotskii kak propovednik*. Moscow, 1886.

Poppe, Andrzej. "O vremeni zarozhdeniia kul'ta Borisa i Gleba." *Russia Medievalis 1* (1973): 6–29.

Pouncy, Carolyn Johnston. "The Origins of the *Domostroi*: A Study in Manuscript History." *Russian Review* 46 (1987): 357–74.

Prinz, Friedrich. *Frühes Mönchtum im Frankenreich: Kultur und Gesellschaft in Gallien, den Rheinlanden, und Bayern am Beispiel der monastischen Entwicklung*. Munich and Vienna, 1965.

Prokhorov, G. M. "Poslaniia Nila Sorskogo." *TODRL* 29 (1974): 125–43.

——. *Povest' o Mitiae: Rus' i Vizantiia v epokhu Kulikovskoi bitvy*. Leningrad, 1978.

Protas'eva, A. N. *Opisanie rukopisei Sinodal'nogo sobraniia (ne voshedshkikh v opisanie A. V. Gorskogo i K. I. Nevostrueva)*. 2 vols. Moscow, 1970–1973.

Prozorovskii, A. A. "Sil'vestr Medvedev." *ChOIDR*, 1896, no. 2, pt. 4:1–148; 1896, no. 3, pt. 4:149–378; 1896, no. 4, pt. 3:379–606.

Prutskov, N. I., ed. *Istoriia russkoi literatury*. 4 vols. Leningrad, 1980–1983.

Pushkarev, L. N. *Obshchestvenno-politicheskaia mysl' Rossii: Vtoraia polovina XVII veka*. Moscow, 1982.

Puzikau [Puzikov], V. M. "Novye materyialy ab dzeinastsi Simeona Polatskaha." In *Vestsi AN BSSR, Seryia hramadianskikh navuk*, 4:71–78. Minsk, 1957.

Puzikov, V. M. "Obshchestvenno-politicheskie vzgliady Simeona Polotskogo." In

Nauchnye trudy po filologii Belorusskogo gosudarstvennogo universiteta im. V. I. Lenina, vol. 2, pt. 2:3–50. Minsk, 1958.

Raab, H. "Über die Beziehungen Bartholomäus Ghotans und Nicolaus Bulows zum Gennadij-Kreis in Novgorod." *Wissenschaftliche Zeitschrift der Universität Rostock: Gesellschafts- und sprachwissenschaftliche* Reihe 8 (1958–1959): 419–22.

Rauch, Georg von. "Moskau und der Westen im Spiegel der schwedischen diplomatischen Berichte der Jahre 1651–1655." *Archiv für Kulturgeschichte* 34 (1952): 22–66.

Robinson, A. N. *Bor'ba idei v russkoi literature XVII v.* Moscow, 1974.

———, ed. *Russkaia staropechatnaia literatura (XVI–pervaia chetvert' XVIII v.): Simeon Polotskii i ego knigoizdatel'skaia deiatel'nost'.* Moscow, 1982.

Rolland, Peter Allen. "Aspects of Simeon Polockij's Early Verse (1648–1663)." Ph.D. diss., Indiana University, 1978.

———. "'Dulce est et fumos videre Patriae'—Four Letters by Simiaon Połacki." *Harvard Ukrainian Studies* 9 (1985): 166–81.

———. "Three Early Satires by Simeon Polotsky." *Slavonic and East European Review* 63 (1985): 1–20.

Romodanovskaia, E. K. *Russkaia literatura v Sibiri pervoi poloviny XVII v.* Novosibirsk, 1973.

Rotar, Ivan. "Epifanii Slavinetskii, literaturnyi deiatel' XVII v." *Kievskaia starina* 71 (October 1900): 1–38; (November 1900): 189–217; (December 1900): 347–400.

Rumiantsev, Ivan. *Nikita Konstantinov Dobrynin ("Pustosviat").* Sergiev Posad, 1916.

Rumiantseva, V. S. "Kruzhok Stefana Vnifant'eva." In *Obshchestvo i gosudarstvo feodal'noi Rossii,* 178–88. Moscow, 1975.

———. *Narodnoe antitserkovnoe dvizhenie v Rossii v XVII veke.* Moscow, 1986.

Runciman, Steven. *The Great Church in Captivity.* Cambridge, 1968.

Rüss, Hartmut. *Adel und Adelsoppositionen im Moskauer Staat.* Quellen und Studien zur Geschichte des östlichen Europas 7. Wiesbaden, 1975.

Russkii biograficheskii slovar'. 25 vols. St. Petersburg, 1896–1913.

Rybakov, B. A. *Iazychestvo drevnikh slavian.* Moscow, 1980.

Rzhiga, V. F. "Boiarin-zapadnik XVI v. (F. I. Karpov)." *Uchenye zapiski instituta istorii RANION* 4 (1929): 39–48.

———. "Opyty po istorii russkoi publitsistiki XVI v.: Maksim Grek kak publitsist." *TODRL* 1 (1934): 5–120.

Savich, A. A. *Solovetskaia votchina XV–XVII vv.* Perm', 1927.

Schulze, Bernhard. *Maksim Grek als Theologe.* Orientalia Christiana Analecta 167. Rome, 1963.

Semenova, E. P. "I. A. Khvorostinin i ego 'Slovesa dnei.'" *TODRL* 34 (1979): 286–97.

Serbina, K. N. *Krest'ianskaia zhelezodelatel'naia promyshlennost' severo-zapadnoi Rossii XVI–pervoi poloviny XIX v.* Leningrad, 1971.

Sevčenko, Ihor. "A Neglected Source of Muscovite Political Ideology." In *The Structure of Russian History,* ed. Michael Cherniavsky, 80–107. New York, 1970.

Shapiro, A. L., ed. *Agrarnaia istoriia Severo-zapadnoi Rossii: Novgorodskie piatiny.* Leningrad, 1974.

———, ed. *Agrarnaia istoriia Severo-zapadnoi Rossii: Sever, Pskov, Obshchie itogi razvitiia Severo-zapada.* Leningrad, 1978.

————. *Agrarnaia istoriia Severo-zapadnoi Rossii: Vtoraia polovina XV–nachalo XVI v.* Leningrad, 1971.

Shchapov, Ia. N. *Gosudarstvo i tserkov' drevnei Rusi X–XIII vv.* Moscow, 1989.

Shevyrev, S. P. *Istoriia russkoi slovesnosti.* 4 vols. Moscow, 1846–1860.

Shmidt, S. O. *Rossiiskoe gosudarstvo v seredine XVI stoletiia: Tsarskii arkhiv i litsevye letopisi vremeni Ivana Groznogo.* Moscow, 1984.

————. *Stanovlenie rossiskogo samoderzhaviia: Issledovanie sotsial'no-politicheskoi istorii Rossii vremen Ivana Groznogo.* Moscow, 1973.

Shmurlo, E. *Rimskaia Kuriia na russkom pravoslavnom vostoke v 1609–1654 godakh.* Prague, 1928.

Shpakov, A. Ia. *Gosudarstvo i tserkov' v ikh vzaimnykh otnosheniiakh v Moskovskom gosudarstve.* 2 vols. Kiev and Odessa, 1904–1912.

Shul'gin, V. S. "'Kapitonovshchina' i ego mesto v raskole." *Istoriia SSSR*, 1969, no. 4:130–39.

Sigal, Pierre-André. *L'homme et le miracle dans la France médiévale (XIe–XIIe siècle).* Paris, 1985.

Sinitsyna, N. V. *Maksim Grek v Rossii.* Leningrad, 1977.

Sivak, S. I. "Ivan Isaev—stroitel' Iverskogo monastyria." In *Pamiatniki kul'tury— novye otkrytiia 1979*, 456–58. Leningrad, 1980.

Skrynnikov, R. G. *Ivan Grozny.* Moscow, 1975.

————. *Nachalo Oprichniny.* Uchenye zapiski Leningradskogo gos. pedagogicheskogo instituta im. A. I. Gertsena 294. Leningrad, 1966.

————. *Oprichnyi terror.* Uchenye zapiski Leningradskogo gos. pedagogicheskogo instituta im. A. I. Gertsena 374. Leningrad, 1969.

————. *Rossiia nakanune 'Smutnogo vremeni'.* Moscow, 1980.

————. *Rossiia v nachale XVII v.: Smuta.* Moscow, 1988.

Skvortsov, Dmitrii. *Dionisii Zobninovskii, arkhimandrit Troitse-Sergievskoi Lavry.* Tver', 1890.

Slukhovskii, M. I. *Bibliotechnoe delo v Rossii do XVIII veka.* Moscow, 1968.

Smentsovskii, M. *Brat'ia Likhudy: Opyt issledovaniia iz istorii tserkovnogo prosveshcheniia i tserkovnoi zhizni kontsa XVII i nachala XVIII vekov.* St. Petersburg, 1899.

Smirnov, P. A. "Ioakim, patriarkh moskovskii" *Chteniia v obshchestve liubitelei dukhovnogo prosveshcheniia*, 1879, no. 2:192–230; 1879, no. 4:417–36; 1880, no. 5:556–602; 1881, no. 4:469–529; 1881, no. 5:575–605.

Smirnov, P. P. *Posadskie liudi i ikh klassovaia bor'ba do serediny XVII veka.* 2 vols. Moscow and Leningrad, 1947–1948.

Smirnov, S. K. *Istoriia moskovskoi Slaviano-greko-latinskoi akademii.* Moscow, 1855.

Smolitsch, Igor. *Russisches Mönchtum: Entstehung, Entwicklung und Wesen 988– 1917.* Das östliche Christentum, n.s., nos. 10–11. Würzburg, 1953.

Sobolevskii, A. I. *Perevodnaia literatura Moskovskoi Rusi XIV–XVII vekov.* St. Petersburg, 1903.

Solov'ev, N. A. "Saraiskaia i Krutitskaia eparkhiia." *ChOIDR*, 1894, no. 3, pt. 1:1– 226.

Solov'ev, S. M. *Istoriia Rossii s drevneishikh vremen.* 15 vols. Moscow, 1960– 1966.

Solov'eva, T. B. "O vzaimootnosheniiakh tsarskoi vlasti i patriarshestva po zemel'nomu i finansovomu voprosam vo vtoroi polovine XVII v. v Rossii." *Vesi ... moskovskogo universiteta: Seriia istoriia* 5 (1978): 60–72.

Southern, R. W. *Western Society and the Church in the Middle Ages.* Harmondsworth, 1970.

Speranskii, M. N. *Istoriia drevnei russkoi literatury.* 3d ed. Moscow, 1921.

Sreznevskii, I. I. *Slovar' drevnerusskogo iazyka* 3 vols. St. Petersburg, 1893–1912; reprint, Moscow, 1989.

Stashevskii, E. D. *Ocherki po istorii tsarstvovaniia Mikhaila Fedorovicha.* Vol. 1. Kiev, 1913.

Strakhova, Ol'ga B. "Attitudes to Greek Language and Culture in Seventeenth-Century Muscovy." *Modern Greek Studies Yearbook* 6 (1990): 123–56.

———. "Problema 'Nestandartnogo' perevoda sv. pisaniia v Moskovskoi Rusi." *California Slavic Studies* (forthcoming).

Stroev, P. M. *Spiski ierarkhov i nastoiatelei monastyrei Rossiiskoi tserkvi.* St. Petersburg, 1877.

Sumtsov, N. F. "Innokentii Gizel': K istorii iuzhnorusskoi literatury XVII v." *Kievskaia starina* 10 (October 1884): 183–226.

———. "Ioannikii Galiatovskii (K istorii iuzhnorusskoi literatury semnadtsatogo veka)." *Kievskaia starina* 8 (January 1884): 1–20; (February 1884): 183–204; (March 1884): 371–90; (April 1884): 565–88.

———. *K istorii iuzhnorusskoi literatury semnadtsatogo stoletiia: Lazar' Baranovich.* Khar'kov, 1884.

———. "O literaturnykh nravakh iuzhnorusskikh pisatelei." *IORIaS* 11 (1906): 259–80.

Syrtsov, I. Ia. *Vozmushchenie solovetskikh monakhov staroobriadtsev v XVII v.* Kostroma, 1889.

Sysyn, Frank E. *Between Poland and the Ukraine: The Dilemma of Adam Kysil 1600–1653.* Cambridge, Mass., 1985.

Tazbir, Janusz. *Piotr Skarga, Szermierz kontrreformacji.* Warsaw, 1978.

———. *Szlachta i teologowie: Studia z dziejów polskiej kontrreformacji.* Warsaw, 1987.

Tatarskii, I. *Simeon Polotskii, ego zhizn' i deiatel'nost'.* Moscow, 1886.

Thomas, John Philip. *Private Religious Foundations in the Byzantine Empire.* Dumbarton Oaks Studies 24. Washington, D.C., 1987.

Thrēskeutikē kai ethikē enkyklopaideia. 12 vols. Athens, 1962–1968.

Tikhonov, Iu. A. *Pomeshchich'i krest'iane v Rossii: Feodal'naia renta v XVII–nachale XVIII v.* Moscow, 1974.

Titova, L. V. *Beseda ottsa s synom o zhenskoi zlobe.* Novosibirsk, 1987.

Torke, Hans-Joachim. "Gab es im Moskauer Reich des 17. Jahrhunderts eine Bürokratie?" *Forschungen zur osteuropäischen Geschichte* 38 (Berlin, 1986): 276–98.

———. *Die staatsbedingte Gesellschaft im Moskauer Reich.* Leiden, 1974.

Tsourkas, Cléobule. *Les débuts de l'enseignement philosophique et de la libre pensée dans les Balkans: La vie et l'oeuvre de Théophile Corydalée (1570–1646).* Institute for Balkan Studies, Publication 95. Thessalonika, 1967.

Turilov, A. A. "Maloizvestnye pamiatniki iaroslavskoi literatury XIV–nachala XVIII v. (Skazaniia o iaroslavskikh ikonakh)." In *Arkheograficheskii ezhegodnik za 1974 g.,* 168–74. Moscow, 1975.

Undol'skii, V. "Uchenye trudy Epifaniia Slavinetskogo." *ChOIDR,* 1846, no. 4:69–72.

Uspenskii, B. A. *Filologicheskie razyskaniia v oblasti slavianskikh drevnostei (relikty iazychestva v vostochnoslavianskom kul'te Nikolaia Mirlikiiskogo).* Moscow, 1982.

Uspenskii, N. D. *Drevnerusskoe pevcheskoe iskusstvo.* Moscow, 1965.

Vasil'ev, V. *Istoriia kanonizatsii russkikh sviatykh. ChOIDR,* 1893, no. 3:1–256.

Vauchez, André. *La sainteté en occident aux derniers siècles du Moyen Age d'après les procès de canonisation et les documents hagiographiques.* Bibliothèque des écoles françaises d'Athènes et de Rome 241. Rome, 1981.

Veriuzhskii, V. *Afanasii, arkhiepiskop Kholmogorskii.* St. Petersburg, 1908.

Veselovskii, S. B. *D'iaki i podd'iachie XV–XVII vv.* Moscow, 1975.

———. *Issledovaniia po istorii klassa sluzhilikh zemlevladel'tsev.* Moscow, 1969.

———. *Selo i derevnia v Severo-vostochnoi Rusi XIV–XVI vv.* Issledovaniia gosudarstvennoi akademii istorii material'noi kul'tury 139. Moscow and Leningrad, 1936.

Viktorov, A. E. "Opis' biblioteki Ieromonakha Evfimiia." In N. Tikhonravov, ed., *Letopisi russkoi literatury i drevnostei,* vol. 5, sect. 3, 50–56. Moscow, 1863.

Vinogradov, I. P. *Istoricheskii ocherk goroda Viaz'my s drevneishikh vremen do XVII v.* Moscow, 1890.

Vinogradskii, N. *Tserkovnyi sobor v Moskve 1682 goda.* Smolensk, 1899.

Vodarskii, Ia. E. *Dvorianskoe zemlevladenie v Rossii v XVII–pervoi polovine XIX v.* Moscow, 1988.

———. *Naselenie Rossii v kontse XVI–nachale XVIII veka.* Moscow, 1977.

Vorob'ev, V. M., and A. Ia. Degtiarev. *Russkoe feodal'noe zemlevladenie ot "Smutnogo vremeni" do kanuna petrovskikh reform.* Leningrad, 1986.

Vozniak, Mikhailo. *Istoriia ukrains'koi literatury.* Vols. 1–3. L'vov, 1920–1924.

Vryonis, Speros. *The Decline of Hellenism in Medieval Asia Minor and the Process of Islamization from the Eleventh through the Fifteenth Century.* Berkeley, Calif., 1971.

Ward, Benedicta. *Miracles and the Medieval Mind.* Rev. ed., Aldershot, U. K., 1987.

Yanoshak, Nancy. "The Author of *Poslanie Mnogoslovnoe*: A Fontological Inquiry." *Slavic Review* 50 (Fall 1991): 621–36.

———. "A Fontological Analysis of the Major Works Attributed to Zinovii Otenskii." Ph.D. diss., Georgetown University, 1981.

Zabelin, I. E. *Domashnii byt Russkogo naroda v XVI i XVII st.* 2 vols. Moscow, 1872.

———. "Zametka ob odnoi staropechatnoi knige." *ChOIDR,* 1880, no. 1:1–10.

Zaozerskii, A. I. *Tsarskaia votchina XVII veka.* 2d ed. Moscow, 1937.

Zen'kovskii, S. *Russkii raskol staroobriadchestva.* Munich, 1970.

Zernova, A. S. *Knigi kirillovskoi pechati, izdannye v Moskve v XVI–XVII vekakh.* Moscow, 1958.

Zhdanov, I. N. "Materialy dlia istorii stoglavogo sobora," In *Sochineniia,* 1:171–272. St. Petersburg, 1904.

Zhegalova, S. K. *Russkaia narodnaia zhivopis'.* Moscow 1975.

Zhmakin, V. *Mitropolit Daniil i ego sochineniia, ChOIDR,* 1881, no. 1:1–256; 1881, no. 2:257–762.

Zhukov, E. M., ed. *Sovetskaia istoricheskaia entsiklopediia.* 16 vols. Moscow, 1961–1976.

Ziborov, V. K. "Ob avtore tak nazyvaemoi povesti Katyreva-Rostovskogo." In *Istochnikovedenie literatury Drevnei Rusi,* 244–50. Leningrad, 1980.

Zimin, A. A. "Feodal'naia znat' Tverskogo i Riazanskogo velikikh kniazhestv i moskovskoe boiarstvo kontsa XV–pervoi tret'i XVI v." *Istoriia SSSR* 1973, no. 3:124–42.

——. *Formirovanie boiarskoi aristokratii v Rossii vo vtoroi polovine XV–pervoi treti XVI v.* Moscow, 1988.

——. *I. S. Peresvetov i ego sovremenniki: Ocherki po istorii russkoi obshchestvenno-politicheskoi mysli serediny XVI veka.* Moscow, 1958.

——. "Kniazheskaia znat' i formirovanie sostava Boiarskoi dumy vo vtoroi polovine XV–pervoi tret'i XVI v." *Istoricheskie zapiski* 103 (1979): 195–241.

——. *Krupnaia feodal'naia votchina i sotsial'nopoliticheskaia bor'ba v Rossii (konets XV–XVI v.).* Moscow, 1977.

——. "Obshchestvenno-politicheskie vzgliady F. I. Karpova." *TODRL* 12 (1956): 160–73.

——. *Oprichnina Ivana Groznogo.* Moscow, 1964.

——. *Reformy Ivana Groznogo.* Moscow, 1960.

——. *Rossiia na poroge novogo vremeni (Ocherki politicheskoi istorii Rossii pervoi tret'i XVI v.).* Moscow, 1972.

——. *Rossiia na rubezhe XV–XVI stoletii.* Moscow, 1982.

——. "Sostav Boiarskoi dumy v XV–XVI vekakh." In *Arkheograficheskii ezhegodnik za 1957 g.,* 41–87. Moscow, 1958.

——. "Suzdal'skie i rostovskie kniaz'ia vo vtoroi polovine XV–pervoi tret'i XVI v." *Vspomogatel'nye istoricheskie distsipliny* 7 (1976): 56–69.

——. *V kanun groznykh potriasenii: Predposylki pervoi krest'ianskoi voiny v Rossii.* Moscow, 1986.

Index